*The Musician as Philosopher*

∴

# The Musician as Philosopher

∵

NEW YORK'S VERNACULAR
AVANT-GARDE, 1958–1978

## Michael Gallope

THE UNIVERSITY OF CHICAGO PRESS
CHICAGO AND LONDON

The University of Chicago Press, Chicago 60637
The University of Chicago Press, Ltd., London
© 2024 by The University of Chicago
Published 2024
Printed in the United States of America

33  32  31  30  29  28  27  26  25  24      1  2  3  4  5

ISBN-13: 978-0-226-83174-9 (cloth)
ISBN-13: 978-0-226-83176-3 (paper)
ISBN-13: 978-0-226-83175-6 (e-book)
DOI: https://doi.org/10.7208/chicago/9780226831756.001.0001

Publication of this book has been supported by a generous contribution
from the Claire and Barry Brook Fund and General Fund of the American
Musicological Society, supported in part by the National Endowment for the
Humanities and the Andrew W. Mellon Foundation.

Library of Congress Cataloging-in-Publication Data

Names: Gallope, Michael, author.
Title: The musician as philosopher : New York's vernacular
    avant-garde, 1958–1978 / Michael Gallope.
Description: Chicago : The University of Chicago Press, 2024. |
    Includes bibliographical references and index.
Identifiers: LCCN 2023027618 | ISBN 9780226831749 (cloth) |
    ISBN 9780226831763 (paperback) | ISBN 9780226831756 (ebook)
Subjects: LCSH: Avant-garde (Music)—New York (State)—New York—
    History—20th century. | Modernism (Music)—New York (State)—
    New York—History—20th century. | Music—20th century—Philosophy
    and aesthetics. | Tudor, David, 1926–1996—Criticism and interpretation. |
    Coleman, Ornette—Criticism and interpretation. | Coltrane-
    Turiyasangitananda, A. (Alice)—Criticism and interpretation. |
    Smith, Patti—Criticism and interpretation. | Hell, Richard—Criticism
    and interpretation. | Velvet Underground (Musical group)
Classification: LCC ML200.8.N4 G35 2024 | DDC 780.9747/1—dc23/
    eng/20230623
LC record available at https://lccn.loc.gov/2023027618

♾ This paper meets the requirements of ANSI/NISO Z39.48-1992
(Permanence of Paper).

# Contents

# Introduction

From 1958 to 1978 in New York, a series of irruptions emerged in the history of music, irruptions fraught with dissonance, obscurity, volume. The musicians behind these irruptions were not merely expanding musical resources into dissonance and noise with a familiar polemical edge. They were thinking with sound: crafting metaphysical portals, aiming one to go somewhere, to get out of oneself. For many artists and thinkers of the postwar period, the self was taken to be ideological, given, normal. Their musical irruptions—this strange, intense, disorienting music—was a way out, a way beyond, through the other, through the collective, through an ecstatic mystery. Their work also had new techno-material underpinnings: radios, amplifiers, televisions, multitrack recording studios, and long-playing records. Some of the results were intricate, esoteric, and fractured; some of them were massively oceanic and inconsistent. It was often difficult to tell the difference.

This book discusses the work of several musicians who played key roles in these musical irruptions: David Tudor, Ornette Coleman, the Velvet Underground, Alice Coltrane, and a final chapter on Richard Hell and Patti Smith. Their work involved a larger group of collaborators: John Cage, Merce Cunningham, Don Cherry, Denardo Coleman, Billy Higgins, Charlie Haden, Maureen Tucker, La Monte Young, Tony Conrad, Lou Reed, Christa Päffgen, John Cale, Sterling Morrison, Andy Warhol, John Coltrane, Jack DeJohnette, Jimmy Garrison, Lenny Kaye, Richard Sohl, Jay Dee Daugherty, Tom Verlaine, Ivan Julian, Marky Ramone, and Robert Quine. This book is a history of the thinking embedded in their collective work, and it is a critical exposition of this period of time.

Consider brief sketches of the five scenes: David Tudor, the iconic virtuoso pianist of the midcentury avant-garde who staged a deadpan commitment to esoteric atonal structures; Ornette Coleman, a jazz revolutionary with a background touring on the Chitlin' Circuit, who celebrated a cacophonous play of contrapuntal lines accompanied by thoughtful riddles few could understand; the Velvet Underground, a decadent experimental rock band that fused together doo-wop, noise, Indian music, and Warhol's avant-intermedia spectacle; Alice Coltrane, an extraordinary gospel and bebop pianist who became a visionary of unheard transcendental landscapes; and finally Patti Smith and Richard Hell, poets of the underground, Rimbaud freaks, who sought the force of rock to deliver their vision, unpredictably ravishing and flailing in ways that ruptured their audiences' expectations.

These musicians all worked in New York, but they came to the city from Fort Worth, Lexington, Detroit, Los Angeles, Chicago, South Jersey, rural North Carolina, Philadelphia, and the suburbs of Long Island. They generally circulated downtown, often in distinct scenes that were very aware of one another but rarely overlapped. Their scenes variously crossed, reinforced, and confronted the color line. Tudor hustled with Cage in a generally white scene of classical music, avant-garde performance art, and professional dance. Coleman and Coltrane managed to carve out a space atop a prestigious corner of the jazz world, originated by Black musicians and joined by many white musicians. The Velvets struggled to find a platform for experimental rock in the late 1960s, though by the time Hell and Smith arrived in the early 1970s, a downtown avant-rock scene had emerged. Also originated by Black musicians, by the late 1960s and certainly the mid-1970s, rock scenes were overwhelmingly white. Their various scenes intersected with broader historical trajectories. Quite famously, the social inequities of this period fueled a thirst for freedom and universal self-consciousness from the civil rights struggle and the feminist movement to the anticaste movement and the decolonization of the Global South. In this context, racialized and gendered spaces of contested mimicry, turf, and genre mirrored underlying material inequities and structured the social imagination of their experimental work.

There were also a number of commonalities. Each of these artists stretched the boundaries and scraped at the corners of their genres. All, to various degrees, recognized a spiritual or mystical dimension to the creative process. Their influences also clustered and overlapped. Tudor, Cage, Coltrane, and the Velvets were inspired by Indian music and philosophy. Cage and Coleman's utopianism was indebted to Buckminster Fuller. The Velvets, Smith, and Hell were influenced by the Beats and Bob Dylan, who were in turn influenced by Black genres of blues and jazz. Coleman, the Velvets, Smith, and Hell were directly revolutionized by—or were practitioners of—rhythm and blues.

These musicians' touring was commonly transnational, as was their influence on others. They all went to Europe at some point in their careers, and Tudor, Cage, Coleman, Reed, Cale, Coltrane, and Smith toured in

Japan. Though Warhol, Reed, and Smith became celebrities, the avant-garde's in person appeal was limited. Their live audiences were all generally of a modest size: a CBGBs or a Five Spot audience was similar to an uptown new music ensemble of the 1970s—a few dozen people, maybe peaking at one hundred. An audience of hundreds turned up for the rare but well-promoted spectacle (Tudor or Coltrane at Town Hall in 1958 or 1966, respectively, or the Velvets at the Dom in 1967). Their work also commonly elicited widespread critical fascination—everyone discussed here, for example, was written about in the *New York Times*.

None were composers who were content with writing music in the form of published scores. They were invested in vernacular, deskilled, and non-Western traditions that were made newly accessible to large numbers of musicians following the birth of the LP and an explosive mass culture of music on radio and television. The postwar media ecosystem made possible radically new patterns of learning by ear outside the locality of oral transmission. In this context these musicians responded to and fused oral and self-taught traditions with a range of knowledge gained from piano lessons to church services and school bands, and in doing so they engaged in all manner of improvisation and collaborative play. Benjamin Piekut has described this mode of reproduction as a "mixed scriptural economy" that was native to the vernacular avant-garde.[1] These musicians were interested in participatory frameworks, regarded recordings as important influences and finished works more often than traditional scores, and often worked with stakeholders and firms in the music industry while institutions of music education played only a muted and peripheral role (if any at all).[2] Even Tudor, who began his career as a pianist of new music, transitioned to collaboration, improvisation, and electronic instruments in a practice that sidelined musical notation. For these reasons, I use the term *musician* instead of *composer*. By centering vernacular technicity, this book seeks to broaden and complicate what counts among scholars as a musical avant-garde.

Yet exactly what they did eluded academic and analytical understanding. This is partly by design: these musicians sought—quite purposefully—to occlude the precision of precise, teachable musical techniques. They left traditional conventions of music history behind (or "forgot" them, to use Coleman's term) and took off into esoteric techniques and games into the alchemy of electrical amplification, an oblique metaphysics, and theatrical and visual hallucinations. Rules and criteria were made metaphorical, left unspoken, joked with, ironized, and scrambled. They sought to elude the philosophical coordinates of reasoned judgment. These musicians even tried to disrupt their own intentions; they sought detachment or tried to stage confusion about what was being done in the first place. Self-taught amateurs and children could be virtuosos. Their positions were painterly, spiritual, and loose, as if one were there and not there at the same time. For they did not just fracture the rules for creating music; more philosophically, these musicians fractured the rules for recognizing the rules. In this book, I call this questioning of recognition a second-order modernism. I develop this concept more fully in chapter 2.

In this book I use the terms *avant-garde* and *modernism* in mutually reinforcing but not identical ways. I define modernism broadly as any art that foregrounds the self-consciousness of modernity. The avant-garde is a pointed provocation within the broader movements of modernism. It polemically and controversially foregrounds the self-consciousness of modernity. An avant-garde musical irruption makes people think. These musicians tried to stop listeners in their tracks and then electrify them. In an era when the norms, rules, and ideas about music changed so quickly and went to so many extremes, critics frequently found themselves running low on synonyms for *insanity* and *noise*. New sounds—alongside the ideas, words, and images of the avant-garde—amplified emotions, echoed social fractures, and opened cutting-edge metaphysical paths.

Though they could be critical of the music industry and its effects on musical creativity (particularly Coleman and Hell, who ran into conflicts with record companies), these musicians eschewed Adornian and Greenbergian models of modernism that claimed the work of art was a monad of historical techniques that negated the specter of mass culture. Instead, they developed alternative critical methods based in the mimicry and historicity of the vernacular and the non-Western. They practiced a multifocal dialectics that questioned what musical form was—that is, through sound, they pressed audiences to wonder whether it could be perceived accurately at all—with the aim of scrambling the coordinates of the self. And by the 1960s their audiences were tuned in to what they were doing; their communities and fans were themselves literate in these emerging idioms and guided by an intellectually minded sphere of critics.

Though these musicians protested the social and material conditions of modernity, like any artist, they offered no material escape from capitalism. At the same time, as musicians invested in vernacular, deskilled, or non-Western traditions, their music was marked by a distinct response to social power. They commonly insisted: Do not assent to the aesthetic education of the already empowered authorities of Western civilization. Remake it yourself. Be yourself. Go get it elsewhere. And then get rid of yourself. Have the confidence or the positioning to discover for oneself, or in a group, a new grammar of art. It would be misguided to climb the intellectual heights of modernist composition; in a "mixed scriptural economy" of the vernacular avant-garde, the creative process was an abyss; find your own relationship with music's technicity. Insist that aesthetic education exist outside established institutions; that is, laterally, or circuitously, or experimentally, or even terminally and nihilistically through the historicity of the dispossessed. It all had a utopian drive: these musicians sought a dissonance that sounded an escape from the self that was also an inversion, a thwarting, or a dissolution of established social hierarchies. For them, the self was both hypostatized and in crisis. With their irruptive dissonances, they sought a paradoxical goal: to be yourself and to get out of yourself—at the same time.

All these musicians thought deeply about their creative practice, and in this way, they acted as philosophers. That is, through their work, they posed foundational questions about music, life, society, and being. Each one also philosophized about the ineffability of musical sound. Of course, in doing so, they did not act as professional philosophers; their thinking did not unfold in the organized form of a reasoned argument or take on the form of a scholarly publication that patiently interrogated the assumptions guiding our beliefs. Their positions were more typically expressed as blunt provocations woven through language, music, visual appearance, and other performance choices that spanned media. As Joanna Demers notes, music's ineffability was often acknowledged through "doing rather than just writing."[3] Along these lines, these musicians' philosophy unfolded as stylistic choice, atmospheric calibration, dialogue, suggestion. It was developed above all in the complex social terrain of this music, often amid what Brigid Cohen has described as a racialized avant-garde marked by "largely unspoken history of mutual fascination, crossed signals, and complicated negotiations of authority."[4] These musicians, who navigated what Cohen describes as the "ambivalence and uncertainty" of avant-garde spaces structured by social and racial difference, often insisted that something was wrong with the trajectory of modernity even if their perspectives were richly varied, and even incommensurable.[5] Their musical atmospheres dissented along the lines of a loose historical thesis of the 1960s: stop repressing and remaining silent about subjugation; we are living with and catering to far too much repression and authority. Even when they did not explicitly insist on this thesis, many at some level presumed it to be the case.

In the realm of language, the philosophy developed by these musicians was informed by different kinds of texts: religious scripture, bits and pieces of non-Western thought, spiritual writings, anthroposophy, New Age books, poetry, novels, essays, and the discourse of other musicians. Many of these influences, with all their conflicting epistemologies and vague beliefs, are sometimes presumed to be intellectually sloppy, unserious, or embarrassing.[6] But the music of this historical period is enriched considerably by reading and grappling with the thought that was widely read at the time and that informed the terms of their creative work. Indeed, there is much to be learned about music and its histories if we credit a wider sphere of human reflection as philosophy. For this reason, this book frames philosophy as an inclusive multiplicity, an expansive definition that could entail vernacular philosophy, ethno-philosophy, and oral philosophy. At the same time, it does not disregard widely circulated texts that are traditionally designated as philosophy, particularly when a philosopher's influence is historically integral to the musicians at issue. Canonical figures of intellectual history remain backdrops for the postwar avant-garde. At some level, for example, widely read texts by Hegel, Marx, Nietzsche, Freud, Bergson, Wittgenstein, and the existentialists inform the terms of the philosophy at issue in any one chapter.

This book is a history of a messy and bustling mix of sounding and thinking that asks to be listened to, thought about, illuminated, and compared. Thus, in the pages that follow, philosophy is not applied to music; instead, it is shown to be woven into its historical and social making. In this way, this book is not a contextual history, nor is it modeled on the connective empiricism of an actor-network. Rather, what determines its emphases and shape is the problem-driven detective work of an imminent critique. These dissonant irruptions perplexed; they induced thought; they exemplified profound tensions of social imagination. How should we understand them? What did the musicians think? How did they think through the shaping of musical sound? What does their work allow others to think? Why did their work matter? How should the utopian aims of their work be positioned in the broader arc of social history and music history?

An immanent critique is guided by more than the available historical evidence. In *The Musician as Philosopher*, it is guided by critical explanations of social problems and their perplexing and inexhaustible relationships to histories of musical sound. Rarely are these relationships explicitly presented in historical sources themselves; to hear them requires the interventions of critique, analysis, and synthesis. In the tradition of critical theory, to critique the normativity of received wisdom, to relate ideas to their genesis in material circumstances, or, with respect to historiography, to have the confidence to reframe what counts as a historical problem—all these interventions are based in the human capacity for reason, or *Vernuft*.[7] For thinkers like Herbert Marcuse in particular, the capacity for critical reason (*Vernuft*) was understood to be potentially utopian, offering emancipatory alternatives to the normative regularities of traditional research and understanding, or *Verstand*. Insofar as critical reasoning has the power to dislodge the norms of the past, in ways both subtle and explicit, the philosophers

I have studied—that is, those who have informed my own capacity to reason—have inevitably shaped the questions and values I have brought to this historical study. In this way, this book's method of immanent critique also functions as a critical reflection on the present, because what counts as musical and philosophical literacy, rigor, or competence today continues to remain ideologically restricted in a way that elevates certain traditions of music and philosophy while devaluing others.[8] The final section of chapter one explores my approach to immanent critique in greater detail.

The musical examples in this book are sound recordings, both of live performances and from sessions in recording studios. In writing about them, I favor a mode of criticism that I take to mirror or find a consonance with the creative process as the artists undertook it. My approach is interpretive and places emphasis on what I infer would have been decisive choices for the musicians in question. This results in a minimal style that I hope is transparent and directs the ear in a way that is accessible to most readers and reflective of the underlying collaborative processes. As a medium, to me it seems self-evident that music is foundationally sonic. And in music, the precise contours of "thought patterns" (to use a locution shared by Coltrane and Coleman) can be elusive, to say the least.[9] As I discuss in chapter one (and have argued elsewhere), music is a perplexing and ineffable ride, what Ryan Dohoney calls "affective atmosphere," a fiery locus of social desire and erotic entanglements.[10] At the same time, it is inescapably structured by techniques, economies, and forces that are integrated with feeling, anger, love, and cathexis, spoken and unspoken. Raymond Williams once gave this composite phenomenon the name "structures of feeling."[11] All that gets unleashed in the complicated flux of practicing, tinkering, composing, arranging, rehearsing, collaborating, performing, recording, and playing back. For this reason, I try to listen dialectically. Sometimes this means the affective heights of music are held in tension with a disturbing inequity or blindness; indeed, aesthetic production is never ideologically blameless.[12] In fact it may be that such contradictions are the medium's most honest moments. For music is the intertwined traffic of sounds, desires, anxieties, and affective and intellectual worlds in their deepest and messiest insolubility. This book seeks to bring to life the speculative polyphony at work in its resounding dissonance.

∴

This book is organized into two parts.

Part 1, titled "Maps," develops some key concepts that circulate throughout the book and positions its method and outlook. Chapter 1 discusses aesthetic properties of music generally: the inconsistency of sound, music's affective intensity, its ineffability, and musical praxis as a basis for thought, in dialogue with writings by Susanne Langer, Angela Davis, and Fred Moten. It focuses particular attention on a conception of musical affect that is dialectically mediated by social praxis, modern technology, and economic structure. Affective praxis is not unique to postwar music; it is a general way of regarding musical practice. But it is especially important for this book, for a meaningful history of the period requires recognizing the peculiarity of music's affective praxis as a historical object and agent. Along these lines, the chapter situates the project in relation to methodological debates in the fields of music studies: the question of ineffability; the status of semiotics, the mediation of affect by cognition, institutions, and politics; and the political question of practicing immanent critique when normative definitions of what counts as music, philosophy, and sound practice are ever widening.

In chapter 2, I revisit the question of what kind of dialectics animate the musical avant-gardes of this historical period. It begins by developing the idea of a *second-order modernism* that emerges during the 1960s. As noted above, a second-order modernism goes beyond the expansion of musical materials and resources and begins to fundamentally question our capacities of perception and recognition. Chapter 2 then proposes two interrelated trajectories of the postwar avant-garde: tense and intricate patterns of intersubjectivity (or "plays of recognition") and new ruptures in style history conditioned by revolutions in the electrification of and social access to the sphere of musical reproduction. I then explore the dynamics of intersubjectivity through a discussion of raced and gendered inequities in late capitalism as they relate to fantasies of otherness and modernist resistance.

The final section of chapter two develops three concepts of stylistic change in the second-order modernisms that cut across the studio chapters—atmosphere, hyperfracture, and alchemy. In this book, modernist *atmospheres* transgress the positive certitude of musical elements and the fracturing of known musical grammars in order to envelop perception and alter its conditions. *Hyperfractures* are modernist atmospheres in which a fascination with abundance and excess results in a loss of transparency of the virtuosic object. Hyperfractures tend to involve esoteric, aleatoric, mystical, elaborate, illogical, or exotic forms and rules; they fuss over numbers and numerologies, code books, elaborate procedures, or intricate logics that may or may not make sense to listeners. *Alchemies* are modernist atmospheres that use electricity and modern recording techniques to develop a more empirical relationship to sound; through experimentation with collaboration, mixing, editing, and loud volumes, they seek out a transformative, even hallucinatory, sense of intensity. Each of these stylistic concepts describes musical forms that challenge the midcentury norms of traditional Western musical literacy.

Part 2 turns to the musicians themselves in the form of "studio" chapters. Here, I write as historian, critic, and comparatist to develop philosophical problems on the terrain of social and collaborative musical life. Some studio chapters are focused on notable musical events that range out into associated activities; others are focused on albums that are part of a time line and a network of cultural life. These chapters reason from the work of musicians, taking their thinking and action as itself philosophical, as a critical reflection of society. In the space below I offer brief summaries of each of the studio chapters:

"David Tudor, Esoteric Spectacle . . . c. 1958" explores Tudor's departure from the philosophical parameters of traditional Western notation via a study of his premiere of the graphic notations in John Cage's *Concert for Piano and Orchestra* (1958) at Town Hall. An iconic avant-garde pianist of the 1950s and early 1960s, Tudor developed a philosophical approach to performance that blended a rigorous method of realizing existing scores with a surprisingly open-ended performance style that anticipated vernacular practices in experimental music of the coming decades. By sight reading customized realizations of indeterminate scores in live performance, Tudor kept the drastic vitality of the performance alive while cleaving to the guardrails of esoteric procedures that involved elaborate calculations. The result had a philosophical effect on his perception that was akin to meditation. In his words, "my mind had to completely forget and not relate the next incident to the previous one."[13] The chapter reconstructs the key influences on Tudor and Cage's collaboration through discussions of writings by Antonin Artaud, Carl Jung, Ananda Coomaraswamy, Mary Caroline Richards, Rudolf Steiner, and Daisetsu Teitaro Suzuki. By treating notation as a means to defamiliarize the act of performance, Tudor staged a hyperfracture—which sounded to many critics as a cacophonous, even absurd, violence at the piano—that aimed to decircuit the Westernized, ego-driven capacity to perceive musical sound.

"Ornette Coleman, Utopian Intentionalities . . . c. 1966" focuses on *The Empty Foxhole* (1966), Coleman's collaborative recording session with Charlie Haden and Ornette's ten-year-old son, Denardo Coleman. Before recording, Coleman had taken it upon himself to teach his son to play the drums and then invited Denardo to collaborate at the session in New Jersey. The album also features Coleman's debut of solos performed left handed on the violin, an instrument he taught himself to play, with no aim of learning to play it "correctly." Critics responded with bewilderment as to how to evaluate the latest collaboration from the by-then-notorious figure of the jazz avant-garde. Based in a range of historical reviews, interviews, and articles on Coleman as well as close study of his recordings, this chapter argues that *The Empty Foxhole* presented a hyperfracture that challenged the horizon of intentional and perceptual criteria held by US jazz critics during the 1960s. The chapter positions Coleman's hyperfracture in context with two discourses: one is Amiri Baraka's dialectical conception of Afro-modernism in *Blues People* (1963, initially published under the name LeRoi Jones), the other Coleman's own vernacular philosophy of "harmolodics" as it is expressed in various interviews and writings from the 1970s onward. It concludes by showing how his words about his music skate around ambiguously, mirroring a sense of music's ineffability by evading the assignment of precise technical terms to the album's sounds and techniques. Coleman's harmolodic philosophy aspired to a socially inclusive utopia that both affirmed the multiplicity of vernacular grammars while thwarting their synthesis by way of numinously indeterminate rules and intentions.

Chapter 5 is titled "The Velvet Underground, Eleven Rooms . . . c. 1967." Like Tudor, Cage, and Coleman, the Velvet Underground harnessed music's ineffability by withholding communication and refusing to adopt a transparent intentional stance. Yet in their eschewal of notation and in their emphasis on collaboration and improvisation, the Velvets' second-order modernism reconfigured hyperfractures into electrified alchemies. They fused together Lou Reed's Beat-influenced songwriting and singing, John Cale's droning experimentalism, Nico's unmappable, ambiguously gendered vocals, and Sterling Morrison and Maureen Tucker's hypnotic grooves into an atmosphere that was equal parts physiological and characterological. Like Cage, Tudor, and Coltrane, a calibrated fantasy of India was a crucial element, but the stylistic framework of their music foundationally appropriated Black rhythm and blues and doo-wop. In a further layer of racialized appropriation, the Velvets adapted Afro-modernist techniques of modal improvisation and deskilling, which they associated with musicians like Coleman and John Coltrane. Philosophically, the band's cacophonous approach to rock music sought to excavate the darkest and strangest depths of the self and the psyche. The philosophy embedded in their work—one that staged a complex intersubjective scenario of erotic and psychological excess—came across in interviews, in critical responses to their work, and through the layered choices embedded in their first studio album, *The Velvet Underground & Nico* (1967).

Chapter 6, "Alice Coltrane, Divine Injunctions . . . c. 1971," explores the ways Alice Coltrane's spiritual philosophy underpinned a mystical ascent to registers of self-consciousness in her solo LP, *Universal Consciousness*

(1971). By contrast to Tudor, Coleman, and the Velvets, Coltrane's alchemies aimed to challenge the norms of musical perception by reimagining the stylistic parameters of Afro-modernism via an explicitly devotional stance toward metaphysical truth. Musically, her work traversed a number of stylistic boundaries: her talents as a keyboardist had moorings in gospel, bebop, and her late husband John Coltrane's increasingly free and ecstatic "sheets of sound" that lent her music a certain historical basis in hyperfractures. But by the early 1970s, Alice Coltrane had developed an alchemy that abandoned the acoustic conventionality of jazz in favor of concept albums that featured genre fusion, tape splices, tanpura, solo harp improvisations, and surprisingly exact transcriptions of works by Stravinsky and her late husband. This chapter shows how her work as a philosopher became key to her musical experimentalism, specifically in the way she mobilized song titles, liner notes, and her spiritual writings to ask philosophical questions about her music's alchemical ineffability. To do so, the chapter positions her work in broader social histories of the Black reception of Hindu spirituality, for philosophically she had discovered in Hinduism a distinctly utopian vision of human universality that mirrored the social desires of the civil rights era. Like Coleman, Coltrane's work challenged her listeners' perception about what musical sounds could metaphysically accomplish. At the same time, Coltrane went further than the many musicians of the 1960s (like the Velvets) who sought to appropriate Indian motifs; she actually invited listeners to join her practice of ecstatic devotion. The chapter concludes by positioning Coltrane's work in dialogue with emergent discourses on Afrofuturism in the humanities.

Chapter 7, "Patti Smith—Richard Hell, Forces . . . c. 1974," explores Patti Smith and Richard Hell's transitions from poets to rock musicians in the Lower East Side as the long 1960s evolved into the postindustrial 1970s. Commonly influenced by bohemian icons like Rimbaud, Artaud, Jackson Pollock, the Beats, Bob Dylan, and the Rolling Stones, Smith and Hell were poets keenly interested in the way language could excavate levels of reality repressed by the fabric of social norms in the US. During the years 1971–76, they became performer-icons in the downtown scene around CBGBs, Smith as a singer, and Hell as a singer and bass player. In finding their way as artists, they both discovered that the ineffability of rock music's affective force could set loose an alchemy that transformed their poetic reflections into primitivist, atmospheric rituals. As was the case with the Velvets, the energizing, dissenting realism of their work was built on an inversion of gendered and racialized inequities. Smith in particular achieved notoriety in producing a newly assertive grammar for women through a combination of existential affirmation, popular accessibility, and cheeky rebellion. But

Smith's and Hell's musical and poetic debts were Black: with formal grammars based in ecstatic vocals, backbeats, repetitive riff-based grooves, and the use of minor pentatonic scales. Their primitivism—which would prove to be foundational for the emergent genre of punk—was both blind in its appropriative whiteness and remarkable in its use of an irruptive dissonance to elevate the possibilities of indeterminate dissent.

In these studio histories, there is much to listen to, meditate on, and be excited by in their rich confluences of irruptive dissonances and philosophical thought. There is also, particularly in the instance of the white musicians who appropriated and profited from traditions they only superficially understood and whose social history they did not share, much to critique. I hope the reader embraces this messiness, even when it makes for uncomfortable reading. The complexity of these entanglements is endemic to the history at issue, for the very substance of the postwar vernacular avantgarde was fueled by the traffic of racialized and sexualized otherness across lines of social inequity. In this way my choice of musicians is not merely about changing who is recognized in music history; its comparative scope aims at the deeper conditions and meanings for how and why what counted as an avant-garde dissonance changed so drastically in the 1960s. At the same time, though the book is comparative, critical, and explanatory, no effort is made to be comprehensive. Given that these studios cross genres (classical, jazz, rock) that have distinct scenes and histories, I realize the diversity of figures could give the impression that they are representative of New York experimentalism as a whole. They are not. Scholarship on experimental music has continued to broaden its ears and definitions, and this book can only be a small effort in this direction.[14] The social and aesthetic complexity of this period is staggering, and part of its magic is that it has resisted summary.

But that does not mean broader historical conclusions cannot be drawn. Indeed, it is key that an immanent critique reasons dialectically and ventures critical perspectives on underlying patterns of social and stylistic change. Along these lines, the book's conclusion takes a step back to consider the larger methodological question of a materialist approach to music history. It argues that musical sound should be regarded as having a distinct sense of historical agency in relationship to social and economic changes in late capitalism. It specifically proposes that a key inflection point in style history—the transformation of hyperfractures into alchemies—dramatized or "electrified" the crisis of the self during the long 1960s with unprecedented irruptions of dissonance that were at once "popular" and "insane."[15] That is, following an argument in Amiri Baraka's *Blues People*, just as the late modern self acquired social advancement, these irruptive vernacular atmospheres brought the self under critique by inviting questioning, disturbance, and a thirst for transcendence. The final section positions the book's method against the neo-Dahlhausian strains of historiography in musicology that quietly allow conventional style histories to underpin increasingly contextual and material inquiries; it instead argues that music history ought to think of music and its historical styles as a distinct kind of historical object and agent. From this perspective, a music history can seek to explain the medium's role as a fundament of social change.

I invite the reader to choose their own path forward through the text. Some readers may want to read it in its published order: to first work through the conceptual "Maps" in part 1, and then hear how they connect elements of the studio histories in part 2. Others may want to begin with the vernacular philosophies in part 2 and return to part 1 to reflect on the broader conceptual questions that emerge in the studio chapters. Either approach works.

∵

When writing my first book, *Deep Refrains: Music, Philosophy, and the Ineffable*, I was enthralled by the conceptual intricacies of philosophers: from Schopenhauer and Nietzsche to Bloch, Adorno, Jankélévitch, and Deleuze and Guattari. My fascination with these authors and their thought remains. A basic political question haunting any philosophy of art is the deceptively simple one of what is included and made literate, audible, and visible. And for all their astounding virtuosity, the philosophers in *Deep Refrains* had only the thinnest sense of the racialized and gendered social tensions of late modernity, let alone all the magical, electrical, improvised, loose musical techniques and atmospheres of the postwar period that bent the social imaginary into unprecedented territory. If this book began as an effort to address music that I am convinced these philosophers should have written about, over time it became a far more exciting project of listening to the way the musicians themselves thought about the powers of sound during this extraordinary period of social upheaval.

In his essay "Music Discomposed" (1967), Stanley Cavell noted that "convention as a whole is now looked upon not as a firm inheritance from the past, but as a continuing improvisation in the face of problems we no longer understand."[16] Cavell did not propose to restore any "firm inheritance from the past"—that was not his project—but, as I will contend in chapter 2, his way of hearing the "improvisation" of social life might be reworked for the philosophical dramas of a broader avant-garde than the narrow world of serial composition addressed in his essay. And in recovering and reconstructing a wider array of forms, intentions, and metaphysical positions, we might avoid simple token inclusions and instead elevate the thinking of a broad swath of practices themselves that cross all manner of social and generic boundaries. As each of these musicians show us, the indeterminacy of unknowing is a new world, a portal, and a critical philosophy. Its forms of sound soared with a force that was at once peculiar and magnetic.

∴

Part One

# MAPS

∵

## CHAPTER ONE

# Affect—Praxis

In *Philosophy in a New Key* (1942), Susanne Langer claims that human societies are foundationally invested in the ideation of meanings and symbols. The source of our investment is not, however, an a priori capacity of cognition; rather, our ideations are spawned by the ineffable grip of affect. In her discussion of the anthropology of ritual, she illustrates her claim with a memorable—and somewhat terrifying—example: "An arriving train may have to embody nameless and imageless dangers coming with a rush to unload their problems before me."[1]

The affective response it triggers in us is already somewhat specific, and what a strange nightmare it is: the train cars themselves are somehow loaded with dangers and problems—but indistinct ones. Their numinous qualities ("nameless and imageless") add to the terror. Spurred by anxiety and instinct, our mind makes sense of the threat by drawing up a governing image, a "first symbol." It is initially somewhat diffuse: "Under the pressure of fear and confusion and shrinking, I envisage the engine, and the pursuant cars of unknown content, as a first symbol to shape my unborn concepts. What the arriving train represents is the first aspect of those dangers that I can grasp."[2]

The image of the engine and the "pursuant cars of unknown content" do not saturate the experience; underneath the mind is ablaze, working to structure the particular dangers that await. At a remove from conscious, well-ordered reasoning, such cognition is largely the work of instinct. The mind is scrambling for meaning:

> The fantasy that literally means a railroad incident functions here in a new capacity, where its literal generality, its applicability to trains, becomes irrelevant, and only those features that can symbolize the approaching future—power, speed, inevitable direction (symbolized by the track), and so forth—remain significant. The fantasy here is a figure; a metaphor of wordless cognition.[3]

"Wordless cognition" grows from affective reflexes. The mind draws up metaphors, relations, and associations, symbols devoid of specific denotations that manage to structure the inconsistency of its affective grip. It is a messy cognitive improvisation. Note that the linguistic capacity for generalization associated with signs, reasoning, and the philosophical power of abstractions are basically irrelevant. Langer confirms elsewhere: "wordless symbolism, which is non-discursive and untranslatable, does not allow of definitions within its own system, and cannot directly convey generalities."[4] Nondiscursive ideation cannot mean anything in particular, nor is it in any sense a matter of categorizing phenomena. Rather, the job of the fantasy's "wordless cognition" is simply to make thinkable the train's overwhelming sense of "power, speed, inevitable direction."[5]

For Langer, music exploits exactly this kind of numinous cognition: the wild, intuitive processes through which feelings flounder toward symbolic expression, where metaphor and association flood us with metaphysical significance, where affective attachments structure an almost mythical sense of belief. Since music lacks semantic elements, its meanings remain permanently unresolved and ambiguous, allowing them to dance in the abyss between the magnetic powers of affect and the structuring powers of cognition. To be sure, one's affects are always mediated by certain regularities such as sonic forms and elements.[6] Yet what she describes as a unique "presentational symbolism" in music ultimately must remain "unconsummated" or incomplete. For Langer music is a "significant form *without* conventional significance."[7] It is thus ineffable, but in a generative sense, not a silencing one. We might say that music is a train rushing at us, devoid of any particular message. Its ontology is the sonic exploitation of the furious and almost theatrical space of affective attachment, temporal drama, and nonconceptual intuition.[8]

With respect to affect, music does not transmit specific feelings; rather, its ambiguous and overlapping temporalities loosely convey "the morphology of feeling."[9] Within this loose morphology (of tension, relaxation, and the like), it is striking that Langer goes on to develop a claim once made by Felix Mendelssohn that music provides—quite paradoxically—a *more precise* externalization of affects than can otherwise be articulated by language.[10] She writes, "music can *reveal* the nature of feelings with a detail and truth that language cannot approach."[11] This is because affects, for Langer, are themselves transient, ambiguous, and ineffable; we can only describe their causes or situations (as in the thought experiment of the train). So music gives us an alternative path toward the recovery and externalization of affects. Because of its uniquely "transient play of contents" and its "ambivalence of content," music can present "a sentient and emotional reality" or "be 'true' to the life of feeling" in an inimitably powerful and specific way that is nondiscursive.[12] Music thus externalizes, articulates, exploits, and amplifies affective inconsistencies in ways that are otherwise ineffable.

Langer's line of thinking—which considers the messy, socially differential wiring of physiology, sexuality, and cognition to be ontologically primary over the well-ordered properties of works—owes a debt to Schopenhauer and Nietzsche and is echoed in Friedrich Kittler's more recent media-theoretical view of music. Schopenhauer heard music as an "immediate copy" of a prediscursive will, which he understood to be a blind striving that operated beneath the mediated domains of representation. Nietzsche, who endorsed much of this in *The Birth of Tragedy* (1872), ultimately formed a physiological view of aesthetics that ridiculed Kantian aspirations to bracket out the vicissitudes of desires and affects. Kittler, for his part, in turn cast Schopenhauer and Nietzsche as visionary philosophers of music in his essay "Musik als Medium" (1995).[13] There, he argued that the advent of algorithmically based music technology (from the basic discovery of the Fourier series to advanced digital sound engineering) developed an unprecedented grip on the physiology of the real. Sound reproduction effectively dethroned nineteenth-century conceits about poetic lyricism and the human soul and opened our ears to the affective alchemy of Pink Floyd's psychedelic crooning and Jimi Hendrix's electric feedback.[14]

Langer's writings on music also anticipate a number of recent interventions in the field of what has become known as "affect theory." Since the late 1990s, this body of humanities scholarship emerged as a materialist reaction to the dominance of discourse, semiotics, and cognition in the wake of the linguistic turn. Affect theorists have drawn attention to the way moods, atmospheres, feelings, desires, and the erotic function as central elements of social life. To do so they have drawn variously on Deleuze's metaphysics, feminist and queer theory, phenomenology, psychoanalysis, and cognitive science.[15] While affect theory has become a powerful corrective to humanists' hypostatization of language, it has routinely wrestled with dialectical questions about what mediates affect and how.[16] Some have redeveloped a Nietzschean ethics focused on actualizing one's inner potential (as a "will," "life," or a Deleuzian "body without organs"). Eugenie Brinkema emphasizes the importance of aesthetic form as a mediator of affect.[17] A significant number of affect theorists, perhaps most notably Lauren Berlant, study the structural consequences of affect in the realm of political and social identification.[18] Langer, as an adherent to two forerunners of the linguistic turn (principally Charles Sanders Peirce's semiotics and Ernst Cassirer's symbolic logic), balanced her attention to affect by emphasizing the powerfully governing mediations of cognition, language, and symbols.

One of the things Langer theorized vividly was the unique cognitive grip of musical affects. In her view the spell of music's immediacy is formidable. Like the arriving train that we scramble to comprehend, music's impacts appear to us as arresting and direct. But such experiences also have cognitive and symbolic reach. Since, for Langer, music has little use for "consciously abstracted" symbols, music's affective significance is instead conveyed through what she describes as "an 'implicit' symbolism" often associated with the irrational but efficacious powers of myths, rituals, and fetishes.[19] Under this condition, music's effects are "regularly confused with the things they symbolize."[20] We effectively hallucinate affects when listening to music.

One of the arguments of this book is that music never really escapes the condition of a magnetized, unconscious belief. Listeners and musicians are continuously imbricated in cathexes that cannot be readily understood or known; they tend to both elicit and evade cognitive awareness. Moreover, in focusing our powers of reflection on them, we are likely to discover quite ambivalent thoughts about their personal significance and social power. As Suzanne Cusick famously asked, Is music sex?[21] To which one might answer, Of course it is . . . and of course it isn't! Such contradictory answers are familiar to anyone who has sung along to the radio: just listen to those voices, iconic personalities, and beats—the egos and fantasies, the superheroes! Is that me in the car by myself, singing along? (Nobody I would publicly admit to be . . . at least while sober). Is this affective blur, or ambivalence, or disavowal between self and music (it can easily be all three oscillating at once) a mere imitation or representation? How can its powers feel so real? In this book, music's affective inconsistency—somehow precise, intense, and vague all at once—serves as the locus of music's ineffability.

And its sheer intensity harbors layered desires and social charges that invite explanation. Consider here just two examples. In *Blues Legacies and Black Feminism* (1998), Angela Davis describes the recordings of women blues artists like Gertrude "Ma" Rainey, Bessie Smith, and Billie Holiday as agents for what she describes as "unacknowledged traditions of feminist consciousness in working-class Black communities."[22] As she explains, though still under the condition of subjugation and impoverishment, following emancipation, Black women could for the first time make their own decisions about sexual partnership. While, in reality, most heterosexual Black couples had children, Black women blues singers tended to sing about existentially charged topics far from the domicile: heartbreak, promiscuity, erotica, damnation, and substance abuse.[23] For Davis, the recorded music effectively served as medium for Black women to cathect to larger ideations about an independent sexuality "free of the domestic orthodoxy."[24]

Electrified by the blues' ineffable abundance of affect, the recordings triggered a sexual emancipation that was numinous, utopian, and highly self-conscious. Its power derived from the fact that the recordings were irreducible to—and in a sense permanently confusable with—the physiology of sexual experiences.

Fred Moten's discussion of Duke Ellington has similar valences. In his book, *In the Break: The Aesthetics of the Black Radical Tradition* (2003), Moten writes that music of the Black radical tradition is fundamentally erotic. He describes it as a nondiscursive "surplus lyricism," an "improvisation" that "continually erupts out of its own categorization."[25] This surplus has a specific social meaning. For Moten, Blackness is historically and ontologically inseparable from the brutality of modern imperialism, colonialism, and slavery. In this context, the affective, erotic, nondiscursive power of radical Black music makes palpable both the unspeakable trauma and resistant potentiality of subjugated Black life. At the level of ontology, it even challenges categories of alienated being; it "exceeds itself," exemplifying "blurred, dying life; liberatory, improvisatory, damaged love; freedom drive."[26]

In a way that parallels Langer, Moten hears the significance of Ellington's music as stemming from the affective weight of its sensory power. He writes, "Swing is given only after the fact of the content—again, the weight and energy in and of sound—of Ellington's drive, which is to say his love."[27] Moten describes this as an affective abundance, the nondiscursive collectivism of Ellington's music as overwhelming. It envelops traditionally discursive spaces like libraries, turning philosophers into soloists: "[Ellington's] sound of love infuses rooms, ruptures walls and hallways, collides with the friezes and carved-out names in library facades, building ever greater unities, making his band (featuring special ghost soloists Sigmund Freud and Karl Marx) swing with the force of a new, another, content."[28] In elaborating this claim, Moten asserts powerful affinities between Ellington's "sound of love" and Freud's theory of Eros (a life force akin to Schopenhauer's will) and claims that both Freud's text and Ellington's ensemble exemplify the coordination of drives.[29] Yet unlike the relatively schematic dualism of Freud's drive theory, Ellington's "sound of love" is built on an erotic ensemble of asymmetry, cuts, ruptures, augmentations, events, eclipses, and nonlocalized origins. For Moten, the nondiscursive qualities of Ellington's music parallel Langer's understanding of what makes music's affective power unique: like the transience and ambiguity of Langer's affects, Ellington exemplifies the numinous, resistant, and liberating polyphony of Black Eros.

For Davis and Moten, music is a complex of affects that embodies real social desires. It is a haptic fight—it's fire. Set aside for a moment conceits of beauty, or conceptions of organized sound in which music is appreciated as art or cognized in rarefied and ethical ways. From the perspective of affective physiology, music is a social imperative; one *has to do it*. And its sensuous character is inseparable from the existential charge of a certain risk; performances are more often humiliating than triumphant just as utopian gestures outnumber political victories. If you are doing it well, you are trying to make it, or be it, or go with it, or use it to do or have your own thing, to recast categories of being. This is what I take to be the underlying phenomenon that Roland Barthes responds to in his famous essays "The Grain of the Voice" and "Musica Practica."[30] Or that Carolyn Abbate engages in her injunctions toward the "drastic."[31] Or that Jankélévitch develops in his writings on the virtues of improvisation.[32] Music's affective inconsistency irrupts from the granular inconsistency of articulation, from the physiological surfacing of lived production. In grabbing you, music is there to make you feel genuinely alive, or to mess your life up, or to release all manner of inarticulate truths, or simply allow you to linger over a sensuous abyss, devoid of goals. Or just to be there to induce euphoria like a tank of nitrous when your teeth are drilled, as Cavell says.[33] Music's ineffability is *that* physiological.

We are perpetually inclined to forget such affective qualities of the medium, which have a way of challenging the aptness of our words and the certainty of our knowledge. The likelihood of forgetting the real is a central leitmotif of Clément Rosset's writings, where he argues that intellectuals routinely turn to abstractions and overlook the intolerable inconsistency of reality itself.[34] With less of an existential charge (and a heavy dose of neoclassical chastity), it is a point Jankélévitch elaborates at length in *Music and the Ineffable* (1961). He contends we are addicted to hearing music *as* language metaphors and systems and are allergic to the blank charm of music's power to fascinate.[35] Cathexes to language metaphors are endemic to modernity and are inescapable. For Lacan, adaption of the symbolic order is constitutive for subjectivity to exist at all. One can also take a sociohistorical view. In music scholarship, orders of thinking, rationalized procedures, and bureaucratic consistencies have a way of translating music into forms of teachable, reproducible knowledge—what Michel Foucault once described as "regularities of discourse."[36] Such regularities facilitate intellectual perspectives on music that tend to frame it as a well-ordered form (perhaps with some loosely assumed moral value), a therapeutic balm, a speech-like form of expression, or an art form saturated by webs of semiotic codes.

Modern discursive frameworks are formidable in their power to structure and incentivize patterns of thought. Thus, from a critical perspective, facing the blank efficacy of its sensory impact requires something of an extra dialectical step, a meditative pause. Abbate has put it in the form of an injunction, a simple reminder to keep reasoning one step further: because disciplinary incentives align with the translation of music into teachable knowledge, we are *likely to overlook* the sensuous inconsistency of musical experience.[37] On this view, it is a gesture of critical and dialectical reflection to repeatedly pause over a moment of unknowing: to face that surplus of that sonic impact—its sensuous particularity—and to be deliberately uncertain of one's interpretation, and to rethink what one thought one knew about what one heard. This itself, I would argue, is an exercise in what Marcuse understood as critical reason. For pausing over affective inconsistency is a reflective gesture that has the potential to induce its own kind of meditative rigor. As an exercise, consider a version of Adorno's critical approach to modernist music in shorthand: find a piece of music you think genuinely resists the march of late capitalism because of its compositional features. Reconstruct this interpretation in your mind or on paper. Then press play on the stereo and ask yourself—with the sound hitting you—does the sounding object truly support the meaning I thought it might hold? When I do this, the meaning is not lost entirely, but the music seems to be constantly pulling away from it. Far from an evacuation of reason, or a fetishistic elevation of the affective and preconceptual, such an exercise maintains an imperative to repeatedly think the medium of musical sound and its strange properties of noncompliance.

If, as an interpreter of music, one can enjoin listeners to the meditative rhythm of pausing over the ineffable, as a historian of music's ineffability, it is possible to attend to and reconstruct vivid and elaborate instances of music's affective inconsistency from within generative historical situations. This is the approach taken by *The Musician as Philosopher*. In the case studies (or "studios") featured in part 2 of this book, several exemplars of the postwar musical avant-garde are framed as socially complex and philosophically productive—as mind-bending forms of affective praxis. Hardly instances of mere liberation or vitality, these musicians' works are elaborately structured, variously linked to and disjoined from histories of all kinds, and often contentious, expensive, even difficult to pull off. This existential charge of music is essential to the way it operated in the long 1960s, which is why the question of ontology is not a mere addendum to an otherwise historical book; affective praxis is exemplary of the way music effected change and was itself transformed during this period of time. The arresting sonic quality of these events and recordings are the historical agent and object. Certainly the traditional coordinates of what Lydia Goehr has termed the "work concept" continue to live on as displaced variants of their nineteenth-century predecessors: for instance, in the role of the music publishing industry's

Platonic commoditization of lyrics, melodies, and chords.[38] But this book casts its historical attention on the existential fabric of music's affective praxis: sounding performances and recordings that are woven into the electric atmospheres of concert halls, smoky clubs, and art galleries, the intoxicating powers of drugs, and varied dramas of social capital and sexual desire. The significance of these irruptive dissonances was mediated by the successes and humiliations of public debates, the structural hierarchies of social prejudices, and the metaphysics of spiritual belief. By attending to the words and actions of musicians themselves, this book tracks the philosophical significance of music in a way that is inseparable from networks of transformative social and material praxis.

How this took place at the level of musical techniques is a complex question. By the late 1950s, affective praxis was technologically reproducible—and transportable—through LPs, photographs, gatefolds, liner notes, record labels, distribution networks, star systems, ephemeral publications, even living room couches. In fact its condition was technological reproducibility. Indeed, in a Benjaminian vein, for a recent generation of scholars like Alexander Weheliye and Beth Coleman, technologies of mass reproduction have proven to be explosively powerful for philosophically and politically minded forms of affective praxis, particularly to those whose styles and idioms have not conformed to normative, institutionally disseminated ideals of what counts as "music."[39] Michael Denning has shown how sound recording in the early part of the twentieth century enabled a range of traditional music to be heard as a "vernacular musical revolution."[40] The development of jazz through the middle of the twentieth century is unthinkable outside the process of recording and the response to past recordings. The same holds for all kinds of popular music at midcentury and for a range of other postwar experimentalisms. With respect to disco, house music, and hip-hop—key genres of the 1970s—writers steeped in the discourse of Afro-futurism have offered some of the most powerful visions of the ways modern technology has enabled new forms of sensory illumination. For Kodwo Eshun, the drum machines and synths of house music need to be understood as a medium for the actualization of a specifically Black posthuman imagination.[41] In all such instances, modern technology amplifies and multiplies access to music's affective inconsistency.

Affective praxis is thus technologically mediated, socially and materially grounded, and philosophically generative.[42] By now I hope it is clear that I am not advocating a solipsistic vitalism shorn of disciplinary grammar and socioeconomic structuration. As Ruth Leys famously contended in her 2011 critique of affect theory, it would be a mistake to assume that such attention to music's affective inconsistencies then renders all ideation, intention, and sociohistorical structures moot and irrelevant.[43] This is why I began my turn to affect with Langer, who cannot discuss affect without the irruption of "wordless cognition." In an encounter with music, this affective inconsistency is far from inaccessible or silencing—our minds, so inspired, furiously respond. We inevitably seek to understand. And just as this is true for listeners, so is it equally true for practitioners. There is nothing more natural than to speculate, fantasize, or feel spiritual when making music; no musician in this book does away with the social power of abstractions, objects, economies, or ideals. On the contrary, the atmospheric weight of their praxis is saturated by structures and ideas.

For these reasons, *philosophy* will remain an important term because there is a certain kind of perplexity emitted from the space-time of the event, which is also a way of making metaphysics, intoxication, or transcendence, or of warping perception. Contra Wittgenstein and his followers, the social use of music is not transparently accessible to the production of examples in the form of the ordinary or everyday. Its affective praxis entails knotty and opaque registers of intellectual and unconscious mediation; when a performance is working there is a complex polyphony of beliefs and fantasies on all sides of the event. This is one place Langer is useful. She derived insights from practitioners, famously arguing, "the most vital issues in philosophy of art stem from the studio."[44] In working, Langer understood that artists themselves continue to ideate about their musical practices, particularly while they are technically invested in the medium. Imaginations and libidos run wild, unencumbered by the disciplinary protocols of academic philosophy or the dogma of organized religion. Musicians rework personal beliefs into homegrown, esoteric spiritual thoughts and speculations. They seek to explain why they are drawn to an activity—being a musician—even when it makes life quite difficult or the resulting explanations fall drastically short. This widespread desire to explain, I contend, forms the basis for a rich linkage between music and philosophy. Tracking its dialectical life on the terrain of affective praxis will be this book's central aim.

If ideation is so central to music's affective praxis, is music not semiotic? If semiotics only entailed a basic ontological claim *that* meaning is woven into musical events, it would be impossible to find grounds for disagreement (short of finding oneself persuaded by an unreconstructed Pythagorean). But semiotics typically promises more; it aspires toward a systematic method for recovering meanings by proposing alignments between cognitions and discrete musical forms. In so doing, it aspires to transform hermeneutics into an analytical metalanguage that parses music into what Andrew Chung calls "basic units of sense."[45] The upsides of such an approach are interpretive legitimacy and crediting the cognitive reach of musical expression; scholars in cultural studies and anthropology have used semiotics (and before that, symbolic logic) to frame a multitude of social practices as "texts" deemed worthy of interpretation. Gary Tomlinson has even postulated that semiotic (namely, indexical) gesture-calls gradually, in the course of human evolution, evolved into systematic and nonreferential music.[46] The downside for semiotics in its application to modern musical analysis is that proliferating language metaphors have a way of latching on to discrete elements of scores and transcriptions, allowing scholars to play with potential meanings in a cognitive space separate from the sounding event. At a basic level, such discretization too easily allows us to feel as though we have solved the problem of musical meaning at a remove from music's sounding affective charge. And ethically, it risks closing our ears to the object's inconsistency by privileging existing alignments with institutionally established grammars and formalisms over the words and actions of musicians themselves.

As an alternative to the semiotic model, consider instead that meaning and significance might exist in the generic form of the purposive artistic intentionality. In this generic form, the potential for meaning is occasionally little more than a skeletal conviction about music: someone made this music for a public, and here I am trying to make sense of it. Such a listener may bring little in the way of formal coordinates or grammatical overlays (harmony, voicing, counterpoint, rhythm, form, stylistic tropes and idioms) to the cognition of such intentionality; the open and hospitable recognition of the complete humanity of a musician is its primary foundation. This approach to listening has an ethical orientation that is compatible with the work of critique: it allows us to eschew the a priori filters of styles and grammars associated with existing authorities and disciplines, minimize prejudices about the presence or absence of such intentionality, and attempt, in light of historical knowledge, to recover interpretive possibilities generated by grammars we do not yet know from objects that have been silenced, marginalized, or misunderstood. We can learn to listen to what we do not and may not ever know—and to interpret it as a purposive object created by a human—with a generosity, an earnest commitment to understanding, and a modesty that it will not be exhausted or may not be understood. In this way, the intentionality of such works elicits fascination.

From the perspective of privileged and powerful institutions, it is ethical to keep expanding that sphere of what is understood by existing disciplinary frameworks to count as legitimate, fascinating, and worthy of philosophical attention. This is particularly the case for individuals themselves: who counts as a philosopher or musician has remained far too narrow for too long. In expanding the map, it remains instructive to pay attention to the sonic medium in its specificity, which is also a way of attending to its ineffability. This gesture ensures that we do not forget the point-blank inconsistency, which, yes, will at some level continue to elude understanding because the desires, fantasies, and beliefs it supports are disordered, layered, and endlessly ambiguous. To be reminded of the critical dimensions of that perplexity is the principal meditation of this book.

∴

Finally, a historical question of method. In the introduction of this book, I described my approach as that of immanent critique. Hegel devised the method of immanent critique as a way to build "immanent coherence and necessity" into forms of dialectical knowledge.[47] Across his writings, he built dialectical reasoning out of a range of phenomena or domains of inquiry (self-consciousness, art, history, nature, religion, the state) in order to understand their immanent conditions, properties, and processes. Marx, for his part, extended Hegel's method into an analysis of capitalism's inner workings and contradictions. Immanent critique is immanent because it is focused on the concrete sphere of the real and local; it is a critique because—in its Marxist variants—it detects the conflicts, disparities, and contradictions of various social norms in order to critique these norms by way of the local processes and norms themselves.[48]

Adorno's approach to immanent critique, in turn, contends that the contradictions, resistances, and utopian yearnings of society are vividly registered in the aesthetic sphere. But, as mentioned above, the habits and values of Adorno's method—irrevocably shaped by European modernism of the early twentieth century—cannot simply be extended to other locales. In the modernism of the 1960s, the categories of philosopher, artist, and what counts as aesthetic form were themselves subject to blurring and experimentation. Thus, my approach to immanent critique works with an abundant range of sources and contexts, dialoguing with people, works, and situations directly related to it, or loosely affiliated, or that function as instructive points of comparison. Though I admire and have learned a great deal from books on this period that demonstrate some alliance with actor-network theory, as a dialectical method, this book abjures any sense of affirmative connectivity or a focus on material objects and media and instead casts a spotlight on vernacular philosophy as a key mediator between music's affective praxis and larger aspirations of social critique.

Thus, the method of this book is a dialectical one that interweaves intellectual, musical, and cultural history as coconstitutive forces. If cultural history in this book recovers the locality of power dynamics and their mediated articulations, broader currents of intellectual history furnish resources for connective explanations of the music as it was practiced. Sustained attention to the productive philosophical questions expressed in these musicians' work allows us to dig beneath the self-evidence of testimony provided by actors in search of underlying structures, regularities, and questions. With actors, ideas, and their material sounds in perpetual dialogue, we can take the grip of belief seriously—the cathexis that is required for music's affective praxis—while developing a comparative bird's-eye view of recurrent issues. For the affective grip of belief—including all manner of cathexes to music's ineffability—is the social fact at the center of this book, and it is one that is irreducibly complex and productive, something Erin Huang evocatively describes as a "torsion between socially constructed interiors and exteriors."[49] As such, though affective praxis is structural, economic, and socially produced, its sheer intensity cannot be deflated as an ideological by-product; to do so would only repress what needs to be historically thought. But tensions arise in the effort to excavate, clarify, and compare what these artists did and how they thought against the backdrop of the forces and tendencies of late capitalism. If I had to say this book had its own philosophy, it would be the critical effort to navigate this challenge. Ineffability may be perennially inassimilable to the orders of knowledge, but a social production it is and was, with a genesis that has always and only been practical.

## CHAPTER TWO

# Veils—Atmospheres

Chapter 1 presented a theory of music's ineffability that rejects conservative associations with formalism and absolute music. It argued that music's ineffability is instead based in a more fundamental sense of the medium's affective praxis and that this affective praxis attracts a complex polyphony of concepts that populate efforts to grapple with the significance of musical experience, from the ethical and utopian to the numinously spiritual and metaphysical. This chapter turns to a featured group of avant-garde musicians who emerged from a broadly modernist context at midcentury. Specifically, it develops a dialectical framework for understanding how these musicians (Tudor, Coleman, the Velvets, Coltrane, Smith and Hell) uniquely exploited the capacities of music's ineffability. Through their practice, they exploited its philosophical paradoxes, amplified its affective powers, and built it out into socially engaged scenarios of self-reflection.

In the introduction, I described the avant-garde musicians in this book as "second-order modernists." First-order modernists—familiar to Adorno and his followers—fracture a given musical style such that a public could more or less agree about what counts as a chord or a note. But second-order modernists more fundamentally question our capacities of perception and recognition. In ways that resonate with Jankélévitch's inconsistency, Adorno's writings on Mahler's use of the vernacular, and Moten's approach to Black improvisation, second-order modernists rendered unclear a basic matrix of musical materials: the notes on the page, the tones comprising themes that are developed, the chords and keys structuring a composition, and even the skilled execution of any of the above. Thus, while we might hear arresting, unsettling, or hypnotic sounds in their works, second-order modernists were not simply sculpting and fracturing music's ineffable forms. Their inventive practices of writing, collaborating, recording, and improvising created philosophically puzzling instances of noncommunication. The sounding result could entail what I will call esoteric hyperfractures, in which broken grammars and styles multiply to the point that any

underlying intention seems to dissolve. Or it could pass into the more po-
rous inconsistencies of an alchemy—a compositional empiricism without a
priori rules and built with amoeba-like puzzle pieces, leaky boundaries, and
murky conventions. A range of newly valued phenomena emerged: cloudy
intentions, nonprecision, hallucinations, nonconsciousness, and the paradox of virtuosos devoid of traditional skills.

Modernist movements that question our capacities of perception are
hardly unusual, particularly in the visual arts, cinema, and literature. For
instance, European painting since the Renaissance had a readily accessible
relationship to visual perspective. As this representational illusion broke
down in the decades after 1860 with innovations from impressionists, ex-
pressionists, fauvists, cubists, and abstractionists, modernist paintings were
often understood—by painters and critics at the time as well as by later
scholars—to defamiliarize our faculty of vision itself.[1] In the broader sweep
of modern intellectual history, Gestalt psychology, art theory, and film theory have periodically explored the way modernist visuality responded to
and reshaped our capacities of perception in ways that have been influential
in the work of artists themselves.[2] And at the register of popular culture, the
1930s writings of Walter Benjamin illuminated broader transformations of
the sensorium in modernity. As Miriam Hansen and Jonathan Crary have
shown, everything from photography to traffic lights, cinema, and later
television reshaped the capacities of our sensorium in ways that were decisive for the trajectories of modernism.[3] Histories of perception in modernity driven by technological and cultural change were no less central to
many detailed, reflective texts of modernist literature.[4] In music, however,
what I am calling a second-order modernism unfolded in response to the
medium-specific particularities of the way music was taught, heard, and
composed in the West. That is, within the disciplinary frame of music produced and reproduced through Western notation, one first had to know,
hear, and believe that music was *made of* notes.[5] It is from this perspective
of midcentury musical literacy as a dominant ideology that one can grasp
the significance of its postwar avant-dissolution.

Amid these conditions, these musicians posed a thoughtful and provocative dissolution—precipitated through esoteric notations, improvisations, or alchemical layering of loudness and rhythmic synergy—of one's
perceptual ability to recognize what counts as musical form. And among
the second-order modernists of the postwar musical avant-garde, some became metaphysicians of their own experimental techniques. Their thinking
is the central topic of this book. This chapter introduces a few recurring
philosophical questions their work poses to us. Such questions orbit the
topic of music's ineffability, but instead of considering ineffability as some-

thing transcendent and inaccessible, they frame it as a generative, socially grounded experience of noncommunication. These questions include: How does one make a ritual, an experience, or an atmosphere for which the grammar of its assembly is unclear? How does one create music based in an esoteric code, a distant opaque solo, a traumatic recollection, a hypnotic groove, or a magnetic ritual of sheer force? How does one sense someone expressing something one has never heard and yet not be able to grasp the grammar of this expression?

For these musicians, questions of perception and form were tightly woven into the problem of social change. In this way, an irruptive dissonance could ask ethical questions about the representation, acknowledgment, and mimesis of the other, questions that spanned boundaries of social inequity. How does one recognize a work as something built with forms one may not adequately recognize? As a musician, what does it mean to not be—or not want to be—fully recognized in one's sounds? What form of listening might we use today to better understand the fraught terrain of this social history? Such questions are foundationally political and were understood as such during a decade when the scope of social recognition—of who counted— was restlessly expanding. And they circle back to a recurrent philosophical problem at the heart of the irruptive dissonances of the period: the late modern self is acquiring ever more mystical and existential independence and freedom at the same time that it is brought under relentless critique, analysis, and experimental indeterminacy.

## Global Inequities

A preliminary sketch of the social field sets into relief the intricate and charged dialectics of the second-order modernists. The musicians in this book lived and worked in and around New York from the 1950s through the 1970s. But the version of this city they saw differed, often significantly. Capitalism produced surplus value for the socially advantaged while subjugating and managing the "freedom" of innumerable others—women, ethnic minorities, Indigenous peoples, those of African descent who were stolen, killed, tortured, and traded as slaves during the preceding centuries. This surplus value made New York a cultural hub during the postwar period, but racial prejudices toward cultural workers meant white musicians had unique access to education and its attendant social capital (from Tudor's close association with pedigreed modernists to the Velvets' array of college degrees). Even a century after the abolishment of slavery and the gradual decline of Blackface minstrelsy, segregation and racism kept many Black musicians from access to music education beyond neglected public schools, community churches, and military bands. For aspiring Black professional musicians, the privilege of making art was remote. As Gerald Horne has detailed, during prohibition, Black jazz musicians worked in segregated clubs run by organized crime, where they were underpaid, manipulated with alcohol and cocaine, and surrounded by crime and violence.[6] By the 1940s and 1950s, Black musicians were typically barred from employment in orchestras, opera companies, academic institutions, and membership in labor unions affiliated with the American Federation of Musicians (AFM). They were excluded from lucrative agreements with agents, managers, publishers, labels, and presenters and were subject to deceitful agreements at the hands of white accountants, lawyers, and industry executives.

Stuart Hall notes that musicians of African descent nonetheless managed to create and define the salient grammars of popular music in the West: they invented the genres of ragtime, jazz, blues, gospel, soul, rock, salsa, funk, house music, and hip-hop.[7] Yet in a world built on racial capitalism, extraction was more common than opportunity.[8] At the hands of the modern culture industry, Black creativity was stolen and repurposed.[9] Prominent white musicians from Benny Goodman to Paul Whiteman, Elvis Presley, Mick Jagger, and Janis Joplin found fame and wealth by appropriating and reshaping Black creativity for white audiences who felt more comfortable listening to similarly white performers. This left a yawning disparity: Black musicians authored a significant majority of the innovations foundational to modern popular music (backbeats, syncopated grooves, vocal styles, improvisational idioms, attitudes, and expressions) while remaining persistently sidelined from professional recognition and prosperity. It was a large-scale inequity of modernism: the arts of the twentieth and twenty-first centuries—high and low—undertook a structural theft of Black life and labor under the protection of the norms and laws of the state, its markets, and its many artistic institutions.[10]

At stake was not only intellectual property and injustices in the way creativity was credited and compensated; racial difference in the arts underpinned complex social dynamics that would become fundamental to the forms and contents of modernism. At issue was an apparent contradiction between a venerated Black aesthetics and the existence of dehumanizing prejudices. For Hall, apparently conflicting logics of discrimination, veneration, and imitation are all part of racialized processes he has analyzed as the fetishistic dynamics of desire and disavowal. That is, within the locus of the psyche, these dynamics could be thought of as a two-way street of ambivalent attachments. Black expressivity could be prized and celebrated by whites as authentic, instinctive, soulful, a noble and almost metaphysical presence. At the same time—even by the same individuals—it could be denied, devalued, cast as relentlessly other and too sexual, vulgar, or commercial.[11] In Hall's words, toward Blackness, a "desire is both indulged and at the same time denied."[12] Tammy Kernodle has described this contradictory and ambivalent dynamic in blunt terms: "People love Black culture; they don't like Black people."[13]

To be sure, this ambivalent logic of fetishistic primitivism in Western culture—characterized above in terms of Afro-diasporic racialization—has a long history. It reaches backward to the Middle Ages and extends beyond the African diaspora to entail appropriations of Indigenous, Latinx, East Asian, South Asian, and Middle Eastern cultures, among other ethnic minorities in Western metropoles. But a twentieth century marked by a new scale of imperial conflict, globalization, and technological interconnection radically expanded the intensity, significance, and profitability of the cultural appropriations in play. In the arts, a considerable number of avant-garde movements were inspired by the arts of Africa, Asia, and the global periphery: French decadence and symbolism, Dada, surrealism, cubism, expressionism, Beat poetry, modern dance, Artaud and the Living Theatre, and happenings based on anthropological accounts of ritual and myth.[14] As the recording industry began to flourish, composers of Western concert music foregrounded evocations of the archaic and primitive from George Gershwin and Kurt Weill to Igor Stravinsky and John Cage.[15]

John Bramble positions these primitivisms within a varied cluster of modernist trends that are united by an irrational metaphysical fascination with the occult. He characterizes it as a global mélange that he describes as an "occult-syncretic conglomerate" that flirted with a dangerous and regressive politics but ultimately drew from the esoteric reservoir of the other in order to bend, dissolve, or critique the strictures of modern life:

> Including its "mystic East," modernist syncretism was an ever-accretive co-creation of many different figures. Including religio-cultural backwash from empire, the "reconvergence" in the scholarly world, of classics, oriental studies and theology, as well as these from what Griffin calls "social modernism" (life-reform, naturism, the simple life), the occult-syncretic conglomerate, still visible in the countercultural sixties, stood variously for pluralism, diversity, regionalism, utopianism, the fantastic, the indeterminate, sometimes the dark and uncanny, its enemies and opportunities bureaucratic reason and "orthodox closure."[16]

Bramble places front and center modernism's structural debts to cultural and epistemic alterity. While ethical debates about cultural appropriation have become central questions in discussion of the politics of the arts, many such primitivisms have been subtly underplayed. Too often scholars have framed white modernists with a quiet, somewhat ashamed acknowledgment of Orientalism and primitivism so as to leave room to foreground a white-male-authored "apex" of Western style history or a heroic critique of establishment institutions of art.[17] Yet debts to the fantasized other are essential to what modernism is and was; it was no less true of Leonard Bernstein's cosmopolitan sourcing (and erasing) of Nuyorican culture and the mambo craze in *West Side Story* (1957) or of Jackson Pollock's references to Native American painting as influences. Throughout the twentieth century, and in the years since, the vitality, spirituality, authenticity, sexuality, struggles, and pain of racialized others (African, Asian, Latinx, Indigenous, and so on) have been repeatedly resourced and erased by white Euro-Western artists in the name of critical reflection.

In a parallel process that intersects with the racialization of the avant-garde, modernism has also famously been predicated on global patriarchy. It has been widely noted that the most prominent postwar modernists were overwhelmingly male.[18] Within the frame of visual and cinematic arts or under the masculine gaze of the camera, women were routinely objectified, gazed at, consumed, idealized, and silenced.[19] In music, women were often confined to the role of an eroticized singer or chanteuse (a queer fascination of Andy Warhol's, and a type both inhabited and disrupted by Nico); though the dissenters grew over time, in postwar popular music, women largely served as numinous sexual vehicles for male fantasy.[20] Iconic figures of the era—like Joni Mitchell, Nina Simone, and Patti Smith—variously masculinized their approaches to creativity in order to forge a viable path for female-authored creativity. In these ways modernism has been no less structurally reliant on the dominance of white patriarchy: an overwhelming number of modernist works were fueled by a mystified, often misogynistic, desire for the woman-as-other.

And yet, as revisionist approaches to the history of modernism have detailed, great number of dispossessed artists—women, minorities, migrants, and others suffering under political, imperial, and economic oppression—devised modernisms with rich, individuated histories in ways that productively reshape familiar narratives of cultural appropriation.[21] Because of the prejudices described above, in these artists' lifetimes, career advancement was consistently difficult, and just as was the case for fantasized cultural others, socially dispossessed artists themselves tended to remain peripheral to or absent from lucrative publishing agreements, recording deals, concert programming, and dominant histories of style. Academic biases have elevated and sanctified white men at the expense of subjugated and unnamed artists whose innovations were reduced to passive sources of inspiration and sidelined from historical accounts. This was as true of Pablo Picasso's co-optation of the ingenuity of African masks in 1907 (which he saw in ethnographic museums) through the cipher of feminine prostitution as it was for the Rolling Stones' gender-bending co-optation of Muddy Waters's Afro-modernist blues (which they heard on commercial recordings) in the early 1960s. Thanks to significant work by Eileen Southern and Samuel Floyd since the 1970s, actual works by Afro-modernists have been acknowledged in new curricula in Africana studies, cultural studies, jazz studies, and in courses on African American literature, music, and art.[22]

Global modernisms have not only been inseparable from the underlying fact of inequality; their appropriative forms have mirrored social tensions that stemmed from the persistence of subjugation in modernity. On a planet of interdependent but persistently unequal social relations, modernist musicians with all kinds of identities and positionalities responded to perpetual crises through intricate processes of fantasizing, escaping, stealing, amplifying, distorting and critiquing across lines of race, gender, and social class. Laura Doyle's concept of "geomodernism" grapples with this kind of global modernism. In her words, such modernisms are variegated by "diverse, interacting conditions of multiple empires and multiple resistance movements since the later nineteenth century, conditions which are intensified by new technologies of finance, travel, communication, labor, and war."[23] Chika Okeke-Agulu's parallel concept of "postcolonial modernism" highlights the decolonial intentionalities of Nigerian modernists of the 1960s, which feature perspectives and artworks that are inassimilable to a white colonizer's style histories of modernist innovation.[24] Thus, amid the inequalities of conflicting empires and social movements, postwar modernisms were more than a reaction to the dehumanizing tendencies of late modernity; they were symptomatic of dialectical crosscurrents between unequal global systems from colonialism and racial capitalism to world-historical patriarchy. In this context, music, among the arts, serves as a vivid exemplification, or an affective heightening—at once sounding and spectral, formal and atmospheric—of what it meant to live a modern life that is alienated, damaged, fractured, or multiplied by an emergent global consciousness of inequality and social dismemberment.

The damage heard therein was never simply general or philosophical; pain, exploitation, and suffering was always specific, lived and unequally felt across racial, gendered, and class hierarchies. In fact Doyle contends that oppressed peoples have a unique, if not exemplary, relationship to key modernist themes of historical fracture and temporal multiplicity.[25] For this reason, the music in *The Musician as Philosopher* will be interpreted with the textured coordinates of biography, social history, and political economy in view. For the traumatic histories of dehumanization gave the African American and women musicians featured in this book very different perspectives on social inequity. To return to the book's social field: Coleman and Coltrane grew up in working-class households in Fort Worth and Detroit. Coleman worked as a saxophonist in R & B bands in the segregated Chitlin' Circuit of clubs of the Jim Crow era. In northern cities after the Great Migration (1916–1970), scenes of the avant-garde remained subject to de facto racial segregation. Coleman echoed the concerns of many of his predecessors in jazz when he persistently complained about being mistreated by promoters and club owners.[26] Through the emergence of the postwar avant-garde, the forward-thinking jazz scenes of Chicago remained notoriously segregated, a point George Lewis discusses at length in his history of the Association for the Advancement of Creative Musicians (AACM).[27]

Alice Coltrane's difficulties were compounded by her gender. She learned music from her upbringing at a Baptist church, a place where it was easier for women musicians to acquire skills and maintain some measure of respect and recognition.[28] She moved to New York but found she did not have the money to attend Juilliard. After finding a foothold in the bebop scene and meeting John Coltrane in 1963, she put her career on hold to have three of his children in 1964, 1965, and 1967 in the suburbs of Long Island while her husband wrote *A Love Supreme* (1965). That same year, Patti Smith put her child up for adoption and moved from New Jersey to Manhattan with her closeted boyfriend Robert Mapplethorpe. Smith's iconic masculine charisma—like the unconventionally gendered personae of Nico, Maureen Tucker, and Lou Reed—would be essential to her ascent in New York's gritty male-dominated downtown scenes of the 1970s.

At a broader register of popular culture, the explosion of rock music—a genre central to chapters 5 and 7—joined patriarchy to the white theft of Black forms. The fashion for rock was typified by Norman Mailer's archetypal white hipster who stole and reshaped the complex tropes of Black cool and Black masculine sexuality into profitable Dionysian fields of imagination and sexual and social rebellion.[29] Strident critiques of the hipster emerged from Black writers like James Baldwin, who heard Mailer's archetype as prejudiced and retrograde and his identification with the counterculture thin and aspirational.[30] But the Velvets, Hell, and Smith—whose hipster icon, Arthur Rimbaud, regarded the "children of Ham" as his fantasized ancestors—would be unthinkable without this racially and sexually charged trope.[31] It named a powerfully operative fantasy: to borrow the sexual bravado of a forbidden Black masculinity and reposition feminine sexuality as a mystical object to be appropriated, possessed, and controlled. In playing a rock LP, and letting one's imagination run wild, white bourgeois consumers acquired street cred—white authorship in the form of cultural capital—by appropriating the veneer of Black struggle.[32] This ideological field meant the women musicians featured here (Coltrane, Maureen Tucker, Nico, and Patti Smith) had to thwart—or in Nico's case, engage—sexualized expectations to earn legitimacy as artists themselves.

As mentioned earlier, a new generation of Black musicians in jazz, blues, and R & B opened new vectors of desire, expression, faith, and utopianism that those in power scarcely could imagine themselves. Thwarting domestic servitude, women gradually became critical and empowered subjects of aesthetic production. Concurrently, critics responded to the musical results with a sense that madness had overtaken the present. The reality of collective psychosis was fresh in public memory: during the 1930s and 1940s, a technologically supercharged racism flourished in a shudder of genocidal delusion and experimentation. But the postwar "economic miracle" ushered in a new consumer-driven psychosis: the spectacularized, eroticized, suffering of liberalism's resubjugated others.[33] Black, Indigenous, and people of color, women, the expendable, fascinating, and addicted were elevated and exploited as mass fetishes—as ciphers, gurus, and mystics of a new collective unconscious. Out of the opportunistic churn of the postwar culture industry—after centuries of white patriarchal silencing—this psychosis became foundational for new utopian grammars. Such contradictory trajectories—those of recognition and renewed exploitation—together formed the complex dialectics of the postwar avant-garde. And at the experimental heights of this contradiction, the music at issue in this book released unheard, indeterminate atmospheres. The pain and pathos inflected by a racist, sexist, neoimperial liberalism—its exploitations, its incommensurable standpoints, its electrifying traumas, and its soaring quest for freedom—underpinned the music's affective pull.[34]

## Intentionality and Grammar

In his 1967 article "Music Discomposed," Cavell argued that artists wage meaning in a way that is irrevocably bound to the assumed presence of human intentions. To make sense of the intentionality underpinning artworks, artists and audiences made use of "grammars"—a term I will reuse in this book—conventions of art traditionally based in lived processes of discovery and improvisation.[35] Yet in his view, postwar modernism—particularly serialism—had brought the humanizing presence of intentionality to a point of crisis by allowing formalized, a priori criteria to get in the way of the intention-driven grammars of art. This precipitated a threat of fraudulence: one could no longer, without question, presume that an artwork's grammar was the meaningful outcome of an artist's layered intentions and decisions. Instead, in this new postwar climate, modernists were posing, in their work, and in the responses to it, foundational questions about what even counted as aesthetic form.[36]

Productively, however, Cavell notes that improvisation—the exercise of practical freedoms within normative aesthetic conventions—continued onward in the age of postwar modernism. But this improvisation was displaced on to socially gregarious and vague grammars in something like an ever-expanding and increasingly philosophical set of inquiries. With modernist painting he says, now "the criteria are something we must discover, discover in the continuity of painting itself."[37] And, for the critic, "we need to discover what objects we accept as paintings, and why we so accept them."[38] As a result, the grammar of art migrated from normative aesthetic conventions within the work outward to broader fields of philosophical debate that are loose, social, and discursive. Amid a crisis of potential fraudulence, artists and audiences found themselves navigating the complex, improvised grammars of a deeper and more philosophical conversation in order to maintain trust, legitimacy, and sustainability.

In a sense, Cavell's diagnosis of postwar modernism suggests that a turn to philosophy—vernacular, literate, and otherwise—is essential to its history. For, in his view, the postwar era was, on the whole, no longer amenable to the humanist principles of intentionality, expression, and sincerity. It had even become hostile to the possibility of human communication. His diagnosis of the zeitgeist runs as follows:

> In a time of slogans, sponsored messages, ideologies, psychological warfare, mass projects, where words have lost touch with their sources or objects, and in a phonographic culture where music is for dreaming, or for kissing, or for taking a shower, or for having your teeth drilled, our choices seem to be those of silence, or nihilism (the denial of the value of shared meaning altogether), or statements so personal as to form the possibility of communication without the support of convention—perhaps to become the source of new convention. And then, of course, they are most likely to fail even to seem to communicate.[39]

To fail to seem to communicate: whether about statements or artworks, it is a now familiar midcentury claim about alienation and dehumanization. One can find variants of it in Adorno and Horkheimer's *Dialectic of Enlightenment*—a critique of the Hegelian metanarrative of universal history—and

Martin Heidegger's "Letter on Humanism"—a critique of the metaphysics of ego consciousness—both from 1947.[40] One might also think of the rise of antihumanist scientific methods like positivism, cybernetics, and structuralism, or of Marshall McLuhan and the emergence of techno-deterministic media theory. In the sphere of cultural history, one might note the intertwined emergence of Jungian archetypes, perennialism and world religions projects, the fashion for Western Zen popularized by Alan Watts and Daisetsu Teitaro Suzuki, and the popularity of Cage's conception of indeterminacy and its naturalist metaphysics of contingency inspired by the *I Ching*. In the sciences themselves, quantum mechanics and relativity theory vastly provincialized the anthropomorphic scale of Newtonian physics. Indeed, in the postwar US, a wide range of philosophy, spirituality, science, psychology, and art called into question the human intentionality of the self, which had heretofore—or at least, since the European Enlightenment—been taken as central to the expressivity of art.[41]

But ubiquitous discourses of noncommunication at midcentury were not only a symptom of formalism, structuralism, modern science and technology, or a fashion for Western Zen occluding the Enlightenment humanism of the self. Newly dynamic social identities associated with the uneven advancement of African Americans and the cultural revolutions of the 1960s brought about intricate asymmetries of perspective in ways that significantly complicated the question of intentionality in postwar aesthetics. As discussed earlier in this chapter, by sheer force of innovation, Black music of the postwar era upended the normative coordinates of Western music and started quickly changing the rules of what Jacques Rancière has termed "the distribution of the sensible."[42] As James H. Cone, Emily Lordi, Alexander Weheliye, Shana Redmond, and Daphne Brooks have emphasized, for Black audiences, this new era of Black music fueled by the record industry became a revolutionary medium for desire, pain, transcendence, and social consciousness.[43] The historical significance of this era cannot be overstated: in the twentieth century, Black musicians dramatically altered the course of global music history, and in doing so they powerfully rerouted its social history as well.

Yet, dimensions of this revolution were recognized with ambivalence and anxiety. White musicians and audiences, for their part, could be said to have taken up a variety of dialectical responses to Black musical revolutions: negation by refusal (moral panic at the hedonism of backbeats, alluring vocals, and swiveling hips), sly appropriation (a hipster's fetishistic imitation of or proximity to its resistant aesthetics), or negation by overcoming (via an academic modernist's fantasy of intellectual supremacy). Gendered dialectical formations of identity similarly structured the male-dominated sphere of cultural production. As mentioned earlier, women in nearly every corner of the modern music industry were rare presences, audible virtually only as eroticized singers. While Alice Coltrane's pianistic talent, her education in a Baptist church, her marriage, and her eventual status as a spiritual leader allowed her to step out of her normative gender role, Maureen Tucker and Patti Smith both espoused tomboyish refusals of femininity. Nico, in an unusually deep and inexpressive contralto, projected an ambiguously gendered sense of authority in her singing with the Velvet Underground (a critic once described her vocals as "perfect mellow ovals").[44] Insofar as postwar modernism was structured by a number of these racialized, sexualized, and gendered negations, the "studios" of the avant-garde featured in this book could be said to exemplify complex social dynamics in which identities and plays on identities multiplied and blurred. Normative social roles receded far into the background as these musicians took the frames of modern social life to their outer utopian limits.

Amid the zeitgeist of dehumanization, postwar modernists questioned the transparency of the self through dialectical polyphonies of fantasy, cathexis, and negation. Social differentials of race and gender were fundamental to these dynamics. Its traffic of mimicry engaged the philosophical imagination in plays of recognition, misrecognition, and disavowal.[45] In the process, complex triangulations of cathexis and identification produced hallucinatory and otherworldly forms. The artistic results were both affectively pronounced and socially transformative. To critique norms, institutions, and commoditized regularities meant to challenge, in Cavell's terms, the transparency of artistic intention ("to fail even to seem to communicate") by stepping in and out of oneself, making work that inhabits, amplifies, and makes atmospheric social tensions. In this situation, music's ineffability is a symptom of the fact that its attendant social charge—built on the numinous dynamics of desire and identity—holds sway over creators and audiences without causes that can be explained by reference to conscious action.[46]

## Plays of Recognition

The dynamics of intersubjectivity are crucial to this process. For this reason, Hegel's philosophy and the grammar of dialectics are productive tools for explaining the modernist imaginary even as one discards virtually all of his empirical judgments and conclusions about art. Key to the afterlife of his philosophy—and an insight that has been influential for social theory in particular—is the way an individual's self-consciousness and freedom acquire social acknowledgment, an acknowledgment that is in turn dependent on social and historical circumstances. Hegel's basic argument is that the emergence of the free and self-conscious subject is logically and materially built out and actualized through the self-conscious *Geist* of history. But getting that acknowledgment is complicated. It cannot come about through just a pure, balanced, and unchanging recognition of commonality among a group of people. In his famous master-slave dialectic, Hegel turns to the dynamic appearance of recognition between two people, and all manner of intertwined seesawing takes place.

Take two people who each desire recognition of one another's self-conscious freedom. They could assert their own self-worth in a fight to the death, but a dead person is, of course, no longer capable of recognition. So suppose the weaker one decided it was worth being a slave to the other to stay alive. The power struggle continues. First of all, the recognition the master gets from the slave is hardly satisfactory; though the slave is not dead, the master has effectively dehumanized the other, calling into legitimacy their capacity to recognize the master. Worse, as the slave does everything the master wants, the master gets lazy and hedonistic. The gluttony of being a pure consumer shades into a philosophical insecurity of "inessential consciousness" once the master realizes the extent of their dependence.[47] Meanwhile, endowed with a human mind filled with the potential for freedom, all kinds of exciting things happen for the slave. The slave begins to understand their own capacity for labor as something linked not only to their own desires but to another's desires as well. And in working for someone else, after fearing for their own death, the slave has learned to be modest about managing their own desires. All of this is empowering; the slave's sense of self grows into a socially and materially rich form of consciousness.

In this dialectic, an unstable situation based in a lopsided power dynamic boils over in an eruption of self-consciousness. It is unquestionably one of the most influential passages in Hegel's philosophy, and its interpretations have been multiform. Marx recast the self-consciousness of the slave's struggle as the collective struggle of the working class to achieve self-consciousness and take control of the means of production. In the 1930s Alexandre Kojève's lectures on Hegel foregrounded an extended reconstruction of the master-slave dialectic, which in turn helped make the questions of intersubjectivity and social consciousness central to the writings of a number of French intellectuals at midcentury, principally Jean-Paul Sartre, Maurice Merleau-Ponty, Simone de Beauvoir, Jacques Lacan, Emmanuel Levinas, and Frantz Fanon.[48]

Among them, Fanon had made the simple point that slave revolt was simply not what happened in history. Structural inequalities kept barriers in place. Consider the context more broadly: among the many costs to modern "progress" were the slaughter of Indigenous peoples and the systematic theft of Black life from Africa to the Americas. In so doing, white Westerners adopted the concept of race and social hierarchies in the nineteenth century atop existing social and economic inequalities in order to explain and justify their dehumanization of Indigenous and Black life.[49] This produced structurally unequal discursive fields. In Fanon's view, across racial lines, inequality meant asymmetries of recognition and epistemology that could not simply be overcome through self-awareness. After all, the master retains the ability to leverage an official language and state power.

Thirty years before Kojève's lectures in France, W. E. B. Du Bois, a descendant of slaves and a student of Hegel's writings, had developed his own version of this critique.[50] Du Bois spent considerable time thinking through the way the problem of recognition across the inequality of the color line continued to afflict the advancement of African Americans following the abolishment of slavery. He coined two famous concepts. One was the veil, a surface that denotes the elegance and singularity of Black skin, and an epistemological barrier that interrupts one's ability to easily translate lived experiences across the color line. This difficulty results in a blockage to mutual recognition that appears differently to Blacks and to whites. Du Bois's related concept of double-consciousness describes a social and epistemic consequence of the inequality underpinning the veil's appearance. Whereas privileged white-male citizens may be able to think of themselves as free and self-conscious individuals, those of African descent have to be aware of themselves both as individuals and as constructed as Black from the perspective of empowered whites.

Equally versed in Hegel's philosophy, Fanon's *Black Skin, White Masks* (1952) mirrors elements of Du Bois's double-consciousness theory in the context of the Black Caribbean. With his expertise in medicine and psychiatry, Fanon goes into more depth explaining the underlying torments that afflict the modern Black subject. In his view, "the juxtaposition of the white and Black races" is a social fact caused by whites that produces a "psychoexistential complex" in need of diagnosis and overturning.[51] In arresting language, and in ways that became foundational to subsequent theories of Afro-pessimism, Fanon recounts the experience of being reduced to crippling stereotypes—biology, brutality, and sexuality—and thus rendered ontologically deficient, cast by histories of racism into "a zone of nonbeing."[52] In ways that echo Du Bois, Fanon argues that Black subjects of the postcolonial Caribbean are often eager to don a "white mask," learn to speak French from white colonizers, and pursue white sexual partners, only to in turn find themselves afflicted by a split subjectivity in which Blacks never again feel at home either with Blacks or with whites. At the same time, a parallel sense of anxiety emerges for the white colonizer over the potential of Black intellect, genius, and sexual potency, which are each framed as recurring threats to white supremacy.[53] For Black subjects, the structured inequality of recognition and perception results in neurotic and despairing complexes of inferiority or dependency.[54] The ethics of *Black Skin, White Masks* aimed to elicit a sense of empowerment, self-awareness, and mutual recognition that would "put him in a position to *choose* action (or passivity) with respect to the real source of the conflict—that is, toward the social structures."[55]

Blackness as a "zone of nonbeing" is a theme that has been developed extensively in the writings of Fred Moten and Achille Mbembe. For Mbembe, the ontology of Blackness elicits fascination, an affective magnetism that presses against one's capacity to think: "the Black Man unleashes impassioned dynamics and provokes an irrational exuberance that always tests the limits of the very system of reason."[56] Race as he frames it is a charged topic that defies organized and rational approaches. In his view, skin color can appear as a "primal representation," an almost prelinguistic category but with its own plentitude of socially determined affects attached: resentment, condemnation, even hatred.[57] Tongue-tied when trying to pin down the horrible weight of such affects and prejudices, racism harbors its own variations on the ineffable but with a crippling social charge. He writes, "We can speak of race (or racism) only in a fatally imperfect language, gray and inadequate."[58] As a consequence, for Mbembe, there is quite simply an ineffability to Blackness itself, one predicated on persistent devaluation:

> The Black Man, a sign in excess of all signs and therefore fundamentally unrepresentable, was the ideal example of this other-being, powerfully possessed by emptiness, for whom the negative had ended up penetrating all moments of existence—the death of the day, destruction and peril, the unnamable night of the world.[59]

Even as injustices underpinning racial prejudice have remained historically constitutive, in the sphere of art, Black artistry has managed to press beyond despair and powerfully reconfigure this ontological devaluation. In doing so, these artists have challenged the dehumanizing aims of Enlightenment philosophy and nineteenth-century racial thinking. For Moten, who was influenced by Adorno and Baraka, such challenges took shape as irruptive resistances or utopian pivots, many of which were articulated as advances in Black music.[60] He frames the Black avant-garde of the twentieth century as a locus of resistance to categorical subjugation; in his view, Blackness is a gap, a break, and a multiplicity of being. It exemplifies an evasive movement of differentiation—an escape, a fugitivity, a freedom, an improvisation.[61] This freedom is a rupture within a specific racialized history. Building off the work of Saidiya Hartman, Moten's *In the Break* (2003) recast this fugitivity as a paradox: a dehumanized humanity. Having been ontologically framed as a dehumanized commodity by slavery, in Moten's view, the Black artist is nonetheless capable of resistant human speech. And in speaking and improvising—particularly through music and avant-garde performance—modern Black subjects express the unspeakability of historical and social trauma.[62]

An influential lineage of feminist theory has been no less dialectical in its critique of the structural asymmetries of recognition. Simone de Beauvoir's *The Second Sex* (1949) forwarded a comprehensive explanation of the historical oppression of women that mirrors the Hegelian arguments made by Du Bois. Though sexual difference has linkages to processes of biological reproduction, de Beauvoir argues that men have needlessly doubled down on the burden of reproductive labor in a way that has left women captive in a sphere of natural immanence and caretaking. Patriarchal laws and social conventions, which were developed and maintained historically, codified male dominance; men were freed to become the citizens, engineers, philosophers, and social creators of the world while women's physical, social, and intellectual capacities were suppressed as they were consigned to servitude in the domestic sphere. In Hegelian terms, de Beauvoir argued that patriarchy rendered women ontologically dependent; while a man's social freedoms underpinned his subjective independence, women were comparatively defined as secondary, objectified, and derivative. In her words, "she is the Other at the heart of a whole whose two components are necessary to each other."[63] In a manner that parallels histories of racial and ethnic oppression, patriarchy in the arts underpinned a male-dominated modernism in which femininity was routinely consumed as sexual, desired, and dangerous rather than creative, emancipatory, and lawgiving. As a corrective, de Beauvoir advocates an ethics of subjective freedom, emancipation, and transcendence for women predicated on the possibility of historical change.

Since then theorists of gender and sexuality have underscored the malleability and complexity of this kind of recognition. Judith Butler famously sheared de Beauvoir's historical critique of gender from its grounding in biological reproduction and emphasized the way the historical dimensions of becoming women are constructed as performative actions requiring repetition and reiteration.[64] Through an approach influenced by poststructuralism, Butler's extraordinarily dynamic Hegelianism highlighted the inescapable need to reenact social conventions. She effectively repositioned gender ontologically as a malleable source of empowerment capable of resisting norms and allowing one to readily articulate more ethical, inclusive, and queer modes of reshaping one's—or recognizing another's—social identity. Her theory also created space for a broader range of nonconforming genders and queer sexualities and established philosophical underpinnings for the advent of third-wave feminism. Since then, intersectional feminism has proposed an open-ended synthesis of these dialectics of race, gender, and class and other axes of oppression, providing a more complex and integrated view of the struggle for recognition.[65] The enduring inequality of intersectional relations are dizzying: Amia Srinivasan has argued that secular frameworks of consent do little to address the subtle and powerful traffic of power and fantasy that underpins twenty-first century sexual encounters.[66]

These lineages of feminism and critical race theory have reframed Hegel's master-slave dialectic to show how the self, in late capitalism, is consistently mediated by irruptive and unequal dialectical frameworks. If humanism presumes the need for mutual recognition and the logic of its historical accomplishment, the social inequality of modernity—ironically but inescapably—provides no basis for intersubjective symmetry. In this context revivals of Enlightenment humanism, such as that espoused by Kant or Cavell, are an insufficient condition for aesthetics in late modernity; an epistemic rift based in the discursive and historical dialectics of inequality routinely interrupts the communicative transparency of Cavell's comparatively dehistoricized conception of "improvisation." It is along these lines—of inequities of history, meaning, and grammar—that I have understood George E. Lewis's ideological critique of the midcentury schism between Afrological and Eurological approaches to improvisation.[67] To return to Du Bois's terminology, we might frame this epistemic rift in terms of the veil: a rupture that disjoins—often productively, in the form of what he calls a "gift"—the purported universality of humanity.[68]

Given the unsettled—and incessant—struggles for modern social equality, how might we adequately theorize the struggle for aesthetic recognition? Cavell would argue that what makes this such a tense complication is that artists, by making art at all, nonetheless always presuppose something minimally universal—the bare existence of shared intentionality. Without it one could not even begin to raise the question of recognition. Yet the weight of underlying asymmetries sets into relief a tension that is foundational to modernism: why and how questions about the meaning of art must grapple with the ingenuity of subjects who have been historically devalued. In this context, Cavell's desire to attend to the importance of intention and intersubjectivity—within a postwar circumstance he diagnoses as alienating, industrializing, fraught with nonrecognition and noncommunication—can be understood as allowing epistemic tensions and gaps to remain productively animated and activated. A renunciation of humanism altogether—aside from its chilling loss of grounds for social justice or the ethics of human history—would abandon our histories to a gray and functional sociology or a wholesale fetishization of the posthuman. Thus, Hegel was correct to claim that mutual human recognition is fundamental to social change (as in the Black Lives Matter movement) even if his master-slave scenario was exceedingly teleological and optimistic. Along these lines, art, which Hegel regarded as self-consciousness in sensory form, emerges emphatically amid a dehumanizing modernity as an epistemic and affective mess, where traces of humanity manage to survive.

The lessons one can derive from aesthetic encounters are fraught with risk, but they invite puzzlement over what the self ought to be, or what the self is attracted to, even perversely, amid the most horrifying and insoluble of social problems. Cavell is a productive interlocutor for this problem, notwithstanding the naivete of his humanism, in part because of his hesitancy to base his thinking in the grammars of a particular aesthetic form, a trap Adorno fails to escape. In fact his prose occasionally mimics such hesitancy, which in a way shows us that the socially embedded guiderails (or "forms of life" to use Wittgenstein's parlance) can be hard to see and even harder to describe and understand. As mentioned in the previous chapter, a recognition of the other's intentionality could then acknowledge the possibility that the other uses a grammar that a given self may not know.[69] This communicative difficulty may not be overcome; it does not follow, for example, that one ought to "solve" the problem of noncommunication by simply prescribing humanism universally in order to flatten out the inequalities of race, gender, or social class. One can instead follow Cavell and acknowledge the contentious and sometimes uncomfortable terrain of improvised debate surrounding the noncommunicative perplexities of a modernism that makes inequality audible. Within this debate, it is legitimate to conclude that there is no common humanity or that it cannot be actualized or spoken of because trauma and devaluation cannot simply be erased from history. Patterns of subjugation continue to structure late modernity.

In this context, Du Bois's veil—or in another context, Édouard Glissant's concept of "opacity"—marks an intersubjective hiatus, a relation that troubles transparency, or one's ability to ask "why" questions about another's intentions, or to be sure a musician "means it" (to use Cavell's phrase), which is also a humanizing acknowledgment that musician and listener may never connect.[70] After all, modern art is not itself predicated on reciprocal humanism—it externalizes, consumes, and fantasizes. In terms theorized by Michael Taussig, it is foundationally mimetic.[71] The other, in this instance, is not merely an arresting infinity that enjoins us to compassion (à la Levinas); in the context of modernism the other is socially entangled, historically attuned, and overdetermined by patterns of consumption. In this sense, the veil does not function merely as an epistemic gap; it also marks the physiognomy of the other's intentions. The other may appear beautiful and fetishized—as magnetic, irresistible, and cool, as bearing an inscrutable attitude, or as harboring an impossibility of exhaustion or communion. The other brings to life a theatrical and ontological space of play in which racial difference underwrites fundamentally unequal—even incommensurable— competitions and fantasies for the self. As Miles Davis once described this dialectics of noncommunication,

> People will go for anything they don't understand if it's got enough hype. They want to be hip, want always to be in on the new thing so they don't look unhip. White people are especially like that, particularly when a Black person is doing some-thing they don't understand. They don't want to have to admit that a Black person could be doing something that they don't know about. Or that he could be maybe a little more—or a whole lot more—intelligent than them. They can't stand to admit that kind of shit to themselves, so they run around talking about how great it is until the next "new thing" comes along.[72]

The raced and gendered magnetism of noncommunication: Du Bois, de Beauvoir, Fanon, Davis, Butler, and Srinivasan complicate Cavell's principle of intentionality into a maze. The earnest recovery of an artwork's meaning becomes the most difficult thing, perhaps far more complex a philosophical problem than Cavell even imagined it as he mulled over music as high mathematics in a journal like *Perspectives of New Music*. Consider the queer opacity of Tudor's Orientalist separatism. Prestigious, solemn, and above all charismatic, he positioned himself beyond the Western ego and behind the cloak of a Chinese aleatoric logic fused to the sonic equivalent of an Artaudian violence. Or consider the notoriously insoluble puzzles surrounding Ornette Coleman's perplexing term *harmolodics*.[73] Or ponder the unsettling injunction of Nico blithely and somewhat disquietingly singing "I'll Be Your Mirror" from a home stereo.

When the other's intentionality is a puzzle, music's ineffability can serve as an exemplary medium—an aesthetic form with an affective grip—that carries unspeakable difficulties and desires for the self as a paradoxical locus of late modernity. For intersubjective drama is not merely a modernist question of individual selves who may no longer be able to communicate; modernity is built on a fraught mirroring of unequal, intersectional epistemologies.[74]

Music is an instance of noncommunication sublimated into forms, sensations, and atmospheres; it is congealed into personae, collaborations, and recorded worlds. It appears not only as aesthetically noncommunicative (in the familiar Adornian sense of an aesthetic work being noninstrumental and thus potentially resistant). It is also socially noncommunicative because musician and audience are mimetically fantasizing about one another in a differential field predicated on unequal perspectives. Its technological reproduction amplifies the affective proximity of the social imagination while leaving the inequities of its material underpinnings unspoken.

## Atmospheres

In these unequal social fields, what music does one make? How does one listen? As noted earlier, by rewiring one's faculties of perception, a second-order modernism engages the capacities of the self, the other, and its social field at a fundamentally affective level. Going this deep with audiences generally entails seismic experiments in the crafting of dissonances. Thus, in the closing sections of this chapter, let us consider a trio of concepts proper to a second-order modernism that mark key stylistic shifts in music of the postwar avant-gardes.

The first is one that can act as a comparative link across the collaborative poetics of this avant-garde generation: atmosphere. An atmosphere is a transformative presence. Its structure moves beyond the positive certitude of musical elements and the fracturing of known musical grammars in order to envelop perception and alter its conditions. It is a presence because its powers of transformation are metaphysical: the experience of music affects one's coordinates of perception. It causes you to forget where you are, to hallucinate, or it opens a void in the floor.[75]

In Jean Baudrillard's *System of Objects* (1968), the author disassembles the symbolic infrastructure that underpins the appearance of mainstream postwar consumer commodities. In his analysis of interior design, the systematic assembly of various elements forms an affective charge, a fetishistic situation or an enveloping scene that provides a sense of symbolic cohesion. A five-star hotel is not simply a question of cleanliness or better materials; the semiosis of its design is calculated in order to telegraph an encompassing inconsistency, an atmosphere of distinction or social class. Baudrillard compares this "systematic cultural connotation" to glass; glass appears as a transparent signification—a metaphysical buoyancy—with a certain ideological power above and beyond its material uses.[76]

The postwar avant-gardists in this book similarly encode their social desires into musical atmospheres; these are fantasies built on delicately wrought elements. Their underpinnings are material, relational, systematic, but they are rarely formally consistent; the underlying grammars in play are diffuse. Such musical atmospheres can have any manner of affective charges: they can be jarring, disturbing, cathartic, ecstatic, lulling, or erotic. Tudor's atmospheres of the 1950s juxtaposed a conservative deadpan theatricality with pianism of esoteric excess and violent physicality. What did it mean? Some journalists heard "nihilist" implications; others called it "far out." Cage framed it with his trademark charisma: here is an exotic tool from China that will utterly confound all your expectations.[77] Coleman's early performances were met similarly by a magnetic feeling of fascination and bewilderment ("I like him, but I don't have any idea of what he is doing").[78] John Cale once remarked that the Velvets aimed to "hypnotize audiences so that their subconscious would take over," adding that "I think it worked because people who tell you they love the band are never able to tell you why."[79] In recorded works by Coltrane and the Velvets, atmospheres could irrupt in entire theatrical-visual scenes, as in "Venus in Furs" (1967) or "The Ankh of Amen-Ra" (1971). Or, in songs like Patti Smith's "Land: Horses / Land of A Thousand Dances / La Mer (De)" (1975), they could turn into an ecstatic ride led by an incantation that breaks rules and has no god while managing to channel a gospel preacher. In Hell's "Blank Generation," (1977) the French decadence is transduced into a cathartic blast of indeterminacy.

These irruptions of affective praxis were inseparable from advances in recording technology. Atmospheres are often mixed, engineered, and manipulated with effects and other studio techniques that were becoming prominent during the 1960s and 1970s.[80] Michael Veal has noted this with particular care in the parallel experimentalism of Jamaican dub during this period, which used deconstructed song forms bathed in echo and reverb in order to evoke what he calls an atmospheric "songscape."[81] The aims were nothing less than utopian. He writes,

> All the talk of circuits, knobs, and switches can distract one from the fundamental reality that what these musicians were doing was synthesizing a new popular art form, creating a space where people could come together joyously despite the harshness that surrounded them. They created a music as roughly textured as the physical reality of the place, but with the power to transport their listeners to dancefloor nirvana as well as the far reaches of the cultural and political imagination: Africa, outer space, inner space, nature, and political/economic liberation.[82]

Musical atmospheres, engineered and mediated in any number of ways, convert electricity into metaphysics in ways that parallel Baudrillard's analysis of 1960s consumer atmospheres. Its poetics are an ad hoc empiricism rather than an intentional sculpting of forms. They can make use of all manner of strange inscriptions: graphic notation, calligraphy, mistranscribed instrumental parts, solos that do not correspond to the head of the song, deskilled collaborators and solos, or tinkering with knobs and sliders of the recording studio. As a stylistic tendency of second-order modernisms, all of them question the transparency of knowable musical forms and reach deep into our ears to trouble our coordinates of perception.

In line with midcentury intellectual fashions, the result both elevated and liquidated the coordinates of the self; the intentions embedded in such atmospheres were at once interrupted and maintained. But the way these musicians effaced the self and its grammars is socially complex. In atmospheric compositions and collaborations, the physiognomy of the other, built out in objects, rooms, and spaces, is refracted by contrapuntal intentions. The musicians may have intended one thing to happen or may not have entirely been on the same page when collaborating, and this indeterminacy—keeping the possibility of a humanism in suspense while enraptured by sensory immersion—is paradigmatic. Thus, the atmospheres of second-order modernisms can exploit the indeterminacy of such intentions to scale new heights of self-consciousness. In an echo of Hegel, musicians in these scenarios may be seeking recognition with a restless, even urgent, intentionality. But built out in the ineffability of a collaborative atmosphere, a musician may come across as cool or distant almost to the point of phoning it in.

In *Blues People* (1963), Amiri Baraka writes evocatively of the Black modernist's proclivity for secret languages, which were developed into tightly knit cultures of exclusivity that reflected a "cult of redefinition, in terms closest to the initiated."[83] The cult was that of Black cool, which Baraka framed as a practical response to racism; it allowed the suffering of racial subjugation to be resisted through a form of strategic withdrawal—the withholding of criteria. He writes,

> It is perhaps the flexibility of the Negro that has let him survive; his ability to "be cool"—to be calm, unimpressed, detached, perhaps to make failure as secret a phenomenon as possible. In a world that is basically irrational, the most legitimate relationship to it is nonparticipation.[84]

This kind of deliberate nonparticipation may question the valuation of the time given to intentionality. Or, seen in a relational field where more or less earnest critics like Cavell really want everyone to "mean it" when they make art, coolness can be a metastrategy to give off aggression and heat by way of refusal—either compulsively, or deliberately, or a bit of both—as one or the other in this or that context, at once perpetuating and unsettling the traffic of social fantasy. Such atmospheric games are relational and dialectical and can stage strikingly complex instances of the ineffable. Made with elaborate awareness of the social field, their complex dynamics underpin the experience of being affectively enthralled by an ineffable situation such that "one fails even to seem to communicate."

As these dynamics were built out into scenes, even as artistry was often collaborative, the scenes themselves were rarely communal in any idealized sense; they were in fact quite socially competitive. To harness the ineffability of hipness was an aspiration; like the Beats, these musicians used their social intelligence to retain power and value in the competitive social climate of New York in ways that could require virtuoso strategizing and gaslighting. The rulebook for hip could not be formalized; real answers had to remain elusive. We might even say that hip developed its own negative theology, since no one would espouse it directly or simply clue you in.[85] And across racial lines, hipness could appear in dramatically contrasting ways. If Baraka described this obscure hipness as something that was resistant to racism, Mailer, a white man, thought of it as a fetishistic primitivism that could not be taught. James Baldwin, in his response to Mailer, indeed had confirmed that the diagnosis itself missed the mark.[86]

### HYPERFRACTURES

Finally, consider two kinds of atmospheric techniques: hyperfractures and alchemies. These are admittedly categories that freely shade into one another and hardly exhaust the uncountable ways of producing atmospheres. But they help set into relief a stylistic trajectory for the scope of this comparative study. Tudor and Coleman are explorers of hyperfractures, whereas the Velvets, Smith, and Hell most vividly turn to alchemies. All these figures could be said to adopt elements of alchemy, but Coltrane most explicitly hybridizes them.

Hyperfractures go beyond the fracturing of a known form recognizable to the listener. When we know the rules of a performance (classical music's "compliance" with a score at midcentury, Schoenberg's principle of developing variation dependent on the recognizable variations of a single theme, or predictable jazz improvisations based on a known theme or a set of changes), it is possible to hear what the fracture is and come to a determination about what it might mean.[87] But hyperfractures break the rules for perceiving what is significant in the forms and thus dramatically reduce one's transparency of expression. Listening to a hyperfracture, one is overwhelmed by plentitude and effectively loses grip on what is being played. Key characteristics are an excess of material that results in a perceptual disorientation and a loss of ability to discern precisely what counts as form. Opacity and perceptual uncertainty come to dominate one's experience of the object. Hyperfractures can involve esoteric, aleatoric, mystical, illogical, or exotic forms and rules; they fuss over numbers and numerologies, code books, recipes, elaborate and extremely ornamented solos, or multiplicative logics that may or may not make sense to listeners. A number of musicians in this period could be said to explore hyperfractures. Beyond Tudor, Cage, and Coleman, one might include Iannis Xenakis, Cecil Taylor, Sun Ra, Cathy Berberian, Anthony Braxton, Michael Finnissy, and certain works of Alice Coltrane. Instead of a clear and impressive spectacle—an exemplary instance of a known accomplishment—hyperfractures press listeners to mull over detailed and opaque sorcery.

In the 1950s Tudor always appeared in a suit, conservative, ready to be a reliable mediator for compositions. But what came out was very far from anything language-like. At Cage's notorious and well-attended twenty-five-year retrospective at Town Hall in 1958, the pianist executed realizations that were actually quite literal. That is, Tudor made Cage's extravagant and calligraphic notation more conservative by determining specific notes and laying it out in transparently legible spatial notation that could be performed loosely. In some instances, Tudor compounded Cage's calculative methods, most famously in his second realization of Cage's score of *Solo for Piano* (1958). Cage's compositional processes and sound palettes involved appropriations from India, China, and Japan, which he fused to Dada theatrics, Artaudian spectacle, anarchism, mushrooms, and experimental pedagogy in order to intimidate audiences with an atmosphere they could not understand. Tudor, who by comparison wore his influences lightly (Artaud, Rudolf Steiner's Anthroposophy, and Indian cooking), was Cage's charismatic salesman, a dispassionate, traditionally prestigious priest and mediator.

In Coleman's hands, hyperfracture resulted in an exacerbated problem of Cavellian "fraudulence." For jazz audiences, there was often an expectation that an improvisation was thematically and expressively linked to its melody and virtuosically attached to a repeated series of chord changes.[88] In this context, Coleman's work raised particularly vivid communicative questions, ones that compounded the problem of fracture, such that one might have to guess about the intentions in the composer's mind. After all, he composed his own tunes and had his collaborators build linear improvisations around them with little harmonic context in the form of a comping piano familiar to bebop. This could easily challenge the credulity of knowing what jazz grammar was fractured (say through complex, fast-paced harmonies in bebop of the 1940s or modal unspooling in the late 1950s). Coleman's work from the 1960s onward—particularly in light of his coinage of the term *harmolodics* in the 1970s—instead asks us to mull over the possibility that the very capacity to name, know, and hear a note is made indeterminate by the collaborative ethics of vernacular creativity. The result seems to let recognizable fragments of individual motives and styles pile up to the point where one might ask a question such as, Is this time valuable? Is there enough intentionality here for me?

Hyperfractures are detailed, fussy, and hypermediated; they take mediation to the extreme. When a hyperfracture calls into question the governing intentionality of its own artistry—as if its authorial subject has been largely occluded—it can become a philosophical provocation about authorship. Along these lines, both Tudor and Coleman were methodical and cool in ways that could be read as effacing the grounding of their respective egos. And because debates about their intentions unfolded socially—as something like Cavellian improvisations—effacing their own egos could also be a way of intentionally creating a stir and blowing themselves up. Conceptually driven, these musicians could thrive amid the confusion.

Coltrane's decisions were no less perplexing, and she, too, occasionally engaged hyperfractures. In works like "Universal Consciousness" (1971), she fractured the real time of an individual take with tape splices and collaborated with Coleman on string arrangements and overlaid materials to produce fiendishly dense textures. At the same time, she experimented with provocative literalisms. In the early 1970s, Coltrane controversially covered and transcribed excerpts from her late husband's legendary 1961 version of "My Favorite Things" (*World Galaxy*, 1971) as well as excerpts from Stravinsky's *Firebird* (*Lord of Lords*, 1972). And during the same period, she pressed beyond hyperfractures. Coltrane's trademark improvisational style at the keyboard was what her late husband described as "fleet"—it was built on trills and tremolos, and on the harp, glissandi. In allowing the material to grow into fields of overabundance, her work repeatedly tipped into inconsistencies and visual hallucinations.[89] In this regard, Coltrane went further than her husband with his famed "sheets of sound."[90] In her records, she pressed hyperfractures into alchemies.

## ALCHEMIES

Historically, alchemy was ancient chemistry that sought to create value through the transformation of substances (lead into gold, elixirs for immortality, and the like). Though the alchemists were guided by myth and speculation (unbound by the rigors of modern scientific skepticism), they were nonetheless resourceful pioneers in the experimental method.[91] In a remarkably similar fashion, modern musical alchemists—whose experimental laboratory was often the recording studio—were essentially speculative thinkers. With sound as their substance, the alchemists' studio techniques were guided by numinous ideals, and aimed at the production of apparitions and environments. King Tubby and Lee "Scratch" Perry, experimenting in Kingston, Jamaica, in the 1970s, are paradigmatic examples. Moreover, in line with ancient chemistry, alchemical music was not only powerful, atmospheric, and compelling, in line with Baudelaire, Verlaine, Rimbaud, Artaud, and Jung—modern enthusiasts of alchemy who were broadly influential on this generation—it sought physiological transformation.

Philosophically, alchemies enacted a Hegelian sublation of hyperfractures.[92] If hyperfractures stage an unprecedented density of fractures such that they start affecting the rules of perception, alchemies jump overboard from tens of thousands of notes to the liquid inconsistencies of electronic mixes. If hyperfractures are akin to elaborately detailed blueprints or schematics, alchemy is the perfecting of a sauce on the stove. Alchemies sublate or dissolve various codes and layers of mediation to the point where they attempt to cook dinner with the real itself; though they never overcome mediation—in practice, they layer it in ever more elaborate ways—their chosen mediations are electrified and resist positive isolation in an empirical search for pronounced intensities of affect and spiritual transformations. Alchemies were also more closely associated with drugs. They were inspired by 1960s generational enthusiasm for marijuana, LSD, and psilocybin experimentation as well as the writings of French decadents and symbolist poets.

Mediation, even for the most mind-bending alchemies, remained inescapable.[93] The Velvets were so drawn to alchemy that they started trying to then build a grammar with it—or at least they tinkered with the possibility of building one. Each of the tracks in *The Velvet Underground and Nico* (1967) could feel like atmospheric rooms, as Lou Reed and Nico took turns embodying and observing characters with whom you could (or could not) identify. By the late 1960s, as a new generation of immigrant Yogis became iconic fixtures of new religious movements, an entire culture industry developed around Bramble's broad zeitgeist of the modernist occult: the Velvets could buy and sell exotic Indian or French atmospheres in stores. Meanwhile, Western philosophy appeared normative by comparison: the tenured logicians and political scientists were modeling their inquiries on the sciences and looking to center reasoned deliberation and instrumentality as the foundation for civil society. By negation, the Dionysian inconsistencies of the postwar avant-garde—as an outgrowth of the counter-Enlightenment—took on a dissenting role in a prestigious space of morally transgressive fantasy. For Reed, Cale, and Hell, the sensory plunge of heroin, a risky and effortful ploy for a white musician to feel as "real" and precarious as the Black beboppers, emerged as a nihilistic, postindustrial limit point. As Hell once put it in one of his notebooks, as if he were surfing Schopenhauer's will in a universe devoid of politics: "I'm pure energy."[94]

In the 1950s it was crucial that Tudor was heard as a traditionally competent virtuoso. But many of the musicians in this book—including Tudor himself following his self-taught turn to electronics—questioned normative ideals of competence, took an interest in varied abilities, or even went down the paradoxical path of deskilling themselves. This was especially true of a postwar alchemist like Lou Reed. Reed's vocals artfully meandered around the notes of a melody in an imitation Bob Dylan, who himself imitated a range of vernacular singers from Woody Guthrie to Rosetta Tharpe.[95] In some instances, traditional instrument setups were abandoned. As noted earlier, Coleman invited his ten-year-old son to drum with his band professionally and later invented his own style of improvising left handed on the violin. Coltrane turned to singing later in the 1980s and 1990s when reimagining Hindu *bajans* with a pitch-bending Oberheim synthesizer and gospel choruses.[96] Punk was perhaps emblematic above all of this move toward deliberate deskilling. Smith and Hell considered themselves to be poets first and foremost, and only secondarily regarded themselves as musicians. In Hell's band, one finds a guitarist like Robert Quine, who seems to be deliberately and self-consciously undoing his own sense of self-conscious virtuosity (in ways that were celebrated by Lester Bangs, another exemplary instance of tortured self-consciousness who deified the Dionysian inconsistency of "The Party" with a capital "P").[97]

Scholarly approaches toward musical modernism have had a bias toward the cognitive and technical—labors of the ear are heard as labors of the mind. This is the basis for academic formalism, writ large, which had its heyday in the 1930s through the 1970s when the institutionalized arts sought siloed, vertical methods in the manner of the natural sciences in order to establish creative work as a form of research. But the artists in this book by and large were not accepted by any academic institutions; they did their work in the marketplaces of New York, European festivals, and in the margins of commercial music industry—in spaces that coincide with what Anthony Reed and Benjamin Piekut have termed the *vernacular avant-garde*.[98] Rather than knowing—and fracturing—rule books for established techniques of composition, they tended to prefer empiricisms of trial and error, of studio experimentation, of repeating without a known grammar, or troubling, tinkering with, and overdeveloping the grammar to the point where it is no longer transparent. In this context, if we still cared about the personal grounds for what Cavell understood as improvisation, it could result in riddles of intentionality. Because these musicians were imagining themselves and their art across unequal social lines (blurred gender lines, racial mimicry, slumming it across boundaries of class, etc.), their intentions, and labors of perception, were foundationally driven by fantasies about transforming who and what a modern self could understand itself to be.

Thus, notwithstanding the near dissolution of individual intentions and selves, hyperfractures (combinatory excess) and alchemies (recipes or calibrations of inconsistencies) had ways of nonetheless thrusting icons to the front of the stage. As performers, these icons could be positioned variously as gurus, mystics, mediums, ciphers, chanteuses, or heroes. Maybe it is not even clear that they exactly knew what they were doing and that is what made them so exciting and real—their genius was that they at once invited and thwarted mimesis. They could easily come across as dangerous, desirable, divine, or shamanic. The scenarios and spaces presented in their recordings were in this way fraught with intersubjective dramas built on the dynamics of desire and disavowal, to return to the formulation by Hall. But their intentions were generally kept obscure. In purportedly trying to hide the ego, they might fuss over perfecting the sound of divine ornaments or stage ancient and exotic rituals that seem to promise metaphysics even if it is only a touristic, temporary metaphysics and not one of sustained or all-encompassing devotional belief.

This all was accomplished by attending to the distinct affordances of music's affective praxis. Their works could be primitivist in their aesthetic choices but not because they were simply reviving esoteric myths of the past in earnest. Instead, these musicians were rethinking ritual in a modern world that was losing track of its meanings and traditions. They altered collective coordinates of mind as much as they altered social coordinates of perceiving sound. All of it—constructing these atmospheres, exploiting the ineffable, and asking foundational questions about self, other, perception, and metaphysics of space—involved creating and changing one's own rules along the way, covering one's tracks, chasing the elusive, ineffable power of music to transform and repositioning it in ever more obscure ways. Dialectics were constantly redeployed even as they were perpetually evading their normative forms.

∵

The dialectics of social tensions and atmospheric forms swarm, mirror, and pinball in the chapters that follow. Supporting this speculative traffic is the ineffability of music's affective praxis, which recurs as a generative leitmotif. At a great remove from the pious, transcendent Platonisms of European Romanticism or the structural listening of its academic afterlife, for these musicians, music's ineffability took flight as an affective praxis in a contested field of social experimentation. It could appear as the spellbinding plenitude and excess of the other, the unspeakable embarrassment of wanting to be the singer, pianist, guitarist, or drummer while listening, or to pretend quietly that the other is mine, when they ought not to be. Here, ineffability could be racist, sexist, productive, critical, and desiring all at once. Or it could be the basis for an aspiration to self-consciousness through work that seems to unsettle social norms. For these musicians, things tended to be ad hoc: one finds tangles of informal social and intellectual life built around affectively charged atmospheres. A musician's metaphysics could be unabashedly spiritual and religious, ecumenical, satanic, decadent, ecstatically protesting, and escapist. Their chosen musical elements may not break down into a pedagogically transparent set of forms either because the music is overgrown by layered hyperfractures or is dissolved into alchemies and inconsistencies governed by elaborate attitudes, calibrations, and metaphors. Across these instances, some musicians attempted to speak of the ineffable; others just had a way of showing us its magic.

∴

Part Two

# STUDIOS

∵

## CHAPTER THREE

# David Tudor,
# Esoteric Spectacle . . . c. 1958

At 11 p.m., on May 15, 1958, with almost a thousand in attendance at New York's Town Hall in midtown, choreographer Merce Cunningham took the podium, a man with no traditional skills as a conductor, and led the world premiere of Cage's *Concert for Piano and Orchestra* by turning his arms in the manner of a clockface (figs. 3.1, 3.2). Pianist David Tudor was the soloist. He sat in front of a small ensemble of thirteen players.

The moment is storied. Nearly a thousand were in attendance, making the concert itself financially profitable. One Cage biographer, Kenneth Silverman, describes it as the most pivotal and consequential of his concerts.[1] Producer and major-label A&R executive George Avakian (whose sister-in-law was pianist Maro Ajemian, dedicatee and Town Hall performer of Cage's *Sonatas & Interludes*) was enlisted to record the concert for release and wrote this in his liner notes: "Few concerts of unusual music have provoked so much interest—before, during and after."[2] Cage himself beamed at the buzzy intensity of the scene that night, remarking, "What pleased me most was that so many people told me they saw friends they hadn't seen in six or seven years."[3] Indeed, after May 15, 1958, following decades of on-and-off support from his parents, Cage—already a notorious provocateur used to groans and eye rolls from critics and audiences and who, during the prior winter, had to take on freelance graphic design work for pennies—would become professionally busy enough to be financially independent.

The opening portion of the program was dominated by works that came from Cage's early period of the late 1930s through about 1950. Scholars have struggled to draw strong lines of influence from South and East Asia to the sound world of Cage's music during these years in part because Cage had little interest in technically specific borrowings. Evocative and often compelling on their own terms, like much exotica, in these works Cage was unconcerned with authenticity or even verisimilitude. One critic described Cage's work as a "sophisticated primitivism" that, in effect, still paled by comparison with actual non-Western music.[4] The *Sonatas & Interludes*

FIG. 3.1. Merce Cunningham conducting the premiere of John Cage's *Concert for Piano and Orchestra* at Town Hall, May 15, 1958. Original courtesy of the Cunningham Trust.

(1946–48) for prepared piano were emblematic; they were influenced by Ananda Coomaraswamy's writings on the Indian concept of *rasa*, which entails eight (or nine, depending on your count) ineffable but permanent moods (*bhāva*).[5] But there were no exact correlations between these moods and the various sonatas and interludes. With a mix of experimentation and fantasy, Cage was aiming for atmospheres. In the words of one reviewer of Ajemian's live recording of the *Sonatas & Interludes*, they "ring fascinating changes on faintly Oriental themes—like an atavistic memory of a gamelan gong."[6]

While his compositional method during the 1930s and 1940s involved sophisticated rhythmic structures and formalisms, in the sphere of philosophy Cage's borrowings from Asia were often superficial even as he repeatedly and heavy-handedly advertised them. Edward Crooks has shown, for instance, how Cage's famous dictum "to imitate nature in the manner of her operation" is ironically not at all Asian; it is in fact an Aristotelian phrase. Its source was Thomas Aquinas, whose phrase *Ars imitator naturam in sua operatione* (art imitates nature in its workings) from his *Summa Theologiae* (1485) appears in Coomaraswamy's *The Transformation of Nature in Art* (1942).[7] Coomaraswamy's book, which Cage read enthusiastically during the 1940s, draws parallels between Asian and European aesthetics.[8] As Crooks explains, the phrase is a simple affirmation of mimesis linked to a conception of nature, one of the most common motifs in Western European aesthetics; Aquinas himself was referring to writings on mimesis by Plato and Aristotle. Of course, playing fast and loose with sources was something of a deliberate strategy: in his writings of the 1940s, Cage insisted that the looseness of Asian influences allowed his own creative voice to emerge.[9]

The last third of the concert drew attention to Cage's more strident chance-derived works and showcased Tudor's premiere performance of the *Concert for Piano and Orchestra*, the composer's first largely indeterminate score. Cage's turn to chance procedures, and its attendant principles of "chaos," "purposelessness," "unimpededness," and "interpenetration," were indebted to several East Asian sources that were newly fashionable in

FIG. 3.2. David Tudor and Merce Cunningham at the rehearsal for the premiere of John Cage's *Concert for Piano and Orchestra*, May 15, 1958. George Avakian Papers, New York Public Library. Photo by George Moffett. Used with permission from the Chicago History Museum.

the West: the Chinese *I Ching* (ninth century BCE), the *Tao Te Ching* (sixth century CE), Huang Po's *Doctrine of Universal Mind* (ninth century CE), and the modern philosophical writings of Daisetsu Teitaro Suzuki, whose lectures on Zen Buddhism at Columbia University Cage attended in the early 1950s.[10] Among these influences, Suzuki became crucial for Cage; the composer cited his work frequently in his teaching and lectures from the 1950s onward. Suzuki's version of Zen was heavily influenced by the "single faith" thesis forwarded by theosophists; in his view, Zen was neither religious nor philosophical—he framed it as a wholly ineffable, nonsectarian, and singular experience that underpinned all world religions. It was Suzuki's somewhat oversimplified, Westernized Zen that became influential on Cage.[11] In his references to Suzuki, Cage was oblique and imitative. At a remove from Zen monasteries or any practice of meditation, he frequently riffed on his own version of the Zen koan. In a philosophical vein, Cage praised Suzuki's belief in an affirmative and inclusive immediacy of the here and now that stood opposed to the causal reasoning of Western thought.[12]

In anticipation of the premiere, Robert Rauschenberg and Jasper Johns, two of the sponsors of the Town Hall Retrospective (alongside filmmaker Emile de Antonio), encouraged Cage to display the score for the *Concert's Solo for Piano* at the Stable Gallery in midtown, a venue strongly associated with the rise of abstract expressionism in the 1940s. He did so and included a flyer for the exhibition in the Town Hall program. In the gallery, Cage's scores received recognition as visual works of art (and in fact, individual pages from the score were sold at the gallery).[13] In her review of the exhibition, art critic Dore Ashton described the visual impact of Cage's scores having "calligraphic beauty" and "a delicate sense of design."[14] The score for the *Solo for Piano* also had a peculiar physical form. Like a thick deck of 11 × 17 cards, Cage's lettered "graphs" (as he referred to them) were visually scattered, often stretching over two or three pages (fig. 3.3). For this reason, the sheets were nearly impossible to view as a totality. Physically handling the score— shuffling it, recombining it, marveling at its many intricacies—mirrored, from a visual and tactile perspective, the indeterminacy of the work. With its overlapping tapestry of inventive notations, the score of Cage's *Solo for Piano* was also redolent of a Chinese or Japanese scroll painting, only cut into pieces of card stock that could be shuffled. Though unlike a scroll painting, no directional narrative or journey is implied from left to right.

Then there is Cage's idiosyncratic calligraphy, with its characteristically heavy blocked serifs rendered in India ink with a calligraphic pen and redolent of the traditionally intimidating French Clarendon typeface familiar from the popular culture of the American Wild West. Lettering from *Water Music* (1952) (fig. 3.4) is a bit more curvilinear and boldly discontinuous

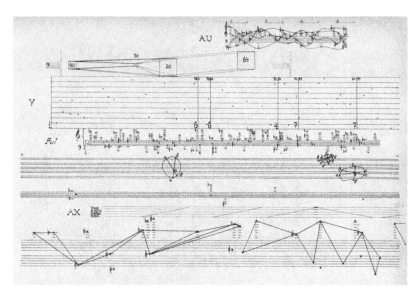

FIG. 3.3. David Tudor's copy of John Cage, *Solo for Piano* (1958). David Tudor Papers, 980039, box 176, folder 1, Getty Research Institute, Los Angeles.

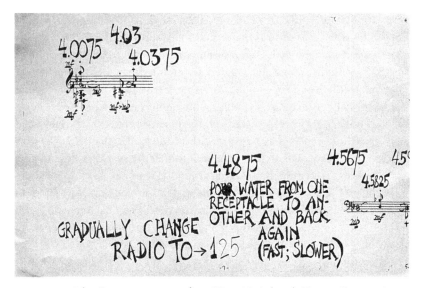

FIG. 3.4. John Cage, score excerpt from *Water Music* (1952). Henmar Press, 1960.

FIG. 3.5. Advertisement for The New Mandarin Inn (1919–21). Public domain.

enough to be redolent of a Chinese restaurant advertisement, a familiar sight in Manhattan during the 1950s (fig. 3.5).

It is inevitably difficult—and speculative—to try to understand what kind of fantasies and desires underpin Cage's appropriations. Though his lettering has a similar feel, Cage was not attempting to reproduce Chinese script. As with his sounds, he avoided direct imitations; he was loosely reimagining with the aim of evoking atmospheres. But it is instructive to note the historical context: Cage's calligraphic choices echoed the exoticized typefaces of a resourceful group of immigrant entrepreneurs who had faced state-sanctioned racism as a result of the Chinese Exclusion Act (1882–1943).[15] The appropriative choice reminds us that the avant-garde's engagement with social inequity was as often grounded in popular atmospherics as it was in intellectually rigorous experiments. In fact, for Cage and Tudor in particular, the culinary point of comparison was hardly far-fetched. Tudor himself compared the unique discipline of these ego-annihilating works of the avant-garde to developing one's taste for Indian cuisine.[16]

The sensational premiere was Cage's, but Tudor—the concert's soloist and the composer's muse—is the central subject of this studio chapter. Tudor's performance of Cage's *Concert for Piano*, by turns confrontational and playful, was a spectacle with exceptional elegance and showmanship; but it had no plausible explanation as to its meaning. Confronted with program notes that made the non-Western debts of Cage's work explicit, their largely white audience was asked to contemplate esoteric appropriations from India, China, and Japan in a way that purported to challenge the philosophical assumptions of Western reason and self-expression.[17] And Tudor's presence was key to this mystique; it evoked for the audience an atmosphere of what Harold Schonberg later described as associated with "that furious mélange [of] modern art, mysticism, Zen Buddhism, higher mathematics, polemics, and a type of musical aesthetics that surpasseth man's imagination."[18] Tudor's spectacular and vaguely mystical presence was an invitation to escape 1958 in New York, or even to get out of oneself, or to spectate as others proposed (or pretended) to get out of themselves in order to commune with nature. In questioning the basic rules of engagement, it was a noncommunicative hyperfracture that, like many piano concertos, elevated the self in a dramatic virtuoso display; this particular concert also asked listeners to consider the self's dramatic liquidation in the form of a meditation into the underlying discontinuity of nature.

Cage's and Tudor's atmospheric evocations, with their loose sense of a global spiritual consciousness, should not be idealized as progressive or universal. A spiritual flight to Asia—in whatever caricatured form—was often routed through an elite discourse of international theosophy that, as we shall see, had minimal understanding of its appropriated sources and relied on a fantasy of the cross-cultural supremacy of global ancient civilizations and, in many cases, a negation of racialized others. Of course, much of this ideological traffic circulated below the surface. In his press release, Cage described the sheer variety and indeterminacy of the score as "the situation being presented being one of that disparateness which may be observed in nature."[19] Yet amid all the apparent "disparateness," it was never entirely clear why exactly audiences were asked to reconnect with the ineffable contingency of the natural world in such an arresting and confrontational form.

Though this chapter focuses on Tudor's role in the performance, Cage also figures prominently. In the years leading up to 1958, Cage and Tudor were living in close proximity at the Gatehill Cooperative Community in Stony Point and acknowledged that their creative work of this period was effectively inseparable. In fact Cage famously said of Tudor, "In all my works since 1952, I have tried to achieve what would seem interesting and vibrant to David Tudor. Whatever succeeds in the works I have done has been determined in relationship to him. . . . David Tudor was present in everything I was doing."[20] This was during a period when Tudor's role had become itself an inspiration for a number of avant-garde composers. In the words of Morton Feldman, "This [avant-garde] kind of music is more than merely a specialty of Tudor's. In some ways he's entirely responsible for it. Meeting David enabled me to hear and see possibilities I never dreamed of."[21]

## Tudor's Pianism of the 1950s

John Holzaepfel, who has done foundational research on Tudor's realizations of the 1950s and 1960s, aptly called the *Solo for Piano* an "encyclopedia" of Cage's notational techniques up until 1958. As Martin Iddon and Philip Thomas have shown in detail, some of the *Solo for Piano*'s graphs were entirely new; others Cage reworked from scores from the 1950s, including the *Music for Piano* series (1952–56), *Winter Music* (1957), and the graphic notation for *Variations I* (1958), all of which were written for Tudor. To perform Cage's unconventional scores, Tudor created his own musical translations of Cage's notation, which he called *realizations*.[22] And to prepare his realizations, Tudor chose forty-eight of Cage's sixty-three lettered graphs, and wrote realizations for each, first as sketches in pencil before making a final copy in ink on short, compact, staff paper that could fit on the piano's pin block (with the music rack removed) so he could read the notation while performing extended techniques with various preparations inside the piano.

Tudor had a more or less consistent philosophy around his approach to realizations. Early in his career as a pianist and organist, he espoused a commonplace view of the work concept built around a composer's Platonic ideal (a "spirit" or "structural thought").[23] His studies as a pianist took place with Irma Wolpe Rademacher, while he concurrently studied analysis and composition with her husband, Stefan Wolpe.[24] In learning to play Stefan's dissonant and monumental *Battle Piece* (1947) for its premiere in 1950, Tudor played from memory and learned to analyze the composer's work in depth to understand its interior logic.[25] In Tudor's words: "I was taught as a performer to be very faithful to a given score. It's important for me to look at every detail and make sure I perform in the spirit of what is indicated."[26] Tudor's thinking began to change as his studio practiced evolved. As he began performing realizations of indeterminate and graphic scores during the 1950s, the Platonic "spirit" or "structure" beyond the score itself began to recede, and the sign systems themselves began to carry the ontological weight of the work. An underlying nominalism emerged: the visual particularity of the notation itself—not an underlying structure or ideal—became the essence of the music even when confronted with a score that was indeterminate. In his words, "what's in front of you becomes the composition."[27] When making the requisite choices entailed in a realization of an indeterminate score, Tudor would remain faithful to the composer's written material:

> I began to look at the parameters and I made certain decisions as to what
> was important and that enabled me to make a score of my own. I looked

at it and I said, "well, this whole proposition is so fraught with chance-happenings, that I have to be able to have a score which itself incorporates all those possibilities, at the same time being faithful to the readings which I make from John Cage's material."[28]

Elsewhere he emphasized a bit more of his own agency: "you choose among the possibilities what you want to appear, and then it's the task [of the performer] to make those things appear."[29] To be sure, Tudor's own skills and inclinations as a pianist guided many of his choices. In fact, Tudor's realizations were custom built for his famed sight-reading ability; he wanted to make a score he could read off in the heat of a performance.[30] This mirrored how he practiced. In a response to John Holzaepfel's question about Tudor's practice habits, Tudor insisted that he basically sight-read:

> My way of doing it is to get instantaneous information from the page that I'm looking at, and do it. The more graphic the notation, especially, the more you don't want to see anything but the music. . . . When I began to play contemporary music, I needed to see the score in front of me. You know, it's very suggestive.[31]

The real-time nominalism of Tudor's realizations was built on his own notational system, or what he calls "directions to myself," which (fig. 3.6) had their own exacting penmanship.[32]

The basics (the notes, clefs, etc.) were written in black pen. Tudor used blue pen for bar lines, dynamics, pedaling, and short phrases of language that describe specialized techniques. Following an approach to dynamics in Bo Nilsson's *Quantitäten* (1957), an important work in Tudor's repertory at the time, Tudor also used blue for precise numerical notation for dynamics (0.5 being the quietest, up to 10.5 being the loudest).[33] Tudor used red pen to mark off unusual sounds and group attacks in a way that corresponds to a given specialized technique or diagrams parts of his realization in a way that mirrors visual elements of Cage's graphs; in such instances, Tudor drew something from Cage's graph into his part. In pencil, one finds labels corresponding to Tudor's sequencing, which includes the letter of the graph and the page of Cage's original score, among other miscellaneous annotations.

Tudor also rejected playing from memory, which he found to be wrapped up in ego-driven idealisms, as when the performer internalizes the work in order to appear as if expressing it ex nihilo from the "heart" or "soul." Tudor, at least by this stage in his career as a pianist, felt no need to practice commonplace techniques like scales and arpeggios. Instead, he made his own exercises customized to the unusual tasks he found for himself ("exercises

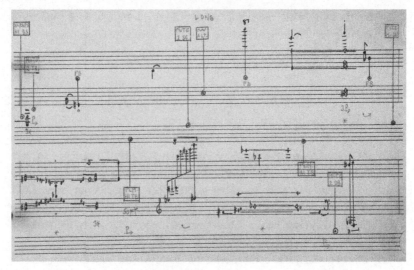

FIG. 3.6. David Tudor, first realization of John Cage's *Solo for Piano* (1958).
David Tudor Papers, 980039, box 6, folder 13, Getty Research Institute, Los Angeles.

dealing with the density of sounds" or "jumps and things").[34] These unique
physical challenges led to one exception: if something was physically so
tricky that Tudor needed to practice it, he would strategically memorize
the single passage so as to smoothly execute it.[35]

Through his studio practice in the 1950s, Tudor developed his own vernacular philosophy based in the experiential valuation of real time. The
idea was that sight reading, as well as its attendant customized technical
problem-solving, allowed him to keep the drastic vitality of the performance alive. By contrast, he regarded the Platonic techniques of memory
and understanding as forms of reification that removed him from the active
and responsive moment-to-moment flux. It was a distinctly esoteric kind
of anti-Platonic, loosely post-Western approach to musical performance:

> That's the point with contemporary music: you don't want to memorize
> it, because if you do, you'll be missing something, because you're creating
> it. And you have to give the music the chance to speak. So if something
> occurs to you, at the moment when you're doing it, you don't want to be
> encumbered by something you remember.[36]

Though Tudor would not extensively improvise until the 1960s when he
turned to the amplified piano, the bandoneon, and eventually modular synthesizers, as a pianist who effectively sight-read avant-garde scores during

the 1950s, he felt it was important to remain oriented toward the vitality of real time. In his view, the dramatic atmosphere of the performance affected the making of the work: "many's the performance (*Music of Changes* is but one example) where I found out the way to do it by having performed it. So the next performance was quite different."[37] The sight-readable quality of each individual sheet in scores like his first realization the *Solo for Piano* allowed Tudor to experiment performance to performance with the sequencing of various sheets so long as the score allowed it. In his words: "if you look through my materials, you'll see that some of the scores are made [by] notating all the choices that I would have, so that, if I were bored by having to repeat it, I could change it instantaneously."[38] Tudor, who professed the need to constantly innovate throughout his career, could barely tolerate a performance that sequenced the same sight-read realization sheets from gig to gig. He changed them in order to sustain an atmosphere of affective vitality on stage.

For the premiere of the *Concert for Piano and Orchestra*, Tudor created a sequence of forty-eight realized graphs across forty-two half pages. Held together in a binder, these realized sheets could be easily resequenced from performance to performance. Consider Tudor's performance sequence for the Town Hall premiere (fig. 3.7). Notwithstanding the scandalous reception of Cage's chance-derived work at the Darmstadt Summer Courses just a few months later in 1958, it is instructive to note that Tudor's chosen performance sequence for the premiere has a surprisingly classical sense of balance. He alternates between dramatic performances of individual graphs and stoic silences; only in a few places are multiple graphs superimposed in any kind of elaborate way.

Though Tudor's preparations were fastidious, certain things about the premiere were less than desirable from Cage's point of view. The ensemble was notoriously loud. Some of this was the fault of the brass players, whose extraneous riffing Cage would later describe as "foolish" and "unprofessional." But there were also issues in the writing of the parts, which indeed asked for a fair number of boisterous and nontraditional sounds.[39] We might also note, as well, that Cage had only rarely written for orchestra, and when the orchestration of a concerto is aleatoric, things you want to hear are inevitably buried.[40] Moreover, a specialist new music performer wasn't exactly a thing in 1958. All three brass players Cage hired (trombonist Frank Rehak; tuba player Don Butterfield, the improviser of Stravinsky's *The Rite of Spring* around 3'25", and Trumpeter Melvyn Broiles, who mischievously sprouts a jazz riff around 6'40") had some familiarity with jazz. Considerable disorder also came from the audience.[41] They cheered many of Tudor's auxiliary sounds: the tape playback, the noises made on the strings of the inside of

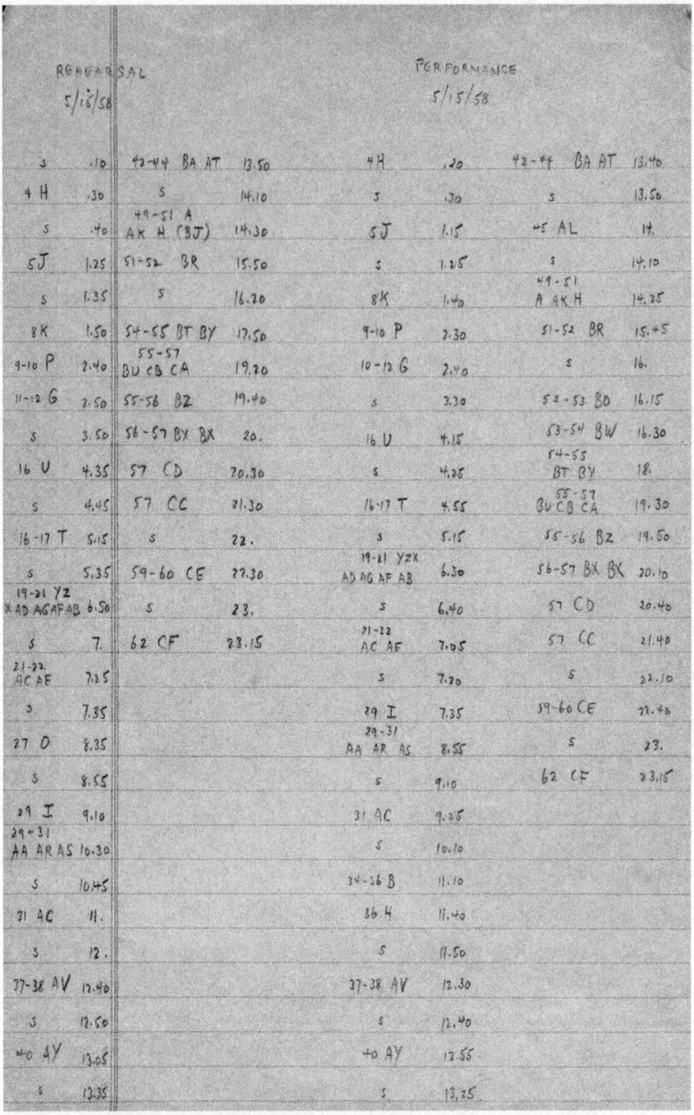

| REHEARSAL 5/16/58 | | | | PERFORMANCE 5/15/58 | | | |
|---|---|---|---|---|---|---|---|
| s | .10 | 42-44 BA AT | 13.50 | 4H | .20 | 42-44 BA AT | 13.40 |
| 4 H | .30 | s | 14.10 | s | .30 | s | 13.50 |
| s | .40 | 49-51 A AK H (BJ) | 14.30 | 5J | 1.15 | 45 AL | 14. |
| 5J | 1.25 | 51-52 BR | 15.50 | s | 1.25 | s | 14.10 |
| s | 1.35 | s | 16.20 | 8K | 1.40 | 49-51 A AK H | 14.25 |
| 8K | 1.50 | 54-55 BT BY | 17.50 | 9-10 P | 2.30 | 51-52 BR | 15.45 |
| 9-10 P | 2.40 | 55-57 BU CB CA | 19.20 | 10-12 G | 2.40 | s | 16. |
| 11-12 G | 2.50 | 55-56 BZ | 19.40 | s | 3.30 | 52-53 BO | 16.15 |
| s | 3.50 | 56-57 BY BX | 20. | 16 U | 4.15 | 53-54 BW | 16.30 |
| 16 U | 4.35 | 57 CD | 20.30 | s | 4.25 | 54-55 BT BY | 18. |
| s | 4.45 | 57 CC | 21.30 | 16-17 T | 4.55 | 55-57 BU CB CA | 19.30 |
| 16-17 T | 5.15 | s | 22. | s | 5.15 | 55-56 BZ | 19.50 |
| s | 5.35 | 59-60 CE | 22.30 | 19-21 YZX AD AG AF AB | 6.30 | 56-57 BX BX | 20.10 |
| 19-21 YZ X AD AG AF AB | 6.50 | s | 23. | s | 6.40 | 57 CD | 20.40 |
| s | 7. | 62 CF | 23.15 | 21-22 AC AE | 7.05 | 57 CC | 21.40 |
| 21-22 AC AE | 7.25 | | | s | 7.20 | s | 22.10 |
| s | 7.35 | | | 29 I | 7.35 | 59-60 CE | 22.40 |
| 27 O | 8.35 | | | 29-31 AA AR AS | 8.55 | s | 23. |
| s | 8.55 | | | s | 9.10 | 62 CF | 23.15 |
| 29 I | 9.10 | | | 31 AC | 9.25 | | |
| 29-31 AA AR AS | 10.30 | | | s | 10.10 | | |
| s | 10.45 | | | 34-36 B | 11.10 | | |
| 31 AC | 11. | | | 36 H | 11.40 | | |
| s | 12. | | | s | 11.50 | | |
| 37-38 AV | 12.40 | | | 37-38 AV | 12.30 | | |
| s | 12.50 | | | s | 12.40 | | |
| 40 AY | 13.05 | | | 40 AY | 12.55 | | |
| s | 13.35 | | | s | 13.25 | | |

FIG. 3.7. David Tudor, sequencing chart for May 15, 1958, rehearsal and performance of John Cage, *Solo for Piano* (1958). David Tudor Papers, 980039, box 7, folder 2, Getty Research Institute, Los Angeles.

the piano, and the slinky with an attached contact microphone. It resulted in what critics described as a "jungle," as "crazy," "mixed up" as "the clash of extreme phenomena," "sheer anarchy," or as a "grotesque comedy."[42]

## Cage's Noumena of the 1950s

Because of the sheer variety of Cage's notation and the complexity of the interpretive task, Tudor had to be a performer both skilled and trusted. Tudor, who began collaborating with Cage in 1951, played the part of the composer's faithful virtuoso, the deadpan soloist, impeccably accurate and well prepared. He carried considerable legitimacy with critics, audiences, and by extension, with composers in the 1950s, receiving routine—almost universal—praise from critics.[43] But Cage's scores never made it easy. Consider his instructions for Graph J (figs. 3.8, 3.9). I will return to the confounding ambiguities of these instructions, but for now suffice it to say that Cage's *Solo for Piano* is rife with them. His instructional sentences tend to be short—almost too economical, to the point of being convoluted.

How did Cage decide what should and should not be said with regard to the performance of his own music? The bracing emptiness of Cage's instructional language has a strange way of satisfying the ear, perhaps because of their lack of emotional content. In the notes to the Town Hall LP, Cage describes his pieces in the manner of formal recipes; he never describes how they sound. Philosophical clues to the thinking behind Cage's rhetoric emerge early in his writings. His 1934 essay "Counterpoint" divides the utterable from the nonsensical by way of a Schopenhauerian distinction tinged with a bit of Wittgenstein.[44] Cage writes, "There are, it seems to me, two sides to music as well as to everything else, including life: the side we can know something about (knowledge which is communicable) and the side which we can know nothing about (knowledge which is personal, emotional, etc. uncommunicable)."[45]

Cage's answer to this dualism is positivist, almost as if it had been adapted from the ending passages of Wittgenstein's *Tractatus* (1921), only without the strict injunction to silence as found in proposition seven ("whereof one cannot speak, one shall remain silent"). Instead, he proposed a kind of ethical passivity or modesty in the face of music's ineffability: "I prefer to communicate those things which are communicable rather than those which are not. . . . It seems to others that I just let the emotions, the uncommunicables, take care of themselves, communicate themselves."[46] Thus, Cage's performer ought to be a formalist and refrain from any more than what is

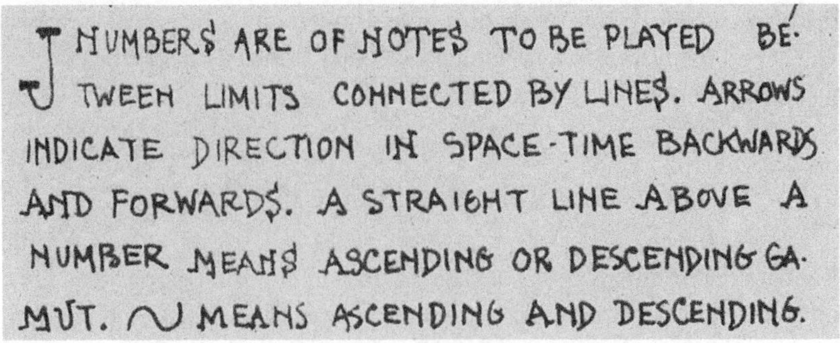

NUMBERS ARE OF NOTES TO BE PLAYED BE-
TWEEN LIMITS CONNECTED BY LINES. ARROWS
INDICATE DIRECTION IN SPACE-TIME BACKWARDS
AND FORWARDS. A STRAIGHT LINE ABOVE A
NUMBER MEANS ASCENDING OR DESCENDING GA-
MUT. ∿ MEANS ASCENDING AND DESCENDING.

FIG. 3.8. David Tudor's copy of John Cage, *Solo for Piano* (1958). Graph J instructions. Edition Peters, 1960. David Tudor Papers, 980039, box 6, folder 10, Getty Research Institute, Los Angeles.

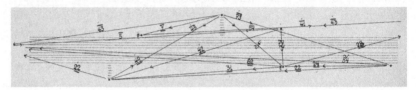

FIG. 3.9. David Tudor's copy of John Cage, *Solo for Piano* (1958). Graph J notation. Edition Peters, 1960. David Tudor Papers, 980039, box 6, folder 10, Getty Research Institute, Los Angeles.

technically specified by avoiding self-consciously expressive means. Instead, one should trust that all that is "uncommunicable" organically comes through the "life-attitude"—a vitalism of the other—in the performance.[47]

For Cage, the ineffability of such a "life-attitude" came to be saturated with potential meanings. For instance, though it is rarely noted, Cage thought of his methods as bearing links to Carl Jung's concept of the collective unconscious, which Cage had absorbed through his friendship with Joseph Campbell.[48] One text of Jung's that Cage found particularly memorable was also closely linked to the composer's turn to chance procedures in 1951. Jung had written a foreword to Richard Wilhelm's translation of the *I Ching* (the edition Cage consulted). In the foreword, Jung extols the modern relevance of the ancient oracle; in his view the *I Ching* was nothing short of a prophecy linked to the latest principles of modern science:

[Today] the axioms of causality are being shaken to their foundations: we know now that what we term natural laws are merely statistical truths and thus must necessarily allow for exceptions. . . . If we leave things to nature, we see a very different picture: every process is partially or totally interfered with by chance, so much so that under natural circumstances a course of events absolutely conforming to specific laws is almost an exception. The Chinese mind, as I see it at work in the *I Ching*, seems to be exclusively preoccupied with the chance aspect of events.[49]

Substitute intentionality for causality, and you have a surprisingly accurate picture of Cage's Orientalist philosophy of composition at midcentury. His works sounded an esoteric oracle of indeterminate simultaneities—akin to an anarchic release of the collective unconscious—in order to repeatedly stage an erasure of expressive Western intentionality. The association of Asian spirituality with Western psychologies of the unconscious or "subconscious" would become a ubiquitous cliché of the bourgeoning culture industry of the New Age. Allied with what Kimberly Jannarone has described as the modern "Counter-Enlightenment," in his forward to the *I Ching*, Jung framed it as a binary fantasy of the Chinese other, a plainly reductive stereotype:[50] "While the Western mind carefully sifts, weighs, selects, classifies, isolates, the Chinese picture of the moment encompasses everything down to the minutest nonsensical detail, because all of the ingredients make up the observed moment."[51]

"Down to the minutest nonsensical detail, because all of the ingredients make up the observed moment" is also a powerfully apt characterization of Cage's formalism of the 1950s.[52] And in crossing the threshold into the "nonsensical," musical inscriptions and scores were put in the service of a hyperfracture that questioned normative boundaries of musical perception. Because far more than mere affirmation of chance, in his compositions Cage intentionally specified "the observed moment" in detailed and visually expressive forms: the esoteric instruction, the unnecessary decimal point, the graph-plotted articulation values of *31'57.9864" for a pianist* (1954), the fiendishly dense score of calligraphic inventions that circumvented the normative facility of expressive hands and minds. It is the strange inscription of an indeterminacy latent in the powers of mind that is the opposite of an intentional act; at a deep register, sounds might then become unfettered from the normative guiderails of social life.[53] Such is the logic of Cage's hyperfracture: to leave behind Western intentionality was to repeatedly perform the disassembly of grammars into an infinite regress of nonsensical detail.

The philosophical sources underpinning Cage's aesthetics of the 1950s were a mélange. In his polemical 1958 lecture "Indeterminacy," first delivered during his legendary visit to Darmstadt later that summer, Cage described a series of frameworks for indeterminacy by interweaving the impersonal externality of the *I Ching* with Coomaraswamy's writings on Indian aesthetics, Christian mysticism, and a Jungian conception of the collective unconscious.

> Or he [a performer] may perform his function of colorist in a way which is not consciously organized (and therefore not subject to analysis)—either arbitrarily, feeling his way, following the dictates of his ego; or more or less unknowingly, by going inwards with reference to the structure of his mind to a point in dreams, following, as in automatic writing, the dictates of his subconscious mind: or to a point in the collective unconscious of Jungian psychoanalysis, following the inclinations of the species and doing something of more or less universal interest to human beings; or to the "deep sleep" of Indian mental practice—the Ground of Meister Eckhart—identifying there with no matter what eventuality. Or he may perform his function of colorist arbitrarily, by going outwards with reference to the structure of his mind to the point of sense following his taste; or more or less unknowingly by employing some operation exterior to his mind: tables of random numbers, following the scientific interest in probability; or chance operations, identifying there with no matter what eventuality.[54]

This delirious sequence, which spirals outward toward indeterminacy, returns three times nearly verbatim in Cage's lecture and repeatedly routes its telos through the pancultural totalities of the Jungian collective unconscious. Here, in a departure from Wittgenstein, the "nonsensical detail" of Cage's score was nonsensical because its performer was oriented toward the numinous field of a collective unconscious, a deep sleep, an underlying reality, or the contingency of nature, all of which eluded expressive and communicative meaning. A key source here is again Coomaraswamy's writings, which explicitly connected Indian aesthetics to the mysticism of Meister Eckhart in the manner Cage does in his lecture. This lecture's explorations of the indeterminate presents us with novel variations on music's ineffability, but not because Cage believed that musical forms were transcendent of language. Rather, for him, the esoteric spectacle of Tudor's sounding *Solo for Piano* at a specific time and place—the confrontational acoustics of sleep, the unconscious, or natural contingency—could not have made sense. The excess of abundant nonsensical sounds created an atmosphere that questioned the capacities—and even relevance of—normative musical perception; it was an exemplification of a postwar hyperfracture. In its sensuous particularity, Cage's version of the ineffable took shape as an esoteric spectacle without content while its nonsensical forms clung to silent procedural details.

## Tudor—Cage—Graph J

Still, as an esoteric practice, the credible performance of forms—or at least the appearance of credibility—remained crucial. And for Cage, as well as for many other experimental composers of the 1950s, Tudor's reputation functioned as a public guiderail capable of sustaining the traditional model of what philosopher Nelson Goodman once called "compliance" between the score and the performance.[55] When sounds unfolded without grammar, Tudor had to be trusted so that a specific kind of noncommunication could emerge as an oracle of the indeterminate.

In the workings of their collaboration lies a still more obscure layer of action. In Cage's instructions for Graph J, Tudor, as elsewhere, simplifies. He seems to ignore Cage's logically convoluted instruction about "direction in space time" and simply obeys the number of notes (with a little fudging) and the outer pitch parameters (quite strictly) by playing the number of notes indicated in the graph in ascending or descending gamuts. In other places, Tudor's approach is similar. In line with his desire to produce a result that can be sight-read, when Cage's instructions for graphs get confusing, he defaults to a fairly straightforward interpretation, trying to salvage whatever traditional left-to-right, top-to-bottom logic the graph may hold.

Consider Tudor's realization of Graph J (fig. 3.10). He chose to play it early on, thirty seconds in. It is a ferocious series of clustered glissandi that uses the whole range of the piano, a prime example of Tudor's pianism at his most spectacular. Note that Tudor's trademark deadpan stage presence often conveyed to audiences a solemn and self-negating commitment to high modernism. But at Town Hall, in front of the largest audience of his career, Tudor engineered a bombastic solo entrance in a venerable tradition of piano concertos from Beethoven to Rachmaninoff.[56] Cage's graph does not prescribe clustered glissandi; it was Tudor's choice to compress the entirety of the graph—all the diagonals—into thirty seconds of arresting virtuosity. Counterfactual realizations, which can now be easily constructed thanks to Martin Iddon and Phillip Thomas's innovative software, are equally compliant with Cage's graph and provide valuable perspective on Tudor's choices.[57] One could imagine loosely chromatic scales ascending and descending relatively slowly (or very slowly, even glacially). Tudor could have sequenced each gamut in a relatively even rhythm. He

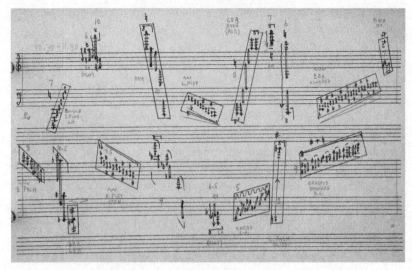

FIG. 3.10. David Tudor, realization of Graph J from John Cage's *Solo for Piano* (1958). David Tudor Papers, 980039, box 6, folder 11, Getty Research Institute, Los Angeles.

could have played the entire graph quietly, or with vast gaps and silences interspersed. He could have spread out Graph J over the course of twenty minutes with other graphs in between. But Tudor chose to play it as a single, drastic module, punctuated with a dramatic sense of urgency. (And his sketches of the realization show that Tudor sketched out a realization in a different ordering, only to decide finally on this one.)[58]

This was also a man with adrenaline on stage. Consider a comparatively low-key performance of the *Concert for Piano and Orchestra* six years later. As Benjamin Piekut has argued, by this time, Tudor had become a far more improvisational performer.[59] Unlike the 1958 premiere, this 1964 performance at Mills College featured an all-star orchestra of seasoned West Coast experimentalists that included Pauline Oliveros and Morton Subtonick.[60] In this performance the orchestra gives him plenty of space to be heard. It is also an example of how flexible Tudor's performances of his own realizations could be; his timing in 1964 is far more spacious.[61] More broadly, Tudor rarely used determinate rhythm or tempo; neither did he always use—or accurately play—proportional notation. He typically just played within the time limits indicated on each page. As he described it in an interview, "It was like a sign to me saying that you have to realize this within a certain time bracket."[62] His realizations might best be described as a convenient shorthand of choreographed gestures that simplified what he would have to visually process on stage.

## Ferocious Ineffability

There is nothing like a conservative critic embroiled in a moral panic to unintentionally hit the nail on the head. In 1959 Paul Henry Lang mercilessly attacked Tudor's stable of experimentalists as "little boys . . . who do not know the value of what they destroy."[63] Lang heard the aim of this avant-garde music as violence, as a polemical repudiation of Western concert music and its intertwined indebtedness to harmony, personal expression, and the moral strictures set forth by Christianity. Yet might we reclaim the latent violence of Tudor's performance from the protest of Lang's conservatism? On some level, he is of course right. The alarming disorder of Tudor's performance of Cage's *Concert for Piano and Orchestra* is plain and incontrovertible. What then was the significance of this violence in sound—placed on a historical pedestal, in the mysterious and speechless combat of a piano concerto? To paraphrase a question posed by Richard Taruskin in his *Oxford History of Western Music*, Why was this violence desirable?

In the final sentences of a review of the 1959 recital Tudor gave at New York University, which included the discontinuous pointillism of Cage's *Music for Piano* series, the reviewer seemed to accept its disturbing "implications" for the sake of innovation: "The philosophic implications of works like these may be disturbingly nihilist. So be it. Whatever their motivation, the pieces are giving us new and usable procedures to add to our musical vocabulary. This, if nothing else, makes them valid."[64]

The fashion for this controversial and dissonant sound world was at least ten years old. For many, it took shape at the beginning of Tudor's career. On December 17, 1950, in New York, Tudor had given the American premiere of Boulez's *Second Sonata* (1947–48). Cage, who turned pages for Tudor at the premiere, seems to have been overwhelmed by the ferociously fractured atmosphere of Boulez's work. In a letter to the composer the following day, Cage wrote that the *Sonata* gave him "a feeling of an exaltation . . . an arousing and breathtaking enlightenment," and with a nod to the challenge of all the dissonance, he proclaimed, "Those who had no courage to directly listen are troubled; you have increased the danger their apathy brings them to."[65] In this same letter, Cage tells Boulez, "My music too is changing" and then describes the move from a music based in organic breathing and rhythm that more mimetically evoked an Orientalist musical atmosphere into the more impersonal and confrontational hyperfracture of "throwing sound into silence."[66] Tudor reports that in fact Cage's excitement dated back to his first hearing of Boulez's work: "[Cage] heard Boulez play his Second Sonata—or part of it—and was very struck by the disorder and chaos of the music."[67] Tudor continues, explaining that Cage's approach was to use exacting procedures to achieve a similar effect: "His way of coming to terms with that [chaos] was that it was exactly the same as perfect order."[68] The following year, Cage embarked on a monumental atonal solo piano work for Tudor titled *Music of Changes* that would put the "order" of chance procedures into esoteric practice.

Boulez had credited Artaud with inspiring his stylistic turn to push atonal disorder to its limit. In particular, Artaud's *Theater and Its Double* (1938) inspired Boulez by advocating a primitivist violence that would tear through the conventional fabric of language, character, and plot with the force of brute, creaturely sensation.[69] Tudor, having been referred to Artaud by Boulez while wrapping his hands around the *Second Sonata*, taught himself French to read excerpts of Artaud. Early in the 1950s, Tudor, Cage, and Tudor's partner at the time, Mary Caroline (M. C.) Richards in turn also began to read Artaud.[70] By the time of his courses in experimental composition at the New School in 1958, Artaud had become part of his lessons for a new generation of aspiring artists and composer-students.[71] Richards, who played an underrecognized but key role in facilitating collaboration among Cage, Tudor, and others in her leadership role at Black Mountain College and the cooperative at Stony Brook, would spend the next few years preparing an English translation of *Theater and Its Double*, which she published in 1958. The year following the publication, Richards delivered a lecture on Artaud for the Living Theatre in 1959.[72] Her lecture paints an explicitly confrontational portrait of Artaud's significance for those in their scene:

Set your audience by the throat, by the breath. Seduce their bodies with scientific precision, transfix their nervous systems, pulverize them, and THEN, when they cannot resist the experience, give them the treatment, give them the poetry, give them the transcendent cosmic reality; dissolve their guard; blast away their armor. . . . Artaud was right. Passive appreciation must be struck from our curriculum. It is a dead and meaningless mausoleum of the spirit. Actors must act. And audiences must re-act. And the fountains must gush, the sleeping members rise, the language of dream speak through the proscenium of the event. . . . THE PARADOX, THE KOAN, THE PARABLE, THE INCANTATION, AND THE RITUAL GESTURE. . . . Inseparable from the concepts of alchemy, the chemical marriage, disintegration and reintegration. Experiences on the path to wholeness are excruciating, insupportable, unavoidable. It is wholeness that we want, but that we fear, as we fear our own unknown. . . . To launch ourselves into the unknown, the untried, into SPACE. That's what Artaud said.[73]

In her lecture Richards connects all the dots. She links Artaud with Jung, mysticism, metaphysics, and world religion projects—many of the key ideas and authors that absorbed Cage in the 1940s. She also emphasizes the spiritual and redemptive qualities of Artaud's aesthetics of the real as opposed to its more nihilistic leanings. Finally, Richards convincingly evokes the sound world of the Cage-Tudor collaboration of the 1950s, for which atonality—and its Boulezian affirmation of violence as rebellion from convention—was heard as a force of life. As You Nakai has examined in detail, one essay by Artaud sticks out in particular as a crucial influence on Tudor's practice of the 1950s—the essay "An Affective Athleticism," which is also the only chapter from *The Theater and Its Double* Tudor seems to have recopied himself in typescript.[74] The essay suggests that the work of the technical virtuoso is metaphysically linked to the numinous flexibility of a skilled actor's capacity of emotion.[75] In Artaud's words, "the actor is an athlete of the heart."[76]

Artaud's theory of "An Affective Athleticism" is compellingly echoed in Tudor's own philosophy of musical time during the 1950s.[77] The principle governing Tudor's fidelity to real time was a form of liberation through an acceptance of discontinuity. While preparing his performance of Boulez's *Second Sonata*, Tudor had come to feel that there was nothing conventionally hierarchical or linear in Boulez's composition; any bit of musical material could be taken as background or foreground. In Tudor's view Cage's chance-derived *Music of Changes* took this acceptance of "moment-to-moment differences" still further. Here, the performer had to be "ready for anything at each instant."[78] At root it was an effort to renounce the human inclination to link together or narrate continuities where none in fact exist. In Tudor's words, "my mind had to completely forget and not relate the next incident to the previous one."[79] On the one hand, this was a novel form of physical discipline; he had to keep his body ready to change anything at any instant. But it also had a profound philosophical consequence on his "frame of mind."[80] As Tudor described it, "I had to learn how to be able to cancel my consciousness of any previous moment, in order to be able to produce the next one. What this did for me was to bring about freedom, the freedom to do anything, and that's how I learned to be free for a whole hour at a time."[81] The evacuation of mental intentionality was loosely evocative of Zen practices of meditation.

Thus, atop his aforementioned interest in real time, Tudor developed a fascination with extreme discontinuity. It was a philosophy oriented away from the normative metrical and linear frameworks of human consciousness and instead toward an inhuman materiality of contingency. The aim was a form of ego detachment. That is, in performing these dissonant, hyperfractured scores, Tudor found freedom in feeling unmoored from a normative consciousness. He described it in terms of a new atmosphere, as if it numinously had enveloped the coordinates of one's capacity to perceive: "I was in a different musical atmosphere. I was *watching* time rather than *experiencing* it."[82] Instructively, Tudor also described it in terms adopted from Indian philosophy in which embodied practice and metaphysical assertions were understood to be inseparable: "it became quite a yoga for a while—any yoga takes a bit of time."[83] In this context, it is instructive to note that Coomaraswamy himself had described Yoga as "dexterity in action."[84] In Coomaraswamy's words, "Yoga covers not merely the moment of intuition, but also execution."[85] The altered physical and experiential conditions pushed Tudor's practice into a second-order modernism; it was not simply about fracturing continuities. He was interested in changing the conditions of perception. In Tudor's words, "the differences were like changes in color perception—that's something that comes about through a totally different type of musical experience."[86] Tudor's thinking paralleled the second-order aspirations of Cage's philosophical works of the period. Their hyperfracture aimed to change the atmosphere produced by, in turn, affecting one's surroundings. For Tudor, "If you can open yourself to [a change of mind] you'll have an experience—when you leave the concert hall you'll hear the environment differently, as many people have found."[87]

In contrast to Cage's outsized public persona, the articulation of Tudor's own philosophy and spirituality were relatively muted; his thinking was expressed largely in recopied readings and personal notes rather than lectures or publications. Tudor was a member of the Anthroposophical Society starting in 1957, remained a member until the end of his life, and was a devotee of the writings of its founder, Rudolf Steiner.[88] Steiner, like many philosophers of his generation, sought to preserve and rethink spirituality in an increasingly material and scientific age and was keenly interested in underlying commonalities of global religions.[89] Anthroposophy followed its Theosophical forebears in positing a hidden, esoteric, occult, and unseen reality that could be obscurely disclosed through intuition. This reality was fundamentally spiritual; beyond a physical body, one could find access to etheric bodies, astral bodies, and ultimately an ego. Though historically conditioned, the individual ego could achieve a form of transcendent awareness through meditation, imagination, concentration, control, equanimity, positive attitudes, and openness to the complexity of the world. (In this regard, Steiner was heavily influenced by a fusion of German Idealism, Hinduism, and Christianity.) In *How to Attain Knowledge of Higher Worlds* (1908), Steiner writes about a mode of listening that would be adequate to the occult contemplation of nature. This mode of spiritual listening is remarkably impersonal and strongly parallels Tudor's revelatory philosophy of liberated discontinuity that he arrived at early in the 1950s via Boulez, Artaud, and Cage:

> For the sake of practice the student is obliged to listen for a certain period to the most contradictory thoughts, and at the same time to suppress all assent, and more especially *all adverse criticism*. The point is that in such a way not only all intellectual judgment is silenced, but also all sense of displeasure, denial, or even acceptance.[90]

One of the sounds Steiner describes at length is the sound of animals in pain. A properly occult form of listening to these sounds requires suspending one's own pleasure or displeasure; one has to concern oneself with "the inward experience of the animal."[91] From this place, then, one can attempt to begin to listen to the whole of nature in this radically empathetic and loving way. The goal was an inclusive and compassionate realism; listening to the harshness of the violence and finding a certain self-discipline in attending to it, thus attuning oneself to a spiritual dimension of nature in all its complexity, which for Steiner entailed recognizing the cyclical recurrence of karma and reincarnation. This attunement cannot be achieved simply through the intellect or by way of language; art's mediation of the senses plays a special role. Steiner writes of it as a form of empirical receptivity and openness:

> The occult explorer ought never to lose himself in speculation on the meaning of this or that. By such intellectualizing he only directs himself away from the right road. He ought to look out on the sense-world freshly, with healthy senses and quickened observation, and then to give himself up to his own sensations. He ought not to wish, in a speculative manner to make out what this or that means, but rather to allow the things themselves to inform him.[92]

Steiner puts in ethical and spiritual terms what Tudor and Cage described largely in aesthetic terms. It is ego attenuation as receptivity and a naturalistic, disciplined acceptance of the diversity of the world.

These writings of Steiner's are relatively breezy, open-minded passages of metaphysical speculation. But it is crucial to acknowledge that the shared "Counter-Enlightenment" fusions of vitalism, primitivism, and esotericism that unite the writings of Steiner, Coomaraswamy, Artaud, Jung, Campbell, Suzuki, Cage, Tudor, and many others, were not necessarily progressive or oriented toward a universal horizon of recognition often associated with the social movements of the 1960s. In fact this generation of global spirituality could easily tip into forms of regressive social thought or outwardly fascist and white supremacist tendencies that devalued Black and Indigenous cultures of the global periphery. For instance, a number of these advocates of global spirituality forged their comparative projects in ways that naturalized social hierarchies or archetypes. Jung, whose comparative approaches to religion and myth are occasionally mentioned as broadening Eurocentric horizons of the time and were an important influence on Cage, was explicitly bigoted in his opinions about race.[93] Jung amplified pernicious ideologies of racial hierarchies that were common in the 1920s through the 1940s and framed Blackness as a primitive temptation to which white Americans "have to maintain the moral standard against the heavy downward pull of primitive life."[94]

Others subscribed to an often not-so-veiled fantasy of Aryan supremacy. Decades earlier, the "syncretic faith" of Helena Blavatsky's Theosophical Society supported an Indo-European fantasy of cultural supremacy that would in turn become a foundational theory for Nazi ideology.[95] Notwithstanding its later association with the social revolutions of 1960s US counterculture—which would evolve in response to the civil rights era, second-wave feminism, and the antiwar movement—the idea that India or Tibet might lay claim to a shared spiritual heritage to Westerners had roots in theories of racial supremacy. Edwin Dingle, the leader of the Mentalphysics movement of Los Angeles, whose pamphlets and literature of the 1950s were collected in Tudor's spiritual papers, made the fantasy explicit, saying what many others likely thought silently to themselves: "What giant intellects these white cousins of ours in ancient India must have had to discover this twenty-five hundred or three thousand years ago!"[96] Dingle's white supremacy is explicit: "What was the secret of this great race? Why was it later to take the leadership of the world?"[97] Politically, many of Dingle's New Age affirmations were allied with what is now described as the evangelical "prosperity gospel"—they were light on principles of compassion and justice and heavy on promoting the self-interested influence, luxury, and personal flourishing of white elites. Coomaraswamy, who supported the social hierarchies of the caste system, placed his political hopes for a globalized world in the hands of a select tribe of Aryan "aristocracy." He wrote, "The chosen people of the future cannot be any nation or race, but an aristocracy of the earth uniting the virility of European youth to the serenity of Asiatic age."[98] Thus, the spiritual movements that influenced Cage and Tudor bore a certain proximity to implicit fantasies of transpacific whiteness, of global supremacy. Suzuki himself supported beliefs in social hierarchy during the lead up to Japanese imperial aggression and fascism during World War II, going so far as to assert that Buddhism was the product of a superior evolution of Japanese spirituality.[99]

In acknowledging the supremacist fantasies of this generation, the social tensions constitutive of modernism first introduced in the previous chapter ("Veils—Atmospheres") come into vivid relief. George Lewis has argued trenchantly that Cage's indeterminacy emerged as a "Euro-logical" disavowal of the work of Afro-modernist bebop musicians, many of whom had been dealing with a combination of formal sophistication and so-called open forms since the 1940s by way of improvisational techniques and competitive jam sessions.[100] As we shall see with Coleman (chap. 4) and Coltrane (chap. 6), Afro-modernists in the wake of bebop would take a very different approach to this social tension by resisting racial inequality among modernists (Coleman) and upending the racialized and gendered expectations of spiritual leadership (Coltrane). In support of his thesis, Lewis's article shows that Cage's deafness toward Afro-modernism is obvious in his disparaging statements about jazz and improvisation.[101] As is evidenced by the sources discussed above, the ideological critique Lewis stages was also mirrored in the racism of the intellectual and spiritual movements that influenced Tudor and Cage. This cross-cultural whiteness revealed in bald terms how Cage's indeterminate music of the 1950s could justify the ignorance if not outright rejection of parallel strains of Afro-modernism.

Artaud's influence is less ideologically clear. He was widely read as a figure of cultural liberation in the artistic movements of the 1960s and was undoubtedly key to Cage and Tudor finding their dissenting voice. Moreover, the need for this liberation was real: as prominent critics like Paul Henry Lang made clear, the Euro-Western aesthetic norms Cage and Tudor rejected had a powerful and conservative grip on the valuation of art at midcentury. But the political outlines of Artaud's thought were complex. Though Artaud never explicitly espoused a nationalist or racist ideology, Kimberly Jannarone has argued that the nihilism of *The Theater and Its Double* was inseparable from the broader interwar revival of mysticism, primitivism, and Orientalist irrationality that would form the basis for what she has described as a fascist culture of "decadence, corruption, death, destruction."[102] Yet in sonic form, Cage and Tudor never presented Artaud's vision of unbridled violence as a system of belief that one could simply adopt. That is, whereas Artaud himself seems to have fantasized about a Wagnerian manipulation of his audiences, in practical terms little was spiritually inviting about making esoteric indeterminacy into an arresting spectacle.

If a panicked critic, clinging to the traditional virtues of Western aesthetics, could be startled and provoked by the horror of this nihilism at Tudor's performances, at best this nihilism landed in the form of an ephemeral shock. It is noteworthy that Artaud was never a public point of reference for Cage; he focused on the spiritual affordances of Suzuki and the *I Ching*. Thus, Cage and Tudor's Artaud might be best framed as performative or hypothetical rather than indoctrinating. Indeed, if Richards's lecture is any guide (and, while together, she and Tudor influenced each other closely during the 1950s), Cage and his circle's interest in Artaud emphasized decidedly spiritual and liberating affordances (Zen "affirmation," or the positive attributes of Steiner's "intuition") over any sense of apocalyptic nihilism.[103] In this way, the *Concert for Piano and Orchestra* was less an outward attempt at reproducing myth and more an extravagant—and highly publicized—rejection of aesthetic criteria. Far from mythical, their hyperfracture, however spectacular, came across as deliberately empty: an abstracted violence at the piano without narrative or context without relation to any specific body, person, or instance of social life. An occult exercise in spiritual freedom, it was a provocation delivered with charisma and authority yet devoid of explanation or meaning.

If Cage and Tudor never explained their dispassionate—and occasionally playful—atmosphere of sonic violence, it is nonetheless important to note that their spiritual underpinnings remained somewhat remote if not inaccessible to audiences. In their responses to Cage and Tudor's performances of the 1950s, critics heard far more Artaud than they did theosophy or spirituality. They associated their music with armed conflict, weaponry, space-age rhetoric, science fiction, and a panic over a loss of traditional aesthetic values. One reviewer of the Town Hall concert interprets Cage's three-hour marathon as a sign of the times.[104] Writing just seven months following the launch of Sputnik, he writes that Cage's music, in all its desires to channel natural forces rather than human intentions, was akin to a cosmic form of alien communication "based in a revised Morse Code," and he devotes the final third of his review to questions of ontology ("Is it music?"). In his view, it was the seriousness of Cage's efforts at earnestness and compliance—while the abyss is plainly screaming—that made his nonintentional music worth attending to. Another referred, quite critically, to the *Concert for Piano and Orchestra* as "sheer anarchy" and an "evolutionary cul-de-sac" (using phrases that ironically may have pleased Cage.)[105] He compared Cage's *Imaginary Landscape No. 1* (1939) to two pressing cultural phenomena of the 1950s: horror films and air-raid sirens. In response to the electronic sounds Tudor used in a 1961 performance of Cage's *Solo for Piano* (possibly the second realization) in Minneapolis, a third critic remarked the inverse: like a wrestling match on television, or a sports game that entails violence, he hears the electronic aspects of Cage's music as a "fearful bombardment."[106]

A WHISTLE, A "SLINKY" AND A BUNCH OF SCREWS—These, too, make music which will be heard in a retrospective concert of the works of John Cage, left, at Town Hall Thursday. David Tudor tests the "prepared" piano; the composer listens.

FIG. 3.11. Preview: "A Whistle, a 'Slinky' and a Bunch of Screws," photograph by Sy Friedman, *New York Times*, May 11, 1958. David Tudor Papers, 980039, box 62, folder 13, Getty Research Institute, Los Angeles.

Though critics supportive of Cage often defended his music as "serious" (and this included a bemused Leonard Bernstein doing his best to persuade his subscription audience in 1964 when conducting the premiere of Cage's *Atlas Eclipticalis*), when staged and responded to in such affective and atmospheric terms, dramatic violence is also an attraction—it could be fun.[107] A preview of the Town Hall performance in the *New York Times* (fig. 3.11) makes a spectacle of what ordinarily would go unseen by an audience seated below the level of the stage—the innards of the prepared piano, with its bolts and screws wedged in between strings.

This photograph appears somewhat staged, with Cage staring blankly into the piano and Tudor staring a bit off camera as he knocks the amplified slinky with his hand. (In actuality, Ajemian, not Tudor, performed on the prepared piano at Town Hall. Cage and Tudor seem to have attached the slinky from the *Concert for Piano and Orchestra* to the prepared piano for the sake of the publicity photo.) By all accounts, the spectacle delivered. Composer and music critic Virgil Thompson described the result as "certainly his most entertaining"—"a jolly row and a good show."[108] In his review of the LP, Alfred Frankenstein writes, "[The *Concert*] has an absolutely epical spine-tingling quality to it, rather like that of Varèse's orchestra works but less massive, and with an element of humor in its improvisation which Varèse never affords."[109] Later that fall, while on tour in Europe with Cage and Cunningham, Tudor described a Düsseldorf performance of *Music Walk* (1958) to his partner, M. C. Richards, as follows: "3 pianists at one piano & 4 radios around the room. Very entertaining."[110] In a period when composers stretched the limits of the hearable as well as the determination, compliance, and expertise of performance, these quasi-theatrical collaborations—an atmosphere structured by visual and theatrical cues as much as technical expertise—insured minimal ontological scaffolding for the experiment. The popularization of the avant-garde was show business even if it was rarely profitable.

Lang, in his disgusted reactions, knew this, remarking in the *New York Herald Tribune* that for Tudor and his compatriots, "public recognition is mandatory."[111] Certainly, if a work were not public, how could it achieve minimal ontological status? The challenges remained significant. The atonal idiom, exacerbated by the chaos of these most experimental works, made inaccuracies less audible and transparent to the audiences. Along these lines, in 1960, Fred Grunfeld, in his review of the Town Hall LP, worried about the inability to discern good from bad in a performance.[112] Such worries parallel what Stanley Cavell would later call "fraudulence"—the paradigmatic risk of modernism.[113] As we may recall from the previous chapter, Cavell felt music should retain some minimum effort of meaning it, of language-like elements and sequences. But philosophers trained to think along the lines of ordinary language like Goodman or Cavell wouldn't find reliable grammars, criteria, or traces of intentionality in Cage's works; they would never have been sure Tudor meant what he did.

Eschewing the transparency of normative virtuosity was, of course, a deliberate strategy. Art historians have emphasized Cage's participatory and neo-Dadaist tendencies from the 1950s onward.[114] He enthusiastically incorporated readymade works that made use of vernacular and everyday items that required no particular skills for performers and artists. Cage's course in experimental composition at the New School for Social Research was hugely significant during this period (1956–60), which, particularly in its summer 1958 version that was attended by figures like George Brecht, Allan Kaprow, Jackson Mac Low, Al Hansen, and Dick Higgins, encouraged artists without much in the way of musical skill to make novel use of the score format for experimental performances and avant-garde intermedia.[115] Outside the developed esotericism of Tudor's 1950s realizations with their calligraphy and calculations, Cage's works increasingly made use of amateur and deskilled performers, eschewing complex rhythms and timings for clock time and sidelining rarefied, established techniques for the populism of recipes and household items. Cunningham's human stopwatch conducting of the *Concert for Piano and Orchestra*, mentioned at the beginning of this chapter, was a case in point: his timekeeping was devoid of a conductor's familiar expressive showboating. This turn toward the amateurism of participatory theater is preserved in Cage's iconic performance of *Water Walk* (1959) on the television show *I've Got a Secret*, which featured an array of domestic technologies resulting in something like a randomized cooking show in which no particular food resulted from the performance.[116] Bits and pieces of this "ready-made" work—particularly the amplified slinky—similarly elicited laughs at Town Hall that night.

But it is important to not too easily assimilate Cage's and Tudor's work to this metanarrative toward participatory, deskilled intermedia. Though Tudor had been performing experimental intermedia like *Water Music* (1952) since the early 1950s and would do more of this work during the 1960s, many elements of Tudor's practice remained traditionally formalist. Tudor's reputation of this period was overwhelmingly due to his credibility as a traditional virtuoso performer of technically demanding scores. His reputation was mirrored by his habits. Tudor was an introverted copyist, archivist, and pack rat with tremendous natural talent, a certain consistent but understated energy for innovation, and a flair for deadpan performances. He studied languages, particularly Latin, as well as archaic forms of musical notation. He also copied down and compiled hundreds of recipes, spiritual texts, and other miscellaneous printed materials of interest to him. In the late 1960s Tudor famously switched from piano to amplified piano, the bandoneon, and ultimately analog electronics and synthesizers, and he developed complex schematic diagrams and schemas for modular synthesis. But even as his repertoire of inscriptions expanded, a devotional compliance to some kind of form or system was central, even if the exact code had been ruptured.[117]

Transfixed into a position of calculated perplexity, we arrive at a novel and practical account of the ineffable—one based in a theater of opaque, nonsensical, and arresting appearances of the violent, disparate, and liberating contingency of nature. The impression that the music emanated a diffuse, Orientalist metaphysics allowed meaning to linger around a hyper-fracture—a strange inscription—of nonsensical detail. A concluding rewind to 1946 brings more of Cage's latent intentions into focus. In his essay "The East in the West," Cage offered something of a dictum about music's ineffability: "The composers who today wish to imbue their music with the ineffable, seem to find it necessary to make use of musical characteristics not purely Western; they go for inspiration to those places, or return to those times, where or when harmony is not of the essence."[118]

Viewers, remembering the esoteric visual design and the intimidating calligraphy of Cage's graphs, were treated to the priesthood of Tudor—the sacred medium for an exotic violence of natural contingency that took place beyond all language. It was a riff on Jung's collective unconscious, but in something like Artaudian panic mode, cloaked in unspoken ritual. Their guiding principles were self-negating discipline and procedural execution. But what mattered far more than its underlying structural integrity was the staged appearance—the atmospherics—of formalism. The *Solo for Piano's* esotericism, a seemingly inexhaustible compendium audiences were asked to gawk at in visual form, was the point. Cage and Tudor together used visual media (the Stable Gallery exhibition; the didactic, recipe-like program notes; the behind-the-scenes press releases; the deadpan performances in suits; and even Avakian deliberately raising the sound of the crowd noise in the recording mix to produce a sense of live atmosphere, something that would become standard practice for mixing of live concert recordings)—all these curated decisions cued viewers and listeners to the complex registers about all that was "really" going on formally.[119] Amid their theater of appearances—the imitation, play, and rhetoric surrounding this aleatoric formalism—a polyphony of metaphysical influences open our ears to the music's explosive interiors.

## CHAPTER FOUR

# Ornette Coleman,
# Utopian Intentionalities . . . c. 1966

A little over a year after Cage and Tudor's packed spectacle at Town Hall, Ornette Coleman took the stage at an equally historic performance at the Five Spot Café in Cooper Square downtown on November 17, 1959 (fig. 4.1). The Five Spot had been open for three years and had an unparalleled reputation for being the trendiest spot in town for cutting-edge bebop. The club's atmosphere, at the edge of what would eventually be known as the East Village, attracted a range of avant-garde artists, writers, and intellectuals. Cecil Taylor had already had a residency that began in late 1956. Thelonious Monk—with John Coltrane in his quartet—had a six-month residency in 1957. For the many weeks of their performances, Coleman was accompanied by Don Cherry on pocket cornet, Charlie Haden on bass, and Billy Higgins on drums.

The Five Spot had become an atmospheric epicenter of New York bohemianism. As with Cage and Tudor's premiere in 1958, Coleman's 1959 residency was a breakout New York gig. Around the same number of people—several hundred—saw each of them, though in Coleman's case, attendance was spread out over weeks of shows. The Five Spot stood on now-demolished buildings at the southeast end of Cooper Square and was remarkably modest; the live room was plain and filled with tables that sat less than seventy-five people (described in *Time Magazine* as a "shabby cave" and by Amiri Baraka as "greasy" and an "avant-garde beer garden").[1] The stage was tiny—barely raised above the level of the floor—and the musicians played around a piano with their backs up against a wall. The room was wallpapered with posters, programs, and photographs. Audiences were dominated by white bohemians, though not entirely; here was a place that everyone from John Coltrane, Charles Mingus, and Miles Davis to Leonard Bernstein could turn up for a gig. Following the initial two-week stint, the café's publicist reported Coleman's "overflow crowds" in a press release that advertised his "style of jazz that is causing much controversy."[2] As with

FIG. 4.1. Ornette Coleman and Don Cherry at the Five Spot, 1959.
Photograph by Bob Parent. Courtesy of Granger Images.

Cage's Town Hall concert, it was an electric moment.[3] One critic reported "the largest collection of VIP's in the jazz world seen in many a year."[4]

Coleman's debut at the Five Spot had not simply irrupted organically from the scene. He came armed with endorsements from the major figures of jazz criticism—Nat Hentoff and Martin Williams—who contributed detailed and persuasive liner notes to Coleman's first three LPs. Williams partially engineered the reception of Coleman's debut, coordinating the performances with the owners, who themselves arranged a preview for a select group of critics. While Coleman's quartet earned praise from many quarters, one critic, less than impressed, complained that "[Coleman's] reputation is completely the result of artificial promotion by a small group of king-makers."[5] Another bemoaned the "many pretentious solos" he had heard on *Change of the Century* (1959). Still others remarked on his lack of a beat, wobbly tuning, incoherent forms, and the blaring, sometimes harsh sonority of his white plastic Selmer "Grafton" saxophone.[6] Riffing on a familiar middlebrow response to the avant-garde as a kind of psychosis, another described Coleman's music as "a great boon to psychiatrists."[7] Other critics compared his music to abstract (or what was then called "nonobjective") avant-garde painting.[8]

The word *modernism* draws Cage, Tudor, and Coleman together under a single banner. But notwithstanding a number of commonalities that will emerge over the course of this chapter, the differences of social and material circumstance for Tudor's life as a musician versus Coleman's were stark. Tudor's relatively quick emergence as a catalyst of the New York avant-intelligentsia was a product of institutional and racial privilege. He had steady employment as a church organist at seventeen, and his family was middle class enough to provide him with the privilege of music lessons as a child that culminated in a valuable period of study with Irma Wolpe Rademacher, a noted European pianist. The institutions and collaborators they performed with had proximity to wealth and social status. Cage, who had a cushion of hereditary wealth, was on and off a trust fund for much of his early career. Though both men had queer or nonnormative dimensions to their sexuality, their whiteness would ensure they would routinely be given social privileges.

Coleman grew up poor in racially segregated Fort Worth, a city that was only 10 percent Black during the 1940s. While he grew up in a musical family, he was largely self-taught on the saxophone. Coleman taught himself the basics of Western notation and developed an idiosyncratic understanding of the transposition of his saxophone's scales. Self-taught musicianship was common in jazz at the time—the genre developed predominantly through oral tradition and apprenticeship until the 1970s—but Coleman's resourceful and independent ways of thinking about music led him to develop his own approach to composition and improvisation. As a soloist, he was a free spirit even then; he was reportedly expelled from the school band for improvising improperly.[9]

Coleman found early work in the culture industry of Black entertainers in the South largely playing the newly fashionable genre of rhythm and blues. At the time, steady work for Black musicians was very difficult to find. Location jobs at hotels or theaters discriminated against Black musicians, which left Coleman doing all manner of occasional gigs. In 1949 Coleman found work touring the South in a brutally depressing tent show, *Silas Green from New Orleans*, which featured minstrelsy, ragtime, and comedy among other acts; a more rewarding touring gig with famed R & B singer Pee Wee Crayton arrived two years later. On the road, bands, audiences, and the touring circuits were often segregated. Booking agencies of this period catered to lucrative markets for white performers, so for Black bands playing to Black crowds, money on the road was slim, and the schedules were onerous. On one occasion, Coleman was beaten and had his saxophone destroyed by audience members while on tour with a blues singer in Baton Rouge. Touring logistics were made nightmarish under Jim Crow: Black musicians frequently had to wait on tour buses while a white person (often the driver) retrieved food to go; Black hotels were rare and not as well financed as white hotels, which often left musicians staying with local families or spending a night in the bus. Black musicians confronted harassment, intimidation, and the risk of violence on the road. Frequently presumed to be "elite" Black northerners (or New Yorkers), their very presence could be seen as a threat to white southern masculinity.[10] Coleman was himself subject to harassment by the police.

During this early period of Coleman's career, the bebop pioneered by Dizzy Gillespie, Charlie Parker, and Thelonious Monk had grown into an iconic genre of Afro-modernism. Parker's records in particular had captured Coleman's attention as a high schooler and inspired all manner of imitation. Beginning in the early-to-mid-1940s, these musicians experimented with frenetic linear improvisations over increasingly complex chord progressions that involved pungent chord substitutions with flat nineths and sharp elevenths. Dance-oriented syncopations and rounded eight-bar phrases gave way to jarring and ornate patterns of meandering. Phrases ended on weak beats or in unexpected places, giving the impression of a roving motion, or, in the imagination of jazz historian Ted Gioia, a journey through a vexing labyrinth.[11] Solos could stretch to great length. The technique of executing all this was driven by a competitive scene of after-hours jamming among relatively small groups uptown at Minton's Playhouse in Harlem.[12]

After making his way to Los Angeles in 1952, Coleman hustled and floundered for a few years to little success during the height of the bebop craze. Criticized for not being able to follow changes properly, he struggled musically, and subsisted on low-paying jobs in domestic labor (as a houseboy and a babysitter) and as a department store elevator operator, common jobs for African Americans who were discriminated against when pursuing other lines of work. Coleman continued studying music theory and composing independently until he eventually met like-minded collaborators: Don Cherry, Billy Higgins, and Charlie Haden among others. It was with them that Coleman managed to forge a distinctive idiom based on his own original compositions. A major break came in an audition for Lester Koenig, founder of Contemporary Records, who was impressed, and signed him to his initial releases.

In some ways, what Coleman and his quartet were playing at the Five Spot was a radicalization of the fractured, modernist bebop of the 1950s. Coleman's saxophone tone tended to be harsh and cutting as opposed to lyrical or expressive. His phrase lengths were often irregular, even more so than his bebop forebears. Texturally, there was an emphasis on the contrapuntal linearity of multiple, often simultaneous, melodic lines that extended into long, occasionally overlapping solos. He used recognizable motives and specific intervals to drive his compositions, though the result was rarely developmental in any large-scale formal sense. Coleman's arrangements could be quite spare; a key choice was to omit the comping piano in bebop, which traditionally fleshed out a harmonic grid of changes that provided context for improvisations that arpeggiated, ornamented, and meandered around the harmonies.

The freedom afforded by this decision was radical: the missing piano left a yawning gap between the bass and the horns, which gave any implied harmonies routine in bebop saxophone lines only a transitory effect. This allowed Coleman to abandon the aural cues of bebop's unusual chord substitutions. The resultant tonality is not so much atonal; it was better described as "pan-tonal" by George Russell in 1960.[13] In fact, Coleman's solos contained a lot of diatonic meandering, often over a tonic or even blues progressions. The harmonic result is often one of a thin and ephemeral tonality, delicately held together by Haden's careful and responsive counterpoint. This open design, punctuated by familiar and often virtuosic recitations of the head, gave the ear considerable space to follow the linearity and emotional skittishness of Coleman's and Cherry's improvisations.

But in leaving the harmonic alignments forever ambiguous, Coleman and his collaborators had bent the formal experimentation of bebop into perceptually uncertain territory. His work featured complex and layered simultaneities that Kwami Coleman (no relation; and in this paragraph I will use their first names for clarity) has described as a "heterophony," which he defines as "the dense and opaque sound of decentralized simultaneity" built on "multiple subjectivities" that had "both creative and political significance."[14] By way of Glissant's theory of opacity, Kwami describes Ornette's "heterophony" as a dissenting utopia that refuses the normative politics of assimilation as well as the "hegemonic model of formal coherence" associated with traditional jazz modernism.[15] In ways that resonate with Kwami's concept of "heterophony," this chapter explores the way Ornette's utopian philosophy of harmolodics reflected experiments that playfully brought into question the transparency of an improviser's intentionality. For by rendering the intentionality of improvisation indeterminate, Ornette devised a novel approach to the postwar hyperfracture.

## Bebop Historicity

How are we to position Coleman's innovations conceptually and historically? Amiri Baraka was an iconic Black intellectual of the period and a fixture in the scene around the Five Spot. His perspective on this moment of Afro-modernism, as well as the postwar avant-garde more broadly, was as significant for the musicians involved as Adorno's was for Cage, Tudor, and the Darmstadt modernists at the very same time, and thus warrants some extended summary and exegesis.

Baraka came of age as a writer during the emergence of the postwar avant-garde, and was associated with the Beats during the early part of his career. He became increasingly influenced by Marxism as his career developed, which inspired the broader historical turn of his subsequent work. Baraka's book *Blues People* (1963) (then he was known as LeRoi Jones) offered a dialectically woven account of Black social life and musical style that does equal justice to the significance of both halves. In its simplest formation, he argues that in Black music, one hears the subjectivity, history, and social imagination of Black Americans. Baraka writes, "The most expressive Negro music of any given period will be an exact reflection of what the Negro himself is. It will be a portrait of the Negro in America at that particular time. Who he thinks he is, what he thinks America or the world to be, given the circumstances, prejudices, and delights of that particular America."[16]

*Blues People* emphasized that the Afro-diasporic experience is both unwanted and perpetually alienating for Blacks. Blacks in sub-Saharan Africa may have practiced slavery, but they did not dehumanize their slaves through the invention and imposition of a racial hierarchy. White Europeans enacted a brutal history of racial subjugation by devising social and legal hierarchies to acquire and maintain the cheapest possible source of agricultural labor. As Du Bois and Fanon have emphasized—both of whom were important to Baraka—this resulted in a complex, doubled sense of subjectivity. For these philosophers of the modern Black experience, no matter the degree of assimilation to normative white culture, the trauma of this historical subjugation was inescapable and haunted the emergence of Black subjectivity. Coleman himself similarly remarked about the experience of Blackness: "A white American can wake up in the morning without having any past on his mind. But I can't at least not yet. Persecution stays in the memory."[17]

In an echo of Du Bois, Baraka argued that the traumatic inequalities of Blacks in the New World were powerfully preserved through music, notably in work songs and spirituals. In his view music has a special status among the arts; the "emotional significance and vitality at [Black music's] core" endured throughout the history of Afro-diasporic people in the United States. It provided a special kind of knowledge and memory "that the white man was the master and the Black man the slave. . . . It is this knowledge—with its attendant muses of self-division, self-hatred, stoicism, and finally quixotic optimism—that informs the most meaningful of Afro-American music."[18]

Baraka offers a striking philosophical perspective on how this knowledge became congealed into musical form. In his view, Black musical forms were the result of "thought perfected at its most empirical, *i.e.* as *attitude*, or *stance*."[19] If Hegel regarded an artwork as an ideal in sensory form, and Adorno insisted on its cognitive, formal character as a reflection of the society that produced it, Baraka would have agreed, but he insisted that what was sedimented within the work of art was an empirically textured attitude—a relational social, existential, and emotional comportment that is also a form of philosophical knowledge. In "Jazz and the White Critic" (1963), Baraka put it as follows: "this music cannot be completely understood (in critical terms) without some attention to the attitudes which produced it. It is the philosophy of Negro music that is most important, and this philosophy is only partially the result of the sociological disposition of Negroes in America."[20] That is, it is not only socially determined, it is also found in the forms, styles, and contents of Black music. This dialectical philosophy echoed the logic of Du Bois's veil; white jazz musicians, for example, could not reproduce the existential charge of what it felt like to be Black. But Black music could affectively convey something of it, quite powerfully.

Baraka describes at length the ways in which Black music was amplified, appropriated, and deauthenticated by the forces of upward mobility, capitalism, and whiteness. In effect, the externalization of attitude in Black music was both enabled and threatened by the racialized prospect of social and economic advancement. In his account Baraka was often skeptical of if not directly opposed to assimilation. For example, though he regarded spirituality in general as an important resource for the Black imagination, Baraka viewed the impact of Christianity on Black slaves largely as an alienating force. Taking a materialist perspective on the question, Baraka framed Christianity as a compensatory remedy (a "metaphysical resolution") for subjugation at the hands of whites.[21] Consider only the aesthetic cost: this was a period, after all, in which the use of musical instruments by slaves was banned by slave owners. Following emancipation, as Black Americans had increased access to musical instruments, they pioneered a series of innovative genres around the turn of the century (minstrelsy, vaudeville, ragtime, boogie-woogie, and blues, among others) that were the product of complex dialectical mimicries. In minstrel shows, for example, whites imitated Black culture with comedic aims, which were in turn adopted and appropriated by Black musicians. Fueled by the techniques of the machine age, the popularity of these genres provide a new era of affective praxis that opened innumerable axes for the reimagination of social relationships.

In the process Black musicians transcended the "base" of agricultural production and entered what Marx termed the cultural sphere of the "super-structure."[22] This slow and uneven process of emancipation was both material and ideological. One might note that Du Bois's *Souls of Black Folk* (1903) emphasized the sacred emancipation of Black modernity by reframing the white reception of Black musicality from comedy (Blackface minstrelsy) into tragedy (spirituals), thus enjoining whites toward compassion rather than mockery or dismissal. Baraka's *Blues People* took this narrative a step further and emphasized the blues as an independent secular and engaged emancipation of self-consciousness. In his words: "There was a definite change of *direction* in the primitive blues. The metaphysical Jordan of life after death was beginning to be replaced by the more pragmatic Jordan of the American master: the Jordan of what the ex-slave could see vaguely as self-determination."[23]

Grounded in the dynamics of Black social advancement, Baraka similarly framed the modern emergence of jazz as starting a new narrative of emancipation, cosmopolitanism, and intellectualism. Early jazz was based on a "widening of Afro-American culture" that incorporated both the blues tradition and an emergent Creole tradition from New Orleans that was oriented toward a "Franco-American middle class."[24] Culminating in the rise of iconic figures like Duke Ellington and Louis Armstrong, jazz of the 1920s sustained the spirit of the blues but in a way that was mediated by the political economy of cities. This novel, Afro-modernist movement mirrored the rise of a Black middle class during the Great Migration to industrializing cities of the north, resulting in what Baraka calls an emergent Black "citizen."[25] For the first time, a genre of Black music could produce a "legitimate feeling" translatable to a public of white Americans.[26]

All that notwithstanding, structural inequalities thwarted the broader autonomous and self-conscious advancement of Afro-modernism. Whites owned the recording industry; their executives and musicians appropriated jazz and turned a significant profit by imitating, redeveloping, and watering it down during the swing era. This cultural theft resulted in the Americanization, popularization, and formalization of jazz as well as the deauthentication of its social, attitudinal origin in the blues. Consequently, Baraka argued that white audiences, in a veil-like logic, could never wholly understand a musician like Louis Armstrong. In parallel fashion, for Black audiences, it meant swing music—increasingly popularized by Paul Whiteman, Glenn Miller, and other all-white "jazz" spectacles—would gradually lose affective and social significance. On this point, note that Baraka and Adorno would have been in agreement.[27]

Baraka frames the fractured grammar of 1940s bebop as a critical response to these early decades of jazz history, and here Baraka and Adorno would have parted ways. With its separatist focus on interiority, complexity, and autonomy and its orientation away from dance and mass entertainment, for Baraka bebop represented a collective rejection of the stereotypical Black entertainer. It presumed an oppositional stance toward the homogenizing, whitening imprint of commercialized swing and instead foregrounded Black frustration with the possibility of social advancement. In the surrounding scene, the affective atmosphere of "Black cool" became a form of strategic nonparticipation, the use of heroin became a form of decadent perceptual separatism, and an emphasis on social intelligence ("procuring his 'shit'") and its attendant capacity for dissent became a way of asserting cultural capital in a tense and changing social world.[28] Baraka articulated a separatist defense of this moment that anticipated the famous 1958 headline attached to Milton Babbitt's high modernism: "musicians . . . were all quoted at various times saying, 'I don't care if you listen to my music or not.'"[29]

In both the economic and cultural spheres, whites supported and appropriated bebop for their own purposes. The jazz industry remained owned and run largely by whites whose audiences were likewise predominantly white. These audiences and industry executives consumed and imitated bebop dissent through the social practice of the white hipster whose cross-racial mimicry fueled their fantasies of rejecting the oppressive norms of American society.[30] This mimicry was far from a form of interracial solidarity. Not only did whites persist in extracting a considerable profit from Black creativity, they also enjoyed significant social privileges. To be a hipster—and to fetishize all that was "deep" or "weird" in bebop—was, for whites, a choice.[31] By stark contrast, Baraka emphasizes that, for Black beboppers, nonconformity was an inescapable existential condition imposed by whites. This induced a complex social tension. Black musicians authored the aesthetic innovations and worked with a white culture industry in order to interface with the cosmopolitan power of a modernist, artistic, elite culture. In response, Baraka makes clear how Black musicians had to safeguard the social realism of an attitude that could only be watered down by white hipsterism.[32]

The paradoxes of these complex social tensions abounded and were fundamental to the art form. In particular, Baraka discusses the way Coleman exemplarily captures such tensions. At a basic level, Coleman was a dissenting, modernist bebopper who refused the stereotype of the blues entertainer. But he was also compelling to critics because of his vernacular authenticity. After all, Coleman built much of his early improvising vocabulary taking solos on tour with R & B star Pee Wee Crayton. In his own unique dialectical fusion, Coleman emphasized the traditional blues virtues of emotional expressivity and individuality alongside the modernist abandonment of conventional grammar. Baraka heard the most iconic avant-jazz sax players (Coleman among them) as retaining a distinct sense of Black vocality: "These young musicians also rely to a great extent on a closeness of vocal reference that has always been characteristic of Negro music. Players like Coleman, Coltrane, and Rollins literally scream and rant in imitation of the human voice, sounding many times like the unfettered primitive shouters."[33] For Baraka, the vernacular blues elements captured the existential grip of racism and terror. Hearing the affective negativity in his music required an exact mode of dialectical listening that was attentive to Black sociality: "Ornette Coleman's screams and rants are only musical once one understands the emotional attitude he seeks to recreate."[34] The result was a unique synthesis of vernacular Black traditions and emergent Afro-modernism.

It has been remarked by historians that many beboppers were not necessarily focused on Black liberation and the social politics of race.[35] Though Coleman spoke powerfully to the press on behalf of Black injustices that he and others experienced (more on that below), he tended not to foreground racialized dissent or political motives in his works. As he once put it, "Music is a sound not a vote."[36] There are rarely sung or spoken words in Coleman's compositions and little in the way of political song titles, poems, and liner notes. He did not, for example, protest racism outwardly in his music in the manner of Max Roach, Oscar Brown Jr.'s, and Abbey Lincoln's *We Insist! / Freedom Now Suite* (1960), Nina Simone's politicized songs after 1964, or the work of Gil Scott-Heron, which was often driven by spoken word. Rather, the politics of Coleman's music was dialectically mediated by formal innovations—what he described as a "thought pattern"—in the music.[37] In doing so, he tended to emphasize general themes of creativity, inclusion, and egalitarianism. Philosophically, however, one should also note that Baraka's theory is not an empirical account of Afro-modernism. Rather, it is a dialectical interpretation of bebop, an immanent critique of the genre. Under this logic—echoed in the recent work on jazz by Fred Moten and Fumi Okiji—musical form was heard as an abstracted reflection of the injustices of Black social life.[38]

At the same time, when speaking in practical terms to the press, Coleman was adamant about the racial and economic injustices of the jazz industry. For example, after Coleman's initial rise to fame around 1960, he soon realized that he was earning considerably less money than his white modernist colleagues. He protested by imposing an early retirement on himself in 1965 and complained of routine exploitation by white-owned clubs and record labels (as of that year, he was sent statements from his labels with no sales figures, and publishing royalties that amounted to little more than a single dollar.) Coleman had also developed concerns about maintaining artistic autonomy. In his words, "Of all the problems that the Negro is confronted with, none is worse than the Negro artists trying to achieve individuality and human dignity without the approval of some organization that wants to control him."[39] During this period, he found little support from patronage; the nonprofit and moneyed institutions that supported white modernists (painters, writers, composers, and the like) had, in 1965, still offered scant support for Black jazz musicians. To a writer for the *Toronto Daily Star*, Coleman remarked the following year, "If you're a Black pianist who wants to learn to play Beethoven, you have a pretty good chance of getting a grant. That's that . . . liberal idea of uplifting the Black man by destroying his culture. But if you want to enlarge on culture, forget it; your money will have to become from bars and that cutthroat record industry."[40]

On the side of reception history, notwithstanding the cultural importance of the Black avant gardes of the 1950s to the 1970s to the emergence of Black nationalism and critiques of capitalism, racism, and colonialism, the wider appeal of avant-garde jazz was also limited for Black audiences. Part of the reason was the rising popularity of other Black genres: during the 1950s R & B and soul music had evolved from their origins in blues and gospel into a mass medium for collective expression and catharsis. In the words of cultural historian Eric Porter, "Not only was the avant-garde's appeal to the Black community tenuous, but jazz as a whole risked losing favor with audiences of all hues. With increasing frequency in the 1960s, musicians tried to rise to the artistic challenge of the avant-garde, theorize their own duty to their communities, understand the broader creative aspects of their projects, and grapple with the reality of surviving as professional musicians."[41] Given the reality of limited commercial appeal, there ensued a series of pioneering DIY innovations among Afro-modernists in the later 1960s and 1970s, notably the Black Arts Movement (for which Baraka played a key role) and a number of other nonprofit organizations such as Chicago's AACM.[42]

At the same time, white critics eager to write about an emergent Black avant-garde were hardly an uncomplicated audience. There was often a tone of condescension in their responses to Coleman as they tried to maintain intellectual authority over what counts and does not. As mentioned above, a broader audience of white hipsters was interested in extracting the cultural capital of Black authenticity via a touristic or "cool" proximity to Blackness. As Coleman put it in a 1967 editorial for *Down Beat*: "How does one play or write music today, since there is a vast number of nonwriters and nonperformers who might not like music and whose only connection with it is to make money and gain social prestige from it?"[43] For white audiences, proximity to the jazz avant-garde could easily collapse into a tokenistic fantasy that functioned as an alibi—a deluded sense of feeling exempt—from the persistent historical traumas of structural racism. It is in this context that Baraka's militant refusal of whiteness in "Jazz and the White Critic" (1963) should be read. But it may also help illuminate the strategic thinking behind Coleman's philosophical approach to Afro-modernism. After all, insofar as Coleman's music embodied a self-conscious attitude about this predicament, one could argue it deliberately aimed to both satisfy and thwart the racialized perspectives of his critics' judgments.

As noted in chapter 2, for Cavell, when modernist criteria question every norm of aesthetics, a principle of intentionality remained the minimal starting point for art. Their works could trigger interminable public debate, but artists nonetheless had to mean something by taking the risk of making art at all. Yet unlike the total serialism at issue in Cavell's "Music Discomposed" or Cage and Tudor's chance procedures, Coleman's intentions and emotions were never simply erased by the procedures of an esoteric formalism. Afro-modernist beboppers may have shared with the Darmstadt modernists a competitive spirit of formalist cognition, one that was also foundational to Coleman's complex hyperfractured compositions. In fact, the insistence on what Adorno would call an *Erkenntnischarakter* (or character-as-knowledge) was in many ways aligned with the way Dizzy Gillespie described bebop: it requires a style of improvisation where performers have to "think all the time."[44] As Baraka put it in the opening epigraph: "It is about thought." But the "thought patterns" that underpin Coleman's modernist hyperfractures were no longer transparent to critics. In a manner that parallels the fractured, polyphonic complications of Black modernist intentionality discussed in chapter 2, Coleman's hyperfractures reconfigured critical and perceptual expectations around Black expressivity.

To venture a brief comparison with the previous chapter: Coleman, Cage, and Tudor commonly provoked the public with indeterminacy and dissonance though a disciplined, intellectualized approach to composition and performance. In Cavellian terms, these modernists were all invested in questioning the coherence of the intentional self and spawning a heated sphere of public debate over art's criteria and definitions. Politically, there were crucial differences: the racialized "attitude" (to use Baraka's term) of Coleman's Afro-modernism was inflected by a sense of social dissent by comparison with the disengaged affect of Cage and Tudor's Orientalizing naturalism.[45] Compositionally, Cage and Tudor had disassembled the intentionality of the individual artist through a formal, esoteric, and highly abstract hyperfracture. Coleman, by contrast, removed the grammatical transparency of bebop harmony and instead developed a loose, collaborative ensemble of playful simultaneities that perplexed audiences with its abandonment of criteria. In a way that would challenge the assumptions of Cavell's essay, Coleman's work embodied a layered sense of self-consciousness that projected intentions that were at once sincere and unwoven. The modern self was both affirmed and evacuated.

## Deskilling Intentionalities

In *The Empty Foxhole* (1966), Coleman developed this philosophy of an unwoven intentionality by exploiting ambiguities in the perception of skill that question the normativity of expressive legitimacy and transparency. In the visual arts, the relevant term here is *deskilling*. Deskilling commonly refers to the automation of skilled labor, but in the realm of aesthetics, it indicates a deliberate refusal or forgetting of traditional techniques. In the words of conceptual artist Ian Burn, deskilling entails a "rupture with an historical body of knowledge."[46] Such a definition might suffice if a more or less coherent body of European historical style could be assumed; in Coleman's case it is far from clear exactly what history is being ruptured.

*The Empty Foxhole* features Ornette, Haden, and Ornette's ten-year-old son, Denardo (and in this section only I will use their first names to distinguish them). In 1962 Ornette had purchased his son a drum set for his sixth birthday, and after only four years invited him to a recording session. In preparation for the session, they rehearsed a few of Ornette's compositions. Track three, "Sound Gravitation," features the debut of Ornette's left-handed violin playing, an instrument he had recently started to learn, though he apparently "purposely avoided learning standard techniques" (figs. 4.2, 4.3).[47] Ornette also played trumpet on the album, an instrument he taught himself during the early 1960s, and chose a close-up of one of his own abstract paintings for the artwork. As a whole, *The Empty Foxhole* foregrounds the creative innocence of childhood. In the liner notes, each of the six tracks is accompanied by a short poem, many of which evoke some kind of childhood experience.

Aforementioned details of Ornette's biography already set the stage for an album about deskilling. We may recall that he had taught himself the saxophone, experimented on his own with different kinds of tone and techniques, and learned to read musical notation in a way that was unconventional. Initially, this presented problems: because of his idiosyncratic literacy as a musician, Ornette reported that others—particularly early in his career—routinely treated him as if he were incompetent. Yet he was in

FIG. 4.2. Ornette Coleman playing violin at *The Empty Foxhole* session, Van Gelder Studio, 1966. Photograph by Francis Wolff. Courtesy of Blue Note Records.

fact profoundly aware of the creative value of his idiosyncratic method. (When Gunther Schuller tried to "correct" Coleman's unique approach to clefs and transpositions around 1960, Coleman allegedly vomited in Schuller's apartment and promptly quit his composition lessons.[48]) In his 1965 interview for the *Liberator*, Ornette strikingly asserts that forgetting technique is a forward-thinking form of self-consciousness. In his view, the truly progressive and creative act is not—in Adornian fashion—to remember and fracture a known historical technique or norm but to find a way to begin to forget the system. In a paradoxical sense, to forget is to make a step forward. In his words, "I not only knew what they [my musician-critics] were doing, I had already forgotten it. I play the way I do because I believe that there is a certain music in America that must exist. . . . I'm dedicated to that cause."[49]

With its norms deliberately displaced and forgotten (or "ruptured" to use Burn's formulation), jazz critics and fellow musicians were predictably bewildered in their responses to *The Empty Foxhole*. For drummer Shelly Manne, "That is unadulterated s——. It sounds like I was standing in the middle of some kids' rehearsal hall and all these people were playing in different rooms. . . . You just don't pick up an instrument and start to play and because you are Ornette Coleman, it is immediately great—that's a lot of crap."[50] In the words of Cannonball Adderley, "I don't like what those other people are doing. I can't even identify with them. It's almost like interruptions to me."[51] It presented a profound challenge to musicians' and critics' criteria for judgment and fracture. Was the ten-year-old Denardo skilled? Ornette refers to his son as "Young Master Ornette" who "knew the music as if he had written it himself."[52] But was Denardo's hereditary relationship to

FIG. 4.3. Denardo Coleman playing drums at *The Empty Foxhole* session, Van Gelder Studio, 1966. Photograph by Francis Wolff. Courtesy of Blue Note Records.

Ornette enough to legitimate his contribution? Was Denardo's intuition assumed to be gifted no matter what he played? What about Ornette himself
sawing away on violin, left handed? The instability of transparent norms of
skill suggests a more abstract question about the degree to which Ornette's
intentions were coherent or consistent. Did he mean it? Was it a stunt? A
misguided experiment? A critique?

The Empty Foxhole activates these questions while evading positive answers. In doing so, Ornette brings to life a Cavellian instance of modernism
by knowingly and philosophically unleashing a sphere of debate. We may
recall that in Adorno's familiar, Eurocentric conception of modernism, an
exemplary artwork fractures a known grammar of art. The grammar is historical, socially conditioned, and for that reason formal. But in order for
the critique to work—for it to recover some kind of ethical capacity to the
work—there has to be some intersubjective agreement about what kind of
grammar, form, or cognition is being fractured. By building his own way
of reading and writing music and by showing audiences how novelty ar-
rives through deskilling and indeterminate openness, the basic assumptions
about what Ornette's materials were and how they could be manipulated
could not be assumed intersubjectively. As a result, Ornette calls into question the intersubjective conditions for perceiving a grammar—the very
essence of a hyperfracture. But unlike Tudor, who sight-read esoteric notations to separate his performance from his intentionality, Coleman staged
novel, concept-driven instances of improvised collaboration that were playfully indeterminate regarding skill, control, perception, and intentionality.
It was a new approach to the perceptual disorientation of the hyperfracture
that made critics and other musicians unsure whether they understood the
criteria for expertise. Perceptions and judgments would be warped in the
face of a new kind of musical object.

Consider a few details from the three cuts on side A of The Empty Foxhole. "Good Old Days" is a blues tune with all the stylistic outlines of bebop.
The head is a five-note motive that appears repeatedly in alternation with
Denardo's thumping drums; it unfolds over a twelve-bar blues progression
with ragged asymmetrical phrase endings; they cadence together, but just
barely. As if he were playing any other kind of bebop, Denardo pivots to
the ride cymbal during the verses as his dad unfurls a tearing, ecstatic four
minutes of soloing. In this extended solo, one has the impression of Ornette
channel surfing between motivic iterations, R & B licks, ornamented runs,
and periodic wailing, while little more than ephemeral implied harmonies
unfold below and around his melodies. Denardo's tempo seems responsive
to his dad's soloing; he uses the snare and floor tom to drop fills in ways
that shadow a skilled bebop drummer. But he does not yet have the muscle

control to maintain a firm tempo. Haden's bass steadies the composition: he plays the blues progression, walking bass lines, and takes a short solo just before the final restatement of the head.

In their blindfold test for *Down Beat*, Manne and Adderley agree that the trio sounds asynchronous. Manne hears the three as obliviously independent; Adderley hears Haden and Denardo as interruptive. For most of "Good Old Days," Ornette, Denardo, and Haden seem to be almost drifting in and out of attention, an apparent violation of Gillespie's bebop requirement that jazz musicians have to "think all the time."[53] To be sure, Haden and Ornette have a track record of productively "thinking all the time" with one another. But this deliberate ambiguity about synchronous thinking leads us to a central paradox to the album: their collective intentionality is purposively vague. Ornette, as ever, frames this as an opportunity: "I found some very new things to play from listening to [Haden and Denardo] play together."[54] Denardo's presence both guides and defamiliarizes their routine; his amateurism pushes Ornette away from his own expectations. (In a favorite moment of mine, Shirley Clarke's footage of *The Empty Foxhole* sessions, a bored Denardo lays his head down on his drums.) But Ornette welcomes the fraying of his own intentionality. *The Empty Foxhole* shows his audience, however implicitly or innocently, open yourself to this. All the while, Ornette's earnest utopian philosophy murmurs in the background. His liner notes poem for "The Good Old Days" expresses an unconditional openness even when one is not recognized ("happy to know someone who didn't know me") with an aim of universal social emancipation ("help to make a stranger free").[55]

A hyperfracture need not be dense; when deskilled, it can be sparse and wondrous. The title track, "The Empty Foxhole," is built on Denardo's wavering metronomic snare drum that flares up for a few stuttered fills as if he is lazily walking home from school. Ornette appears on the trumpet with a simple major key melody, while Haden accompanies him with simple diatonic triplet arpeggios. In a skilled and controlled way, they frame Denardo's juvenile drums with a beautiful, plaintive duet as if they are living inside Denardo's head and finding some kind of latent lyricism in his empty drumming. Ornette and Haden are telling the audience: there is actually a strange sort of poetry here in Denardo's perfunctory snare sound. The poem and song title tell a story: "men sleeping in the ground / hoping to escape death / thinking of their children / and loved ones. / bury not the soul / in a hole, / whose life has yet / to exist."[56] It is a minor hallucination built on little more than the acoustic sounds of a trio: someone hiding in the foxhole, or somewhere else if it is "empty," where they are hoping to see their family. At the same time, after reading the poem, it suddenly seems as if Denardo's snare might be a military drum, or gunfire, or somewhere in between. It is a strangely blended scene of nostalgia and fear.

"Sound Gravitation" is another atmosphere entirely. It is a free-flowing group improvisation with no apparent song structure. The liner notes poem presents us with a kind of Cagean event-score: "hear a sound—feel a sound, speak a sound—play a sound, all the gravitation of silence."[57] By 1966 there were precedents: plenty of avant-garde composers—from La Monte Young to Yoko Ono, George Brecht, and Ben Patterson—had made these kinds of event-scores in the earlier part of the 1960s.[58] In his performance, Ornette the violinist applies a great deal of bow pressure, scraping away, frequently on double-stops, clearly without much precision in tuning. By 5:30, he goes wild with right-hand pizzicatos (his fingerboard hand). In 1959, when Ornette was playing saxophone in unison with Cherry's pocket cornet, he demonstrated to the public that he could be precise. But on violin, Ornette withholds credibility; in hearing him, we might assume he is not skilled enough to play a typical bebop head on the violin and even more significantly that he is okay with his public thinking that. How, then, are we to take the semiskilled expressivity of his gestures? After a few opening pizzicatos, Haden is bowing imitatively with Coleman and manages to outline the makings of a minor cadence around 2:03. All the while, Denardo's free drumming might be concealing his still rudimentary skills. What criteria might be used for this "thought pattern?"

A deskilled avant-garde was common currency for Fluxus; the idea was that anyone could perform a work like Benjamin Patterson's *Paper Piece* (1960).[59] But Ornette's hyperfractures pushed virtuosity and deskilling at the same time: *The Empty Foxhole* contained as much expressive control—particularly in the saxophone and bass—as it did playful experimental abandon. And while he chose these instruments for their embrace of contingency, his aims were still coherent. As he put it about thirteen years later: "Since I've started to play the trumpet and violin I find myself playing only for the compositional manner that is certain to allow one to play or write at random while seeking a perfect compositional goal musically."[60] In *The Empty Foxhole*, the album's sense of compositional unity across the tracks remains elusive. After "Sound Gravitation" one flips the record to side B, where "Freeway Express" depicts the trio on a frenetic, highly responsive journey with Ornette back on trumpet, Denardo at full throttle, and Haden frantic, outlining pitch space. Ornette explicitly positions the experimentation of "Sound Gravitation" within the same boundaries of the album as the more conventional tonal tunes, however unspooled and improvisational those first tunes are. One cannot quite square the free-form experimentalism of "Sound Gravitation" with the criteria one needs to make sense of his nostalgic portrait in "Good Old Days" (or the sultry tonality of "Faithful" for that matter).

Amid this diversity of perceptual criteria, *The Empty Foxhole* appears as a deliberate paradox—a hyperfracture that is alternately simple and opaque. Far from a strong Cagean abandonment of the subject, the intentional stance of this album is playfully unwoven. Ornette positions Denardo's innocence as a guide, quietly relies on Haden's contrapuntal elegance, and switches between instruments and compositional styles that span his most accomplished vernacular skills as a blues-based saxophonist and his amateurism on the violin (an instrument that, we might note, was associated with some of the highest forms of technical competence within the whiteness of the classical tradition). It was a deliberate, self-conscious move not to erase his intentions (as Cage and Tudor purported to do) but to make them unpredictably vernacular, virtuosic, emotional, and experimental. An intentional polyphony stands on the album unwoven, without synthesis.

## Vernacular Utopias

As his career continued to evolve, Coleman increasingly foregrounded the philosophical thinking that underpinned his experiments. He first coined the term *harmolodic theory* in the liner notes to his orchestral work *Skies of America* (1972) to describe his approach to composition.[61] In the ensuing years, Coleman repeatedly announced that he was preparing a book length account of harmolodics, which, despite various editorial efforts from friends and colleagues, never ultimately appeared. Across many interviews, he typically defined the term with koan-like knots of poetry and oblique formulations. By the 1980s and 1990s, it had evolved into a branded leitmotif, particularly after Coleman made it the name of his own record label in 1995. It is through a combination of editorials, interviews, liner notes, and other critical coverage that one might reconstruct harmolodics and its unique engagement with music's ineffability.[62] Given how complex and resistant to summary the term is, what follows is far from an authoritative account, but it is nonetheless an attempt to map many of its basic attributes.

Harmolodics is a portmanteau joining the terms *harmony*, *melody*, and *movement*; it denotes the free and equal transformation of these three dimensions of music.[63] To Coleman's ear, these three dimensions are ontologically intertwined. In his words, "Harmony describes a certain position in an ongoing melody. . . . Melody is how you get to that position. And melody, at its simplest, is just a single interval—a movement from one note to the next."[64] Intervals, in particular, link these three musical dimensions together and facilitate equality and transformation between them. He writes, "that single interval can suggest or be the harmony, it's part of the melodic line, and it shows you the direction of the movement, the interval has three different functions."[65] Rhythm and movement further facilitate musical creativity given the sheer variety of approaches to musical time various collaborators are likely to have.[66] Among the three dimensions, melody has a nominal privilege because it reflects the simultaneous expressions of multiple individuals as well as their ability to interact socially.[67]

The often-cacophonous pluralism that results is something Coleman affirms; harmolodics encourages the expression of individuality by asking musicians to engage with one another with novel melodic combinations and transformations.[68] In his words: "[Harmolodics] means that you can transpose any chord or melody or change and still maintain the original (compositional) design by modulating to any sound that you hear from that design."[69] Philosophically, no two musicians need to agree about the exact idea, concept, or harmonic framework that is used to describe this collaborative polyphony. What ensures the coherence of the result is the limited set of twelve pitches in the equal-tempered scale, coupled with the endless possibilities of conceptualizing their potential relations. In his words, "When you've decided to analyze something called harmolodics, and you find out that that note that's harmolodic is now another note that's giving a different idea, then that's what's going to happen. Because, let's face it, it's only 12 notes, and all the music we ever heard is played by the same 12 notes."[70] On a number of occasions, Coleman illustrated the twelve-tone aggregate to an interviewer by diving them into three tetrachords: a C-major seventh, an E♭-minor seventh, and the dissonant chord D–A–A♭–F.[71]

The likelihood that "note" and "sound" may not align in the minds of various collaborators happens to be a very productive insight for Coleman.[72] As he once put it: "Believe me, the sound of the instrument is not the note of the instrument."[73] Transposed instruments are a perfect example. An instrument transposed to B♭ (as in a B♭ trumpet, for example) will play what they think is a C, even though that same sounding pitch on a piano is a B♭. The B♭ trumpet is trapped in a conventional system of notes that does not correspond to the normativity of the piano's concert pitch.[74] In fact, the piano has a way of maintaining harmonic authority over an ensemble; it lends itself to a single correct grid of chord names.[75] This is in fact the reason Coleman eschewed performing with a pianist for much (though not all) of his career. More commonly, Coleman celebrates the diversity of transposed instruments, which, in his view, lends itself to a similar diversity of conceptual perspectives.[76] Harmolodics affirms this multitude of idiosyncratic musical perspectives from the basic level of arbitrary pitch transpositions and clefs up to the more elaborate level of entire vernacular and self-taught idioms.

How it all manages to come together for an ensemble entails a complex and delicate philosophical formulation. Harmolodics affirms varied conceptualizations of simultaneous sound events as a special kind of harmolodic unison or "same sound."[77] This is a conceptual unison that is not at all the same as a unison concert pitch; rather, it is instead an empirical dissonance that can be philosophically unified as "a clarity, almost a ringing."[78] A 1995 interview around the release of *Tone Dialing* (1995) is particularly synthetic. Here, Coleman compares the dissonance of a harmolodic unison to analogs in language: different words in different languages that sound differently but can be understood as having the same meaning, or conversely, different words in different languages that have different meanings but nonetheless sound identical.

> Harmolodics is a way to describe and use information that has identical meaning but sounds like two different words as the same time. When you hear the guitar, the bass, and everyone else play what is called their tone dialing sounds, they are not so much playing different notes as they are playing their own tones, a form of the notes they have been given in the clef that they read. . . . If a word means something else in another language, and it's spelled and sounds the same, that's very harmolodic. . . . It expresses what sounds could be if they weren't programmed to represent a certain territory. It has to do with what you base a concept of unity on.[79]

The goal is a special kind of pluralized unison. A harmolodic unison asks us to hear identity amid difference so long as that difference is produced collectively, openly, and ethically and remains as true to an individual's vernacular roots as it is to the relational combinations of tones. In 1983 Coleman defined harmolodics in a way that was knotty but comprehensive: "the use of the physical and the mental of one's own logic made into an expression of sound to bring about the musical sensation of unison executed by a single person or with a group."[80] In other words, harmolodics redefines the "musical sensation of unison" in a way that allows it to accept pluralism of perspective "with a group." This challenges us to rehear "what sounds could be" in a utopian sense.

Harmolodics also works against the normativity of competence. The flexibility of harmolodic ideas liberates musicians from the repeatability of notes or any sense of inadequacy one has of not being able to read music or master a given style correctly.[81] What matters above all is the pluralism of perspective. This extends into the way one analyzes or listens to music. In Coleman's words, "The only analyzing that I do is to listen and try to enjoy the performers' concept in relation to the material they are using."[82] By affirming idiosyncratic musical ideas, Coleman gives unbounded credit to the conceptualizations each musician has about what they think they are playing. Along these lines, harmolodic pedagogy asks collaborators to recover idiosyncratic and unreifiable combinations of musical ideas that eschew the normative means of musical literacy.[83] As with *The Empty Foxhole*, Coleman's interest in children, amateurs, or self-taught musicians is a consistent theme.[84] As he once put it in 1978: "creativity does not have an age."[85]

In various interviews Coleman names these unique conceptualizations with a cluster of terms. Beyond "ideas," he speaks of musical concepts, logics, combinations, and information. In a parallelism with French structuralism, which rose to prominence in the Anglophone world during this same period, this vocabulary emphasizes elements and relations from the scale of musical materials up into larger social and ideological structures. Where Coleman would part ways with the structuralists, however, is in his emphasis on the key role of individual expression in the construction of harmolodic ideas. In an articulation of his utopian philosophy of music, he writes: "I think music itself is an idea. It's not a style, it's not a race, it's just an idea. And everybody has ideas. That's why music is so free for people to cherish, and so open—because it's how the idea is affecting you, and how you express what it means to you, regardless of what the style is."[86]

In the above locution Coleman defines harmolodics negatively. He positions musical styles as formulaic and repeatable, while contrastingly describing harmolodics as maximizing collective innovation.[87] By focusing on the socially creative combination of harmolodic tones, one can find their unique individuality within a collective. He states: "I'm not worried about the style, just the idea of how that person hears and expresses what he does on an instrument. I know music will allow any person to participate in it once they find out what their tone relationship is to the other tones."[88] In another instance, Coleman claims that harmolodics avoids measurable or formal regularities. He describes this poetically: "My music doesn't have any real time, no metric time. It has time, but not in the sense that you can time it."[89] And in terms of its harmonic content, harmolodics also eschews any resolutions traditionally associated with tonal syntax (as in the ubiquitous ii–V–I progressions in bebop).[90]

Coleman hears utopian stakes to all this: equality, interdependence, and freedom. Harmolodic freedom and equality reflects the social freedom and equality of individuals: it valorizes independence, creativity, and vernacular know-how.[91] An additive, combinatory melodic freedom works in this way because it is always open to new relationships that are both logical and sociological: "A melody is a repetitive form of construction that has an end and a beginning in relationship to logic—sociologic—[it's] basic. But ideas, inspiration? There's no person in the world that can tell you 'Don't do that.' "[92] By casting aside prefabricated stylistic expectations and norms, one can then openly "[transpose] any sound whatsoever into your own playing."[93]

Notwithstanding harmolodics' openly utopian character, its politics is not straightforwardly instrumental. In an interview with philosopher Jacques Derrida, Coleman made no claim to change the "way people act" "on the political level" or in their "sexual relations."[94] In line with a conception of modernist autonomy, his utopian aims were loose, abstracted, and idealistic; whereas traditional styles and techniques were tied to the social hierarchies of gender, race, ethnicity, and territory, harmolodics has the capacity to "[remove] the caste system from sound."[95]

Buckminster Fuller's writings were a significant influence on the utopian strains of Coleman's thought. His interest in the concept of information parallels Fuller's interest in geometric structures and concepts as analogous systems that could be both socially democratizing and operative regardless of medium.[96] As Coleman once put it, "any project that has to deal with collective information has to make sure that all information can be spread out and used equally."[97] The concept of information led Coleman to draw a parallel with Cage, whose valorized principles of interpenetration, interdependence, and anarchy were similarly influenced by Fuller's writings. Coleman was particularly interested in the way information, like musical notation and the equal-tempered scale, allows for free and collaborative forms of transformation. It is something he considers himself to have had intuitive access to since childhood. Below he relates a story of imitating (or transforming information from) his mother and older sister against their wishes:

> All information has something to do with changing its form, its appearance, to have a wider relationship to those that can use it. . . . Look at John Cage. He went to the point of having four people read from a book with a generator playing and that was advanced information that had to do with music being in the form of words. That transformation of information is something I understood when I was four years old. I remember trying to do something I saw my mother and sister doing, and they like to beat me to death. They said, 'No, you can't do that, you're a little boy.' I said, 'But *you're* doing it, and you're laughing.' Ever since then I've been aware that

human beings do things that translate into other things you can do that might not have the same shape and form you find when they were originally done. To me, harmolodic music encompasses all those things.[98]

In some of Coleman's more speculative moments, the harmolodic ideals of equivalence and transformation crossed specific and textured senses of the body. In a way comparable to other philosophers who sought to demonstrate the linkages between talking and thinking, Coleman once proposed that the five senses of the body were harmolodically linked to five dimensions of living in the world:

> Smell ~ Presence
> Taste ~ Clarity
> Hearing ~ Receiving
> Touch ~ Action
> Sight ~ Territories[99]

In Coleman's imagination, the five senses and five dimensions of life can overlap freely in the harmolodic presence of an individual. Similarly, Coleman heard four traditional Western vocal ranges (soprano, alto, tenor, bass) as exemplary of the ways four kinds of sounds can be drawn together into a harmolodic unison. This unison would take the place of what is elsewhere—and more hierarchically—called a "chord," "changes," "modulations," or "melody."[100]

Though comparisons with language are ubiquitous in Coleman's accounts of harmolodics, the relationship between harmolodics and grammar is complex. Generally speaking, Coleman defines sounds as flexible, indeterminate, and nonsemantic compositional elements. As he says on more than one occasion, "a sound is free of grammar."[101] According to this line of thinking, the abstract transposability of individual sounds is their great virtue: sounds have flexible relationships that can freely and collaboratively be built out into musical ideas. By contrast, Coleman hears traditional song forms and established styles as reified, language-like, and bound by "grammar." According to this binary logic, Coleman places an ethical focus on the unreified capacity of sound and its temporal flexibility to articulate the utopian ideals of individual freedom and social equality.

At the same time, there are occasions where Coleman refers to some language-like elements of harmolodics in order to emphasize the collaborators' vernacular know-how and the combinatorial potential of various sounds. In one instance, Coleman asks musicians to recover and exploit the vernacular rhythms of "talking" insofar as the underlying rhythms are themselves equally interchangeable, nonhierarchical, and nongrammatical: "when people talk, you talk in rhythm, especially if you talk fast it sounds like rhythm. Sound and rhythm is free of grammar, which is why it's so equal to everyone."[102] Following the release of *Sound Grammar* (2005), Coleman took an even more accommodating position on grammar in a discussion with philosopher Andy Hamilton about the ways harmolodics expresses emotions. After denying Hamilton's assertion that Coleman's music includes "bent" notes, Coleman claims that what others hear as "bent" note or a blues idiom is in fact audible in the combinatory grammar of harmolodics: "Sound has a grammar to it—believe me—that will cause that thing that you call bending to open up in a way you won't believe it."[103]

This does not mean harmolodics is a semiotic mode of composition. Any echo of grammar in harmolodics is nonreferential and nonmimetic; Coleman is more numinously asking musicians to translate an emotional intention into a harmolodic idea that is at once deeper, higher, and more abstract. As he explains: "In sound grammar, we can express any form of emotion, of the deepest depth or the highest. . . . Grammar is higher than any figment that has to do with emotion."[104] For the listener, the harmolodic result is thus not expressive of any particular emotion; in modernist fashion, it facilitates an abstracted understanding or affection. Coleman continues in his utopian register: "The emotion, in some way, has no gender, it has no race, it has no goal, it has no purpose. It's only to let you know the state that's affecting you at the moment . . . and then hear something that makes you say, 'Oh my goodness, I understand that'—that's just how [sound] grammar affects you."[105]

In the realm of affect, harmolodics thus does not seek to elicit or communicate specific emotions, as for example, in an artist's own experience of heartbreak. Rather, a musician intuitively or internally applies emotions to sound and thus more abstractly transforms them into the collaborative shape of harmolodic ideas.[106] For example, for Coleman the blues is not an expression of specific emotions through the use of known idiomatic features (flatted fifths, a twelve-bar progression, etc.). Rather, in resonance with Baraka's historicism, the blues is a dynamic form of knowing, an attitude or affection with its basis in Black sociality in which emotions are intuitively applied to sounds. In the words of Greg Tate,

This is the basis of Coleman's harmolodic system which is less a formal system, I feel, than a very Central African way of putting together a symphony. One where the interaction of discrete units of rhythm, line, and timbre fit together in a logic meant to draw each member of the band into a funky democracy that's maybe most akin to watching a room full of agile, creative dancers freestyling.[107]

The result was a hyperfracture insofar as it precipitated a positive, participatory excess of material that eschewed the synchronicities associated with perceiving jazz form in any traditional sense. When taking shape harmolodically in Coleman's music, emotions were similarly transformed—even sublated—into the free-form grammar of a dance party. Listeners can then recognize that a musician's ideas are infused by the sociality of emotion in a way that elicits a higher form of understanding.

Coleman had two motivations in forwarding his theory of harmolodics. One was to have a philosophical response to the racial biases of critics of his music who he felt did not understand it. The other was to popularize harmolodics beyond his reach. The former was a defensive response to a sense that his music had been misunderstood by white critics as a superficial provocation done in bad faith or, as Stanley Crouch once noted, exclusively and inescapably bound to the emotive orientation of jazz.[108] The latter was a reflective of Coleman's utopian aspirations. His ultimate hope was that its collective individualism could be taken up by musicians from all kinds of traditions worldwide, "not just people playing tempered instruments."[109] In learning from his theory, musicians could overcome reified grammars and styles, and find a global and utopian sense of cohesion and togetherness. He writes (and here grammar is negated rather than accommodated), "It must be something everyone can do in their own way. Once the concepts of music become free of grammar, then every person will not be stuck in a style. We'll be citizens of the earth; we'll stop seeing ourselves ethnically and see ourselves instead as humanity."[110]

As mentioned at the outset of this section, though Coleman promised to publish harmolodics in book form since he first announced the term in 1972, he never managed to finish the project. Despite the difficulty many had in understanding his theory, he did not want it to be a secret; Coleman wanted to be as accessible and nontechnical as possible.[111] At one point he imagined making harmolodic theory into a novel, though he more often expressed the desire to simply edit and polish it into a technical and philosophical text.[112] A related dream of his was that he, as the composer, would no longer be necessary; that amateur and professional musicians alike— even professed nonmusicians—could independently practice harmolodics for themselves.[113] Paradoxically, he hoped that by understanding his theory, musicians would no longer need his approval as a composer (though ironically, he said the reason he had not finished the book was because he was too busy performing harmolodics).[114]

## Harmolodic Ineffability

A critic for the *New Yorker* once described Coleman's theorizing as follows: "Coleman talks about his music in coherent bursts or in quasi aphorisms that keep spilling over into philosophy."[115] Even as Coleman hoped harmolodics would be received as an inclusive and accessible theory, it is an obvious historical fact that many of his interlocutors (collaborators, interviewers, critics, fans, and the like) routinely found his aphorisms obscure. One reason is that harmolodics eschewed normative rules and instead prized an indescribable multitude of vernacular creativity. Harmolodics was also, of course, built on the numinous medium of music, which Coleman felt was already resistant to description or explanation. In this final section, I will elaborate on these and other ways in which harmolodics aligns with the perplexing qualities of music's ineffability.

At a basic level, the dynamics of harmolodic collaboration resist explanation. In this regard, Coleman emphasizes the inconsistent qualities of intuition over clear and distinct lines of communication. In harmolodics, communication is not built on a normative syntax or protocol; it is, rather, "a form of energy that allows everyone to have the same equal time or position."[116] This intuitive medium of communicative energy does not necessarily require specific information; rather, it works expressively through inconsistencies of feeling, hearing, and thinking.[117] For listeners attuned to harmolodics, the musical result is atmospheric and therapeutic rather than mimetic or referential. And these atmospheres can become utopian hyperfractures in their capacity to alter the apriorities of one's perception in the manner of a second-order modernism: "I'm just talking about psychological medicine. . . . It's that sound that has something to do with changing the mood of your environment, the way you see it. . . . There must be sounds yet to be combined that are going to mean, that *will* mean, more beautiful things to people, once individuals spend time developing these combinations."[118]

Though Coleman was not a particularly religious or spiritual composer, he also affirmed music's perennial associations with mysticism. In a 1979 interview he reported the following: "There are endless experiences of the mystical experience, they occur in every form of human expression. Yes, music can be and has been a mystical experience for me."[119] In an independent parallel to the writings of Vladimir Jankélévitch, Coleman had particular regard for the inconsistent dynamics of improvisation as a locus of mystical and inconsistent experience. In this same interview, he describes this with a nonsemantic placeholder: the letter X. "In composing as well as improvising exists X, the unknown. That is to say thinking and feeling, when in agreement to an expression, causes the unknown to happen, as in instant perfection."[120] Such experiences depend on access to unconscious forces that short-circuit the mediation of explicable bodies of knowledge. An almost telepathic sense of intuitive communication predicated on the immediacy of a sonic object allows one to be fully open to the input of emotional experience. Just three years later, Coleman reported, "What goes on in my head when I improvise is like human auras. Ideas flow through me the way a child grows. I play the same logic fast or slow. I don't think about feeling, seeing, or thinking. I try to have the player and the listener have the same *sound* experience. I'm not thinking about mood or emotion. Emotion should come *into* you instead of going out. All those things are built into your human fibre."[121]

The underlying content of harmolodics lent itself to ineffability as well. In 1978, when asked by a critic whether language "stands in the way of explaining things," Coleman agreed and responded that the reason was due to the sheer multiplicity of vernacular dialectics that might be used to describe music:

> Musically, I think it does. For one reason, I think the English language in America is really the street language. It's not the ancestral language of all the people. I know myself, I don't speak any other language fluently, but there are many English words that you can use that another person wouldn't understand. Also, it's hard to describe something musically just using a noun, more than the *contents* of it.[122]

In other words, the contents of music are inescapably vernacular and resist categorization by nouns. Thus, in a sense, harmolodics cannot be transparently explained because it so radically pluralizes the concept of musical literacy. In an example of what I have elsewhere termed *a paradox of the vernacular*, we might say that Coleman's harmolodics is ineffable because of its veneration of a vernacularism that is so varied and multiplicative that it is inexplicable. Its internal diversity is an inexplicable multitude.[123] Charles Kronengold describes Coleman's "stance" as "a kind of being-next-to: a position that's proximate enough to make us wonder about the nature of the relation, but not so close as to provide any answers."[124] The polemical claim to hear consonance in the spacing of this internal diversity was at the center of Coleman's utopian, democratized, and unwoven approach to intentionality.

It is a paradoxical philosophy, a communicative immediacy that is nonetheless mediated by elaborate "thought patterns" of vernacular, combinatoric improvisations. By letting these grow to certain excesses of what Kwami Coleman has described as Ornette Coleman's "heterophony," Ornette conjured a novel form of the hyperfracture.[125] As mentioned briefly at the outset of this section, to Coleman's many interlocutors, such paradoxical explanations had a way of skating around, like copies of the ineffable that never quite resolved the question or named the unnameable. As his collaborator, guitarist Bern Nix once remarked, "To me, it's like Zen. There are no exact answers. It's all enigmatic and contradictory. Ornette speaks in puzzles and riddles; you just have to figure it out. It's a metaphysical inquiry into the nature of music."[126] In the formulation of these paradoxes, Coleman was effectively practicing an apophatic approach to his many definitions of harmolodics. Across his many interviews, he did not say "harmolodics is neither x, nor y, nor is it z," while prohibiting positive efforts at definition. He instead performed music's ineffability through playfully elaborate rhetoric, poetry, and imaginative logics. Each definition of harmolodics is plausible, though none is fully adequate or satisfying. His formulations appear like riddles or koans; they ask to be puzzled over. In doing so, he staged perplexity about the harmolodic method without having to tell people "no" in explicit terms.

We would misunderstand his work if our takeaway from his perplexing rhetoric was that Coleman was confused about the scope of his own theory. Rather, in my view, his choices to define harmolodics with paradoxical formulations were more of a deliberate strategy. That is, Coleman was staging a challenge to his listeners and readers by foregrounding an experience of perplexity about musical creativity that he took to be productive and ethically significant—utopian, in fact. It was a philosophical strategy for eschewing prescriptive norms, and it kept any systematic regularities of harmolodics indefinable. That is, he develops his own musical language while performing and staging his and others' perplexity or playfully repositioning positive definitions of what those systematic regularities are.

Coleman's multifarious engagements with ineffability after 1972 can be read back into his earlier work. Consider his use of language in the liner notes to *The Empty Foxhole*. He does not show his cards and say, *This album is a modernist revaluation of amateurism—here is an elaborate theoretical treatise about deskilling and compositional intentions.* Instead, he writes, in effect: *Denardo is the leader here. Just listen to him—he is an expressive human being.* In fact, Coleman expresses intentional sincerity about this whole approach. In his liner notes he states, "Music will never fall short of an honest effort when it has love, talent and sincerity in its performance."[127] Just one year earlier he wrote something similar regarding intentionality: "The reason I am mostly concerned with music is because music has a

tendency to let everybody see your own convictions."[128] Earnest and humanizing words had a pressing social motivation for Coleman: he was com-
bating the racist tendency for white critics to take his experimentalism as
an inauthentic shock tactic ("There's always the tragedy of your not being
totally understood because someone suspects some other motive outside
of you expressing yourself").[129] But his earnest appeals also stage a complex paradox essential to what I have described as Coleman's second-order
modernism: they seem designed to quell Cavell's anxieties about modernist intentionality at the very moment when the album dramatically exacer-
bates them in proposing—in musical form—a deskilled hyperfracture that
occludes its own criteria.

We are left to mull over the effect of this language: Coleman's actual music on *The Empty Foxhole* does every possible thing to thwart the criteria
for judgment and at the same time insists on its intentional sincerity. This is
ineffability as a strategic withholding, a playful, utopian, and gentle engagement with his audience's search for positive criteria. The full philosophical
guide to comprehend this subject position remains withheld, deferred, or
unrealized. Denardo or Ornette—or both—are positioned with a certain
metaphysical aura; listeners may be drawn into an apophatic search for a
compositional method that cannot fully be explained as it insistently points
toward the numinous decisions of his ten-year-old son. As theater, it is both
earnest, socially determined, and ontologically disruptive in Cavell's sense
insofar as fraudulence can and does remain a risk. But if the serialists used
scholarly journals to stage aesthetic justifications and debates over formal
criteria, Coleman brings to life music's perplexity and ineffability on the
couch, liner notes in hand, record on, brain puzzling, reading, listening
to intentions that are both earnest and heterophonic—to return to Kwami
Coleman's term. Thinking that complex reality is an inventive way of staging while also—in the manner of a hyperfracture that question the norms of
one's perception—refusing a definition in public.

According to Baraka, bebop fit the profile of a dissenting Afro-modernism
and reflected a social desire to reject the commoditized stereotype of the
Black entertainer. As a bebopper, Coleman undoubtedly exemplified a
sophisticated, intellectual, competitive formalism that was effective precisely because it so compellingly maintained the vernacular roots of the
blues tradition even as it disrupted and pressed beyond these norms. But
Coleman's own philosophy added further twists to Baraka's dialectical
interpretation of Afro-modernism, in particular by reworking the blues
not merely as an idiom, but as a collaborative vernacular philosophy. The
added dimensions of deskilled "forgetting," his playful engagement with
unwoven intentionalities in *The Empty Foxhole*, and his elaborate utopian

philosophy of harmolodics show that Coleman found novel ways to reconstruct the compositional subject of Afro-modernism into a new form of self-consciousness. In the process, the unwoven intentions of his work revealed novel—and utopian—incarnations of music's ineffability. It seemed to be equal parts negation and affirmation or forever blurring the boundaries between the two.

What Coleman did was exceptionally elaborate, certainly of philosophical significance in its own right. He unearths ontological problems that his audiences only seem to grasp obliquely, dismiss as irritants, or completely miss altogether. Like Cage, as both musician and philosopher of the indeterminate and the utopian, Coleman's influence over the remaining musicians in this book would become immense. By the late 1960s a world of free jazz and free improvisation at a remove from the idioms of jazz altogether—particularly among white musicians in Europe—had emerged in the wake of his experimentation. In fact, much more so than Cage, it was Coleman and the Velvet Underground who would create prototypes for decades of future experimental musicians.

[ CHAPTER FIVE ]

# The Velvet Underground, Eleven Rooms . . . c. 1967

The breakthrough of the Velvet Underground came in 1966 as a result of the management and promotion of Andy Warhol, who had already become a famous icon of pop art.[1] Warhol's first major solo exhibition in New York was at the Stable Gallery in 1962, the same gallery in which Cage had exhibited and sold the calligraphic scores for the *Solo for Piano* four years earlier. Together, Warhol and the Velvets devised a confrontational, chaotic, and immersive intermedia touring show entitled the Exploding Plastic Inevitable (1966–67) that paired the band's performances with film screenings, animated visuals, and live dancing.[2] Though this was ostensibly a multisensory rock show, little about the result went down smoothly with audiences. At an early performance in January 1966 that Warhol booked at an academic psychiatry convention, doctors fled for the doors, reportedly exclaiming, "Why are they exposing us to these nuts?" and "Put it down as decadent Dada."[3] Another doctor exclaimed: "It was ridiculous, outrageous painful. . . . Everything that's new doesn't necessarily have meaning. It seemed like a whole prison ward had escaped."[4] Of a brutally hot residency in Chicago that summer, another critic described the noisy, overabundant spectacle as cornering audiences into delirious participation:

> The musicians occasionally revealed, sweating over their instruments, grinding out a noise that has music in it somewhere. . . . Too much is happening—it doesn't go together. But sometimes it does—suddenly the beat of the music, the movements of the various films, the pose of the dancers, blend into something meaningful, but before your mind can grab it, it's become random and confusing again. Your head tries to sort something out, make sense of something. The noise is getting to you. You want to scream, or throw yourself about with the dancers, something, anything![5]

As with Tudor, Cage, and Coleman, the critics' responses to the Velvets' performances blended accusations of psychosis with testimony of a second-order modernism that contended the very coordinates of perception were undergoing alteration, blurring, and reconfiguration. Despite significant differences in aesthetic process, the Velvets joined Tudor, Cage, and Coleman in harnessing ineffability by occluding the communicative transparency of intentionality. Yet in a break with their virtuosic hyperfractures, the Velvets' experimentalism was focused on alchemy—the transformation of musical substances. Through a collaborative mix of Reed's Beat-inspired songwriting, Cale's searing minimalism, and Morrison and Tucker's hypnotic discipline, the band recombined trance, drone, and ecstasy to produce atmospheres that were equal parts physiological and characterological. More than any other rock band of their era, they recognized that the strident inconsistency of sound could bring the ineffable depths of the psyche to life.

Alchemy lends itself to new methods of musical composition. Cage delivered scores to Tudor for realization and performance. Coleman wrote out charts and worked with favored collaborators to establish improvisational norms derived from bebop that were uniquely open ended. The Velvets worked by ear, spinning out Reed's songs into long-form improvisations.[6] Their alchemical techniques—ad hoc, collaborative, variously skilled and deskilled—challenge our capacity to isolate criteria and elements. For Reed, one of their techniques involved playing so loud that it became difficult to distinguish one instrument from another: "We used to call it the Cloud, and like, on certain songs, we used to consciously enter the Cloud and you just hear all these funny things. They're not you, but you know they're being caused by the guitar, right?"[7] The melodies and chords of Reed's memorable tunes, which tended to revolve around the uplifting feeling of oscillating I and IV chords, were a mere skeleton; the sonic flesh itself was foundational. (Just try reading a sheet music version of "Venus in Furs.") In the studio, they built otherworldly, enveloping versions of these songs indebted to Phil Spector's wall of sound (though devoid of the strings and winds). In the words of John Cale, "We were trying to do a Phil Spector thing with as few instruments as possible. On some tracks it worked."[8] The result was decorative, almost architectural atmospheres with hypnotic grooves, layered reverbs, decadent imagery, and ambiguous intentions. A rich array of historical, social, situated knowledges remained irrevocable from the band's recorded form; it elicited complex layers of affective appeal.

A number of parallels with the previous avant-gardes remained: Afro-modernist techniques of modal improvisation and deskilling were taken up, here by a white, college-educated, hipster "art" band. As with Cage and

Tudor, a fantasized version of India remained a resource. And like Cage, Tudor, and Coleman, the Velvets constructed affective intensities in sensory, practical form that explored mysticism, ineffability, and an oblique desire for social change. Though the Velvets' iteration of the ineffable avant-garde reaches into interviews and reviews, and emerged in dialogue with philosophers, writers, artists, and cultural movements of the period, its central incarnation is in the praxis of the band's recorded collaborations in sound. With their grinding, delirious atmospheres, the Velvets aimed to blow a hole in the floor. As the critic above put it: "The noise is getting to you."

## Drone Alchemy

The idea of an avant-garde rock band had little in the way of precedent; in 1965, rock music had only begun to find its footing as a genre in the culture industry. But minimalist composer La Monte Young's collaborations with Velvets' violist John Cale from 1963 to 1964 would be a key impetus. And the trajectories of these two musicians were meaningfully enmeshed in the scenes discussed in the previous two chapters. During the mid-1950s, Young worked and studied as a jazz saxophonist in Los Angeles and happened to collaborate on occasion with Ornette Coleman and his future sidemen, Billy Higgins and Don Cherry.[9] In 1959, when Coleman and his collaborators moved to New York and were preparing for their breakout gig at the Five Spot, Young had taken a path available virtually only to white musicians and become ensconced in the study of modernist composition at the University of California, Los Angeles, and the University of California, Berkeley. That summer, he made his way to Darmstadt, where he learned of Cage's music, met and heard David Tudor, and found works by Sylvano Bussotti, Christian Wolff, and Cornelius Cardew revelatory.[10]

Upon returning to the states, Young had become a committed and spirited avant-gardist. He moved to New York, enlisted Cage and Tudor to help perform a screeching indeterminate work of his titled *Poem for Chairs, Tables, Benches, etc.* (1960), wrote a series of event-scores for Tudor, and collaborated with Yoko Ono in a famous loft series of avant-garde concerts (1960–61).[11] Young also edited a printed compendium of experimental scores with poet Jackson Mac Low titled *An Anthology of Chance Operations* (1963).[12] With students from Cage's famed course in experimental composition like George Brecht, Dick Higgins, and Allan Kaprow now out in the streets making what Higgins termed experimental "intermedia," a notorious neo-Dadaist zeitgeist had exploded in New York and was quickly attracting notoriety in Europe, Japan, and Latin America.[13] It was in this "experimentalist" climate of New York during the early-to-mid-1960s that the Velvet Underground took shape.

Young's and Cale's histories had a certain parallelism: in 1960, Cale, while attending Goldsmiths College as a violist, discovered modernist composition. He met Cornelius Cardew, who had been blown away by Cage and Tudor's performance of the *Concert for Piano and Orchestra* in Cologne in October 1958. Cardew in turn introduced Cale to American experimentalism through works by Cage, Young, and members of Fluxus. In July 1963 at a concert of avant-garde music that Cale organized at Goldsmiths, he conducted the British premiere of Cage's *Concert for Piano and Orchestra* and performed La Monte Young's "X for Henry Flynt" (1960) as a marathon series of forearm clusters on the piano.

Cale's education and whiteness also gave him access to a privileged social network; he contacted the eminent composer Aaron Copland, who would sponsor Cale's green card via a Tanglewood residency. He arrived in the states during the summer of 1963, studied composition at Tanglewood for a short period with Iannis Xenakis but quickly lost interest in concert music and moved to New York. Like Young, in the early 1960s Cale had been drawn to Cage and contacted him. That September, Cage in turn found Cale a job at the Orientalia bookstore on East 12th St. and arranged for Cale to participate in an iconic performance of Erik Satie's *Vexations*, a piece that requires a haunting atonal chorale to be repeated 840 times.[14] Thanks to prominently featured photographs in a *New York Times* review, Cale's role earned him some modest recognition.[15] (Cale playing a single solo iteration of the piece would soon after be featured as a middlebrow oddity on an episode of the television show *I've Got a Secret*).[16] That same September, Cage also gave Cale Young's phone number.

By the time Cale and Young first spoke, Young had already struck out in a new direction: his newly convened Theatre of Eternal Music had pivoted away from the ontological shock of Fluxus and instead back toward the Afro-modernist idiom of modal improvisation that Young had explored as a jazz saxophonist.[17] Following some initial gigs in the summer of 1962 with Billy Name on acoustic guitar, a lineup emerged that included Young, singer and visual artist Marian Zazeela, percussionist Angus MacLise, and violinist Tony Conrad, who joined in the spring of 1963. The Theatre featured Young's saxophone playing and MacLise's sporadic drumming (something in between tabla and free jazz drums) accompanied by Conrad and Zazeela on violin and vocal drones, respectively. They performed seated on a carpeted floor in the manner of Hindustani classical musicians. When Young learned that Cale played viola (at the time Cale was ready to move on from the world of classical music and put the viola away), Young insisted he join in a rehearsal with the band as a drone performer on viola at their newly established studio in Tribeca.

In traditional style histories of modernism, The Theatre of Eternal Music could be seen as a reaction against both academic serialism and the Fluxus-oriented avant-garde. This is, I suspect, at least in part due to the fact that these recordings remain unreleased. But listening to the informally circulating bootlegs of a 1984 WKCR broadcast makes obvious the band's overwhelming debts to a blend of Indian and Afro-diasporic music. Years before Young's study with Pandit Pran Nath in 1970, a major influence on the group was Ali Akbar Kahn's traditional Hindustani classical music—notably his first LP of 1955 (the first commercial recording of Indian music in the West), which circulated widely among jazz musicians at the time—as well as John Coltrane's modal jazz around 1960, particularly his ubiquitous and accessible reimagining of "My Favorite Things" (1961). The influence of Coltrane's sheets of sound and his tuneful and ecstatic and frantic meandering within a single mode is particularly palpable on Young's sopranino saxophone playing in the Theatre's first recordings between 1962 and early 1964.[18] In these recordings, Young's saxophone is complemented by the aperiodic popcorn of MacLise's hand drums—a blend of pulsing tabla and free jazz atmospherics—and delicately shifting, strangely emotional, tanpura-like drones.

Young's affinity for Afro-diasporic improvisation was essential to both the Theatre's music as well as the sociality that underpinned its mode of collaboration. Beyond his earlier work as a jazz saxophonist, Jeremy Grimshaw has detailed Young's virtuosic pianism and saxophone playing within traditional blues idioms during this period, emphasizing that jazz is what led him toward seventh chords as compelling static harmonies that could prove foundational for large-scale improvisations.[19] Young even leaned into a certain fantasy and fetishism in recalling this formative musical experience with Black music; he would later describe the blues as an "ancestral lineage" to his mature musical style.[20]

By the early 1960s Young had quickly risen to the status of an iconic scenester. He was not only the convener of the Theatre; Young was dealing marijuana, opium, and speed (with Cale as his delivery man).[21] The reserves of social capital acquired through this role had debts to the racialized fantasy of Mailer's and Baraka's hipster (we can recall Baraka's contemporaneous remark that the hipster has no trouble "procuring his shit").[22] Young facilitated the Theatre's jam sessions with weed smoking, an activity with a racialized history linked to Black musicians and to South Asian spirituality. He had the social power to lead rituals that, like many jazz, R & B, and rock musicians of the 1960s, explored a second-order modernism as an altered physiological state: THC facilitated the dilation of time and perception, which helped the musicians focus on particular sonorities at length. More philosophically, it helped to break open and unlock potentialities of the self that were otherwise bypassed by socially ingrained habits of perception.

Early in 1964 MacLise left the band and traveled to India and the Middle East to study percussion while the remaining members moved beyond the aperiodic virtuosity of jazz and more toward drone alone. Around the same time, Young first slowed his saxophone playing down to drones, and eventually—frustrated by the instrument's unstable tuning—put the saxophone away and began singing drones with Zazeela. Conrad, who had a background in mathematics from his years as a Harvard undergraduate, introduced the Pythagorean precision of just intonation to the group, specifically tuning the drone around a perfect fifth (3:2) and the harmonic seventh (7:4), the two intervals that would prove essential to Young's approach to just intonation in *The Well-Tuned Piano* (1964–).[23] Droning for ninety minutes at a time almost daily, in what Young would describe as a newfound "discipline," the Theatre began to focus on carefully tuning harmonies that featured these two "just" intervals of pure integer ratios.[24] "Day of the Antler" (1964) emphasizes the perfect fifth and the harmonic seventh with occasional sharp fourth or natural sixth harmonies as pungent, ephemeral dissonances. "Day of the Millstone" has the same perfect fifth as the drone foundation, but Young sings alternately a perfect fourth and minor third, giving it the lightest suggestion of a tugging, even gripping, plagal flavor. The voicings of the harmonies are always oscillating and the aggregate drone is not consistently anchored by a single fundamental bass pitch.

By the fall of 1964, Cale and Conrad together had devised the use of contact microphones to increase the amplification of their droning. When listening to the recordings, however, one has an overwhelming sense of fragility: each tone is separated by breaths and bowings. The band's music harnessed ineffability by immersing listeners in a surface nearly devoid of expressive or language-like musical features. The texture is organic and overlapping, remarkably steady over large stretches of time. In collectively finding a new consistency out of inconsistent materials, the Theatre was seeking out alchemical transformations and providing Cale with a prototype for collective experimentalism.[25]

## Afro-magnetism

The Theatre of Eternal Music's (fig. 5.1) unmappable, immersive rituals—exhaustively recorded but only fragmentarily released—proposed to suspend

FIG. 5.1. The Theatre of Eternal Music performing in 1965
(*from left*, Tony Conrad, La Monte Young, Mariane Zazeela, and John
Cale). Photograph by Fred W. McDarrah. Courtesy of Getty Images.

and reframe the intentionality of the ego. But unlike the violent disjunction of
Cage and Tudor's esoteric formalism, Young's Theatre blended and stretched
out Indian and Afro-modernist forms in order to bring to life a cloistered separatism from the normative coordinates of Western aesthetics.[26] Aside from
Cage's tape pieces and instrumental use of radios and phonographs, what
Cage, Tudor, and Coleman had done up to that point was largely acoustic
music with occasional amplification and recording. The Theatre's gesture-
driven world of electrical sensation aimed for something—an erasure, a stop-
page, or an ascent of some kind—that modernity could not furnish within its
own historical resources. In Young's words, the aim was to produce "meditative and exalted psychological states."[27] From their perspective, no self-aware
fracture of an existing technique taught by a white Westerner could harness
the metaphysical power of such immersive intermedia. In an imaginary, appropriative space, the Theatre aimed to subtract itself from the social fabric in
the purposeful act of an elite meditation. To be sure, Young's compositional
ego seems to have remained at the center; but this was hardly an uncommon
paradox: Cage often sought top-down control over the process of noninten-
tionality.[28] It was a ubiquitous irony of 1960s utopianism: gurus like Swami
Satchidananda may have claimed that "the guru is within," but a famous male
guru delivered the message, all the same.[29]

From a bird's-eye perspective, Cale and his future collaborators in the Velvet Underground were caught up in some fast-changing dialectics with American popular culture that complicated the traditional Greenbergian distinction between an avant-garde and the kitsch of popular culture.[30] Most simply, the 1960s was a period when the avant-garde itself became a topic of mass fascination.[31] As mentioned earlier, Warhol's pop art was first featured in major solo exhibitions in 1962. Inspired by Robert Rauschenberg, Jasper Johns, and Roy Lichtenstein, Warhol powerfully collided the aspirations of the art world with the accomplishments of commercial culture. This development affected Young as well, whose Theatre had drifted away from avant-antics and instead toward countercultural fashion.[32] Building on Hollywood fashions of the 1930s and 1940s, by 1965 Warhol, Young, and Zazeela (along with Bob Dylan who was seen on occasion at the Factory) all wore sunglasses indoors to project a glamorous and detached affect. In the realm of music and poetry, the commercial folk revival and countercultural rock during the mid-1960s revolutionized the bohemianism established by the jazz-inspired Beats of the 1950s.[33] Rimbaud-reading poets like Dylan and later Jim Morrison brought the avant-garde spirit of surrealism and decadence to a mass audience with unparalleled sensory force in songs like "Desolation Row" (1964), "Visions of Johanna," (1965), or Morrison's "The End" (1967). In the same span of time, the Beatles went from highly controversial in the American press (1964) to acclaimed countercultural geniuses (by 1967).[34]

∵

Twenty years before this watershed moment of the postwar avant-garde, Lou Reed grew up first in Brooklyn and then lived in Freeport, Long Island; his middle-class Jewish family was a product of postwar white flight. Reed had nothing but disdain for his largely well-off, idyllic, though conservative suburban upbringing. As a teenager, he was keenly attracted to the powers of Black popular culture. He particularly admired doo-wop, a genre of R & B invented by Black musicians that rose to popularity during Reed's childhood in the late 1940s. Reed would describe the midcentury explosion of Black popular music as opening an atmosphere of seduction, freedom, and empowerment away from schoolbook positivism and the stifling normativity of upward mobility. He heard R & B as a magnetic medium with unique powers of affective intensity and inconsistency:

> The dusky, musky, mellifluous, liquid sounds of rock and roll. The sounds of another life. The sounds of freedom. As [DJ] Alan Freed pounded a telephone book and the honking sax of Big Al Sears seared the airwaves

with his theme song, "Hand Clappin'," I sat staring at an indecipherable book on plane geometry, whose planes and angles would forever escape me. And I wanted to escape it, and the world of SAT tests, the College Boards, and leap immediately and eternally into the world of Shirley and Lee, the Diablos, the Paragons, the Jesters. Lillian Leach and the Mellows' "Smoke from Your Cigarette." Alicia and the Rockaways' "Why Can't I Be Loved," a question that certainly occupied my teenage time. The lyrics sat in my head like Shakespearean sonnets with all the power of tragedy. "Gloria." "Why don't you write me, darling / Send me a letter"— the Jacks. And there was Dion. That great opening to "I Wonder Why" engraved in my skull forever. Dion, whose voice was unlike any other I had heard before. Dion could do all the turns, stretch those syllables so effortlessly, soar so high he could reach the sky and dance there among the stars forever. What a voice that had absorbed and transmogrified all these influences into his own soul as the wine turns into blood.[35]

Reed is reconstructing a revolutionary affective experience of the 1950s in which millions of listeners from living rooms to high school dances, white and Black alike, heard a new Black grammar of love and desire. His account drifts from a catalog of Black doo-woppers to a lyrical tribute to Dion—a white Italian imitator of Black forms. As Reed's words attest, R & B was an unheard-of language of affects: Black-authored backbeats and soaring choruses were near-automatic smiles painted in frequencies and pulses; indeed, the concluding thought of this passage ventures a comparison with divine transubstantiation. The content of this fantasy is not often spoken about, but it was constitutive. Far from an unstructured immersion, these experiences were transcultural, highly appropriative, and subject forming. In the above quotation, Reed calls it "The sounds of another life." As Dylan similarly remarked about hearing a recording of country music in Hibbing in the 1950s: "the sound of the record made me feel like I could be somebody else . . . like I was maybe born to the wrong parents or something."[36] Radio transmission and 7″ singles allowed innumerable white kids a metaphysical space that crossed racial lines; this kind of listening could be erotic, empathetic, and painfully self-absorbed all at once.

Reed felt compelled to mimic, occupy, and risk living this fantasy. He began to teach himself guitar as a teenager, though his skills on the instrument would remain limited. As a high schooler he played in a Little Richard cover band, a doo-wop band, and a garage-rock band. At this age, Reed was rebellious, sexually promiscuous, and dabbled in same-sex relationships while developing what his childhood friend and collaborator Allan Hyman would call "an effeminate attitude."[37] Reed's teenage struggles with mental illness (he suffered from panic attacks, and had a nervous breakdown during a Freshman year of college at New York University [NYU]) led his parents to pursue electroconvulsive therapy in 1959, a common treatment at the time and one that Reed would bitterly recall as a trauma.[38]

As a college student Reed developed a pronounced interest in the latest trends in modern literature and Black music. While enrolled at NYU in 1959, Reed reportedly heard Coleman, Coltrane, and Cecil Taylor in various gigs at the Five Spot.[39] After transferring to Syracuse University upstate, Reed ran a free jazz radio show, *Excursions on a Wobbly Rail*, named after a cut from Taylor's 1958 album *Looking Ahead!*, and he coedited a literary magazine titled *Lonely Woman Quarterly* (after Coleman's famous 1959 standard, "Lonely Woman").[40] In the coming years, he would become a committed fan of Coleman, Taylor, Cherry, Archie Shepp, and John Coltrane.[41] As a part of his English major, Reed studied with poet Delmore Schwartz and became enamored with the idea of taking what the Beats accomplished in literature (particularly Burroughs and Ginsberg) and fusing it to the immediate, sexual, and subversive affective charge of rock and roll.[42]

For the time being, however, the spheres of music and literature would remain somewhat distant from one another. Reed started a rock band called L.A. and the Eldorados that specialized in Chuck Berry covers and played a circuit of local frat parties and college bars. He and his friends soon ventured out to Black blues clubs in town.[43] As recalled by Syracuse frat boy and Eldorados bass player Richard Mishkin,

> Lou and I would go down to the bars in the black neighborhoods in Syracuse, and everybody would look at us like we were going to die. . . . Most of these bars had pickup groups. I remember asking if we could sit in, and the [black] musicians just laughed. They said, "You white boys can't play this music." But, in fact, that's the music we played. The musical influences that were strong for Lou and me were Jimmy Reed, John Lee Hooker, a lot of Mississippi blues players. When we did sit in on occasion, they were astounded. I mean, we weren't that good, but we were certainly as good as the guys playing there. . . . We'd say, "Listen we have a band and once in a while we need guys who play like you." . . . They'd say, "How much do you pay?" Whatever we paid them was more than they usually got, because we got paid way more than we were worth.[44]

It is worth pausing over a socially pernicious instance of the ineffable here, one predicated on a veiled interaction across racial lines. We may recall that, for Mbembe, Blackness carries a distinct kind of ineffability: it entails a traffic of affects that carry complex, often unspoken attachments and disavowals. In Rishkin's account, he and Reed had an ambivalent combination of personal fear and aesthetic desire toward Black music. They were attracted to the transgression of showing up on the wrong turf (Reed would later sing about scoring heroin on 125th Street in the song "I'm Waiting for the Man"), and yet they had already been reaping the social rewards of imitating R & B in white spaces thanks to recordings and radio broadcasts that allowed them to mimic the idiom from a distance. Between Rishkin, Reed, and the unnamed musicians at this club, Black musical grammar served at once as a common affective nexus and a veiled locus of inequity. Mishkin's story of white privilege is a symptom of the underlying asymmetry: in 1960 these white college boys provided Black musicians access to frat house budgets and campus bars (both underwritten by the pocket books of well-to-do white parents) on white cultural terms.

Reed's affective attachments to Black music and his aspirations as a writer would prove to be central elements of the Velvets' identity as a band. After graduating from Syracuse in 1964, Reed moved to New York and found a job as a songwriter churning out throwaway material for the culture industry at Pickwick Records in Long Island City. At the same time, he was aspiring to compete with a new generation of Rimbaud-reading poet-singers and had a particular admiration for Dylan, whose star was rising fast in the years 1963–64. For Pickwick, Reed cowrote a derivative garage-rock song with a unison guitar tuning under the band name the Primitives. Titled "The Ostrich," it was a song the label thought was worth promoting.

"The Ostrich" would set the stage for Reed's otherwise unlikely meeting with Cale. Over the course of 1964, while Reed worked at Pickwick, Conrad began exposing Cale to pop music in their apartment at 56 Ludlow Street on the Lower East Side. Though Cale had been socially cloistered in music school, by 1964 he was beginning to absorb the fast-developing counterculture. That December, Cale and Conrad—their ears saturated with avant-droning—were invited by friends in their building to a party in the Upper East Side where they happened to meet the Pickwick brass.[45] Among them was Terry Phillips, Reed's Pickwick boss and cowriter of "The Ostrich." He heard Cale and Conrad were musicians, found their haircuts attractive and trendy, and asked them to join the pickup band of Reed and the Primitives to promote the song. Nothing professionally came from the piecemeal touring around the promotion of the single, but the collaboration ignited a powerful friendship between Cale and Reed.[46]

Early in 1965 Reed replaced Conrad as Cale's roommate at 56 Ludlow Street, and they began collaborating. Reed exposed Cale to heroin, known as a musician's drug because of its association with jazz, although reportedly neither ever succumbed to addiction.[47] Cale gradually introduced his avant-garde sensibilities to Reed's songs and provided Reed some sorely needed encouragement. Reed had already written "Heroin" and "I'm Waiting for the Man," which had been of little relevance to Pickwick's shameless practice of copying existing trends. At the time, these songs were little more than acoustic folk arrangements. What Cale found compelling about these songs was less the music and more the lyrics coupled to Reed's complex, depressive personality. Their jamming would soon find company. When MacLise returned from his percussion studies abroad, he moved across the hall at 56 Ludlow, and the two became a trio. That April, guitarist Sterling Morrison, a friend of Reed's from college, joined on rhythm guitar to make a four-piece band. Morrison's confident grooves would bring a sense of hypnotic focus to the band's extended jams. By the summer of 1965, the quartet had named itself the Velvet Underground after a nonfiction paperback about illicit sexual liaisons.[48]

The Velvets' eventual fusion of rock songwriting and minimal avant-garde noise took much of 1965 to coalesce and continued to evolve over the course of 1966.[49] Their first demo recording in July 1965 reveals that Reed, Morrison, and Cale were still having a hard time getting past the folk revival; these early versions of "Heroin," "I'm Waiting For the Man," "Venus in Furs," and "All Tomorrow's Parties" feature Reed singing and occasionally playing harmonica in a style unquestionably derived from Bob Dylan.[50] It seems to have been during the latter part of that year that the band's distinctive alchemy began to come together. Around this time, Manhattan scenester Al Aronowitz took an early interest in the Velvets, and booked them a now legendary gig that December with a $75 guarantee at a high school opening for a folk-rock band that he managed. When MacLise abruptly quit the project in advance of the show, Reed auditioned Morrison's friend's sister Maureen ("Moe") Tucker in her home on Long Island as an emergency replacement. A female drummer was nearly unheard of at the time. The decision was fortuitous: Tucker's minimalist backbeats, nearly devoid of fills, her ambiguously gendered appearance, and her eschewal of the conventional drum set overturned the norms of masculine showmanship. It was a self-consciously deskilled approach to drumming with a primitivist atmosphere that aligned with Reed's and Young's appropriative fantasies (she notably described her drum setup as "African," while a critic noted Tucker was "methodical and steady like some entranced Zulu witch doctor").[51] Along with Morrison's rhythm guitar, Tucker's drumming also provided structure to Reed and Cale's free-form improvising.[52]

## Atmospheric Rooms

As the 1960s zeitgeist quickly evolved, it became increasingly obvious to culture warriors in New York that rock and roll could be a financially lucrative investment. Warhol's collaborator, filmmaker Paul Morrissey, had become interested in producing a profitable intermedia spectacle that featured a live band. At Morrissey's suggestion, Warhol first heard the Velvets in December 1965 at a residency Aronowitz organized at a West Village novelty spot called the Café Bizarre. Though he was initially reluctant, Warhol soon proposed a management deal to the Velvets that provided them with equipment, salaries, and rehearsal space at the Factory, which they enthusiastically accepted. As producer, Warhol provided the band with a platform. They soon became the centerpiece of Warhol's avant-intermedia spectacle, the Exploding Plastic Inevitable, which elicited the heated critical reactions discussed at the outset of this chapter. Over the course of 1966, they became a central component of the Factory scene, and performed shows at the Film-Makers' Cinematheque, on campuses like Rutgers and the University of Michigan, and at The Village Gate (all of which hosted avant-garde artists and musicians), and most famously at the Dom (an East Village venue Warhol and Morrissey organized themselves). In short order, the Velvets went from playing for small, occasionally hostile audiences and empty rooms to promoted spectacles with buzzing, curious listeners who were often already inclined toward the avant-garde.[53]

Always the passive affirmer, Warhol offered no pedagogy other than an environment of permission (Cale described it as an "intellectual location").[54] He was uninvolved in musical decisions but gave the band license to experiment in a way that paralleled the liberating quality of Cage's course in experimental composition just seven years earlier.[55] Warhol's one insistence was the addition of German bohemian singer, model, and Factory scenester Christa Päffgen, who went by the stage name of Nico. Her otherworldly contralto voice and arresting beauty created an iconic and affective focal point opposite that of Reed. In January 1966, the initial month of Nico's involvement, one of Warhol's films shows the Velvets playing in a style openly redolent of Young's Theatre: a formless hour of modal, drone-based improvisations derived from Indian music with Reed's and Morrison's guitar solos loosely imitating sitars and ouds.[56]

While the band kept up a considerable performing schedule that year, it was their debut album *The Velvet Underground & Nico* (1967) that would become an influential object far beyond their immediate milieu, particularly in the years after the Velvets had dissolved. To the ears of some, the band's music opened the very possibility of atmospheric production, possibilities that broadened the ontological boundaries of what a musician could do. Jonathan Richman put it memorably: "I didn't start singing or playing till I was 15 and heard the Velvet Underground. . . . They made an *atmosphere*, and I knew then that I could make one too!"[57] In 1970 a critic described its intended effects on the psyche in noting that the Velvets "saw the need early to push people out of their normally bound perceptions."[58] (A pithy account of a second-order modernism if ever there were one.) Their recordings had an uncanny ability to put listeners in surreal and altered states of being; in a sense, the sounds themselves were metaphysically active. The band found ways to unearth unspoken rules of life through a strange tapestry of images, a theater of sounds that were empirically tweaked until apparitions came to the surface. By dropping the needle, one could fill a room with atmospheres that could not be communicated in linguistic terms. The effect was excessive, terrifying, exhilarating. As Kittler once suggested, in the epoch of gramophone poetics, one could turn on the stereo to transmit a trace of the real directly to the brain.[59] The atmospheres were like wallpaper—they set the mood—and became conditions of possible experience. They were also affective vectors of particular scenarios: each song was a portable transmitter of social and sensory experimentation.

And yet, *The Velvet Underground & Nico* was not carefully engineered as a concept album. The recording quality is generally lo-fi, hissy, and unpolished; it was recorded quickly and inexpensively. The first session took place in April 1966 at Scepter Studios in midtown on Warhol's dime (fig. 5.2). After the Velvets signed to Verve/MGM later that month on the basis of Warhol's agreement to do the artwork, Tom Wilson (a Black producer then working for MGM who began his career by launching an Afromodernist label that released albums by Sun Ra and Cecil Taylor and who produced Dylan's *Bringing it All Back Home* in 1965) took over production of the album. Wilson arranged for a second session in Los Angeles a month later to rerecord "Heroin," "I'm Waiting for the Man," and "Venus in Furs," as well as a final session that November to record "Sunday Morning" as the album's single. Across these sessions, the band's division of labor remained relatively consistent. Reed had written the songs and served as front man with the exception of three songs in which he agreed to let Nico sing lead vocal. Cale, with some consultation from Morrison, acted as musical director, and developed the album's "symphonic" sound by way of experimentation with arrangements.[60] Tucker was a quiet bandmate, but her choices were no less consequential to the result. All that said, when recording, decisions had to be made quickly. There was no time or budget for multiple

FIG 5.2. The Velvet Underground at Scepter Studios, April 1966
(*from left*, Nico, John Cale, Lou Reed, and Sterling Morrison).
Photograph by Steve Schapiro. Courtesy of Getty Images.

takes, elaborate editing, and overdubbing.[61] The band seems to have simply tried to make it through a take without major problems and recorded over takes that fell apart.[62] Much of the innovation one hears is a product of a band that had been cutting their teeth that winter improvising in front of Warhol's trendy, sympathetic audiences.

The album's energizing heartbeat begins with "I'm Waiting for the Man," a song based in a loose blues progression. The feel is driving and relentless. A rhythm section of bass, piano, drums, and tambourine plays accents on every beat to match the marching throb of Cale's Black-authored boogie-woogie piano. It is an exuberant, headbanging party underscored by the clattering momentum of a subway ride uptown. In the mix, the rhythm section is firmly in the background. In the foreground are syncopated and grooving guitars: Morrison's distorted rhythm part turns on a sustained, accented strum on the eighth note right before the backbeat. This is interwoven with Reed's melodic R & B figures. Reed's guitar is mixed loudest during the verses; Morrison's level rises during the instrumental breaks as Cale unspools his piano part into La Monte Young–style tone clusters (these could easily have been sped-up clusters from Young's "X for Henry Flynt"). There are no guitar solos. Reed's vocal is dry, mixed front and center.

Though Reed described the Velvets' aesthetic as a "realism," their music was hardly representational, as if literary works like Sacher-Masoch's *Venus in Furs* (1870) were simply dramatized by a musical arrangement.[63] The songs did not depict spaces in any literal or mimetic sense; they more abstractly produced a sense of enclosure—eleven songs, eleven rooms—that transmitted hallucinations built on inconsistency. Like each of the album's cuts, the atmosphere of "I'm Waiting for the Man" puts us in an energizing, activating room. In this space, listeners see a film with no physical screening. The film is about scoring heroin—sort of. It loosely narrates an adventure. In listening, one can easily opt into the racialized fantasy of a white person buying drugs in Harlem, an experience that parallels the thrill of the drug itself. But by spinning the record, one risks virtually nothing. As Dylan had remarked when listening to records, "I could be somebody else." Anyone with the LP can have this: an exportable hallucination, an invisible movie in the room that smoothly, easily, so quickly puts listeners in a scenario.[64]

"Heroin" audaciously proposes to take us into the experience itself. Like "I'm Waiting for the Man," this song has a hypnotic I–IV oscillation at its core. But instead of periodic cadences, it accelerates and decelerates to mark tension and release. The arrangement is relatively simple. There is no bass; Reed and Morrison's guitar parts interweave, supported by the droning halo of Cale's viola that remains unchanged over the course of the song aside from a frenetic solo at the song's climax. For the drone, Cale seems to have found the perfectly voiced perfect fifth. Morrison's guitar drives the accelerandos. On the take they used for the album, Tucker is not really synched with Morrison. She complained of not being able to adequately hear the guitar, but her patter on this take is redolent of MacLise's free-form drumming with the Theatre.[65] This was also an exemplary instance of deskilling, in a way that is redolent of Coleman's experimental work discussed in the previous chapter. For the band to affirm Tucker's uncertainty was a strategy.[66] Her nonprecision is a mode of looseness, her hesitancy an authenticity. The band did not want a drum part totally edited and synched to Morrison's accelerating guitar; they chose a take that felt shambolic. Deskilled experimentation with happy accidents or affirmations of something working even when it is not synchronized are symptoms of an alchemical method. Tucker herself recalled in 1986, "I think we all had that idea to have a nice vaguely amateurish sound to this."[67] The collaborative messiness mirrored their espoused aesthetic of realism.[68]

Like "Heroin," "Venus in Furs" aims at sensuous extremities. The room presented by this song is a dark, torturous scene, and has inspired no shortage of visualizations by critics and fans.[69] Its atmosphere, marked by high frequency noise, is one of searing heat. Cale's piercing viola drone is unquestionably the distinctive element here; it sits high in the mix, explicitly echoing the Theatre of Eternal Music, with solos indebted to the Afro-Asiatic fantasies of his collaborations with Young. Cale achieved the rhythmic "whip effect" by gently touching the midpoint of the A and D string while bowing with a lot of pressure to get natural harmonics to sear in a hypnotic rhythmic pattern.[70] Beneath it all, Tucker's swaying bass drum and tambourine played at a slow walking speed gives the song a feeling of a processional or a ritual. Reed's guitar has little syncopation; his vocal sits low in his range giving his account of the masochistic scene a feeling of authoritative observation. The short bridge in parallel major that repeatedly walks up I–IV–V–I and switches to the first person pushes Cale into creaky, detuned sonorities. What would normally be an uplifting major key relief feels like the torture has only increased. Perhaps most remarkable of all: though "Venus in Furs" is often hailed as revolutionary, Reed's underlying song form is in many ways familiar. The 1965 demo—which features Cale on lead vocal in his Welsh accent—reveals a melody similar to the English ballad, "Scarborough Fair," which Martin Carthy had released that year.[71]

Consider as well the structured atmosphere of "All Tomorrow's Parties," a song written by Reed as an ode to nightlife decadence. It is designed to show you how to feel about the scene, or to put you in a room to think about it. Nico is a third person observer to an anxious female partygoer, singing with some measure of detachment. The arrangement seems to be inspired by Spector's wall of sound production techniques. Cale's pounding broken two-hand piano chord progression bears resemblances to Leon Scott's piano clatter in The Crystals' "Da Doo Ron Ron" (1963), a hit that also featured a bass drum and tambourine beat similar to Tucker's. The groove on this take is relatively loose—Tucker even comes in a bit late on the first downbeat—but the dilapidated quality, an emblem of purposeful deskilling, adds to the charm.[72] Above Morrison's bass sit two melodic parts at the front of the mix: Nico's vocals, which alternate with Reed's guitar part in an all D "Ostrich" tuning from the 1964 Primitives single.

Little about the "All Tomorrow's Parties" assemblage makes logical sense. Spector-like atmospherics, which famously reproduced Black affective ecstasy of love and sincerity, do not really inflate a romantic scene here. It is somehow both rickety and regal; it puts us into a room at the Factory where something like a DIY Orientalist carnival float emerges. Nico is dispassionate, her intentions somewhat unknown as she tells the story of a woman whose partying is effortful, earnest, and tragic. There is a touch of sweetness to Nico's rising phrases on "And where will she go and what shall she do?" even as other phrases sound characteristically detached. Her double-tracked vocals are front and center in the mix, but unlike Ronnie

Spector's adorable romantic soaring, Nico's message was strange, judgmental, self-aware. Around Nico's vocals sit Reed's sitar-like meanderings.

Finally, we turn the clock ahead ten hours, and return to the album's opening, "Sunday Morning." It is a dream state. Cale's celeste is vintage Spector; Reed's rounded melodies are exemplary of his best songwriting. Reed's woozy, meandering vocal captures a diffuse, affective polyphony shaded with worry, regret, and euphoria. The typical story about the song is that it was written at Warhol's request for a song about paranoia, though the exquisitely sung "watch out, the world's behind you" feels undeniably inspiring and uplifting. The fact that the phrase handles both affective directions—or is a poor carrier of paranoia—is a great illustration of the way an amazingly sung magnetic phrase can itself exemplify music's ineffability. Wilson dials in a playful alchemy; the first vocal is dry, but the vocal reverb is turned up in the second verse; by the instrumental break, one hears a tape delay and further delays in the viola. By the final verse, Nico and Cale's viola are lilting in the background with an eerie and gentile counterpoint.

No song on this album is content to entertain. Some of the best-known songs on *The Velvet Underground & Nico* confront listeners with dimensions of extreme sensory pleasures: "I'm Waiting for the Man" and "Run Run Run" (the anticipation), "Heroin" and "Venus in Furs" (the experiences themselves—existentially fraught, masochistic), and "Sunday Morning" and "All Tomorrow's Parties" (looking back or ahead: reflections, hangovers). Three songs feature an eroticized woman-as-other: "There She Goes" (with Reed on the microphone, singing about a woman as a disrespected prostitute), "Femme Fatale" (the alluring and dangerous woman embodied by Nico singing about a woman in the third person), and "I'll Be Your Mirror" (a woman addressing the listener again, embodied by Nico, as a perplexing reflection of self). In these songs, Nico embodied complex "plays of recognition" (to use the phrase from chap. 2) within individual songs that complicated erotic norms of the alluring chanteuse. The album's final two cuts are noisy avant-jams with extended improvisations. "Black Angel's Death Song" showcases Reed as a delirious, improvising bard accompanied by Cale's searing viola, and "European Son"—with its Fluxus-like crash engineered by Cale—is a repudiation of Reed's college mentor, Delmore Schwartz, that seems to descend into nihilism.

Reed's expressive stance as a singer could be strikingly ambiguous. In the sensory form of his vocals, the sincerity of his intentions could come across as unstable and perplexing. Did Reed mean what he sang? This ambiguity came to life in the wobbly style of his singing, which could veer—sometimes within a single phrase—between sincerity, and sneering, ironic distance. At a thematic level, nihilistic or aggressive moments in his singing could be set in contrast to sincere, romantic, and even theological gestures that renewed a search for transcendence. This yearning for salvation amid depravity is particularly palpable in the self-titled 1969 album, with songs like "Jesus" and "Beginning to See the Light."[73] Nico's vocals are no less indeterminate in their intentional stance. Her bellowing, blank, and wavering expressivity with the Velvets seemed to take place on a pedestal, in an aristocratic, almost cosmic remove from the scenes she set into motion.

If the album's eleven rooms have a common dialectic, it is one that drops listeners into scenes stuck ambiguously between intoxication and sobriety. "I'm Waiting for the Man" is a junkie's walkout music; on the 4-5-6 uptown to Harlem, we meet a dealer in an encounter that may end up sexual. On "Heroin," Reed slows us (and then speeds us) into his decadent affective envelope, with Cale as his droning sympathetic accomplice. He sings about the ambivalence of being taken away by a sensation that inflates and erases his sense of self ("I have made a big decision . . . I don't know just where I'm going."). In "I'll Be Your Mirror," the other—in the form of Nico's iconic voice—is outwardly sincere in her desire to support her partner (and the listener) by insisting that her beauty is a reflection of his inner beauty ("Reflect what you are, in case you don't know"). Of course, in recorded form, Nico is an acousmatic transmission who cannot see the listener. Inaccessible, abstracted, unreliable, we are left to wonder what we might be told by a singer who nonetheless, a blind assemblage of waveforms, continues to insist "Please put down your hands. 'Cause I see you."

The atmospheric hypnosis induced by these eleven rooms was, at its core, an appropriative mimesis of Afro-diasporic and Indian forms. Early in their career, the Velvets eschewed the literal adoption of blues-scale improvisation and vocal styles familiar to 1960s rock (notwithstanding Mishkin's aforementioned claim to blues authenticity) as exemplified by then-ascendant bands like the Rolling Stones.[74] Instead, with largely India-inspired motifs in their guitars, they focused on reimagining the traditional songwriting of 1950s doo-wop while reconstructing echoes of Spector's production techniques of the early 1960s. In live shows, and especially in *White Light/White Heat* (1968), the Velvets took the affective power of the ritual of rock to a noisy and confrontational extreme, earning the respect and admiration of critics like Lester Bangs.[75] By 1969, however, Reed and Morrison were once again sourcing blues licks in their soloing, as is especially evident on the Quine tapes.[76] Like Young's Theatre, the band was also inspired by the chaotic and dissenting atmospheres of Afro-modernist indeterminacy and improvisation. On songs like "Black Angel's Death Song," "European Son," and "Sister Ray," the last of which appeared on *White Light/White Heat* (1968), the band infused their Afro-Indian alchemy with a heavy dose of cacophonous, deskilled improvisation. The dissenting result was both culturally indebted and economically cushioned; after all, their praxis relied on the privileged whiteness of midcentury postcollegiate life.

As mentioned above, the Velvets joined both popular and avant-garde Black influences to Indian-derived elements, which arrived through Cale, MacLise, and indirectly, Young.[77] With his viola, Cale transformed the meditative and immersive tanpura from India into a grinding, electric, blare of pain.[78] Many of Reed's guitar solos—some of which featured the unison "Ostrich" tuning—anticipated the fashion for raga-rock and mimed the meandering modal drone of the sitar.[79] There were also Tucker's tabla-inspired drums on "Heroin."[80] Elements of Reed's songwriting relied on droning, modal sonorities. These debts to "Asia" and "the East"—however vague—were evident to listeners at the time. One critic claimed to hear "Egyptian belly-dance music" at a live gig in 1966.[81] A few years later, another compared the Velvets to "a form of Yoga."[82] Others heard musical details. One noted Reed and Morrison's guitars "droned and sensuously dribbled out notes in a very Eastern way; visions of sheiks and harem girls and plodding camels in the desert."[83] Another wrote, "The sound is harmonic, insistent, pulsing and sustained—suggesting comparisons with Indian ragas."[84] In his 1971 review essay of the Velvets' output, Bangs wrote that Cale "authentically absorbed Oriental influence in the viola track [on "Black Angel's Death Song"] (just compare its originality with the obvious 'rag rock' scales indulged in by so many other groups at the time, and recall that the Velvets were doing it long before the rest, in 1965)."[85]

The Velvets avoided literal borrowings or transcriptions, an approach that was consonant with the band's alchemical poetics and echoed Cage and Tudors arm's-length practice of cultural appropriation.[86] Their imaginative appropriations eschewed cross-cultural mimesis in favor of the atmosphere of a second-order modernism. They aimed to dial in exotic alchemies capable of altering one's "frame of mind." As one critic put it, "While listening to this album [*The Velvet Underground & Nico*], it is best, perhaps, to put yourself in the frame of mind that you might assume while listening to Indian music, for the Velvet Underground produces a type of music that is distinctly different from American popular music."[87] Outside the whiteness of classical music forms, an Indian "frame of mind" could become a stolen warp zone to an obscure dissent, to an atmosphere without function.

## Attitudinal Virtuosity

The intentionality underpinning these eleven atmospheric rooms was also spoken about and acted through. If Coleman's intentionality as an artist was utopian, unwoven, and affirmative and opened on to riddles and paradoxes, the Velvets, from a place of white social privilege, had the luxury of being far more negative in their stance as artists. Their experimental realism came to life through a confrontational attitude. By focusing on the vivid peaks of pleasure and pain—and, like the Beats before them, appropriating materials from India and Afro-modernism—the band could position their music as staging critique by exposing the repressed dimensions of social life. But alignments with historical patterns of appropriation were hardly rote mimicries. Though Reed's attitude appropriated elements of Baraka's conception of Black cool (as discussed in the previous chapter), it was less stylized, more of a deadpan take it or leave it affect.

Interviews are a key site where vernacular philosophy can surface to the public. Reed, like Coleman, approached them thoughtfully. Reed's notoriously bad attitude as an interviewee had a way of amplifying the affective indeterminacy of the Velvets' (and his own) music by projecting an intransigent, noncommunicative atmosphere. His approach had roots: growing up, he was known to be rebellious and disrespectful in a way that others found compelling. In the words of a close childhood friend, "He would love to shock. That's his thing. It was probably one of the reasons I found him so interesting, because most of my friends were not like that at all."[88] As an aspiring rock musician, Reed developed this into a "New York Attitude," a demeanor at once inscrutable and magnetic, an impassive copy of the city's gritty social reality. This character was too weird to be subsumed by the thudding ideologies of rhythm and administered pleasures, too emotional to be dismissed as a provocative stunt. Reed once described it as follows:

> The Lou Reed New York attitude is really just a New York attitude. You can find lots of people with it. [laughs]. I can't really take credit for copying down a New York attitude. But it was like . . . there was no moral stance. I think that was another thing I tried to be really careful with it. There's no moral stance to these songs. It was just: this happened and that happened and [it was] presented kind of dry, unemotional.[89]

Like Warhol's silkscreens, Reed did not claim authorship over New York attitude nor did he intend it as a commentary. He preferred blank reproduction. And in this regard, Warhol's influence could be felt: the artist's philosophy emphasized ubiquity, efficacy, superficiality, coolness, irony, and distance. As with Coleman, Warhol's thoughtful approach to interviews opened a novel space of self-positioning. His method relied on a magnetic passivity: from 1962 onward, Warhol routinely used silence in interviews and withheld explanations of his work in ways that gave his interlocutors space to think even harder. Warhol often answered pointed and complex interview questions with a cryptic nonchalance (Interviewer: "What is Pop Art trying to say?" Warhol: "I don't know.").[90] In *The Philosophy of Andy Warhol* (1975), he articulated it philosophically through the eyes of an absent critic: "Some critic called me the Nothingness Himself and that didn't help my sense of existence any. Then I realized that existence itself is nothing and I felt better. But I'm still obsessed with the idea of looking into the mirror and seeing no one, nothing."[91]

Dylan, equally important for Reed, and no less famous for his cryptic and cantankerous interviews, similarly resisted explanations of his own work. In a notorious San Francisco press conference in 1965, a series of writers ask Dylan to explain his music, his process, and his status as rising cultural icon.[92] Dylan responds, with the occasional mischievous grin, that he has little sense of the source or reason behind the magnetism his work has generated with a fast-emerging 1960s countercultural public.[93] Reed, routinely a prickly interviewee, himself experimented with Warhol and Dylan-style intransigence, and one-word responses.[94] If Coleman's interviews were typically friendly and loquacious but artfully circuitous, Warhol, Reed and Dylan provoked with mordant, difficult responses or silence. For all three, to withhold explanation or enthusiasm, to play dumb, resistant, or disinterested was an intentional strategy of coolness; it was to say little in the face of their art's ineffability.[95]

Parallel engagements with ineffability recur in the erotic literature that was formative to the Velvets' praxis. There were the late eighteenth- and nineteenth-century European classics of sadomasochism by the Marquis de Sade and Leopold Sacher-Masoch that explored the psychological depth of sex and violence unstructured by Christian morality.[96] There was also a host of modern variants that Reed knew and read, from Anne Desclos's openly sadistic *Story of O* (1954) written from the perspective of a woman to Beat writers like Burroughs, Ginsberg, and Kerouac to Hubert Selby's gritty portrait of the New York underbelly, *Last Exit to Brooklyn* (1957).[97] Like Patti Smith after him, Reed was particularly attracted to the Beats' use of plain language. In 1967 Deleuze remarked that erotic literature "is aimed above all at confronting language with its own limits, with what is in a sense a 'nonlanguage' (violence that does not speak, eroticism that remains unspoken)."[98] Across these instances, the medium of literature had unique capacities for explaining unspoken registers of the erotic, for it was in language without images that the public could explore the complex psychological dimensions of sexual deviance at length.

But by comparison with literature, a musical atmosphere is not there to represent or explain. As scenarios for Reed's lyrics, the Velvets' artistry mingled two forms of nonlanguage, two ontological inconsistencies: music and sensuous extremes. In doing so, their atmospheres captured an erotic indeterminacy, a highly mediated affective charge that could be strikingly oblique and abstract in a way that is specific to music. Consider a recent example: in "WAP" (2020), Cardi B does not actually command a billion people in 2020 to satisfy her with oral sex, even though her lyrics literally say that. It is foundationally a magnetic machine for affective production. She can deliver commanding X-rated lyrics because the injunction is cushioned by ineffability—by an indeterminacy of address.[99] A listener can be male, female, trans, or queer, and yet something about her position within the song elicits magnetism. The situation is similar when Muddy Waters sings "Hoochie Coochie Man" (1954). The artistry of these songs lies in carving out an atmospheric fantasy space that elicits unspoken registers of attention, imitation, and cathexis.

The Velvets do something similar with songs like "Venus in Furs," "Heroin," and "Sister Ray," which glamorize drugs, BDSM sexuality, and the bohemian ephemerality of life. These songs hypnotize listeners with a noisy cushion that alludes to, narrates, acts out, animates, and projects the unbridled vitality of sensory forces. But because of the oblique and abstract quality of musical affects and dynamic plays of recognition (as discussed in chap. 2), the songs could became canvases for ambivalence, anxiety, or reflection.[100] Is that not the point of a song like "Heroin," which mimics a high at the same time that it alienates one from the experience by narrating, with ambivalence, its formidable, almost existential grip? However ideal it may be for conveying sex, intoxication, and moral transgression, music is also—due in no small part to Reed's thoughtful but often monosyllabic lyrics—a profoundly defamiliarizing medium.

The Velvets' aesthetic fit Susan Sontag's account of 1960s modernism as sensual and erotic and was aligned with her arguments against loquacious, speculative explanations of art.[101] (Note as well that Sontag herself had a habit of turning up at the Factory.) Reed himself once remarked (like Dylan before him), "The music is very simple. . . . It never was anything else; it's not advanced, doesn't have any messages . . . It's just songs. Anytime anybody says 'interpreting,' I immediately grow scales."[102] For Sontag—as for legal scholars debating obscenity and censorship in the ensuing decades—there remained a rigorous boundary between art and pornography. Porn simply functioned as sexual gratification. Erotic art, by contrast, had an elevated formal, contemplative, or impersonal moment that built on art's ineffability. If Tudor and Cage abstracted the arresting extremes of Artaudian violence into an esoteric form, in songs like "Venus in Furs" the Velvets staged masochistic violence by fabricating visual-affective hallucinations that transmitted an empty scenario. The recorded form of the Velvets—the fact of its being as inconsistent musical sound—provided this essential layer of abstraction and ineffability. A room space incarnated in sound becomes a locus of simultaneous contemplation and immediacy beyond what language alone could accomplish.

In the context of social history, Warhol's scene was a refuge for oppressed transgender and queer people (though his space's safety was a contentious issue; by many accounts, proximity to Warhol was brutally hierarchical, and Warhol's attitude toward others was often cold and exploitative).[103] There were allegations of misogyny in Warhol's scene.[104] Note that the queer dimensions of the Velvets had Black precedents among blues and R & B musicians. Ma Rainey and Little Richard had pioneered queer lyrics and personae.[105] Alongside the Velvets, there was also a queer dimension to the mass flowering of rock in the later 1960s and early 1970s, particularly following the rise of Janis Joplin, Marc Bolan, and David Bowie.[106] The Velvets themselves hardly confirmed to normative gender roles: Tucker was frequently mistaken for a male musician; Nico's vocals were unusually low in pitch, unsettling perceptions of her femininity. Reed was fairly open about his bisexuality and developed a relationship with a trans woman named Rachel Humphreys during the 1970s.[107] The Velvets' gritty, queer realism aligned with a decadent aestheticism that refused the norms of liberal social engagement. In musical form, their droning delirium—even as it incarnated a decadent and amoral Nietzschean vitality—was also a resourceful (and fully clothed) way of confronting a social prohibition, a moralizing, normative ineffability about sexuality.[108]

Like Smith and Hell after them, ineffability in the form of an aggressive, queer attitude was also a response to the ascendant hippie counterculture of the late 1960s, with its loose, free-loving, and optimistic communitarianism. Though the Velvets were sometimes associated with global spiritualities of the 1960s, it was common to find them positioned as dialectical antagonists to hippie idealism.[109] Iggy Pop, a collaborator of Cale's in 1969 and a key inheritor of the Velvets' aesthetic, himself confronted the telos when reporting on television in 1977: "I think I helped wipe out the 60s."[110] As will be discussed in the next chapter, it is notable that key figures in Afro-modernist jazz from Mingus to Bill Evans and the Coltranes drew on India's association with hippie counterculturalism, the civil rights movement, and associated conceptions of political and religious universality in the 1960s. By contrast the Velvets seemed inspired by a vaguely decadent fantasy of India, one associated with a confrontational anti-Western naturalism that stood in opposition to Judeo-Christian social norms. Once this fantasy had been filtered through the confrontational sounds and themes of the Velvets' music, the result had become Artaudian. In the words of one critic, "the message was one of perversion, sickness, and turmoil."[111]

Notwithstanding the sexual utopianism of their scene, along other axes of identity the Velvets' ideals were less than progressive. In the domain of racial politics, the gritty and amoral realism so central to their aesthetic could also sink into complacency if not regression. Morrison once suggested that his artistic proximity to Black music exempted him from investing in the imperative for racial justice.[112] Ironic songs Reed wrote later in his career like "I Wanna Be Black" (1978) trade in crude racial stereotypes and struggle to convey a compelling parody. Nico reportedly slid into regressive if not outwardly racist language in informal conversations.[113] Readers of Nietzsche and enthusiasts of punk, or anyone familiar with their histories—from Eric Clapton's drunken defenses of white nationalism to Bowie's "ironic" admiration for fascism in the 1970s—knows this risk of regressive derailment, pessimism, or nihilism is significant for movements focused on overturning the fabric of social norms.[114] As will be discussed in chapter seven, as the genre of punk emerges in the 1970s, these risks grew further.

How might Cavell, who published "Music Discomposed" in 1967, the same year *The Velvet Underground & Nico* was released, have parsed the Velvets' magnetic atmospheres? Insofar as Mailer's and Baraka's hipsters capture the social imaginary of the Velvets—infused as they were with Afro-diasporic and Indian cultural debts—were they not dialectical foils to Cavell's high formalism? Rather than hyperdeveloped modernist rules that used logic, tautology, and transformation to obviate the transparency of convention (as with the serialists), with the Velvets, Cavell would have confronted themes of deep social provocation alongside endlessly vague impressions without discernible sources or accessible rules of engagement. With the serialists, there was an overabundance of self-verifying consistencies; with the Velvets, there was an excess of inconsistency.

On the Velvets' inconsistencies, an empiricism of alchemies solicited new dialectics that mirrored complex social tensions. Mailer's controversial analysis of the hipster speaks to the racialized fantasizes at work in this process. Here, he unpacks the tensions of the hipster's contradictory psychology:

> It is this knowledge which provides the curious community of feeling in the world of the hipster, a muted cool religious revival to be sure, but the element which is exciting, disturbing, nightmarish perhaps, is that incompatibles have come to bed, the inner life and the violent life, the orgy and the dream of love, the desire to murder and the desire to create, a dialectical conception of existence with a lust for power, a dark, romantic,

and yet undeniably dynamic view of existence for it sees every man and woman as moving individually through each moment of life forward into growth or backward into death.[115]

Mailer thought of the hipster's "dialectical conception of existence" as a "pathology," an exoticizing, appropriative "microcosm" of history, cool and ironic, a walking subject of dissent.[116] In this figure he heard racialized echoes of romantic decadence.[117] For Baraka, by contrast, the coolness of a Black hipster was based in an existential strategy specific to the subjugation of Black life ("the purpose was to isolate even more definitely a cult of protection and rebellion") and was thus inassimilable to the appropriative, draining whiteness of the Velvets' hipsterism.[118]

If the method for overcoming modernist fraudulence was personal for Cavell, the decadent, racialized dialectics that shaped the sound of the Velvets' music made the presence of any personalized intentions inscrutable. Animated by hipster insiderism—or at least projecting the impression of it—their deskilled compositional method sought to imitate a social "pathology" with something prelinguistic. Reed's singing, with its deadpan indeterminacy and ornery earnestness, conveyed a peculiar kind of noncommunication, a poem uttered by a singer addressing nobody, congealed within the form of hypnotic rock. To be sure, their music was not without consistencies. Alchemical inconsistency is a product of woven mediations. There is modality, there is idiom, there are patterns; there are verses and refrains. One still hears what Cavell described as "improvisation," a term that refers to the possibility of a rule-bound form of life. And the band's sounds were magnetic; that was the minimal condition for its life as a work of art. But their alchemies projected dialectical tensions of the psyche—a portrait of modern alienation predicated on the appropriation of Afro-diasporic and Indian others—in ways that resided below the threshold of communicative transparency.

## Vital Tape

At a perpendicular axis, the ineffability of the Velvets' music exemplified the ontological contradictions of modern media. Consider a 1970 bootleg of "What Goes On" at Philadelphia's Second Fret. There were no drums on this gig; Tucker was out taking care of a new baby. Doug Yule, who had come to replace Cale in 1968, was on stage playing bass. Without his organ, the song lacked one of its key sonorities. Reed's vocals were unmoored from the melody of the original 1968 version.[119] In Richie Unterberger's

exhaustive chronicle of the Velvets' day by day existence, the author describes this bootleg as an instance of poor documentation.[120] Indeed, it was
recorded as such a low level that the tape hiss competes for one's attention;
it sounds as if they are being erased by the same tape heads that recorded
them. After all, this performance took place toward the end of the band's
existence. With only fifteen people in attendance, one hears Reed, Morrison, and Yule going through the motions in an undervalued interval of time.

Yet in a way that is still transfixing, the song in the background murmurs.
In 1934 Adorno made prescient remarks about sound recording when he reflected on the mysterious circular grooves of the phonograph.[121] He claimed
that its form embodied a powerful contradiction. Sound recordings capture
and petrify life in the form of inconsistent and ephemeral musical time, but
in a way that mirrors the dark ontology of modernity: the dying ephemerality of life is the only life there is. This Velvets bootleg takes this ontological
contradiction and sharpens it. We hear a band preserved in the very process
of their decay—matched by an occluded, muted, dark medium—as if the
plastic itself, stupid and indiscriminating, was the most apt carrier of a band
that had lost any means of outward expression. In the process the Velvets'
intentionality and motivation—once thought to be crucial to the ontology
of art—seemed to fade. The recording is ready to be thrown away; its ontology became weak.

Recorded songs, in their alchemical specificity, dazzle and burn out like
fireworks. Adorno once wrote of the latter:

> The phenomenon of fireworks is prototypical for artworks. . . . They ap-
> pear empirically yet are liberated from the burden of the empirical, which
> is the obligation of duration; they are a sign from heaven yet artifactual,
> an ominous warning, a script that flashes up, vanishes, and indeed can-
> not be read for its meaning. . . . It is not through a higher perfection that
> artworks separate from the fallibly existent but rather by becoming ac-
> tual, like fireworks, incandescently in an expressive appearance. They are
> not only the other of the empirical world: Everything in them becomes
> other.[122]

Exploding stars at the scale of human life, fireworks appeared to Adorno's
eyes as linear script, a hypermodern form of writing without meaning. They
also had what Hegel called *Geist*: historical self-consciousness in the form
of midcentury engineering and countless indeterminate celebrations. According to this logic, light artists, pyromaniacs, improvising ensembles,
and party promoters of the 1960s managed to create, from inverted perspectives skew to every Western history of art, prototypical artworks for

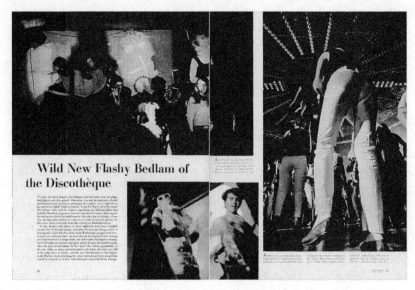

FIG. 5.3. "Wild New Flash Bedlam of the Discothèque," *Life* (May 27, 1966).
Velvet Underground Collection 8105, 1964–2015, box 12, folder 13, Division
of Rare and Manuscript Collections, Cornell University Library.

a modern world.[123] Similarly, the Exploding Plastic Inevitable exemplified
a modernist alchemy of the ephemeral. Spectators to light shows and dis-
cotheques marveled that colored lighting and projectors could so dynamically change the appearance of their clothing.[124] In a *Life* magazine feature
(fig. 5.3), bright yellow pants at a discothèque on the far right are juxtaposed
with photographs of a screeching dance party that featured projections
saturated with blue (above) and red (below) light in the manner of a Warhol silkscreen. By letting forms die the moment they came into being, this
generation avoided worrying about what the rules were, or they deliberately deskilled themselves to focus on unspoken rules, to open themselves
to fantasized histories from another place that was never quite specified or
spoken of. But it was not a resignation or an escape to utterly deterritorial-
ized inconsistencies. It was defined by new feats of self-consciousness; at a
meta-register, the Velvets built modern alchemical worlds.

Adorno does not discuss what it means when a recording of ephemeral alchemies itself decays, but the Velvets' 1970 bootleg at Second Fret
foregrounds this question. The bootleg is a leak, a trace, a faded imprint,
a memento that is far less than a work. The Velvets' are phoning it in to
fifteen people as the band is about to break up, and maybe it is somehow
compelling because they are phoning it in. A voice from the grave, a late

style on cassette, they were temporarily expelled from the culture industry with an emotional charge somewhere around 10 percent. It is even less than a commodity. Its purposiveness is fading. With this obscure ontology of dissent, the bootleg is not just indexing an event at the twilight of the band's existence; its capture of decay has a significance that seems to mirror—even vivify—a symptom of modernity that can only be read as a language of no languages, because its indifference changes the criteria of its comprehensibility in the inconsistent decay of every instant.

Having ripped off the affective magic of doo-wop grammar and Indian ragas, in recorded form the Velvets planted their flag on the ephemeral fantasy of an atmosphere: the unstable and undecidable diffusion of musical languages. Only if one assumes—as Adorno does, unfortunately—that the mediation of sound recording is secondary or "technological" does it neutralize the abyss of music's ineffability, as he contends. To many others, the paths of meaning multiply on the blankness of phonographic hypnosis. It is a hypnosis with no guarantee of reflection, even as it ironically insists on it, by almost allegorizing noncommunication: "What Goes On in Your Mind?" The Velvets were as blank as Warhol's endlessly reproduced silkscreen prints or his films that lasted forever and put spectators in a place of narrative emptiness.[125] There was nothing to say and they were saying it, and not only that—they meant it. Perhaps they meant to make something whereby philosophy might come along and panic about not knowing what it meant, or if it meant anything at all.

## CHAPTER SIX

# Alice Coltrane,
# Divine Injunctions ... c. 1971

1964: Tudor and Cage had largely abandoned the esotericism of their detailed scores and had begun improvising and chasing touring opportunities with the Merce Cunningham Dance Company. Disgusted with the lack of patronage for Black artists, Ornette Coleman was on an early hiatus from the jazz scene in New York. The Velvets had not yet become a band: Nico, while in France, had found work as an actor in television commercials; Moe Tucker, having heard the first Rolling Stones album, started tinkering with the drums while working for IBM; the Theatre of Eternal Music members John Cale and Tony Conrad recently discovered they could put electronic pickups on their droning string instruments, and Lou Reed graduated from Syracuse University before finding work as a songwriter at Pickwick Studios in Long Island City.[1]

That same year, Alice Coltrane was building a name for herself in the upper tier of the downtown bebop scene. She had attracted admiration and attention for her work as a pianist in vibraphonist Terry Gibbs's bebop ensemble. Critics of Gibbs's records at *Down Beat* noted the inventive, proliferating quality of her pianism. Don DeMichael noted that Coltrane (known as Alice McLeod at the time) was "impressive" and "a strong player" while remarking on the inventive directionality of her solos, noting that "sometimes [she] seems unable to contain herself, though, and her solo may go off in several directions during its course" (1964).[2] Another noted that her playing contained surprises: "she double-times unexpectedly (and intelligently) or builds on an idea when one would think her finished with it" (1965).[3] Though still a few years away from establishing herself as a solo artist, as a bebop pianist, Alice Coltrane, leaning toward hyperfractures, was already an inventive soloist experimenting with pushing the grammar of her improvisations past her critics' perceptual horizons.[4]

She first met John Coltrane at a gig at Birdland in 1963. By 1964, John and Alice had moved in together, and by 1966, at the apotheosis of Coltrane's experimental performances, Alice had replaced McCoy Tyner in

John's quartet. That same year, John admiringly described Alice's pianism: "she continually senses the right color, the right textures, of the sound of the chords. And in addition, she's fleet. She has real facility."[5] Critics registered the affective strangeness of what they were hearing in the couple's performances. Their praxis was not really entertainment, but neither was it modernist bebop, with meandering intricacies that could be traced by competent critics and listeners. It was veering into hypnosis—a suspension of artistic intentionality. The late night "Titans of the Tenor Sax" Lincoln Center concert in February 1966 featured Coltrane's quartet with Alice, Jimmy Garrisson, two drummers (Rashied Ali and J. C. Moses instead of Elvin Jones) and an array of guest horns (Albert Ayler, Donald Ayler, Pharoah Sanders, and Carlos Ward). *Down Beat* critic Dan Morgenstern responded in frustration and framed his concerns as a crisis of John's intentionality, one that would seem to fit Cavell's 1967 analysis of modernist fraudulence: "After this display one wonders what happened to Coltrane. Is he the prisoner of a band of hypnotists? Has he lost all musical judgment? Or is he putting on his musical audience?"[6] The Lincoln Center extravaganza was a new kind of hypnosis by comparison with John's and Miles Davis's modal jazz circa 1960; the Coltranes were taking off into noncommunicative cacophony.

Critic Pete Welding responded to the quartet's 1966 live recording of "My Favorite Things" at the Village Vanguard by describing an atmosphere saturated by affective inconsistency: "Now, in fact, his music is more a release of psychic energy than ever before, an emotional Pandora's box, if you will—with streams of cathartic, even exorcistic statements rushing into the atmosphere to implode on the listener's unconscious with almost physical force. It is tremendously powerful, energetic music, often more ugly and brutal than beautiful but always intense and blindingly honest."[7] In these years of collaboration, Alice's pianism could easily be occluded by the shambolic ecstasy of John's ensemble. In this quartet recording, Alice is not high in the mix; still, her chiming chords provide a sense of meditative gravity to John's euphoria and delirium. But with Sanders on flute and tenor sax and Emanuel Rahim on auxiliary percussion, the ensemble itself was the message. Recognizable fragments of "Naima" (1960) and "My Favorite Things" (1961) remained, but the band's aim was both materially grounded and metaphysical. It was a collective search to transform substances, to forget and annihilate the coordinates of the self by turning inward on—and I return to Welding here—"a journey to the center of the self, a dissection—often painful—of the psyche in which every nerve is laid bare, every feeling, impulse, and reaction probed mercilessly for what it will reveal."[8] As the Coltranes slipped into ecstatic cacophony, bebop-based hyperfractures found alternative footing as alchemies, torrents of sensation that were also exercises in how to perceive the divine being of life.

∴

Like the other chapters of this book, this one charts the emergence of an artist's (Alice Coltrane's) second-order modernism. Yet more than any other musician featured in these studio chapters, spirituality was foundational to her musical thought. Coltrane's early musical experiences were as a pianist in a Baptist church in Detroit, though as her career matured, she increasingly drew on the mystical traditions of Hinduism. Following her husband's death, Coltrane traveled to India and studied with the iconic guru of the American 1960s, Swami Satchidananda. During this period, Coltrane's music expanded rapidly from cacophony into compositionally organized, almost cinematic musical fusions of a droning tanpura, string arrangements, harp, and a 1971 Wurlitzer Centura 805 electric organ. From the late 1970s onward, she turned away from steady commercial recording, developed her voice as a spiritual writer, published four volumes of devotional texts, and founded the Sai Anantam Ashram in 1976, which she ran until her death in 2007. Coltrane's beliefs and revelations facilitated a mystical ascent to registers of universal consciousness in the wake of her solo LPs, which had explored a multitude of ornamented, ecstatic, dissonant, and stylistically varied atmospheres.

There are a number of Orientalisms circulating through the studio chapters of this book, and though they have common figures, books, and concepts, they are hardly congruent or monolithic. The Coltranes' spirituality broadly paralleled the idealized, exoticized Asia that provided philosophical underpinnings to Cage and Tudor's esoteric formalism. But Alice Coltrane's political views, aesthetic aims, and level of metaphysical commitment were quite distinct from the musicians featured in the preceding chapters. Tudor and Cage appropriated bits and pieces of texts and techniques from India, China, and Japan to pointedly critique and preserve the autonomy of Western aesthetics with dramatic philosophical inversions of principles such as expression, intention, and form. We may recall that Coleman's philosophy—even as he affirmed music's mystical capacities— was comparatively secular, formed largely on the indeterminacy of interconnected individuals and vernacular creativity. The Velvets, for their part, recovered India through a modal atmosphere of decadence and hypnosis, with lyrics and themes that staged a realist fantasy, a Nietzschean rebellion against social norms instituted largely by Western Christianity.

With Coltrane we arguably return to a variant of Tudor and Cage's Asiatic asceticism. But in a new modality that was quite distinct, Coltrane lived her philosophy and became a spiritual practitioner in her own right. We might note that neither Tudor nor Cage (with their interest in ego annihilation, philosophical musings, and recipes), nor the Velvets (with their mind-bending immersions) ventured to India during this period. Nor did they have any interest in meditation; they adopted fantasies of Asia to position themselves as artists. By contrast, Coltrane—though not without fantasies of her own, to be sure—far outstripped them in her commitments and beliefs. She made a number of trips to India, learned some Sanskrit, and, by the latter 1970s, had become a leader of her own California-based new religious movement. For in conjunction with her late husband, Coltrane heard in Hinduism the holistic metaphysics of a social utopia.

As with the other studio chapters in this book, this chapter draws broader conclusions about the ways Coltrane's creative praxis exploited and transfigured the long-standing philosophical question of music's ineffability. Its culminating focus will be on Coltrane's work as a philosopher—that is, it contends that her work seems to have asked certain kinds of questions—or physically posed them—through a mixture of music, mystical writings, and the album as a material object, all of which were informed by her spiritual thought. In bringing this view to bear on her work, the chapter will discuss the ways her Afro-modernist praxis mirrored and disrupted larger social currents of the period. Coltrane's alchemies departed from the acoustic norms of recorded jazz, dove into psychedelic studio practices, and experimented with a wide multiplicity of styles from bebop, modal jazz, and fusion to solo harp improvisations, reconstructions of works by her late husband, covers of Stravinsky, and gospel-infused Hindu *bajans* in which she sang as a soloist. Like Coleman, Coltrane's liner notes enhanced audiences' sense of perplexity about what musical sounds could affectively and metaphysically do. But Coltrane went even further, challenging listeners to actually join her spiritual perceptions.

∵

Alice McLeod grew up in Detroit in a deeply musical family and played piano and organ at Mount Olive Baptist Church for a number of years. This was the primary site of her education in music. Like Tudor, she had classical instruction in piano, though she chose not to pursue it professionally. Franya Berkman's biography has noted that (1) Coltrane the church musician was a pianist and organist—in church she presumably would have played a Hammond, an organ marketed as a cheaper alternative to pipe organs and inseparable from the emergence of gospel music; (2) in Black churches, which tended to be less male dominated by comparison with the secular world of the music business, women frequently worked as keyboardists and singers; and (3) a mix of oral and literate practice—coupled with ecstatic and intense emotional and spiritual experiences—was central to the Black Baptist church, was foundational on the job training for Coltrane (beyond Mt. Olive, Coltrane freelanced at other churches), and eventually became central to her experimental grammar.[9]

In the coming years Coltrane would leave Detroit in search of musical opportunities. In the late 1950s she began performing in a local band that played a combination of jazz, R & B, and gospel. With her first husband, a bebop singer, Coltrane traveled to Paris in 1960 in search of work. There, she met and learned from Bud Powell, whom she described as "a guiding light" for her musical growth.[10] Often mentioned by critics as the key influence on Coltrane's bebop pianism, Powell was an innovative voice in bebop piano during the late 1940s and early 1950s. He devised novel ways of thinning out piano voicings to foreground the linear and harmonic complexities of bebop. In particular, Powell developed a piercing, ornamented, and transparent right hand that could be accompanied by dissonant left-hand harmonies with all manner of ninths, elevenths, thirteenths, and the like. Coltrane's pianism of this period is documented on a rare television broadcast.[11] Soon after, she moved to New York and explored the possibility of studying music professionally at Juilliard, but for financial reasons—she received a full scholarship but had no family support for living expenses—abandoned the plan and took work as a file clerk.[12] She did manage, for a spell (and while parenting a child as a single mother) to support herself for a period of several months as a gigging musician in New York through connections from Detroit-based musicians. After this initial stint in New York, Coltrane returned to Detroit for three years and put together her own jazz sextet.

By 1963 Coltrane had returned to New York following a successful audition for Terry Gibbs and in turn took up work in his band. In her recordings with Gibbs one hears elements of her later style of keyboard improvising. There is a Powell-inspired right-hand linearity at work, albeit with a unique density of repeated ornamental figures added and repetitive passages that seem to hint at the hypnosis and shimmering stasis that would ultimately prove foundational for her solo work. It was with Gibbs's band that Coltrane would meet her future husband John Coltrane at a 1964 gig opening for John's quartet at Birdland. Their personal affinity was, in Gibbs's own account, powerful. And their subsequent musical collaborations and marriage, in Alice's own words, led her to more experimental territory, though the paths of influence were more double sided than has been often recognized.

## Afrocentric Spiritualties

By 1964 John had become an icon for spiritualized jazz influenced by mid-century conceptions of universal religions, daily meditation, and musical influences from India and Africa. John's spiritual quest had emerged in a postwar climate of "Afrocentric spirituality" that entailed reassessments of Egyptology, Santeria, traditional African religions, and most notably Islam in wide ranging efforts to construct new global histories and geographies that reflected dissatisfaction toward the social legacy of Protestant Christianity in the US.[13] The antecedents to this moment emerged early in the twentieth century as a number of Black leaders became particularly interested in Asian religions as potentially opening a path toward a counterhegemonic spirituality.[14] If the Nation of Islam represented an iconic movement of Black nationalism in the US that rejected vestiges of racial assimilation and whiteness, John's spirituality was universalist by comparison; it sought to incorporate the virtues of Christianity while rising above its limitations. Jayna Brown describes it as a "syncretism," one that "frees [Black] subjects from the organized Christian church and its religious narrative and allows for a sense of self in which slavery does not function as our origin tale."[15] While the influences on John's universalism were multiform, the importance of Hinduism was pronounced.

The warm and exoticized reception of Hinduism among white elites had nineteenth-century antecedents from Western Esotericism to German Romanticism, French Orientalism, and American Transcendentalism. Helena Petrovna Blavatsky's Theosophical Society was among the best known of this universalist tradition around the turn of the century. Its aims were "to reconcile all religions, sects and nations under a common system of ethics."[16] The Theosophical Society had supported the study of comparative religion, promoted Asian religions and philosophies, and held that a single universal truth could be disclosed across a number of faiths worldwide. Theosophical enthusiasm for Hinduism was also underpinned by immigrant labor from India. Since late in the nineteenth century, hundreds of itinerant Yogis (then predominantly focused on self-help, psychology, and fortune-telling rather than physical poses) lectured to and entertained the elite tastes of educated, middle- to upper-class US whites.[17] This was part of a broader fashion for Asian spirituality that Cage and Tudor participated in during the 1930s–40s.

By midcentury, Theosophical universalism became associated with a Neoplatonic term originally coined in the European Renaissance to describe the congruence between Christianity and pagan or Ancient Greek thought—*perennialism*. A key modern articulation of perennialism was Aldous Huxley's *The Perennial Philosophy* (1945), a book that stitched together a global anthology of mystical thinkers with a synoptic commentary. Perennialism addressed a paradigmatic problem for religion and modernity: how can one reconcile the fact that different world cultures continue to have mutually incompatible religious beliefs? For Huxley, a perennial philosophy underlying the world's religions held that transcendence or Being was immanent to all life and matter and that the conscious mind (and its capacity to detach from the particularistic and worldly desires of the ego) could serve as a privileged vehicle for such revelation. Huxley's book connected mystical figures of Christianity (principally Meister Eckhart) with parallel texts and figures in Asian philosophy. It was an important text in a broader network of cross-cultural and universalist religion volumes written or complied by Ananda K. Coomaraswamy, Hazrat Inayat Khan, Sri Ramakrishna, Paramhansa Yogananda, R. H. Blyth, D. T. Suzuki, Joseph Campbell, Carl Jung, Alan Watts, and Rudolf Steiner that circulated in the West during the early to middle part of the twentieth century.

Black affinities with the culture, philosophy, and spirituality of India have their own complex history. In the Harlem of the 1920s and 1930s, Black newspapers advertised Hindu iconography in the context of the ongoing practice of African-derived Hoodoo folklore.[18] Philip Deslippe has referred to this phenomenon as "manufactured Hoodoo," which in effect was an urban syncretism of traditional African magic and Orientalized performances of magic shows, fortune-telling, and hypnosis, often with Swamis in turbaned outfits. There was also sociality between these two minority groups: before the 1960s, it was not uncommon for Indian immigrants to cohabitate and intermarry with African Americans, particularly in cosmopolitan spaces like Harlem.[19] In this era, some African Americans—particularly musicians and other celebrities—repurposed stereotypes to pass as Indian or syncretized various folklores for inventive uses. For an African American, passing as Indian could be a way around anti-Blackness and a means of asserting cultural otherness against the normativity of white Christianity.[20] During the 1920s–40s, a number of Black magicians actually wore turbans and presented themselves as fakirs, fortune tellers, and Swamis. Dizzy Gillespie, for his part, allegedly wore a turban on occasion while traveling in Europe in order to pass himself off as Hindu.[21] This history of "passing" as Indian to thwart anti-Blackness was famously embodied in the work of Korla Pandit for television in the 1950s.[22]

The Coltranes represented a distinct turning point in this complex history between Blackness and India. As the civil rights era emerged and the burgeoning cultural revolutions of the 1960s unfolded, a universalist tradition of "reading" India based in Mahatma Gandhi's increasingly well-known doctrine of nonviolence rose to prominence among African Americans. This new tradition drew on a complex history of cultural exchange between

FIG. 6.1. Byron Goto, left-hand side of gatefold artwork for
Alice and John Coltrane, *Cosmic Music*. Impulse!, 1969.

people of color across continents. As Nico Slate has shown, a number of
African American and Indian intellectuals—notably W. E. B. Du Bois, Mahatma Gandhi, and Martin Luther King—drew analogies between the push
for racial justice in the US and the Indian struggles against colonialism and
social caste.[23] King, in particular, was profoundly influenced by Gandhi
both for his interest in nonviolence and in broader campaigns against poverty and caste discrimination.[24] At the same time, the uneven history of
Theosophy was fast evolving from its unsavory prewar associations with a
fantasized communion of elite, white civilizations (as discussed in chap. 3).[25]
Amid the countercultural revolutions of the 1960s, many perennialists became interested in postwar decolonization, overturning caste hierarchies,
and the civil rights struggle in the US, all of which sought to recognize the
humanity of oppressed minorities. In a set of associations that were popular in the 1960s, the Coltranes would refer to modern figures for social

reform—particularly Gandhi and King, alongside the messiahs Buddha and Christ—as overlapping influences for their thinking.

These icons of 1960s perennialism were strikingly fused together in Japanese American artist Byron Goto's gatefold artwork for the Coltranes' collaborative release, *Cosmic Music* (1969). On the left (fig. 6.1), a spiritual mélange: Jesus is adorned by a mandala, a feature he shares with two Buddhas that extend perpendicularly on each side.[26] On the left appears a South Asian Buddha; on the right, an East Asian Buddha. Directly below is an Egyptian Pharaoh in the form of the Great Sphinx. The two floating icons between the Buddhas and Jesus present an image of Krishna (the Hindu god of compassion, tenderness, and love) and the crescent and star symbol of Islam. At the center of the cross form sits a triplex symbol: a Celtic cross with a star of David in the middle and at the very center, the Sanskrit for "Om." On the right (fig. 6.2), the explosive contradictions of modernity

FIG. 6.2. Byron Goto, right-hand side of gatefold artwork for
Alice and John Coltrane, *Cosmic Music*. Impulse!, 1969.

abound: Goto's circular collage features John at its center, surrounded by atomic warfare, space-age iconography, faces in negative, and a suited figure of Martin Luther King in the lower left. The paring of the two images is as dialectically messy and unresolved as the album itself.

In the preceeding two decades, perennialist framings of Hinduism had an impact on the course of postwar jazz.[27] Charles Mingus, who was close friends with two white bohemian artists in the bay area who were deeply invested in Hinduism, became devoted to Vedanta Hinduism during the 1940s and 1950s because of its inclusive, universalist, and democratic potential as a spirituality. Concurrently, Sun Ra's Afrocentric spirituality began to coalesce during the 1950s in dialogue with Theosophy, Egyptology, and the bourgeoning New Age; his unique visions developed more fully during the 1960s and 1970s.[28] Sitarist Ravi Shankar's first international tours that began in 1956 alongside sarodist Ali Akbar Kahn's parallel rise to fame set the stage for the increased notoriety of Hindustani classical music as well as a broader universalist and countercultural revival of Hindu spirituality in the West. John, who knew Ra's music well and was an enthusiast of Shankar's sitar playing, had a spiritual awakening in 1957 and began to familiarize himself with Hindu spirituality and philosophy from written texts.[29] Sonny Rollins, who would begin studying Yoga in 1963 after a visit to Japan, had recommended to him Paramahansa Yogananda's widely read memoir *Autobiography of a Yogi* (1946).[30] At the suggestion of Bill Evans, Coltrane also read Jiddu Krishnamurti's *Commentaries on Living* (1956–60).

The spiritual atmospheres of John's modal jazz of the early 1960s also had influences outside of India. As Ingrid Monson has noted, the formal malleability of modal jazz (with its open harmonic space for melodic exploration) was understood by jazz musicians as an ideal canvas for projecting fantasies and constructions of non-Western cultures from Africa and India to the Middle East.[31] This could be true even when the influences were not themselves non-Western. George Russell's book *Lydian Chromatic Concept of Tonal Organization* (1953) drew together the modalities of French impressionism and medieval church modes and proved highly influential on a new generation of jazz musicians.[32] Miles Davis's *Kind of Blue* (1959) made use of Russell's theory, revolutionizing jazz harmony with a return to an unspooled modal feel with often only one or two chords over the course of an entire song. John's modal compositions of the early 1960s—notably *My Favorite Things* (1961) and the monumental atmospheres of *Africa/Brass* (1961)—were influenced both by Shankar's sitar playing, Folkways recordings of Indian music (probably Kahn), and Yusef Lateef's modal jazz (which was, for its part, influenced by both Russell and Shankar).

Amid an atmosphere of global fusions, Afrocentric trends in jazz retained a distinct epistemology. Though both John and Alice espoused a broadly universalist spirituality, John articulated a dialectical view of music and politics sympathetic to the Afrocentric historicism forwarded by Amiri Baraka in the early 1960s (as discussed in chap. 4). In 1966, when questioned by Frank Kofsky about his music's relationship to Malcom X, John agreed that music generally—though passively—could mirror Black nationalism. But taking a position that also echoed the broad outlines of Adorno's historicism, John claimed the ethics or politics of his music should be heard dialectically in the formal prism (or "thought patterns"—a phrase Coleman used as well) of musical innovation:

> [social and political issues related to black nationalism are] definitely important. . . . The issues are *part* of what *is*, you know, at this time. Naturally, as musicians, we express whatever, whatever it is. . . . In music I make, or I have tried to make, consciously, an attempt . . . to change what I've found in music. . . . I think music is an instrument. It can create the initial, just, the *thought patterns*, that can create the changes, you see, in the thinking of the people.[33]

More commonly, John presented the relationship between music and politics holistically, as a broader metaphysical effort to construct a social utopia based around love and compassion in opposition to war, poverty, and profiteering. When asked by Japanese promoter Ennosuke Saito about the kind of love he expresses in music (Christian, familial, or heterosexual), John responded,

> I really can't . . . separate any of it. I think they all are certain degrees of that [*unintelligible*] of the one Christ, or maybe Buddha, or Krishna, or all of them. And all of them, I think it's the same one, that *one*, that all of them describe. It's from which it all comes [*unintelligible*] path, the love you have for your work, it's all of the manifestations of that one, to me.[34]

With respect to the question of ineffability, John expressed a similar modesty about being able to define the divine unity of this complex multiplicity: "I don't like to try to define god. Because I think he's beyond any definition that I could give."[35] And in another context, he claimed he did not want to be too aggressive in explaining his own work:

> I think that it's going to have to be, uh, very subtle; I mean it's—you can't, you can't ram philosophies down anybody's throat—and the music is

enough! [*laughs*] You know, and that's philosophy. But I think the best thing I can do at this time is to try to get *myself* in shape, you know, and *know myself*. If I can do *that*, then I'll just play, you see, [*laughs*] and leave it at that. . . . And I think they'll get it, because music goes a long way— and it really is—it, it can influence.[36]

At midcentury, the existentialists regarded the authenticity of the self as a potential backstop against the contradictory ideologies of an increasingly globalized age and a loss of common moral fabric. Here, John similarly turns to the process of self-actualization in order to comprehend a truth that is otherwise ineffable, a process that was also the foundation for the perennialism that underpinned his spirituality. In his words,

> As I look out upon the world . . . I've always felt that even though a man was not a Christian, he still had to know the truth some way. Or if he was a Christian, he could know the truth—or he could *not*. [*laughs*] It's according to whether he knew the truth, and the truth itself doesn't have any name on it, to me see. Each man has to find this for himself, I think.[37]

The lines of influence between John and Alice during those years were complex. While much has been made of Alice's insistent devotion to and crediting of John, Berkman posits that much of John's most experimental work developed while the two were mutually influential on one another (1964–67). It should also be emphasized that Alice produced virtually all of her significant work after John died in 1967, and with regard to spirituality, her adoption of Hinduism went far beyond that of her late husband. As mentioned earlier, following his death, she traveled to India and Sri Lanka and became close with Swami Satchidananda, who would have an outsized influence on her philosophical outlook during the late 1960s and early 1970s and would appear in the form of a voice-over in her album *World Galaxy* (1972). Musically, during this period Alice wrote compositions that built on musical ideas of her late husband, but the atmospherics had evolved significantly. Around 1970 her music changed from an idiom tied to her late husband's avant-garde approach to bebop into an alchemical landscape of musical hallucinations grounded in a new array of instruments: harp, electric organ, string arrangements, and even, on occasion, a droning tanpura.

At the same time, there were gendered obstacles to Alice's quest for artistic autonomy, particularly at this key stage in her career. She was limited both by the actual domestic labor she needed to do to raise three children and by the professional ceiling that wrongly presumed she was bound to be the caretaker of her husband's work. In 1966 Alice (described as "the saxophonist's bride" in the *Down Beat* announcement of the personnel switch) replaced McCoy Tyner as the pianist in John's quartet.[38] Following her husband's death, Coltrane made clear on the liner notes to *A Monastic Trio* (1968), "How many people can devote that kind of time [to music, day and night, in the way John did]? Even if you like it. I like it but I still have responsibilities to my children and household, but John gave it his full and undivided attention."[39]

Tammy Kernodle has contextualized the gendered nature of Alice's struggles more broadly: in her view, the Afro-modernism of the period had a structural bias toward masculinity. It stemmed from the myth that to be a Black avant-garde artist also meant to "liberate oneself and the art from the clutches of women."[40] That is, to the extent Black art opposed social norms, it similarly opposed the inclusion of women insofar as they were taken to represent monogamy and traditional domestic values. Kernodle's hypothesis raises the possibility that it may have been easier for Alice to achieve credibility and status as a religious leader whose exceptionalism was taken to be transcendent of social norms rather than as an artist negotiating a competitive secular and commercial field with few if any comparable woman colleagues. It is worth noting as well that Alice's ashram was both participatory and pedagogical and, in this way, paralleled a new generation of artists making a living as academic workers in the 1960s and early 1970s.[41] At the time it would have been almost impossible for Alice to find that kind of work in higher education, where faculty positions were overwhelmingly dominated by white men with degree credentials that were themselves exclusionary.

## Ornamental Apparitions

Notwithstanding these formidable social barriers, by 1970 Alice was producing a new language of psychedelic tapestries that moved far beyond the conventions of the bebop she had been playing professionally in the 1960s. How are we to position the philosophical dimensions of Alice's solo work of this period? Elliott Powell frames John's spiritual jazz as emblematic of an emergent intercultural solidarity between Afro-diasporic modernism and India rather than a simple act of Orientalizing appropriation. In Powell's words,

> The polycultural wing of Afro-Asian studies, thus, illustrates how African and Asian America are not, and should not be, antagonistic and oppositional—as the model minority myth attests—but instead projects and formations of collectivity. And it's here that the two dominant schools of thought in Afro-Asian studies—political solidarity and

FIG. 6.3. Alice Coltrane, *Universal Consciousness*, album artwork.
Photographer and designer Philip Melnick. Impulse!, 1971.

polyculturalism—demand an understanding of African and Asian (diasporic) comparative racialization as a site of kinship and anti-imperial, anti-capitalist, and anti-racist alliances.[42]

In Powell's view John's spiritual utopianism is hardly a bland depoliticization of Black nationalism; to the contrary, John's music extends well-known Afro-Asian solidarities into a complex utopian register of Black internationalism.[43] There are many subtle moves to Powell's ensuing reading of *A Love Supreme* (1965) that lie beyond the scope of this chapter, but his theory of polycultural solidarity places a valuable spotlight on the dissenting strangeness of Alice's *Black Orientalism* (to use a like-minded term coined by Helen Jun)—one that falls neither squarely on the side of Black nationalism nor on a bland politics of spiritual universality devoid of specific risks and commitments.[44] In his reading, as in mine, polyphonies and paradoxes abound beneath the surface of the Coltranes' perennialism.

We might recall for a moment Cavell's 1967 diagnosis of modernist depersonalization and opaque noncommunication, as discussed in chapter 2. This midcentury artistic and intellectual climate was central to Cage and Tudor's collaborations, and informed the keen ear for Coleman's harmolodic formalism. It also undergirded the more decadent borrowings of Indian tanpura and Black hipsterism in the Velvet Underground's alchemical hallucinations. In this context consider a provocative aesthetic object, with a title that initially appears to promise total emancipation from the obscurity of noncommunication—Alice Coltrane's *Universal Consciousness* (1971) (fig. 6.3). (And hereafter I shall switch back to "Coltrane.") The album's rhetoric mirrors her late husband's desire for expressing the cosmic truth of pure universality. But the resultant music projected an overwhelming multitude that seemed to resist consumption.

Consider just a few basics of the title track. It has a rough ABA form and begins with Coltrane on harp surrounded by a band of four violinists. In the B section, Coltrane plays an organ solo with the rhythm section alone. Finally, in the last minute and a half, we hear the harp and strings return. Beneath it all, bassist Jimmy Garrison and drummer Jack DeJohnette serve as a churning, occasionally volcanic rhythm section.

The beginning has a way of tearing in. Four violinists shriek downward, stuttering, almost as if people are stumbling. Coltrane's harp—given to her by John in 1965 after they had moved in together—decorates the arresting feel of the scene; it is cosmic, glittering, and wild. The harp had become an icon in her sound that she explicitly associated with a past life in Egypt. In Coltrane's words,

> When I play [the harp], maybe the flowingness of it, or the way it is so harmonically and melodically set so different from the piano, for example. It makes me recall Ancient Egypt. It makes me seem to remember that I have a past or a history there somewhere.[45]

In her *Monument Eternal* writings, Coltrane more specifically heard the harp as linked to Ptolemy III, pharaoh of Egypt circa 246–222 BCE:

> Ptolemy was an excellent young musician who played a large golden harp inside the marble courts of the palace. Today, in our home [Dix Hills], we have many musical instruments. They include two grand pianos, woodwinds, drums, two organs, a guitar, a vibraphone, a violin, flutes, a koto, a sitar, a tamboura, and four harps. Ptolemy loved the sound of the harp—oceanic, deep, billowing.[46]

The harp recurred in many of her recordings of the 1970s, reappearing like an involuntary memory, something like a metallic curtain framing the arrival of a divine apparition. Coltrane often tuned it pentatonically, giving her the physical freedom to gliss and pluck at will within a single mode.[47] The string parts, transcribed by Ornette Coleman, are curiously enough redolent of the sawing, ecstatic violin playing we heard on *The Empty Foxhole*.[48] In the opening section, one can count the violin phrases: seven short jabs followed by two longer loops that dip down and up. Then a dramatic unison tremolo, a grand descending theme of nine notes, and a relatively loose and free transitional passage in a higher register.

At 1:08, there is a cross-fade on the tape: Coltrane's organ suddenly appears in a trio with her rhythm section. She is striving for God here, still the church organist, a woman allowed to speak through an electrical instrument thanks to the social and spiritual practice of her Baptist upbringing. In a reincarnation of her late husband, she simulates breathing by inserting small breaks through much of this organ solo, and by the second half of the solo she's beginning to glue together trills and arpeggios in longer phrases. Just before the three-minute mark, the strings are spliced back in with screeching tremolos. It is a retransition to the opening material, but the string themes have now been fragmented; they are meandering wildly, and seem to be echoing elements of Coltrane's organ solo. We hear a fast cross-fade again at 4:20 before hearing the descending string theme once more as a refrain. We finally land in a disorderly and exhausted coda.

The ornate, meandering grammar of bebop—one that, during the 1940s and 1950s, aimed for increasingly dissonant and frenetic languages or a certain distance from the dancing body in its commodity form—here this grammar murmurs as a mere shadow of a past hyperfracture. The fracturing of jazz languages does not seem to be what Coltrane's music is about. Music recognizable as jazz is interwoven with episodes of harp and strings in a landscape that presents an unspeakable challenge. Filled with abundant ornamentation, this music aspires to alchemy—metaphysical transformation—a transcendent sublimation. But striving for God? The challenges of spiritual leader and musician were, to be sure, inseparable for her. And the physical form of the album facilitated points of contact. Each song on *Universal Consciousness* had its own spiritual liner notes, a practice that echoed that of her late husband for *A Love Supreme* (1965). Coltrane writes of this track,

> UNIVERSAL CONSCIOUSNESS: literally means Cosmic Consciousness, Self-Realization, and Illumination. This music tells of some of the various diverse avenues and channels through which the soul must pass before it finally reaches that exalted state of Absolute Consciousness. Once achieved, the soul becomes re-united with God and basks in the Sun of blissful union. At this point, the Creator bestows on the soul many of his Attributes, and names one, a New Name. This experience and this music involve a Totality concept which embraces cosmic thought as an emblem of Universal Sound.[49]

"Universal Consciousness" is a four-minute jumble of dissonance; a block of ecstatic meandering that feels almost as if it is was unloaded backward onto us. It is composed in the manner of a montage; one can feel the subtle artificiality of the splices and cross-fades. By what logic might these episodes follow one another? The track is not a physical room or a scene; the listener has been thrown into some kind of warped cosmic space. In the atmospheres of Coltrane's second-order modernism, sounds can trigger visual hallucinations and begin to question one's normative coordinates of musical perception. Such is the aim of alchemy: apparition, fabulation, and transformation. In the liner notes, listeners are told of a journey toward transcendence; the music is actually telling us "of diverse avenues and channels" that the soul has to pass through. Yet how exactly does this music serve as a medium for such a transformation?

## Coltrane's Philosophy

Key elements of Coltrane's theology—as it evolved after 1968—mirrored a broader set of trends in what eventually became known as New Age spirituality.[50] Taking its name from theosophist Alice Bailey's writings of the 1940s and 1950s, the New Age emerged an international cluster of new religious movements that adapted perennialism to the emergent liberalism of 1960s counterculture.[51] These movements addressed a widespread desire for spiritual cohesion in a time of unprecedented social diversity and interdependence worldwide. In particular, New Age movements mobilized the self's capacity for authentic intuition and inner experience as an alternative to the top-down adoption of traditional religious beliefs. In line with Hinduism, Buddhism, and Christian mysticism, these movements held that this self should be detached from the local desires of a socially contingent ego. Only then could one properly disclose the universal consciousness of the underlying reality immanent to nature—variously referred to as God, mind, energy, or a force of life. This reality was often understood by New Agers to be an ever-changing and interdependent network of elements rather than a harmonious sphere of organisms or eternal proportions. To aid in the disclosure of these revelations, New Agers made use of channeling, meditation, charismatic leaders, voluntary communities, psychedelic drugs, esoteric rituals and appropriations, and alternative lifestyles. Ethically, these movements emphasized collectivism, natural ecology, wellness and natural medicine, and the emancipation from traditional social, moral, and sexual norms.

Within this broad cultural field, Swami Satchidananda stood out as an exceptionally important influence on Coltrane, second only to her late husband. In line with the New Age, Satchidananda's inclusive, accessible, and populist philosophy claimed the "Self *is* God."[52] But far from selfish behavior, for Satchidananda, our true self is one that wants nothing; it has no definition, nationality, race, or tribe; its principles are only sacrifice, generosity, and love. The task of the self is to detach from the identity and particularity-driven tendencies of our ego and discover the ineffable, serene, balanced, and silent universality of the underlying vital truth of what is—forces that are neither good nor bad but should be accepted as they are. Following the liberalism of the 1960s, a spiritual movement based in these ideals ought to be leaderless. As he put it, "the guru is within."[53] Satchidananda placed a particular value on happiness, but it was a happiness detached from any kind of worldly relations, an impersonal and universal tranquility—a purity of mind—unmoored from particular attachments. Ethically, Satchidananda emphasized diet and moderation: meat, alcohol, caffeine, and cigarettes should be avoided, while sleeping, talking, and sexual activity should never be taken to excess. In another vein, suffering, austerity, and adversity could, in his view, bring about happiness insofar as they were a mode of purification, a way of physiologically separating from the ego and of moderating the mind—of "burning out the undesirable impurities."[54] For, ultimately, the mind's ups and downs are the cause of all evil (war, greed, hatred, pollution); if one steps back from the ego, one can moderate these impulses.

In her philosophical texts, Coltrane develops a like-minded metaphysics that fleshes out the spiritual visions conveyed in her liner notes. In parallel with the New Age, she developed a pantheism that fused Hindu mysticism to Abrahamic theology, and she maintained that the perfect and unchanging divinity of God is infused in all matter, from the atomic scale up through the anthropomorphic scale of humanity and outward to the grand register of the cosmos. Consonant with the immanentist strains of the New Age, Coltrane describes the various scales of nature with a vocabulary from midcentury science: atoms appear in terms of quantum mechanics, the human psyche in the terms of psychological testing, and communication with the cosmos in terms of an array of modern technologies: telephones, file cabinets, information code, televisions, cars, elevators, airplanes, and space travel.[55] In this context humanity's ethical challenge is to renounce the locality of our material attachments: the inclination toward self-interest, the ephemerality of our sensory and emotional life, the tendency to exploit others, and the acquisition of wealth.

For Coltrane, ego detachment allows one to dramatically dematerialize oneself while attaining consciousness of the eternal truth of God. Mirroring themes in the Neoplatonic strains of Abrahamic religions as well as in the apophatic elements of Hinduism that were central to Satchidananda's teachings and her late husband's spirituality, Coltrane positions this eternal truth as paradoxically ineffable. In her words, the perfectly eternal, immaterial, and formless truth of the Absolute "defies discovery and description," and "no man, cosmic god, or whatsoever else knows or can measure the length, breadth or depth of My Being."[56] And yet, paradoxically, she enjoins others to be unafraid that they might "not succeed in fathoming My meaning." ("My" means Coltrane's and God's since, in these texts, she understands herself to channel the voice of God.).[57] This is something in *Deep Refrains* I called the "paradox of the ineffable": one can potentially fathom a meaning about something one cannot fully understand or describe. Satchidananda put this paradox playfully: "You can't talk of it. There's no mark, no symbols. It's not located in one place. That's the essence."[58]

Coltrane's theology was more austere and challenging than the breezy tone of Satchidananda's teachings and the affirmative liberalism of the New Age. There were theological reasons for this. Satchidananda's ecumenical spirituality sought to synthesize all six branches of classical Yoga (Hatha, Raja, Bhakti, Karma, Jnana, Japa) while maintaining that the "Self is God" to emphasize the individual over any particular belief system. By contrast, Coltrane's spirituality was based in Bhakti, a branch of Yoga that emphasizes devotion and emotional surrender to God. She put it simply: "I believe that the greatest achievement is devotion."[59] Thus, while Satchidananda understood the conscious self as having a unique capacity to reveal the truth of the Lord, Coltrane's self is not the telos of one's spiritual journey; her aim is transcendent communion with God himself. She writes, "Self-realization, to know your own soul, is not the journey's end in the Lord; *go onward* to the highest attainment of God Realization, where you see God face to face, where you are privileged to dwell with the Lord every moment of your existence."[60] Bhakti (a Sanskrit term entailing devotion, participation, and love) has historically been positioned by scholars of comparative religion as consonant with Christianity.[61] For Coltrane, Bhatki seems to have accommodated a perennialism that allowed her to maintain an Abrahamic view of God as sovereign, omnipotent, and almighty. Along these lines, Coltrane frequently describes being God's disciple, practicing sacrifice and austerity, and being commanded to write down her experiences. In fact, for Coltrane, God is not only all powerful; he is also capricious in the manner of the God of the Old Testament. As she put it in her channeling of God in *Endless Wisdom*, "I, the Supreme Lord, dost teach all, admonish all, and chastise all created beings hereby: Sometimes I heal; somedays I inflict. Sometimes I scorch; somedays I fulfill. Sometimes I summon; somedays I cast out. Sometimes I renew; somedays I rent asunder. Sometimes I build; somedays I destroy."[62]

## Divine Injunctions

Coltrane held that consciousness was divine—a numinous portal to the infinite—while music, in turn, was a medium particularly infused with the potential for revelation. Yet in her spiritual writings, Coltrane does not speak very much of music; she tended to develop her music and philosophy independently. In her liner notes for *Huntington Ashram Monastery* (1969), *Journey in Satchidananda* (1971), *Universal Consciousness* (1971), and *Lord of Lords* (1972), language is more closely indexed to her musical decisions. Beyond the usual personnel listings, in these texts, which appear alongside album artwork on the LP gatefolds, Coltrane issues powerful and complex injunctions or describes spiritual hallucinations evoked by the music. Yet the details and correlations are kept vague. What kind of strategy is this? How might we, Coltrane's listeners and readers, understand the puzzling juxtapositions of her music and her philosophy?

Let us return to *Universal Consciousness*. Consider the question of the album's intentionality. In this album, is Coltrane, the avant-garde church organist, leading her listener anywhere? Or is this listener merely peering in on her ascent to the infinite? A puzzle of this work is in how Coltrane addresses her listener. She is not a singer or a soloist; it is in fact difficult to know where she *is* on the track. By my count, there may be at least two Coltranes: one envisioned the colorful and jagged curtain of harp and strings that frame the central organ solo. These framing episodes produce a sense of magic, of theater, a vaguely Orientalist scene that features an intricately veiled atmosphere of ornaments. In the middle there is a second Coltrane, speaking in the first person. Or, with her hands at the Wurlitzer, she is not so much speaking as she is twirling. Here, the rhythm section plays a more traditional support role derived from bebop. At the organ, we ostensibly hear her ascent, a strange ventriloquism of her late husband's wild, overgrown arpeggios and trills. The Wurlitzer is her cosmic vehicle. Beyond the Baptist church, Coltrane credited her choice of the organ to her recent trip to India where she heard the sustained tones of harmoniums and the shruti box. Incidentally, she also reports feeling as though she could address her audience more powerfully with this electronic instrument: "When I began to play the organ, there came the freedom and understanding that I would never have to depend on anyone else musically."[63]

With this music, what kind of universal consciousness is she aiming to convey? Twirling at the organ in an ecstatic space, orally responsive to congregants who are only implied as they are not in the physical space; in fact, we cannot share that physical space except through the mediation of the record player. The grammar of Coltrane's address—its humanity, orality, and intentionality—is supported by liner notes meant to be read when one is relaxing on the sofa, on one's way to a place one does not yet understand. It is almost as if she knew the music needed a user's guide: "This music tells of some of the various diverse avenues and channels through which the soul must pass before it finally reaches that exalted state of Absolute Consciousness."

Coltrane's music of this period explores diverse variations on this theme: odes to love and compassion, reincarnations and communions with deceased figures (John, Igor Stravinsky), and riffs on ancient Asian, Greek, and Egyptian myths. In the liner notes for *World Galaxy* (1972), Coltrane writes a poem that describes unconditional love as the uncommodifiable creative force of the universe that is the origin of selflessness.[64] And in "Andromeda's Suffering" on *Lord of Lords* (1972), she fuses a Greek myth about the suffering of an Ethiopian woman—Andromeda—to the eponymous supergalaxy with a trillion stars. Her liner note connects this massive cosmic being both to the New Age gospel of love and to a Christianized internalization of Andromeda's suffering. It fully comes to life at the composition's affective climax: "At the coda point of this music (5:26 into the piece), I can hear the Lord's voice as it spoke to me three years ago, saying, 'Do you feel like suffering for My Love?' . . . etc. I feel the Lord's suffering within my being everyday [*sic*]. Mother Kundalina Shakti [a divine feminine energy] pushes inside me."[65]

In ways that echoed the Theosophical cosmologies of Sun Ra as well as those her late husband, Coltrane's peculiar brand of Hindu-Christian mysticism was a life practice that allowed her to disable the material support for her ego. Though this was a broad theme of the New Age, textual foundations for this devotional philosophy are found in the *Bhagavad Gita*, a Hindu text widely read by Westerners. As a practitioner of Bhakti, it was central to Coltrane's devotional reading and teaching.[66] In this portion of the *Mahabharata* epic, Krishna counsels the fretting warrior Arjuna to engage in battle by detaching himself from his desires and sensory attachments in order to discover intellectual fortitude, discipline, and calm. In her first book of devotional writings, *Monument Eternal* (1968–70), Coltrane describes parallel experiences seeking dematerialization.[67] Practicing "tapas"—the Sanskrit word for "heat," which indicates practices of asceticism, cleansing, and self-discipline—she fasted, abstained from sensory pleasures, and physically exhausted herself in order to follow an unquenchable desire to transcend her material foundation and even travel through physically impossible spaces. Her goal was mystical revelation.

In a mystical experience when one becomes conscious of the divine truth—say through a devotional service—one cannot see or explain the underlying absolute truth. Instead, one has only a unique and "secret" glimpse of what truly is.[68] One vehicle for doing so is the discovery of what Coltrane describes as an "astral body," a concept familiar to both Theosophy and Anthroposophy. An astral body is an immaterial copy of one's material existence. Similar to what Coltrane describes in her liner notes as "diverse avenues and channels through which the soul must pass," one's astral body can communicate and travel at the speed of thought itself. When one assumes astral form, time becomes flexible; one can fast-forward, rewind, and cycle through life in ways that transcend material conditions, giving one a glimpse of life processes far beyond the speed in which they are actually lived. Through a consciousness of one's astral body, one becomes fearless, humble, detached, and compassionate by understanding the experiences of others and their deeply unique character, even to the point of communing with the protointelligence of animals and insects. Stars from the night sky can scale down to human size, and older friends and relatives appear in a state of eternal youth, beauty, and genderlessness. In doing so one realizes that one lives "within and beyond the smallest atom" and that one "can see vividly beyond the ken of human eyesight"—that is, we are paradoxically living within and beyond our material conditions.[69]

∵

How are we to experience such transcendence through Coltrane's music, with its forests of trills, ornaments, glissandi, and string arrangements? The alchemies of *Universal Consciousness* are built on an empiricism—an ad hoc making of visions in stereophonic form—of varied styles and modes of address, of narrative hallucinations, and of irrepressible visuality and abundance. Like the Velvets, the music is filled with costumes, makeup, atmosphere, and ritual. In Coltrane's devotional writings, she describes alchemy as a way to achieve divine purification, which "is analogous to the processes and the results of empirical chemistry performed by an alchemist who transmutes base metal into gold."[70] In this music, through transmutation, we are being shown something golden: a transformation of substances. But exactly what is obscure; as a path to universality in sound—a ritualized praxis—it is impenetrably challenging. We might recall Cavell's bleak diagnosis of modernism at midcentury. In this context, Coltrane's appeal to absolute knowledge might be figured as untranslatable; a noncommunication in the form of a beautiful—and fiendishly dense—surface of oblique missives, a polyphony of inconsistencies.

How might Cavell have responded to Coltrane's oblique spiritual injunction with the whiteness of his earnest Kantian humanism? One could imagine Cavell's social grammars, always on the lookout for accessible rules of engagement, grappling with endlessly vague impressions. After all, Coltrane is aiming at the disclosure of an underlying inhuman reality, at once atomic and cosmic. Without an institutionally sanctioned means toward the recovery of an exact grammar structuring such an experience, the recording might simply be there to emit stunning force. Meanwhile, the liner notes furnish its minimal semiotic index: here it is. Just as Warhol once said, "I don't know," confronted by the plain fact of its sound, Coltrane simply says—without saying it—do what you like. You will not hear why certain rules are followed; you will not be shown the techniques in any detail; you will be told only that the music narrates and embodies spiritual ascent, and then you will be left alone. So perhaps we have this: a skeletal claim to artistic purposiveness that contains a multitude of unwoven grammars left strewn about, indeterminate. It is a strikingly novel use of music's ineffability.

It may be instructive to compare Coltrane's spiritual metaphysics to the formalist self-promotion criticized by Cavell just four years earlier. The high formalism of serial composition drove Cavell up the wall; after all, his case in point, Ernst Krenek, had contended that the individual sounds of his music, no matter the apparent disorder, were formally defensible. In the face of hyperspecified formalism, Cavell repersonalized modernism in order to draw attention to the broader sociology of valuation at midcentury. By contrast, Coltrane's "Totality Concept" is massive, numinous, and unlinked to any specific technique of musical analysis. Does this make her philosophy merely of biographical value? As a Black woman, note that critics were already more than inclined to personalize her artistic intentions as a fetishized inner vision—as reflections of her spiritual journey, as idiosyncratic hallucinations, or her mourning of her late husband's absent spirit.

But in the context of Cavell's view of modernism, this off ramp of personalized intentions risks short-circuiting the philosophical complexities embedded in Coltrane's work. If *Universal Consciousness*—as an aesthetic object—is filled with magnetism—a valued object with purposiveness—one ought to keep its intentionality productively open, more or less depersonalized. This at least provides one rich perspective on the philosophy embedded in her music: to point out that one is at a risk of failing to register her thinking, or to remark that her work perplexes the drive to grammatical certitude while being a carrier of intentions that might not be understood. For Coltrane's noncommunicative spiritual injunction sets up an undecidable dialectical tension between personal vision, inconsistent abundance, and cosmic universality. Any residue of hyperfracture, familiar to Alice's meandering variants on John's "sheets of sound" at the organ, was giving way to an alchemical platform of metaphysical intentionalities.

What, then, might we glean from pausing over Coltrane's polyphonic alchemies? *Universal Consciousness* points the listener toward absolute consciousness while tossing us backward into noise, confronting listeners with an elusive promise to convey—or an appearance of conveying—a grammar-like atmosphere in music that refuses humanist intelligibility. Grammar is gestured at and listened to, or imagined to be there, but its divinity cannot really be taken in. The music productively, and in a utopian sense, leaves the work of communication either too ornate or amazingly vague. The listener is left wondering: What is there? What Coltrane says is: this music is maybe like speaking, it is not entirely formless. But it is so distant from language. Way out there. So what we are left with is bare intentionality that is in fact saying little to nothing, or saying something so passionately (or elaborately) as to be implausible as the work of communication. An alchemy is not a statement; it is a conjuring.

While Cavell's method might provide an illuminating path to this puzzle, his resolve to turn away from the musical object toward grammars of social life loses track of an important lesson that Coltrane's work makes explicit. As a channel for devotional spirituality, for her the medium of musical object— its correlations with "diverse avenues and channels"—is vague, inexhaustible, or untrackable. We might say that Coltrane's *Universal Consciousness* foregrounds a new philosophical exercise in what Cavell diagnoses as modernism's problem of fraudulence. She has opened the possibility of letting the atmosphere of an ecstatic grammar multiply, get scrambled, aggressively pile up, or permanently dissolved into wallpaper. In this way, her alchemical experimentalism entails a latent critique of humanism insofar as it asks questions such as: Is this devotional situation eliciting or refusing my participation? Or both at once? How is it addressing me? What are its rules of engagement? In a way, Coltrane is showing us a philosophy of music, showing us at some deep level that this is what music, as a medium, can do.

## Afro-futurity

Among Coltrane's albums, *Universal Consciousness* is unquestionably Afro-modernist in orientation, one carrying echoes of Sun Ra, Ornette Coleman, as well as the avant-garde work of her late husband. In a segment featured in a 1970 film, shortly after the austere exercises of her *tapas*, Coltrane described this spiritual experience as producing her free and autonomous subjectivity in proximity to the icons of perennialism but at a remove from any principle of transaction or exchange.

> I can't say it was the highest price as Buddha or Christ, because that was life. Or Martin Luther King. That was life, you know. But, I've been very close to the end of my life and I feel that I've been given my freedom now. That I can act, I can be, I can live as I want to, and nothing can—there's no claim—no one can buy me. Or there's no action I have to pay; I have no karmas to pay. . . . All of it has been given back to me. That I'm free.[71]

It is a bracing articulation of the underlying intentionality of Coltrane's experimentalism. She positions spiritual transcendence—however obscure or painful, up against the risk of death—as a weapon against the transactional ontology of the culture industry ("no one can buy me"). Coltrane would make consonant points in her later spiritual writings, particularly in a section of *Endless Wisdom* on "materialism" that offered a sustained critique of the modern reduction of life to economic means and worldly commodities.[72] We may recall from chapter 4 that Baraka had argued similarly in *Blues People* (1963) that the very idea of a Black musical avant-garde—particularly in the case of bebop and free jazz—was one that positioned itself as a resistant world of formal experimentation against the commodification and appropriation of Black forms in the entertainment industry.

Divine injunctions from a Black woman guru come from a very different place than they do from an Indian man or a white man. Indeed, assuming the status of a guru was a resourceful way for Coltrane—a woman seen primarily by the jazz press as a widow and a caretaker of her late husband's legacy—to address her audience as a musician with agency. We might even think of Coltrane's status as an Indian spiritual guide as echoing the past tradition of racial "passing," and subverting the racialized expectations of a Black woman that, at the time, made it extraordinarily difficult to achieve recognition as an artist. In the fraught dynamics of self and other which I traced back to Fanon, de Beauvoir, Du Bois, and Hegel in chapter 2, the central dynamic is an independent subject acquiring self-consciousness and freedom through its realization of dependence on the other. In late modernity, the asymmetrical racialized and gendered versions of this process are doubled and short-circuited through unsubvertible subjugation and psychic distress. For Coltrane, it may be that to "pass" as having artistic intentions—to be recognized in dialectical terms—was a mode of survival and a disruption of who a modern composer ought to be. At the same time, the spirituality—being a guru and a guide, and the channeler of injunctions—could be a way to produce a polyphonic, Black, feminist intentionality recognized by others. It was one built of social necessity, but its complex staging makes the layered grammars of Coltrane's work a mind-bending example of second-order modernism in which the processes of questioning and enjoining her audiences are intricately layered and distorted.

As an alchemical experimentalism, Coltrane's resistance also made resourceful use of technology. By the 1990s Black cultural criticism had begun to espouse the term *Afro-futurism* to describe an emergent strain of utopian Black cultural production based around creative adoptions and reimaginings of late-breaking technology.[73] One might note her signature use of pitch bend on the Wurlitzer's embedded Orbit III synthesizer that created a virtual reincarnation of her late husband's saxophone, or her later work with the Oberheim OB-8 synthesizer (1983–85) that recalls what she described in her devotional writings as "etheric sirens" and "a spinning sound whirled and revolved so strongly inside my ear that I fell into an unconscious state."[74] To the ears of Kodwo Eshun, Coltrane's use of overdubbing and tape splices retrospectively harnesses metaphysical energies by anticipating a technological condition that emerged in the 1980s and 1990s: remixing. Her harp overdubs on her late husband's "Living Space" (1965, rev. 1972) were "a resurrection technique in which sounds are rematerialized as spirits on tape."[75] In Eshun's inimitable prose, Coltrane's track projects images that are at once ancient, oceanic, and creaturely; it was a spiritual and hallucinatory fractal of the album's intentionality:

> The *Living Space Remix* is . . . devout, a miraculous mosaic of ceremonial strings, an astralized procession of tamboura drones and chimes. Turbulent tintinnabulation heaves in waves that part like the Red Sea; harps plume like the spume of sperm whales off the Galapagos Archipelago; astringent sax squeals like a pig being skewered. . . . The inside-sleeve picture shows a lineup that never existed, electric ghosts playing phantom jazz in tape space-time. The Sleevenotes are signed by John, but read as Alice. To look at the front sleeve is to fall through fractalized stained glass into nested formations of spirals within spirals, kaleidoscopic iterations as blue as mother sky.[76]

Similarly, for Kara Keeling—whose approach echoes Powell's lens of Afro-Asian solidarity—Coltrane's Orientalism, coming from a subjugated position, was exempt from the traditional dynamics of cultural appropriation in which the colonized are materially exploited and subject to silencing projections and fantasies at the hands of the colonizer. Coltrane's uniqueness—her capacity to displace the historical expectations of exotica from India—stems from the affective power and the utopian charge of what Keeling describes—following Édouard Glissant—as an "errant" future expressed in aesthetic form.[77] This allows listeners to move beyond the disappointments of nation-state citizenship and its ongoing racism and instead toward a promise of a transcendent "World Galaxy" of life that also allows one to reimagine a new "terrain of belonging" within a "vast imagined universe."[78] For Keeling, Coltrane's work amounted to a historical "creolization" of African and Asian heritage into a utopian form of a political solidarity. Similarly, with Coltrane's spirituality as a point of focus, Jayna Brown argues that "to insist on the possibility of peace, joy, pleasure, and serenity is a defiantly political act."[79]

In *Blues People*, we may recall that Baraka wrote evocatively of the Black modernist's proclivity toward secret languages, which were developed into tightly knit cultures of exclusivity, and produced socially what he called a "cult of redefinition, in terms closest to the initiated."[80] For Baraka, the Black cool made legendary by the beboppers of midcentury was a practical response to racism; it allowed the suffering of racial subjugation to be resisted through a form of modern withdrawal or social negation.[81] If white serial composers instituted pedagogy exams to teach students to hear music in terms of set theory, the structured atmospheres propagated by Baraka's Black cool developed and questioned the ephemerality of Black life in a way that would have deliberately resisted transparent pedagogies.

Cavell, the white humanist, might suggest we could just continue to improvise our way through debating the problem of modernism in a social field of discourse. But as Baraka, Coleman, and Coltrane make clear, social languages and improvisations cannot ever be thought of as a flat, unstructured field of actors reassessing and debating the rules of art. American postwar modernism is a powerful ideological landscape riven by racial subjugation. It was a field divided by elaborate mimicries, disagreements about the grammars that constitute possible resistance, and complex efforts at spiritual experimentation. Dialectical identities—built on mobile fantasies and social inequities—overwhelmingly structured the grammar of modernism at midcentury. In this charged context, Coltrane reconfigured ineffability around an appeal to universal consciousness in a way that remains polyphonic, overabundant, oblique. She interpellated her listener with a desire for a transcendence that, in her view, would forever appear beyond the capacities of description.

## CHAPTER SEVEN

# Patti Smith—Richard Hell,
# Forces . . . c. 1974

By the time Alice Coltrane's *Universal Consciousness* was released in 1971, the Velvets had dissolved. It was a new era of atmospheric production aided by synthesizers, ubiquitous LPs, advances in multitrack recording, and the mass popularity of amplified live performances. Tudor transitioned from being a pianist of works by others to performances of his own work on modular synthesizers. Reed moved on to his solo career and would soon release the glam rock masterpiece *Transformer* (1972). In the wake of Miles Davis's *Bitches Brew* (1970), jazz fusion was on the rise. Ornette Coleman was experimenting with new soundscapes beyond the framework of instrumental jazz: the opening track from *Science Fiction* (1972) featured vocals from Indian singer Asha Puthli in a soaring, gorgeous slab of cosmic experimental pop.[1] Beyond the coordinates of modernist hyperfractures, new alchemies of the 1970s, fueled by electricity, were pushing music's affective temperatures ever higher.

On February 10, 1971, a twenty-six-year-old Patti Smith—expressing herself with a full range of awkward banter, poetic verse, ecstatic incantation, and outright singing—gave a debut of sorts with guitarist Lenny Kaye for a relatively sedate but clued in, connected, and partly scandalized audience at St. Mark's Church in the East Village.[2] It was a gig opening for a poetry reading by Warhol's associate, whip dancer, and discoverer of the Velvet Underground five years earlier, Gerard Malanga. Smith's performance had debts to Dylan, but whereas Dylan sang in a numinous drawl, Smith earnestly read, intoned, wailed. There is no question the performance was a debut; endings were ragged, with Kaye's guitar often spilling over an extra bar or two, but her talents as a singer were obvious. Smith's opening rendition of Kurt Weill's "Mack the Knife," programmed as a birthday tribute to Bertolt Brecht, sounds a bit like Bobby Darin filtered through the ears of a drunk Dylan. Smith's poems in this performance—most notably the existentialism underpinning the declaration, "Christ died for somebody's sins, but not mine"—would become germs for some of the lyrics in Smith's debut album, *Horses* (1975).[3] Though her musical career would not take off for another three years, Smith's explosive, earnest, and unpredictable way of soaring over the vamp was already coming to life. And here, again in Manhattan, as with Cage and Tudor in Town Hall in 1958 or Coleman at the Five Spot in 1959, was her first moment of recognition by powerful white insiders. The audience was filled with VIPs: Malanga's Factory crowd including Warhol himself, Lou Reed, Brigid Berlin, and Rene Ricard; the poets Allen Ginsberg, John Giorno, Joe Brainard, Annie Powell, and Bernadette Mayer; producer Todd Rundgren; and scenesters Sandy Pearlman, Richard Meltzer, and Danny Fields, the last of whom had recently signed the Detroit-based musicians Iggy and the Stooges and MC5.[4]

Richard Meyers, a twenty-one-year-old aspiring poet and like-minded Rimbaud enthusiast, was also in the audience at St. Mark's. Like Smith, Meyers took his time finding his footing in New York; he struggled for a few years meandering about the social scene working odd jobs. Both found gigs at bookstores: Smith at Scribner's in midtown and Meyers at the Strand in the village, among others. Following the St. Mark's debut, Meyers saw Smith and Kaye perform again at Le Jardin and a third time in 1973 at an opening gig for the New York Dolls at the Mercer Arts Center.[5] Of all the influences on Meyers during these early years in New York, it was these shows—particularly their sheer affective intensity—that stood out to him, altering the trajectory of his work. Meyers described the Dolls' performances as "physical orgies, without much distinction between the crowd and the band." Of Smith, he recalls feeling stunned by her "electrifying, rock-and-roll-level poetry" and for her "seductive and funny and charismatic" way of holding an audience while improvising in a manner "like a bebop soloist or an action painter, off to a whole other plane beyond the beyond."[6] During these years, Smith and Meyers became acquainted through their shared interest in poetry. In 1973 Meyers recruited Smith to submit writing to his small-run poetry press, Dot Dot Dot.[7]

It was in their mutual discovery of rock music that the two would articulate a new philosophical perspective on music's ineffability. During this same period, Meyers and his high school friend Tom Miller, who had joined him in New York, formed a band they called the Neon Boys. Inspired by Dylan's example, they changed their surnames to reference French modernist poets, choosing Verlaine and Hell, respectively (Meyers derived Hell from Rimbaud's famous 1873 poem, "A Season in Hell"). Energized by the electric atmosphere of performances by Smith and the Dolls as well as the stripped-down, angry, glammy rock of Iggy Pop, the MC5, and T. Rex, Verlaine and Hell wrote over half a dozen songs between 1972 and 1973 ("Love Comes in Spurts" and "Blank Generation" date from this period). It was a phase of learning, practicing, and writing; there was no gig for at least a year.

Scenester and manager Terry Ork set the band up with a rehearsal space in 1973–74; around this time they took the name Television, and their set began to take shape.[8] Their first show was for an invited crowd at the rented Townhouse Theater in midtown on March 2, 1974. Readers familiar with the delicate and meandering guitar work of Television's *Marquee Moon* (1977) should note that this 1974 lineup was a very different band: raw, sloppy, unhinged. Hell invited Smith to hear them that spring at CBGBs, just months after the club opened. The downtown scene was still small: the audience probably numbered around thirty or forty. Smith wrote a glowing review for the *Soho Weekly News*. She found Television to be a revelation: amateurish, cheap, immediate, unpretentious. Smith hailed the band's adolescent sexual energy with reference to Chuck Berry, Dylan, and the Stones. To her ears, they were also an avant-garde. After all, Television exemplified the trend of deskilling central to Coleman and the Velvets, a principle that helped break normative contact with stylistic pasts. And like each of the musicians featured in this book's "studio" chapters, the band's earsplitting performances struck typical listeners as mad. Smith marked herself off as a knowing insider to their avant-technological condition: "A few nonbelievers murmur that [the members of Television] look like escapees from some mental ward but those tuned into TV know better."[9]

Television's unruly performance (fig. 7.1) in turn affected the course of Smith's work. As she put it in her memoir, *Just Kids*, "I liked everything about [Television], their spasmodic movements, the drummer's jazz flourishes, their disjointed, orgasmic musical structures."[10] In the summer of 1974, Smith and Television coheadlined a series of shows at Max's Kansas City. Smith also gave Hell a notebook, a gesture that first seems to have slightly intimidated him; in his first entry, he wondered with a combination of anxiety and ambition about how he would fill the pages.[11] In the coming months, Smith's music evolved from the atmospherics of theatrical cabaret to a more aggressive guitar-driven rock.[12] And Smith began casually dating Verlaine. Verlaine, in turn, contributed guitar to her first recording: a 7" single featuring a cover of "Hey Joe" with an erotic spoken-word intro that imagines sex with Jimi Hendrix and the Symbionese Liberation Army in the form of a fantasy about Patty Hearst (she altered a key lyric to "a gun in *her* hand"). Side B was an original song titled "Piss Factory," a poem about breaking free from the drudgeries of her manufacturing job, which she read over the ecstatic vamping of pianist Richard Sohl.[13] In the first few months of 1975, Smith and Television coheadlined a second residency, this time

FIG. 7.1. Richard Hell and Television at CBGB's, 1974. Photograph
by Bob Gruen. Courtesy of the Estate of Bob Gruen.

at CBGBs. This time, Smith joined forces with Television for a few songs.
Meanwhile, drama had emerged in Television: Hell and Verlaine were embroiled in a tense battle of egos. As Smith and Verlaine's relationship grew
close, Hell felt Smith was taking Verlaine's side in the band's dynamics,
which in turn led to distance between Smith and Hell. Before the end of the
CBGBs residency, Hell had been pushed out.

Though the paths of influence were reciprocal, as musicians, Smith's and
Hell's trajectories would diverge. Having self-released her first 7″, Smith's
ambitions coalesced around releasing a full-length record. She searched
for a label and struck gold: following the CBGB's residency in 1975, Clive
Davis's Arista took her on for four albums, beginning with the eternally remembered *Horses* (1975).[14] Armed with major-label publicity, Smith's rise
from the Lower East Side was quick in a way that was similar to the Talking
Heads (Sire, 1976), Blondie (Chrysalis, 1976), and slightly later, Madonna
(Sire, 1983). (The Ramones didn't exactly blow up in 1976; their legacy
mushroomed over time.) Blowing up in this way was also, to be sure, never
simply an organic event. Like Coleman—but unlike the Velvets during
their active career—Smith was heavily promoted in the mainstream press.
Writing for the *New York Times* in March 1975, John Rockwell noted that
Smith was an "alien muse who has come down and captured the essence of
the stylized punk defiance that is at the heart of rock music."[15] Hell himself

noted in his autobiography that "Patti drew the biggest crowds [at CBGBs in 1975]."[16] She began to headline major tours and developed the stature and longevity of someone like Coleman, who was similarly promoted by Columbia. Though Smith took a hiatus in the 1980s to have a family in Detroit, by then it was a break she could afford. She had already built a significant platform for herself and would release eleven studio albums and publish over twenty books of poetry, art, and memoir over four decades.

By comparison, Hell's career as a musician was short, lasting in modest form until the early 1980s. He wrote "Blank Generation" and "Love Comes in Spurts" in 1972 and performed them with Television in 1974. After leaving Television in 1975, Hell took his songs to Johnny Thunders and the Heartbreakers for about a year and added "New Pleasure" to his catalog. In 1976, he formed Richard Hell and the Voidoids. The Voidoids signed to Sire records and released *Blank Generation* the following year. The album earned Hell a measure of recognition as "the demon-eyed New Yorker who could become the Mick Jagger of Punk."[17] He was christened the progenitor of key punk fashions: short spiky hair and torn clothing with safety pins. But Hell's relationship with Sire, a label that had major-label distribution and was seminal in promoting the weirdos of downtown rock, was acrimonious and short lived, ending in few profits and a threatened lawsuit where blame was thrown in both directions for poor sales.[18] Hell's second album, *Destiny Street* (1982), despite some strong songwriting and good performances, was marred by poor mixing and released to little fanfare on a smaller label with a limited budget.[19]

There were artistic differences between the two. Smith's voice was reedy, precise, and huge—naturally full of expressive dimensions from speech to song. Her band was solid and sonically lean, even if they could sometimes feel distant and a bit too polished. What carried the act was Smith's singular way of producing a larger-than-life atmosphere that could scale up and command large audiences. As a musician, Hell was charismatic but limited: his singing, though not imprecise, had a throaty, clownish, unhinged character—like an angrier electric Dylan. In his own words: "The more people there are the more wound up I get and the physical messages, particularly 'rage/disdain' get very exaggerated. I feel like they are viewing me as a freak, like the crowd gathered at a car wreck."[20] The Voidoids were clangorous and abrasive, albeit musically gifted, particularly given Robert Quine's and Ivan Julian's intertwined guitar playing, though the band itself never had much of a platform beyond the work of supporting Hell. As thinkers, Smith and Hell had different strengths: both were exceptional writers, offering no shortage of penetrating interpretations of the creative process and world around them. But Smith's accessible realism spoke with an infectious and magnetic humility, whereas Hell's blunt confessions, often self-conscious and speculative, reflected his introverted tendencies.

At a vernacular register—through their interviews, writings, and artistic output—Smith's and Hell's encounters of 1974 yielded novel philosophical perspectives on music's ineffability. They had mutually discovered that rock music—namely its ineffable ecstatic force—could act as a unique form of alchemy: it could transform poetic language into the atmosphere of a stunning ritual. In their work, music's ineffable forces carried all manner of unconscious desires and fantasies of living the other that were structured by ideological inversions of racial and sexual inequities. Yet despite the notoriety of their creative output, neither Smith nor Hell saw themselves first and foremost as musicians. They understood themselves as poets, fascinated by the powers of language to capture the unruly intensities of reality.[21] They heard music as an affective platform for poetic expression, an atmospheric incarnation or "transmedial exposure" (to use Erin Graff Zivin's term) of the gritty and unnamable thing-in-itself.[22] Their stated influences were well-known figures in bohemian modernism, encompassing Rimbaud, Artaud, Pollock, the Beats, Dylan, and the Stones, among others. Smith in particular created a newly assertive language for women by using singing to channel an aggressive force of affirmation, uplift, and rebellion that had been historically coded as masculine. At the same time, Smith's and Hell's musical debts were to Black artists: the grammar of their sounds was based in back beats, blues vocals, minor pentatonic scales, and cyclical, riff-based grooves.[23] What they accomplished musically, culturally, and philosophically was foundational for the generational primitivism of punk, a highly appropriative, popular—and ultimately subcultural—avant-garde that embodied an indeterminate mixture of anger, dissent, and empowerment.

## Punk Primitivism

Punk was hardly the first avant-garde movement to become popular. By midcentury, to shock, scandalize, and dissent with one's art was, to large swaths of the American public, both exciting and entertaining. The Beats had become household names during the 1950s. Allan Kaprow's happening, devised in the late 1950s, began to circulate as a pop culture phenomenon in the 1960s. And a range of individual artists had breakout moments: Pollock was featured in *Life* magazine in 1949, Coleman was signed to Atlantic in 1959, Cage was on television in 1960, Warhol was a celebrity by 1963, and by 1972, Lou Reed was no less famous. John Coltrane's *A Love Supreme* (1965) would sell over a half-million copies. With these many precedents, by the mid-1970s, an avant-garde movement like punk could quite credibly claim to be engaging, critiquing, and reworking large totalities of popular culture. The genre was also primed for intervention: rock music had become ultraprofitable. Its styles had fractured into a variegated set of largely white culture industry markets that ranged from the anodyne sounds of soft rock to the middlebrow megaspectacle of progressive rock to the edgy and quasi-satanic fantasies of heavy metal. In this context, Smith and Hell—both late to the party of the 1960s—fit the rock critics' desire for a "punk" spirit that reauthenticated the elements of excitement in rock and roll about 1958–66, in a way that was free of the reified, theatrical pretentiousness of all that had been promoted by the culture industry from the late 1960s through the mid-1970s.

There was also a newly established sense of punk historicity. In 1972 Smith's guitarist Lenny Kaye had produced the *Nuggets* double-LP compilation of psychedelic and garage-rock singles from the 1960s.[24] That same year, Lou Reed's star quickly rose in the wake of *Transformer* (1972), which helped position the Velvets as a precursor. Thus, from the perspective of a newly constructed style history, punk extended the dark realism of the Velvets to harsher territory. Its affects and ideals were resolutely negative, its spatial trajectory the reverse of white flight. Punk musicians, typically white, returned from the suburbs to inhabit the broken postindustrial urban landscapes of the 1970s. Their blisteringly loud music had a way of exposing social norms as searing critique. As Greil Marcus described it,

> Damning God and the state, work and leisure, home and family, sex and play, the audience and itself, the music briefly made it possible to experience all those things as if they were not natural facts but ideological constructs: things that had been made and therefore could be altered, or done away with altogether. It became possible to see those things as bad jokes, and for the music to come forth as a better joke. The music came forth as a no that became a yes, then a no again, then again a yes: nothing is true except our conviction that the world we are asked to accept is false.[25]

Malleability above all. Punk negativity was a radicalized freedom to not commit, to walk away, to oscillate wildly, sometimes ironically, about what one will do (or not) having become an angry, dissenting singularity. In his best-known song, Hell aimed straight for the zeitgeist, claiming this indeterminacy as a mode of belonging to a collective ineffable nothingness. (In his diaries, he even considered "THE INNEFABLES [*sic*]" as a possible alternative band name).[26] Behind the microphone, the famed "beat generation" became the "blank generation" (with Hell occasionally omitting the word "blank" as a rhythmic hit), immediately insisting "I can take it or leave it each time."[27] In making such a declaration, Hell sought to enervate his listeners with an ever more uncompromising version of bohemian dissent. He was effectively elevating indeterminacy to an absolute. It was a gesture akin to unleashing the blind striving of Schopenhauerian will as a blanket gesture of self-deterritorialization. Smith was no less spirited, though her diagnosis of generational malaise became a backdrop for a more uplifting intervention:

> In the early-middle Seventies, there wasn't much happening at all to stimulate the minds of the new generations . . . No centralized communication ground for the youth of the future. . . . I just wanted to inspire kids, get 'em off their ass, get 'em thinking, get 'em pissed off, as pissed off as I was. Get them to look around at what was going on, even in the simplest way. Just get them to ask a few questions. You know, interject a little extra joy and pain into their lives.[28]

Smith and Hell both understood themselves to work in a lineage of avant-garde poets and artists.[29] Their favored French bohemians framed subaltern life—infused with poverty, intoxication, mental health struggle, ephemeral attachments, and unprofitable creativity—as a dissenting escape from the world-historical norms of capitalism that had prioritized the aggressive expansion, exploitation, and reproduction of human life. Smith, whose background was working class and who sought education via osmosis in bookstores and proximity to Robert Mapplethorpe's studies at Pratt, accrued a number of intellectual influences for her work: principally Rimbaud, but also Baudelaire, Verlaine, Genet, Gide, Artaud, Brecht, and the Beats. Hell, a child of academics and a prep school dropout, similarly maintained a pedigreed modernist perspective that extended from Baudelaire to the postwar avant-garde. In 1968 he wrote requests to avant-garde cognoscenti from Cage to Duchamp to ask for intellectual manifestos that he hoped to publish in a DIY literary magazine.[30] During these early years in New York, his most important early relationship was with Claes Oldenberg's ex-wife Patty. Through her social connections, Hell met three icons of avant-garde painting: Robert Rauschenberg, Jasper Johns (both sponsors of Cage's 1958 Town Hall concert), and Willem De Kooning.

Hell and Smith conveyed their avant-dissent through an existentialist vernacular that prized freedom from social norms. The Beats—whose work they both knew well—had popularized this tradition by finding and affirming new cultural freedoms through appropriations of jazz, Westernized

Zen, and populist uses of accessible language. In doing so, the Beats exemplified the liberal indeterminacy of the modern white subject on a socially privileged path of searching, self-discovery, and convention questioning. This philosophy became foundational to the "me generation" liberalism of the 1960s and the associated spiritual movements of the New Age, which, as discussed in the prior chapter on Coltrane, had set out to reconcile the multiplicity of global faiths while centering the liberal principle of individual self-discovery.

Yet the negative temperament of Smith's and Hell's work marked a profound affective shift from the 1960s: while postwar liberal individualism remained at the center, 1970s disillusionment ushered in ever more aggressive—even explosive and confrontational—rejections of normativity in ways that revived Cage and Tudor's Artaudian approach to the avant-garde. (Smith gave Hell a copy of the collected works of Artaud at the Voidoids' first run of shows at CBGBs in December 1976.)[31] Smith could be said to have doubled down on 1960s liberalism; she accused the hippies of hypocrisy and claimed that their attendant social movements fell into new forms of dogma. To renew a sense of emancipation, she shaped atmospheres and channeled the energies of her unique charisma to reconnect with audiences as a kind of existentialist shaman. Smith's approach reflected a continuity with the Beats before her insofar as she sought—like the idealists of the 1960s—higher forms of consciousness through the rhythms and arcs of an ecstatic performance. Smith also, however, went beyond the Beats by following Dylan and using music to build a mass following (fig. 7.2).

Hell was no less interested in the ecstasies of performance, reminding himself in a notebook circa 1976 to "Find a church with a real good minister and go listen to his sermon every week."[32] But he rebuked his Beat forebears with even stronger assertions of the powers of the self. In this same notebook, Hell described it as a combative disavowal of history: "Everyone has enemies / And I have more than most / To live you must be dangerous / to those who'd tie you to the past / You've got to know what scares them / And it's obvious to see."[33] At a Delaware prep school a few years earlier, Hell recalled feeling a new dogma had already grown around the experimental, self-searching individualism of Beats like Allen Ginsberg. As he wrote in his autobiography, "I couldn't respond wholeheartedly to the beat writers because there was that ubiquitous youth group who considered pocket copies of *Howl* to be a secret handshake and I didn't want any part of that. I was suspicious of the mystic dogma too, the insistence on spontaneity. I'll be spontaneous when I feel like it."[34]

As mentioned earlier, the negativity espoused by Smith and Hell was driven by a century-long archetype of Western modernity: bohemian

FIG. 7.2. Patti Smith in performance, 1978. Photograph
by Stephen L Harlow. Creative Commons License.

dissent. Though this concept has recurred throughout the studio chapters, here it deserves a fuller historical sketch. Bohemianism stems from an area of Paris that housed subjugated Romani peoples, an ethnic group with roots in medieval North India, who were falsely presumed to have emigrated during the fifteenth century from Bohemia, a Czech region of central Europe. Initially popularized by Henri Murger's *Scenes of a Bohemian Life* (1851), bohemians positioned themselves as allied to, living besides, and imitating an oppressed social class for the purpose of creativity, critique, and insight.[35] Though hierarchical concepts of social class have roots and histories in cultures worldwide, thinkers of the Western Enlightenment created quasi-scientific racial hierarchies to universally categorize human labor for the needs of industrial capitalism.[36] It was these nineteenth-century hierarchies that subtended the bohemian imagination.[37] Bohemians romanticized and appropriated the lives of the dispossessed because, from their perspective, these others embodied resistance to instrumental reasoning by virtue of their social position.

Bohemianism shared with primitivism an atmospheric fantasy to live and incarnate the authenticity of the oppressed with the aims of escaping the norms of the modern subject. As discussed in the "map" of chapter two, the inequities at the root of the late modern social imagination have long provided a cultural template for modernist critique. Dominant music histories promoted by music scholars in the West—imprinted by a conservative bias toward style history—have emphasized white formalism's critique of the past as the backbone of modernism. But modernism has been consistently invested in mimetic fantasies of overturning social reifications by appropriating and stealing from subjugated others. These bohemian-primitivist fantasies played a central role throughout the studio chapters featured in this book, from Tudor and Cage's Asian-inspired esotericism as a critique of the Western ego and its intentional-expressivist musical forms, to Coltrane's Afro-modernist utopianisms borrowed from India that incarnated hyperfractures and alchemies to stand apart from the norms of the jazz industry, to the Velvets decadent alchemical explosions that sought a perception-deconstructing realism via calibrated variants of African and Indian forms.

To Smith and Hell, Rimbaud was the heroic poet of social negation, the quintessential bohemian. And Rimbaud's bohemianism was profoundly inflected by negrophilia. The symbolist poet positioned Blackness as an inversion of the white bourgeois imperative to work. In "A Season in Hell" Rimbaud fantasized about becoming Black and used the offensive term *nègre* to mark his transformation. Below I have reproduced the Varèse translation, which circulated widely at the time:

> Yes, my eyes are closed to your light. I am a beast, a n——. But I can be saved. You are sham n——s, you, maniacs, fiends, misers. Merchant, you are a n——. Judge, you are a n——. General, you are a n——. Emperor, old itch, you are a n——. You have drunk of the untaxed liquor of Satan's still.—Fever and cancer inspire this people. Cripples and old men are so respectable that they are fit to be boiled.—The smartest thing would be to leave this continent where madness stalks to provide hostages for these wretches. I enter the true kingdom of the children of Ham. Do I know nature yet? Do I know myself?—*No more words*. I bury the dead in my belly. Shouts, drums, dance, dance, dance, dance! I can't even see the time when, white men landing, I shall fall into nothingness. Hunger, thirst, yells, dance, dance, dance, dance! . . . The white men are landing! The cannon! We must submit to baptism, put on clothes, work.[38]

Rimbaud's caricature is symptomatic of primitivism circa 1880: the narrator fantasizes about becoming a dark-skinned cannibal, a shouting, drumming dancer on the void. Kristen Ross has explored the ways Rimbaud's fantasy of becoming Black in "A Season in Hell" (a poem she notes was once titled *Livre nègre*) effectively inverts the narrative of the white, European, normative bildungsroman into a youthful, dissenting narrative of "pure transformational energy" that refuses the capitalist demand for productive labor.[39] This critique of capitalism is no doubt evident in Rimbaud's text, but at the level of social recognition, the poet's fantasy is also internally ambivalent, even fraught. To invert the order of subjugation, Rimbaud seeks out a space of prelinguistic dehumanization: "*No more words.*" Yet any force of dissent that emerges is hardly the simple product of recognizing oneself in the wordlessness of the other. Rimbaud's "barbarian" or "pagan" perspective is in fact a loquacious, reflective one; after all, for him poetry scales the heights of self-consciousness. A paradox emerges in the hubris of Rimbaud's inversion of the social order: it entails a tense and ignorant moment in which his frenzy to be the other overtakes his capacity to listen. In this strange and unstable dialectic, one can never simply recognize oneself as the other; it is a dissenting fantasy that is as uncertain as it is aggressive.

By the time Rimbaud's ambivalent primitivism reached postwar US youth through dog-eared English editions in the 1950s, white bourgeois musicians were already experimenting with their egos by imitating, inhabiting, and enveloping Black musical forms.[40] As discussed in chapter five, rock musicians had begun to appropriate Black life and its forms in the late 1950s and early 1960s, when Black and white musicians alike were playing Black-derived rhythm and blues. A new erotic grammar streamed into high school gyms via electromagnetic waves and live bands in ways that scandalized white Judeo-Christian sexual norms. The aesthetic shock for whites was no less ambivalent: to live, love, and sing Black musical freedom was to imagine other white audiences (and parts of the white self) recoiling at the amplification of moral disorder while narcissistically grabbing the microphone themselves. It was through this ambivalent dialectic that Lou Reed listening to radio DJ Alan Freed aligned with Dylan's love of Little Richard, Keith Richards's fixation on Chuck Berry and Muddy Waters, and Smith's attachment to James Brown. None were reducible to identifications, all were atmospheric experiments structured by a polyphony of hubris, blindness, and disavowal. Then came the philosophy: throughout the 1960s Rimbaud's bohemian poetry would become foundational for white rock musicians—like Dylan, Jim Morrison, Smith, and Hell—who were looking for an icon of mystical negrophilia to deepen their self-consciously modernist approaches to this practice.

A final complicating factor was that 1970s punk was also, in some circles, inspired by Afro-modernists.[41] As noted in chapter five, Reed had been interested in free jazz since his first year at Syracuse and was inspired by Coleman and Albert Ayler while writing "Sister Ray" (1968), a groove-driven edifice of rock hypnosis now recognized as an iconic protopunk song.[42] Verlaine cited Ayler and John Coltrane as early influences on his development as a musician.[43] Hell's guitarist Robert Quine was influenced by Miles Davis's experimental atmospheres of the early 1970s.[44] Smith notes Coltrane as an influence. To these rock musicians, Afro-modernism aligned the pathos of Black subjugation with outwardly noisy, noncommercial dissent. It was a motif familiar to readers of Mailer's "The White Negro" (1957): white appropriation of a Black "freedom drive" (to use Moten's term) could give punk emancipation the weight of a vernacular history.[45] From Cage to Stockhausen, the comparatively white and academic lineages of dissonance, while widely recognized, were of limited use to punk vernaculars. Afro-modernist dissent, by contrast, had the social credibility of a Black vernacular that Reed, Verlaine, and others could appropriate against the repressions, silences, and hypocrisies of suburban normativity.

It is of course a well-known characteristic of whiteness that it purports to go unmarked as a race or ethnicity. The rock culture industry had a way of draining Black musicians and fans from the genre, reshaping its history to center around Dylan, the Stones, and the Beatles, thus ensuring its efficacy as white counterculture. By the 1960s and 1970s—even as Black musicians invented the grammars, and many of its early stars were Black—rock music, as Jack Hamilton put it, "came to be understood as the natural province of whites."[46] As exemplified by Questlove's film, *Summer of Soul* (2021), what was once called R & B had become two largely segregated genres by 1969: (white) rock and (Black) soul with two distinct audiences and countercultures. The 1970s punks only furthered the trajectory of punk's whiteness. As Lester Bangs memorably put it in 1979, "Most of the SoHo bands are as white as John Cage."[47] The racial divide, it should be said, was not absolute.[48] As Maureen Mahon has shown, despite obvious segregation, Black men and women alike were foundational and enduring contributors to rock music.[49] In fact, there were also a number of influential Black punks, notably Hell's guitarist Ivan Julian, Poly Styrene of X-Ray Spex, and the DC hardcore band Bad Brains, among others. White musicians were also presences in a number of important soul bands, notably Sly and the Family Stone.

Yet, in these early years of the 1970s, the ideological terrain of whiteness in rock music was formidable. By mimicking and appropriating Blackness in social spaces that were predominantly white, punk functioned as a case study in white privilege, deflected and disavowed by an obsessive rhythm of self-negation and social critique. In this context, it was a scandalous provocation for Smith, Reed, or any other rock musician to so willfully provoke their listeners that they secretly imagined themselves and their music as nonwhite. When hearing Television for the first time at CBGBs, for example, Smith imagined her compatriots embodying an exotic violence she associated with vaguely Middle Eastern and Caribbean locales. In her *Soho Weekly News* review of the band, she remarked that Verlaine's guitar tuning between songs was "moslem [*sic*]," the band's unconventional sense of timing "persian," and Ficca's drumming a "psychotic calypso."[50] As her career quickly developed in the coming years, Smith deepened her commitment to a brazen primitivism that closely paralleled Rimbaud's.

This was particularly evident in interviews. In 1975 Smith described her adolescent musical interests as focused on Black musicians like Smokey Robinson, James Brown, and Marvin Gaye, until she heard Dylan, Jagger, and later, Reed, and found she could proudly admire—and thus aspire to become a version of—Mailer's White Negro, thus in a literal sense fulfilling Rimbaud's famed declaration that "I is an other" (*Je est un autre*).[51] She imagined Brian Jones tapping into African "roots" and Jagger and Richards—in a dream of hers—speaking a "funny language" to one another that "reminded [her] of voodoo, Haiti or something."[52] With respect to reggae, Smith alarmed interviewers by trumpeting a broader trajectory of white appropriation, remarking that "[Rastafarianism is] not a black thing anymore; it's not even Jamaican. It belongs to us now."[53] The story was similar with Hendrix, who, in her view, actually "became white" in a kind of cross-racial synthesis due to his interest in what she understood as the whiteness of high art, cosmic universality, and poetry.[54]

Then there were the more brazen choices of 1978. Smith recorded a song called "Rock 'n' Roll N——" for *Easter* (1978), featuring lyrics that flagrantly proposed to redefine the offensive and triggering term n—— to entail anyone, regardless of race, who struggled "outside society." The lyrics echoed the passage of Rimbaud's "A Season in Hell" quoted earlier. In the song, she describes Jesus, Pollock, Hendrix to be n——s. In associated interviews, she added Jagger and herself to the list.[55] The liner notes to the LP contain an oblique paragraph, devoid of punctuation that explains her choice:

> n—— no invented for color it was MADE FOR THE PLAGUE the word (art) must be redefined-all mutants and the new babes born sans eyebrow and tonsil-outside logic-beyond mathematics poli-tricks baptism and motion sickness-any man who extends beyond the classic form is a n—— one sans fear and despair-one who rises like rimbaud beating hard gold rythumn outta soft solid shit-tongue light is coiling serpant is steaming spinal avec ray gun hissing scanning copper head w/ white enamel eye wet and shining crown reeling thru gleem vegetation ruby dressing of thy lips puckering whispering pressing high bruised thighs silk route mark prussian vibrating gushing milk pods of de/light translating new languages new and abused rock n roll and lashing from tongue of me n——[56]

With its asyntactic flow of the creaturely, abject, erotic, and metallic, Smith's liner note attempted to define n—— as an avant-garde expression "outside logic-beyond mathematics," as "any man who extends beyond the classic" with musical-poetic "de/light translating new languages new and abused." In another instance she noted it indicated "an artist-mutant that was going beyond gender."[57] There are literary references: that of "rimbaud beating hard gold rythumn," as well as a "plague" that indexes Rimbaud's *Illuminations* no less than Artaud's *The Theatre and Its Double* (1938), with its revitalizing focus on the physicality of violence.[58]

By this point in her career, Smith's influence was considerable, and the choice to amplify Rimbaud's primitivism by deracinating the most loaded racial epithet in English was taken as offensive. In interviews, she defended the choice as one intended to be "off the cuff," funny, and permitted because she grew up as working class around Black Americans.[59] At the level of ideology, one could argue that Smith was simply revealing the underlying primitivism quietly desired by millions of rock fans while her white critics' offense could come off as scandalized and self-righteous. Rock as illicit sexual primitivism was, after all, the opening thesis of Bangs's 1971's famous stream of consciousness essay, "James Taylor Marked for Death."[60] Smith was also hardly alone: the idealized universalism of the civil rights era was something of a faded memory: white rock musicians of the era were seeking to shock audiences with everything from offensive appropriations to outright racism: from the aforementioned (see chap. 5) examples of David Bowie admiring Hitler (1976) and Eric Clapton's racist stage rant in the UK (1976) to the skinhead punk movements of the late 1970s, Sid Vicious's swastika T-shirt (1978), Reed's purportedly ironic song "I Wanna be Black" (1978), and Ian MacKaye of Minor Threat (and later Fugazi) defending his use of n—— because he, like Smith, grew up around Black Americans (1983).[61]

One should not collapse the difference between offensive and hubristic acts of appropriation, purported irony, and explicit white supremacy. But the racialization of punk and rock entailed profound inequities of perspective. Black musicians of the period endured the theft of musical innovations, the repeated trauma of "n——" echoing in one's scene, while innumerable white rock musicians claimed to inhabit the other as a figure, a costume, a provocation with a certain measure of arrogance. The empathetic and epistemic gap between these two racialized experiences meant that rock musicians could not see that their bohemian primitivism—lived as a calibrated atmosphere of rock attitude, sexual promiscuity, heroin addiction, or just feeling cool in New York—for the narcissistic theft that it was. In a sign of how problematic the situation had become, Bangs's "The White Noise Supremacists" (1979) criticized punk's unsettled, ambivalent, and often problematic relationship to racism as a ubiquitous and nagging issue afflicting the scene while acknowledging that Bangs himself had contributed to the problem.[62]

In adapting Black musical idioms, Hell was a Rimbaldian bohemian, to say nothing of the fantasies underpinning the decadence of a narcotics addiction (after all, he named himself after Rimbaud's fantasy). But in lyrics, interviews, and writings, Hell was circumspect on the topic of race. His lyrics tended to engage social issues obliquely and often staged observations of the world through personalized confessions and anxieties. And the racialization of Hell's work environment was complex. On the one hand, in the Voidoids, he collaborated with a Black guitarist, Julian, which one assumes would lead him to be cautious about reproducing racist biases and stereotypes. Yet the spaces in which the Voidoids circulated were hardly safe, racially integrated cultural spaces. Julian reported to Bangs that he often had to endure hearing "n——" and added that it triggered an uncontrollable sense of rage.[63] Bangs himself confesses having used "n——" around Julian and offers a measure of repentance by enjoining his readers to "get rid of all those little verbal barbs," adding that punk "irony" or "misanthropy" was often lost on general audiences. In his words, "anytime you conclude that life stinks and the human race mostly amounts to a pile of shit, you've got the perfect breeding ground for fascism . . . your irony just might be his cup of hate."[64] Indeed, as Sontag noted of a parallel fashion for Nazi-inspired pornography in the early 1970s, a new excess of liberal individualism was turning fascism and white supremacy into a form of regressive theater.[65] Punk primitivism similarly courted a socially dangerous and potentially hateful sense of indeterminacy.

## Poetry, Alchemy, Force

With ambivalent identities built on a romantic industry of theft, mimicry, and racialized fantasy, bohemian punks hardly understood themselves as nihilists; in their view, normative capitalism was the true nihilism as it quietly assented to social hierarchies through its moralizing commitment to repressive norms and upward mobility. And for Smith's and Hell's bohemianism, poetry was an emancipatory vector: to call oneself a poet at midcentury meant to dissent against the parameters of capitalist society and claim the virtue of elevated self-consciousness.[66] Insofar as language was taken to be ideologically saturated with social norms, Smith and Hell understood poetry as breaking through linguistic convention and carrying readers toward the search for the real.

How exactly Smith's and Hell's poetry did this was complex. Influenced by Dylan and the Velvets, in 1972 Smith followed the Beats in prizing immediacy and affective impact. It was a view of poetry diametrically opposed to the esotericism of famed modernists like T. S. Eliot and Ezra Pound, whose work presumed sophisticated efforts of interpretation:

> I can seduce people. I got good punchlines, you know. I got all the stuff that Americans like. Some of it's dirty. There's a lot of good jokes. I mean I write to entertain. I write to make people laugh. . . . Everything I write has a motive behind it. I have to write to somebody. I write the same way I perform. I mean you only perform because you want people to fall in love with you. You want them to react to you.[67]

As a teenager, she thought of poetry as an earnest vehicle for romance, dream, and fantasy and "had no idea of what to do with language." She eventually "started seeing language as magic" and began using short, direct, three-word sentences, a choice influenced by Mickey Spillane's popular crime novels.[68] Smith fused this method to her interest in the erotic, imagining poetry as less a form of romantic expression and more a narcissistic projection of the ineffable dimensions of her own desire:

> I started dreaming of [ Judy]. . . . I had such a strong mental contact with this girl that I couldn't talk to her. So I was at the typewriter. . . . I write with the same fervor as Jackson Pollock used to paint. All the things that we had, like, we loved the movie *Judex*, I started writing down in a line, just words but, you know, words that were perfect, words like "kodak," "radiant," "jellybitch," and I just tried writing these words. . . . I was trying to write her a letter but I had no idea where she was, so obviously it was a piece of narcissism. . . . I was trying to project with words and language a photograph of Judy.[69]

Rimbaud further expanded Smith's imagination during this formative period of the late 1960s. She cleaved to Rimbaud's transcendent aspirations ("to arrive at the unknown through the disordering of all the senses" as she would have read in *Illuminations*) in a way that opened a mode of expression that was at once mystical and esoteric. This elevated sense of self-consciousness helped Smith imagine escaping the normative conditions of working-class labor.[70] As noted earlier, Kristen Ross has investigated in detail Rimbaud's critical relationship to the bourgeois imperative to work.[71] In a poem titled "Piss Factory" that was a live favorite in 1973 and would become her debut recording in 1974, Smith similarly positioned Rimbaud as awakening her emancipation from wage labor.[72] The symbolist poet gave her mystical permission to imagine and dictate the existence of "fantasies" and "obscure events."

> I'm allowing myself to get more obscure. I've always been against that. I like people to say what they mean. But what I'm moving into now is sort of the style of [Rimbaud's] *Illuminations* but more describing situations that have not happened. . . . I like writing like a news reporter about more obscure events. In other words my writing is much more didactic. Documentaries of fantasies. That gives me a chance to get really obscure in terms of actions but it gives the reader a chance because it's written so rigidly they don't know something really bizarre is happening. . . . To me when I am both inspired and have light emitting from me and feel real natural and intuitive but also at the same time clearly walk into my brain and look around.[73]

To "have light emitting from me" or to "walk into my brain and look around" was an affirmation of ecstatic self-consciousness. It powerfully echoed Rimbaud's declaration in *Illuminations* that, in a bout of poetic ecstasy, "I witness the birth of my own thought."[74] Hell was reading the same Rimbaud texts as Smith and similarly described poetry in terms of unparalleled immediacy and penetrating insight. In his view poetry had the power to press beyond conventional appearances, induce exceptional powers of thought, and arrive at the awareness of the truth. And in line with Smith and the Beats, it should also be accessible and powerfully connective. In a diary entry of 1970 he writes,

> In works like my favorite poem I attempt to make a poem occur in the reader's consciousness rather than "make a poem" that the reader has to be ultra-sophisticated to find the poetry in, be moved by. This is the aim to pursue. . . . The premise of metaphysics is the body [. . .] on the same principle that makes telephones sexy, or that makes babies resemble their parents: any thing or concept bears the qualities of its originator.[75]

For Hell, the social immediacy of poetic language had a critical power. It could dissolve the ideological "garbage" of adolescent perceptions. In the same diary entry, he described the meanings of poetry in metaphysical terms indebted to the French symbolism and esotericism he read and admired:

> The world is so fucking rich with magic—poems should be powerful catalysts little capsules to snap open gristle in the mind that grew at ado-

lescence or actually much younger ostensibly to enable us to sort out our perceptions and attend to the "vital" ones. The poetry capsule should dissolve this garbage and reveal marvelous universe.[76]

For Hell and Smith, music's ineffability could elevate these poetic interventions into alchemies. Because for both, rock music carried an exceptional, even scandalous degree of force. It set new standards of intensity for eros in art conveyed by an undeniable, numbing, cathartic loudness. We might note that Smith and Hell were conscious of the way electrified alchemies had already caused ontological scandals, as with Dylan's 1965 turn from the political agendas of the folk revival to the confrontational obliqueness of a raucous band. In something of a nod to Dylan, by adding Kaye's guitar to her performance at St. Mark's in 1971, Smith claimed to have "desecrated" the very medium of the poetry reading.[77] For Smith, the physical presence of sound and rhythm—particularly rhythms influenced by Black music—pointed to poetry's future. And Jagger, one of the most accomplished white blues singers of the era, was the exemplar:

> I think Mick Jagger is one of the greatest living performers. . . . Just the drum beat rhythm and Mick's words or refrains that are always magic could have been very powerful and could have I believe held the audience. And that excited me so much I almost blew apart because I saw almost a complete future of poetry. I really saw it, I really felt it. I got so excited I could hardly stand being in my skin, and, like, I believe in that.[78]

For Smith the future of poetry was a channeling of electric alchemy, which she registers here in terms of its ineffable affective force: "I could hardly stand being in my skin." To feel as if one "almost blew apart" when being enraptured by the Black atmospheric grammars of the blues provided underpinnings for Smith's subjectivity as an artist.

During the 1970s this music grew ever more intense and uncompromising. When recalling his early experiences playing rock music in 1973, Hell offered a complementary meditation on the affective powers of musical sound. It was a quasi-phenomenological analysis of Television's immersive experiments in collective composition. Hell's second-order modernism calls into question one's capacity to parse the band's overwhelming sound into anything more granular than the "magic powers" of an alchemical mass:

> The hilarious incomparable intoxication of materializing into being these previously nonexistent patterns of sound and meaning and physical motion. It was as fraught and sublime as great Renaissance religious

painting; Bellini's *St. Francis*. . . . The power and beauty of it was un-
imaginable until then. It can't be overstated, that initial rush of realizing, of experiencing, what's possible as you're standing there in the rehearsal room with your guitars and the mikes turned on and when you
make a move this physical information comes pouring out and you can
do or say anything with it. It was like having magic powers. The ability
to create action at a distance. The sounds that came from the amplifiers were absurdly moving and strange, the variety of them so wide in
view of the fact that they came from flicks of our fingers and from our
vocal noises, and the way that it was a single thing, an entity, that was
produced by the simultaneous reactive interplay of the four band members combining various of their faculties. We were turned into a sound,
a flow of sound. I remember having a moment of weird revelation once,
that each moment of a phonograph record being played, each mil-
limeter of information conveyed via the needle to the amplifier to the
speaker to the ear, is one sound. A whole orchestra is one sound, altering
moment by moment, no matter how many instruments go into producing it. And, as our band rehearsed, in each moment we made the sound
spray out in arrays we could instantly alter, emanating from inside us and
our interplay and our inner beings combined, playing. And the sound
included words.[79]

Hell's reflection captures, at length, the numinous alchemy of a rock
band made loose and loud by deskilled punks of the period. It also echoed
the Velvets interest in a singular envelope of amplified sound. Cage, the erst-
while scribe of 1950s hyperfractures, had taken notice of the same postwar
stylistic rupture into inconsistency, which he similarly noted was defined
by its distinctive affective force: "If the amplification is sufficient . . . you are
inside the object, and you realize that this object is a river. With rock, there
is a change of scale: you are thrown into the current. Rock takes everything
with it."[80] If Smith "almost blew apart" when feeling this Dionysian force,
Hell links the "absurdly moving and strange" atmosphere of Television's alchemy to traditionally ineffable experiences: that of birth or of the divine.
He continues, musing on its metaphysical intensity:

All through this book I've had to search for different ways to say "thrill,"
"exhilaration," "ecstatic" to communicate particular experiences. Maybe
the most extreme example of this class of moment is what I'm trying to
describe here. What it felt like to first be creating electrically amplified
songs. It was like being born. It was everything one wants from so called

God. The joy of it, the instant inherent awareness that you could go anywhere you wanted with it and everywhere was fascinatingly new and ridiculously effective. It was like making emotion and thought physical, to
be undergone apart from oneself.[81]

"It was like making emotion and thought physical, to be undergone apart
from oneself." This is an instance where a musician, as I put it in chapter 1,
becomes a metaphysician of their own techniques. An alchemical flux, one
that Smith herself described as mad or psychotic, is for Hell something that
unfolds "apart from oneself" (again, Rimbaud: "I is an other"). A sonic and
spectral primitivism takes flight, via amplifiers, hands, and arms, as a warp
zone of empowerment ("you could go anywhere you wanted with it"). Note,
however, that Television's alchemy was not sheer Schopenhauerian will or
unbridled vitality; it was dialectically punctuated by form and structure.
Movements of the arm, wrist, and fingers had to find synchronicity: idioms,
identities, and attitudes had to be calibrated. But the visual transparency of
scored material had firmly been sublimated into a punctuated river of electricity that was "fascinatingly new and ridiculously effective." Hell never
explained this little bit of music philosophy to Smith; he didn't have to. As
praxis, its atmosphere was obvious and seductive when the band was on stage.

Electrified rock alchemy provided a way out of a modern paradox of poetic form: "language as magic" (to use Smith's phrase) could conjure the
most repressed and inarticulable truths, but without the force of music,
poetry could end up an idle meditation. Atmosphere became a key term.
With music, Smith declared in "Gloria," "I move in this atmosphere where
anything is allowed." For his part, Hell similarly noted of his band, "[the
Voidoids] were there to help construct the space consistent with me, a musical atmosphere I could breathe, in which I could act and carry out my intentions."[82] When asked in 1972 what would make poetry becoming a "big
public art" again, Smith responded, "Physical presentation in performing
is more important than what you're saying. . . . If your quality of intellect is
high and your love of the audience is evident and you have a strong physical
presence you can get away with anything."[83] Again, Jagger is the exemplar:
"his presence and his power to hold the audience in his palm. There was
electricity."[84] Smith heard how the metaphysics of poetry, when fused to
the sound of Black-derived R & B grammars, could produce a second-order
modernism: an atmosphere that was forceful, void inducing, beyond san-
ity. Ineffability in action. Like the alchemies brewing in the Velvets, in Coltrane, in Miles Davis, Smith and Hell bent coordinates of perception: What
forms are these, anyway? Two chords?

The accessibility of punk's point-blank force sparked debates among critics and intellectuals about its status in the history of modernism. Smith's work effectively proposed to upend Adornian models of an elite fracture: her charisma channeled a popular anarchism of the spirit, a spirituality of the real. The underlying political economy was primed: by the mid-1970s, the culture industry knew very well that bohemian rebellion could be massively profitable. Eschewing the Greenbergian model for modernism that positioned it as a self-conscious, formal negation of popular kitsch, Robert Christgau framed Smith's total commitment to popular accessibility as its own kind of "formal adventurousness," one that was continuous with the history of the avant-garde:

> Avant-garde anarchists have always been especially fascinated by popular imagery and energy, which they have attempted to harness to both satirical and insurrectionary ends. Patti simply runs as far as she can with the insurrectionary possibility: Her attempt to utilize the popular form authentically is her version of the formal adventurousness which animates all artistic change.[85]

Musicians themselves tended to characterize punk in broader philosophical terms. Hell, in 1976, at the height of his aspirations, subscribed to a variant of musical exceptionalism that was almost Schopenhauerian. He insisted that rock music alchemies had the affective force to summon "passions and ideas too radical for any other form." Celebrating the profit motive with characteristic abandon, Hell joined this to a loosely Hegelian claim that the medium of rock was the most responsive "outlet" for the historical zeitgeist:

> The truest, best work takes into consideration and takes as its territory every bit of information from every source. That's why the occupation of rock and roll is so appealing to inspired people now—it's an outlet for passions and ideas too radical for any other form. (Plus you can get rich and have fun at the same time.) . . . That's simply one of the definitions of the form, like making a sonnet fourteen lines [long]. . . . [A modernist artist] can see the condition you're in and because conditions keep changing very quickly you're only as good as you are modern.[86]

And yet, well-schooled in the idea of modernism as a self-aware dissent, when his mass-cultural aspirations faltered, Hell turned to traditional Greenbergian dichotomies. In a 1978 interview with Sontag, Hell noted that high (or "elitist") art existed to satisfy itself, while popular art had power and influence. What was a dialectical contrast for Greenberg had become, for Hell, a working paradox: he now bemoaned the artistic compromises of working in the commercial sphere of rock music. Sontag effectively drilled home the point and noted the tension: while music and poetry were balanced in his work, poetry alone, without the affective force of music, would have a far smaller audience.[87]

## Paradoxes of the Erotic

Punk's intermedial exposure created complex and powerful atmospheres. The ineffability of social desires—one's shimmering desire to be, or not, or to admire and appropriate, or to empower one's ego and disavow its origins, mimicries, and debts—were made palpable by music's distinct and specific affective forces. And the traffic of the erotic desires in play was often ephemeral, making music an apt carrier for new grammars of sexual rebellion.

Smith's outlandish charisma, ambition, and slender profile hardly conformed to any idealized conception of femininity. Interviewer Susin Shapiro described her in 1975 as "word-crazed and crooning, a cross between Keith Richards and Mia Farrow; an omnisexual high priestess careening freely between the genders, elevating rock n' roll into incantation."[88] In 1976 another critic wrote, "Like all of them—Jagger, Dylan, Bowie, Stewart—intense sexuality was sped along by gender ambiguity. This fascination with androgynous creativity and [Smith's] own ability to exchange sexual roles influenced her early works."[89] Though Smith's famed gender fluidity anticipated twenty-first-century conceptions of queer identity, her underlying thinking reflected popular discourses on gender and sexuality of the postwar period. In fact, Smith's thinking on gender could appear broadly Jungian; she spoke about varied degrees of masculine and feminine tendencies in human societies. It was through this lens that she described her own nonconforming gender: "I don't think I hold any sex. I think I have both masculine and feminine rhythms in my work."[90] In an early poem entitled "Female" (1967), Smith traced this to her childhood desires:

> female. feel male. Ever since I felt the need to choose I'd choose male. I felt boy rythums [sic] when I was in knee pants. So I stayed in pants. I sobbed when I had to use the public ladies room. My undergarments made me blush. Every feminine gesture I affected from my mother humiliated me.[91]

As an adolescent, her mirror for gender experimentation became the Stones, who, in Smith's view, exhibited a strange masculinity infused by counterintuitive femininity that was differently accessible to men and women:

> I can tie the Stones in with every sexual release of my late blooming adolescence. The Stones were sexually freeing confused american children, a girl could feel power. lady glory, a guy could reveal his feminine side without being called a fag. masculinity was no longer measured on the football field.[92]

Smith was struck by queer undertones in the Stones' performative approach to masculinity, for instance, in Jagger's long hair and scrawny frame to his strutting and playful stage presence. In some ways, her persona was an inversion of Jagger's: a heterosexual woman inclined to live and breathe masculinity (as in "a girl could feel power"). Smith's cathexis to masculine empowerment extended to her personal and professional relationships as well. She took comfort in being protected and supported by a man: "If I have a man who believes in me and pushes me, I can do anything. I'm just that kind of girl, y' know. If I'm protected I feel good."[93] And like many heterosexual men, Smith found a queer inspiration in the otherwise normative figure of the feminine muse ("a woman I can be male with"). In discussing the muse here, she distances herself from homosexuality and goes so far as to concede her subservience to men (with a reference to the Stones "Under My Thumb" [1966]):

> Who are most artists? Men. Who do they get inspired by? Women. The masculinity in me gets inspired by female. I get, you know, I fall in love with men and they take me over. I ain't no women's lib chick. So I can't write about a man because I'm under his thumb but a woman I can be male with. I can use her as my muse. I tried to make it with a chick once and I thought it was a drag. She was too soft. I like hardness. I like to feel a male chest. I like bone. I like muscle. I don't like all that soft breast.[94]

This face value affirmation of masculine dominance set Smith apart from second-wave feminists of the 1960s who subjected these ideological norms to deeper critique (and she makes clear: "I ain't no women's lib chick"). Smith considered masculine dominance a historical fact with little ideological power. As she noted elsewhere: "most of my heroes are men simply because most of the heaviest people in the world have been men."[95] But because she identified as a woman and made explicit, often aggressive, use of sexuality in her work (Hell once described her as "a natural born sex waif"), her work could hardly be reduced to the repressive status quo.[96] Paradoxes of eros animate her work: she assented to submission (even "giggling at herself like a five year old" as Hell recalled) while overtly subverting it through her confrontational performances in a worn out white T-shirt and dark pants in ways that could make her appear indistinguishable from someone like Jagger. By maintaining legibility as a woman while subverting both second-wave feminist and normative gender molds, Smith devised a magnetic, queer position that anticipated elements of third-wave feminism.[97]

She accomplished this all by thinking in, though, and with music. The eros of her method was built out of rock's primitivist alchemy: the confidence that allowed a woman to function as a surrogate spiritual leader for youth would have been rare if not unthinkable in a voluntary community of the late 1960s and early 1970s. It was specific to the ambivalent fantasies of punk primitivism, Rimbaldian tangles with social inequity, and a medium of an amplified rock-stage spectacle of the mid-1970s. In building her improvised, unbridled, paradoxically gendered being, Smith opened new grammars for aggressive self-assertion by women singers, establishing a precedent for Poly Styrene of X-Ray Spex, Siouxsie and the Banshees, the Slits, the Raincoats, Lene Lovich, Joan Jett, Pat Benatar, Kathleen Hanna, Kim Deal and the Breeders, Courtney Love, and riot grrrl bands of the 1990s.

These grammars were first individuated in the process of Smith's early musical performances. For their final song of a set at a live-broadcast fundraiser for WBAI-FM at a church on the Upper East Side on May 28, 1975, the band performed "Gloria (In Excelsis Deo)," an R & B song Van Morrison had recorded as "Gloria" in 1964.[98] This was an early lineup before they had enlisted drummer Jay Dee Daugherty. Van Morrison's original featured a loop of three hypnotic chords that were easy to play (E, D, and A); the lyrics grew out of sung improvisations about a woman he lusted after named Gloria. The idea of developing a rendition of the song came from Kaye, editor of the *Nuggets* collection, and an expert on 1960s R & B.[99] Smith and her band stretched it into a propulsive recitation, an ecstatic chant. It is instructive to note that their most distinctive writing in the period was not really songwriting at all; it was based in Smith's improvisations over long hypnotic grooves.

"Gloria" begins with her existentialist slogan from "Oath" (1970), first delivered at St. Mark's in 1971, "Jesus died for somebody's sins, but not mine." This lyrical choice came about when Smith first plucked an E on Hell's bass (which he had recently sold to them) and found herself instinctively reciting the lines.[100] After introducing herself in the song's opening lines as someone with an unmatched sense of self-reliance, she and her band build up the three chords into an ever more rapturous and erotic frenzy. If Van Morrison and his band were dynamically steady, Kaye and Sohl's interlocking guitar and piano is terraced in its energy level: it begins with chill lounge chords and proceeds to a series of escalating hypnotic platforms. It culminates in an obscure sexual act ("she whispers to me and I take the big plunge"). Like the Velvets' "Heroin," the tempo speeds up over the course of the song before eventually slowing to a final cadence. By October 1976, at a performance in Belgium where Kaye's guitar, locked in a groove with Daugherty's drumming, is unusually high in the mix, the level of ecstasy is explosive.[101]

With her vocals, Smith stages a paradoxical sexuality: most concretely, she is a woman desiring Gloria. But she is also inhabiting the voice of a man, arguably even taking it over. At a more abstract level, she is allowing others who desire Gloria to feel indeterminate lust through and about her as a shamanic vehicle. These audiences could be men, they could be women, they could be nonconforming. In "Gloria," Smith functions as a shapeshifting vehicle for all while remaining a focus of desire herself. Through it all, she paradoxically retained a sense of authenticity: unlike Dylan, Smith was emotionally exposed; unlike Bowie, she played no characters. Her vocals were piercing, often speech-like, wailing and shouting around a well-tuned reciting tone, but she had the ear and the accuracy to take these risks. Philosophically, Smith's performance was a demonstration of music's affective electricity (through this song, she contends, the band "became a rock band"). In so doing, Smith also exposed her own sexual desire in music, and thus showed us—in a rare, dangerous, and scandalous instance—what the medium of music really is. As noted in chapter 1, this ontology of music is easy to forget: music is sex and, at the same time, it is also an indeterminate space of desire apart from any physical act. All the while, it is still aiming for physical impact; audiences can't stop dancing and feeling Gloria's charge. Her music set in motion a spectral fantasy that riffed (quite literally) on the atmospheric revolution of Chuck Berry and Alan Freed's DJ sets two decades earlier.

Propulsive immediacy is neither regressive nor is it numbing to the mind; it carries its own autonomies. This is the paradox of music's many erotic grammars: its relationship to the physical body is at once physical and speculative, historically appropriative and socially oblique. As with the discussion of the Velvets in chapter 5, Smith's music was never pornography or sincere romance. To the extent that it engaged the physicality of desire—and that was an important aim of her poetic work—she left things open for audiences. In a way that would have made Cavell both anxious and thoughtful, Smith's work was self-distancing or abstracting in ways that could accommodate multiple interpretations:

> Another thing I do is give people breathing room. In other words . . . I don't mean any of the stuff I say. . . . I don't know what I mean, it's just it gives somebody a new view, a new way to look at something. I like to look at things from ten or fifteen different angles, you know. . . . The other thing is that through performance I reach such states in which my brain feels so open, so full of light, it feels huge. It feels as big as the Empire State Building and if I can develop a communication with an audience, a bunch of people, when my brain is that big and very receptive, imagine the energy and the intelligence and all the things I can steal from them.[102]

Hell theorized rock audiences more passively in terms of their collective desire for self-pleasure. The culture industries of the 1970s had undoubtedly elevated rock singers—Hell, Smith, Jagger—into narcissistic icons, material inflations of the ego. Hell described the role as a "sacred monster." In his view, the job was "to be godlike for teenagers." This theater of "aggressive self-assertion" was the focal point of a process of dialectical mirroring in which the band incarnates the ideal pleasures of the collective.[103] Addressing these desires required considerable psychological-expressive labor for musicians. For Hell it took "an indestructible certainty of one's own irresistibility."[104] And as with Hegel's master-slave dialectic (as discussed in chap. 2 with respect to the question of intersubjectivity), the dependence on the fans often resulted in a contradictory dynamic of pressure and resentment: "It's also usually a monster of stress on its adepts; not really a fate to be desired. Which is another reason the stars are so cranky. They hate everyone for making them into what they've turned out to be, so they rub everyone's faces in it."[105]

To Hell, punk aggression was also never simply about masculine empowerment. Certainly, Hell and Verlaine identified as men and exhibited no shortage of ego-driven masculinity. But in line with the downtown scenes of the 1960s and 1970s, gender experimentation was familiar territory. In 1971 they devised the genderqueer nom de plume "Theresa Stern" for a series of poems they had cowritten (complete with a blended portrait of the two poets dressed as women in makeup and an identical wig).[106] In 1973 they named themselves after two queer poets who were sexually involved. Hell was also attentive to the underlying insecurities and anxieties driving masculinity. In 1971 Bangs had claimed that garage rock triggered a primitivist liberation of adolescent masculine fantasies.[107] But audiences brought complex baggage to this intersubjective space, which was inhabited by people of all genders. And Hell viewed the front person's authority as compensatory: fans and musicians alike were seeking empowerment because of despair, sexual anxiety, and youthful alienation. In his words, "teenagers need to swagger and be sarcastic and furious because they have so little power (or self-assurance either) otherwise and elsewhere, and because sex chemicals are pouring through them."[108] Like Hell's famous short haircut and torn clothing, both of which were crafted as a calculated effort to look ragged and real, punk style had a way of revealing the anxious and theatrical aspects of masculine desire.[109]

## The Aura of Unknowing

At the level of technique, punk musicians deconstructed and democratized the heroics of skill and virtuosity. To make one's own skill an object of unknowing, to problematize technique, or to simply not know how to play very well—these paradoxes animated the field of punk technicity. Deskilling had complex philosophical ramifications: one could create complex ambiguous and ironic relationships to past musical materials, one could earnestly deconstruct the reproduction of known skills to invent something new, or one could create puzzles of intentional and intuitive uncertainty in audiences. The politics of deskilling could similarly move in multiple directions. Bangs considered the essence of primitivist, three-chord garage rock a "superjoke" of seemingly infinite ironic potential, opening portals onto elite dimensions of artistic self-consciousness.[110] In the direction of populism, its limited vocabulary encouraged participation and set in motion decades of hardcore bands shouting, playing loud riffs, and slamming drums for small audiences. Intersubjectively, the thought was *that rock star is not me, but it could be me.*

As with the Velvets, collaborative projects can entail different kinds and degrees of deskilling. A single song of the Voidoids is a case in point. Consider "Love Comes in Spurts," which the Voidoids used to open their first set at a show at the Village Gate on August 26, 1977.[111] Lyrically, the song is an anxious declaration of adolescent excitement for sex and drugs. But as with Reed's "Heroin," there is more angst and pain than there is desire: the addict / lover is "crazed with devotion" and is constantly declaring "oh no it hurts" and "it murders your heart." Though Hell demonstrated variety and expressive range in the singing on his two albums, he was a predictably "crazed" and shambolic singer in bootlegs of live performances, often maintaining a constant fortissimo, as if his nerves caused him to push it over the edge.[112] In his stage banter, Hell presented himself as inarticulate and disoriented, rarely tapping into the insightful dimensions of his written personality. We might say that Hell was less deskilled than he was a semiskilled musician. Supremely self-aware, none of this was lost on him: though Hell was philosophical in his writings about the general affective powers of rock, he also acknowledged that he lacked a sustained investment in music as an art form.

His guitarists—Ivan Julian and Robert Quine—were another story. Hell's songs may have been simple in their formal outline, but the Voidoids' intertwined guitars (often panned left and right respectively in stereo mixes) created an intricate counterpoint. Blues and surf-like riffs were layered and juxtaposed against angular and atonal riffs. Strangely complex or dissonant voicings are found throughout *Blank Generation*. Quine's solos could sound like R & B guitar sped up and fragmented; he would often interrupt himself and not quite land on the beat before jangling up and down the fretboard. On "Love Comes in Spurts," classic Chuck Berry–style R & B riffs and searingly high double-stop figures crash and turn unpredictably.[113] As a fake out to the audience, the Voidoids used dissonant guitar intros that were often a in different key or tempo than the ensuing song. Both Julian and Quine were virtuosos but in a way that had a calculated minimalism and a deliberate sense of disjunction as if they were venerating and worshipping mistakes and sloppiness.

Like Coleman and the Velvets before them, not being totally in control of your instrument was a mode of deliberate thought, regardless of one's level of actual skill. It was itself indeterminate and unforeseen, but its recurrence is canonized periodically in retrospect. As Bangs described it,

> It always begins with that glorious "mistake," the crazy unexpected note kicking out sideways to let us loose again no matter what you call it. It reappears periodically every few years, the next new absurd and outrageous squeak that no one could calculate till ten years after it moulders buried in new clothes![114]

Unlike skilled improvisations that presume a coherent and known model of virtuosity (one often legislated in jazz by the critics of publications like *Down Beat*), for Smith and Hell, being uncertain about one's capacity to control what was happening had become essential to the art form. It was a concerted effort to replace virtuosity with alchemical energy: deliberate unknowing, or a self-conscious forgetting (so crucial to Coleman's music as discussed in "Deskilling Intentionalities," chap. 4), however paradoxical, became the means for creative work. As Legs McNeil, one of the founders of

*Punk* magazine, put it: "We don't know what we're doin' . . . so . . . y'know . . . We keep goin' . . . ta do somethin'!"[115] This deliberate lack of control could be a palpable force to audiences, a sign of authenticity. As Rockwell noted in 1976: "A major part of the thrill of any Smith performance is the sense that she may not be quite in control, and a major source of her priestess like power is that notion that the flames of irrationality are raging within her, just barely contained."[116]

It mattered less what was played than whether the proper atmosphere had been summoned into the room. How this happened varied constantly, as it would with any musical alchemy built on the energetics of inconsistencies rather than the classical architecture of harmonic, melodic, and formal complexity. Smith's band shaped and followed her affective flow; they would experiment over periods of six or seven minutes, and like James Brown (one of Smith's stated influences), ride long waves of energy up and down. Lenny Kaye described their approach, as with jazz and jam-driven rock bands, wanting to preserve the electricity of the live act:

> We want to give everybody who comes to see us a different show. Now, that's pretty difficult, and obviously you're not going to be able to get it totally different. . . . But I think we try to gear ourselves around moods so much, and Patti gravitates so spectacularly from level emotion to level of emotion. . . . I mean, really, when we do something, something we don't know where it's going to, how it's going to end, what ground is going to be covered, whether we're going to have fights on stage—it's a very organic type of situation that we're attempting to set up between us and the audience, and the audience is as much a part of it as we are, by necessity.[117]

There was enough risk involved that Smith and her band occasionally lost their groove (as they do momentarily *sans* drummer in the WBAI performance of "Gloria"):

> There's always surprises because we improvise so much. Sometimes we totally blow it, but we blow it and then get on a new rhythm. Some nights, I'll be trying for a stream, but we'll disconnect, and it'll self-destruct and it'll be like a moment of total pain. . . . Kids are wondering, "How are they gonna get out of this? They've really blown it. They've really fucked up." And usually I run to Lenny. Or I have to get on my knees to one of them. We'll just let anything happen, get ourselves out of the jam, or into a certain kind of ecstasy. . . . To me, performing, worrying about being embarrassed, you just can't worry.[118]

Though both Smith and Hell could be uneven in live performance, the Voidoids were less inclined toward improvisation. Live, they tended to re- produce loose, angry, and drunken versions of their records. This meant Hell had less control over the electricity of a live show, a problem that could be frustrating to him. Following a Heartbreakers performance in 1975, Hell described himself feeling "very nervous" on stage. Four days later, Hell wrote, "I felt true control for first time ever on stage for a few scattered moments during second set of second night."[119] By 1976 Hell worried that his control had devolved into a form of tightness, that on stage he was "not loose enough."[120] By summer 1977, at his musical peak, he recognized that affective commitment may not be enough to help him find a higher consis- tency in his performances:

> How can I make beauty . . . ? That is truly the greatest art and its noblest function. It may be fear that I can't create such a work (in performance or vinyl) in my present line of work that prompted all this thinking in the first place. How can I be sublime in rock and roll? I've always attacked it as performance—believing that I myself could be the "thing of beauty" by giving myself into the total possession of the heart of each song (pre- suming I'd composed hearts into them) but the extremely rare moments when I could feel this happening haven't gotten any more frequent. (I can still hope it will come with a heavier playing schedule than our customary once in two months.)[121]

The affective forces that propelled Smith's and Hell's music to alchemi- cal heights also had the capacity to genuinely overwhelm and even humili- ate them. There were particularities of the medium in play: what poetry could incarnate with language, music brought to life only very imperfectly, particularly because Hell's wild delivery and his earsplitting band were not great vehicles for communicating poetry (unlike, say Smith's band in songs like "Gloria" and "Land"). In a broad sense, we might say that collaborative, deskilled, semiskilled, and ephemeral practices found their force in a resis- tance to inscription. Here we find the genre's inherent existentialism: punk could never have a critical edition. Again, malleability, or inconsistency—in precisely calibrated historical, social, and affective ways—above all. It was fitting, in this sense, that an art form that channels such high levels of acous- tic volume and affective intensity remained studiously devoted to its own documentation, from poetry and journals to interviews, zines, posters, photographs, films, and in recent years oral histories, archives, and mem- oirs.[122] In Hell's journal, for instance, we read words that reveal considerable anxiety, as the steward of affective rituals grapples with the slipperiness of his own capacities to reflect. In his imagination, a void, a blank, a defiant resistance to the status quo, a vulgar surplus of sensations, the punk affect that is taken as a sheer force of indeterminacy, risked becoming adrift in a sea of rituals without autonomy and permanence.

For skilled performers, orienting oneself toward the inconsistency of vernacular peripheries required deconstructing one's own certitude about the history and idiom of what one (and the other) is doing. It was an instance of what I have described elsewhere as a paradox of the vernacular: deskilled punks self-consciously emulated "mistakes" and sought to open themselves to strange alchemical choices.[123] The skilled and self-reflexive always run the risk of becoming too self-conscious in their efforts to embrace mistakes or play in a deliberately naive way. After all, the R & B musicians of the 1950s and 1960s could not have been historically or formally conscious of their playing in the way musicians of the mid-1970s were in their punk emulations (as Bangs put it, "[the music] moulders in new clothes"). In the face of these paradoxical difficulties, punks frequently took recourse to the vitalist escape hatch, swearing fidelity to their own irrational creative fire. This tendency toward self-assertion ("giving myself into the total possession of the heart of each song" as Hell put it) was never only a blanket protest against society's ideologies: there was always a more intricate fantasy of who one was and ought to be. *It must be the reality of life that I'm finding. It is so cool. Is it not mine?* The instability of this epistemic paradox was rooted in the ambivalence that haunted Rimbaud's racialized fantasy: to live the other as liberation meant to busy oneself with a narcissistic mode of dissent, closing one's ears, partially or fully, to the underlying theft of Black life.

Punk supported a dissenting, dangerously indeterminate, and primitivist traffic of desire that aimed to circulate far faster than the rhythms of social life. The intensity of Hell's and Smith's intentions, pinned as they were to the bohemian fantasy of inverting, owning, and imbibing the oppression of racial hierarchies, reflected the paradoxes of vernacular creativity: as the performance fails, or explodes, or both, we sense an exposure of music's inconsistency fueled by an unquenchable desire to live the other. Its alchemy aspired to undo and remake the self, a peculiarly and paradigmatic Rimbaldian gesture, in the hopes of liquidating the remnants of historical consciousness.

# A Materialist Music History

This book is a weave of music history and philosophy, but its underlying purpose is a critical explanation of a period of time—principally the heavily teleological, driven, exuberant, delirious postwar "economic miracle" and the relatively aimless decline and rebirth of economic stagnation and postindustrial decadence in the 1970s.[1] It is the period Ernst Mandel once referred to as late capitalism.[2] Beginning in the 1950s a period of postwar prosperity famously featured a "compromise" between capital and labor built on a so-called virtuous cycle of profit and investment. By the 1960s a series of social movements demanded an end to segregation, racism, patriarchy, caste hierarchy, and colonial rule. Innumerable books have narrated the period's countercultural ethos of "authenticity, individuality, difference, and rebellion," to borrow the words of Thomas Frank.[3] But Frank went on to detail an underlying irony: capitalism was far from a clear adversary. From the 1960s onward the culture industry reaped exceptional profits by popularizing the ethos of dissent.

By the 1970s this trajectory had arguably become an open contradiction: as the culture industry ballooned with profits, influence, and platforms for artists, the social conditions of the underlying economy slipped into serious decline.[4] Industrial labor was gradually exported to the global periphery. Urban factories and warehouses emptied, and the US transitioned to a largely white-collar service economy that entailed intellectual and historically feminized forms of labor (corporate office culture, health care, hospitality, and education). (We may recall, for instance, Alice Coltrane finding work as a file clerk in the early 1960s.) Management approaches evolved from Fordist top-down methods common in the US of the 1920s–40s to increasingly flexible management models in the postwar period. By the 1970s job security became weaker and wages stagnated. Organized labor was blamed for inflation. Smith's early career exemplifies this transition: in the late 1960s she worked in a factory in South Jersey, a day job almost unthinkable for an artist in the US today. By the time she wrote "Piss Factory"

(1974), an antiwork ode to her discovery of Rimbaud, New York, and emergent self-consciousness as an artist, manufacturing work in the US was already becoming less common.

How did the music discussed in this book relate to these material changes of this historical period of time? In thinking through the surrounding scenes of 1960s experimentalism, many scholars have turned to intellectual history for guidance. A number of scholars have focused attention on broader principles of indeterminacy, improvisation, conceptualism, or intermedia that circulated at the surface of the postwar avant-garde.[5] Political readings of these key ideas tend to bolster the well-worn narrative that artists of the 1960s were rebellious liberals whose ideals were ultimately co-opted and exploited to spectacular effect by the profit-driven imperatives of neoliberalism and Silicon Valley. The neoliberal reading of postwar experimentalism is historically compelling, though it tends to emphasize conceptual positions and representational contents over the sensory and formal character of the medium at issue. Regarding conceptual positions, the "open forms" that seemed so radical and antiauthoritarian in the postwar period can indeed appear, in retrospect, as mere prototypes of the illusory freedoms of the gig economy. And for many works of literature, theater, and film, one can claim that concrete representational work of the social and material world of the long 1960s is being tangled with at some level of determinate detail.

When it comes to modernism's tendency toward abstraction, the dialectical links to material history tend to be more speculative. Famously, Marxist critics of the postwar period regarded the nonrepresentational qualities of high modern formalisms—for Adorno, modern music; for Greenberg, abstract painting—as self-aware refusals of the culture industry's monopoly on consumable representation that was so fashionable in the era of late capitalism. Their common conceit was that a Hegelian modernist abstraction can, by feat of formal self-consciousness, short-circuit vestiges of the commodity form. There are, of course, reasons to be skeptical of their heroic view of Webern and Pollock. Either because abstraction won its significance by sacrificing its broader social relevance (as in Milton Babbitt's 1958 polemic, "Who Cares If You Listen?") or because it was easily reappropriated as a midcentury commodity anyway: as luxury art object and elite cultural capital, or in the commercial sphere, as the allover patterns of household linoleum and the arresting dissonances of horror film soundtracks.

Of course, *The Musician as Philosopher* has eschewed the idea that music is fundamentally abstract. At a remove from the poles of representation and abstraction, this book's irruptive dissonances position the electrifying vectors of live, recorded, and broadcast music as a third category of the aesthetic with its distinct creative processes, affective intensities, and pronounced sense of metaphysical and social weight. It has asked why—amid unprecedented economic growth, a new consciousness of social universality, and subsequent decline into postindustrial malaise—musicians were so keen to use this new media environment to confront audiences with extremes of sonic psychosis and disorder. Even when a musician in this book seems to spell out the connection themselves, the dialectical links can feel elusive. In "Piss Factory," we may recall that Smith essentially read aloud a prose poem about her transition from exploited factory worker to artist with an electrifying vamp in the background. But explicit, biographically narrated relations between base (in this case, the production of commodities) and superstructure (a social reflection and critique of this work) rarely played out so explicitly. Arguably, Smith's narrative was only a surface symptom of this dialectic; the alchemy between the music and her oral delivery is what made her work magnetic and historically consequential.

Martha Feldman and Nicholas Mathew have noted that music's ineffability and affective intensity (as discussed in chap. 1) make it a peculiar historical object: "vibrational, ephemeral, footloose, politically mobile, and semiotically uncertain," it is at once a generative, galvanizing, and destabilizing historical actor. And for these reasons it is a source of troubling difficulties for historical method and for a materialist historiography.[6] Indeed, the complex nexus between music and history poses provocative and enduring questions. How did those irruptive dissonances of the long 1960s precipitate social and material historical change? How did they underpin new forms of self-consciousness? What did they indicate, reflect, or amplify about history itself? And how can we listen to music to better understand its relation to social change, notably changes that were linked to seismic developments in capital, labor, and in the material reproduction of life?

A sense of social alienation and persistent inequities were the material condition for the postwar irruption of music's inconsistency. The 1960s was marked by a utopian thesis of universality in the face of these inequities: decolonization in the global periphery, anticaste struggles in India, the civil rights era, second-wave feminism, and the New Left.[7] These movements exemplified an ideal that meanders in the background of Cavell's "Music Discomposed": we all count. At the level of the classed subject, these movements precipitated contradictions: the emergent bourgeois self, in its trajectory and its freedoms, had a way of yielding its own underlying critique. It was one Baraka analyzed in *Blues People* (1963) as endemic to the formation of a Black middle class: no advancement without ambivalence, no upward mobility without a growing consciousness that becoming American was also participating in an ongoing history of racialized exploitation.[8] The bohemian romanticization of the subjugated was no less a raising-to-consciousness of this underlying inequity of modernity. Rimbaud's poetry—a rebellious path to independence for many—was also queer, appropriative, primitivist, and its material aims were a refusal and a critique of work as a bourgeois imperative. In sum, as the self and its social groups were acquiring more mobility, malleability, and freedoms than ever before, its rise fueled a growing sense of unease. A concomitant sense of alienation emerged that drove a thirst for a greater transcendence, a deeper truth, a realism beyond any social norm. With freedom came ambivalence, with utopia a form of critique.

In this way, Tudor, Coleman, the Velvets, Coltrane, Smith, and Hell did not simply stage an escape from the self or a desire for emancipation or an affirmation of collectivity and participation against the authority of aesthetic autonomy. Their irruptive avant-gardes electrified the historical contradictions of the self in its ambiguous thirst for freedom, justice, transcendence, realism, and rebellious erasure. In giving voice to what Reed describes as "the sounds of another life," they engendered an affectively disturbing—yet productive and honest—refusal of a normative self.[9] That is, during the period when cries of cultural, political, and economic liberation were widespread and spiritual leaders pushed aside dogmas of the past to declare, with Swami Satchidananda, "the guru is within," these musicians venerated the self while also insisting—in the same stroke—to question and even liquefy it.

In the medium of musical sound, the techniques of a second-order modernism infiltrated the machinery of consciousness. Like the LSD, booze, heroin, and marijuana that soaked the subcultures of the period, these musicians sought to invade, inflate, and decenter the perceptual coordinates of the late modern self. They produced a breathing, fragile contradiction: at once an impossible transcendence and a dissenting erasure, they presented the modern self as a confounding tangle of intentions, esoteric blockages, seductive magnets, elite closures, and opacities. In following Rimbaud, Cage, Berry, Dylan, Sun Ra, or just the paths and atmospherics of sound, these musicians experientially renewed the claim that one is an *other*. If the politics of 1960s universality was a key backdrop for the second-order modernists, it is nonetheless important to note that it was rarely at the surface of their work. These musicians expected listeners to do the work of getting there, thinking and feeling their way through a strident esoteric space, learning a bit about what is going on, then getting inside and losing oneself. It invited, without explicitly prescribing, what Frederic Jameson has described as a "collective reeducation" of the oppressed self's capacities insofar as their music refused the authority of institutionally sanctioned forms and pedagogies.[10]

Supporting this thesis involves no easy methodological tools or short-cuts in part because variously racialized, gendered, and sexualized perspectives on this process remained incommensurable, unequal, and without synthesis. For this reason, there exists no homology between the base of changes in political economy and the superstructure of musical style. No single philosopher has the key to unlock the paradoxes of the medium's electric ineffability: no cosmic Schopenhauerian will, no negative Adornian *Schriftcharakter*, no Attali-like anticipatory "code," no diffuse magic of Jankélévitchian *Charme*, no ontological creativity of Deleuzian deterritorialization can serve as a master explanation of the many calibrated atmospheres of this period. The method of immanent critique I have used here instead attempts to give the social cacophony of the 1960s space to breathe on its own. It asks readers to listen to the localities and detect the relations in the thinking that is immanent to the atmospheric operations of the medium. To understand the kind of formal object that music is, without overthinking or deluding oneself about the historicity of its form, one must press play —*pause*, as I note in chapter one—and face its inconsistent depth: a loud, nocturnal atmosphere of psychosis is what was made and circulated among these musicians. The significance of that inconsistency, in all its affective disorder, is the historical and social question at issue in this book.

It was not a particular method of composition, but in the musical sounds, in its affective praxis, one can hear complex mirrors of self-and-other utopianism and dissent. Its forms were built on idiosyncratic decisions and discoveries woven of complex histories that are themselves murky, occluded, or deliberately undefined. For this reason, vernacular philosophy is key to its disclosure. Music's ineffability is a magnet for so much that is spiritually, affectively, and socially too intense or complex to think about clearly and logically. In this book's studio chapters, one finds that music's ineffability is not only complex in its articulation but it is philosophically undecided; that is, musicians might not be very articulate about how they are doing what they are doing. And yet in their creative decisions—in their rehearsals, performances, recording processes, chord choices, lyrics, manuscripts, and solos, and in their relationship to their world, their audiences, their styles, and their place in the culture industry—what they made was influential and electric in its forms and intentions.[11] Something worked, however unevenly. Thus, what we hear in the studio histories is a mobilization of the ineffable that is immanent to history itself. The actors may not fully be able to tell you why; the detective work of immanent critique discloses its power.

Their creative processes entailed what I referred to in the book's introduction as a "multifocal dialectics." No one style history or social history conditioned the postwar development of hyperfractures and inconsistencies. There were more than a few social and musical histories in play, histories that were not always well defined, certainly not by discourses at the centers of institutional power. The sonic objects themselves were complex, mimetic, atmospheric. Their forms and grammars were not reducible to positive elements; they were made with what Cavell described as varied sequences of improvisations and discoveries. These congealed decisions made by musicians are what make these atmospheric objects worthy of historical explanation. For through these decisions, they electrified the self into a place of profound dissonance and ambivalence. It was not simply a populist call for participation (although Smith tried this in her own way by riffing on Dylan). This music was a series of places where you could dive down and feel lost. The musicians said we are weird and lost, and we are living in a strange and inhospitable atmosphere, so feel free to join us and lose your mind. Perhaps it will help, perhaps not. To feel that "I is an other" (Rimbaud) means to cancel one's consciousness of a previous moment (Tudor), to open oneself to a harmolodic freedom (Coleman), to affirm a dissenting realism of desire (Velvets, Hell, and Smith), or to seek the obscure transcendence of a universal consciousness (Coltrane). All these atmospheres stop the norms of life with a strangely refracted form of social beauty. Their work proposed to rewire the mechanism of perception itself.

The historicity of these second-order modernisms was conditioned by technologies of sound recording and broadcast, which produced a complex rhythm of relay, playback, and erasure. That is, as music captured the immanence of a social crisis or desire, it continued to be played back and riffed on in a way that both carried that history and did not carry that history, or carried it only in an abstracted, affective shell of musical sound. (Recall, for instance, the discussion of the Velvets bootlegs from 1970 in chap. 5). This was a nonsynchronous process that was dynamic, subtle, and epistemically textured. While activating transportive atmospheres, the music could have intensity but could also lose it with time, translation, and even failure as the sometimes yearning, sometimes erased, sometimes critical self was played back; its social desires could be relived and unwound at the same time. This ambivalent process of playback was a condition for the racialized and gendered dynamics discussed in chapter 2. By making atmospheres acousmatic, replicated, and incessantly displaced by space and time, the music's efficacy was rarely clear in its social intent: recordings echoed past historical moments with unstable mixes of represencing and uncanny emptiness. Because of this underlying nonsynchronicity, the history presented in this book is irreducible to a discrete series of events. It was more like a political-affective complex of intricately wired dialectical processes, a transformative blend of sound and social imagination funneled into strange and ambivalent trajectories. It enabled glimmers of a collective psychoanalysis, but one that could constantly undo itself in its historical rippling aftereffects.

∵

In closing, we might review the technical infrastructure of this music history. As noted in the introduction, it would be misleading to categorize any musician in this book as either "literate" or "oral"—all straddled this boundary. Musical notation and literacy functioned differently here than it did in the world of classical music. Notation and its attached systems of discipline had the social and institutional power to dictate the complexity, sophistication, and legal boundaries of music. For Tudor, notation provided an esoteric discipline of creating a secondary realization of an indeterminate score (at least until he began turning to improvisation and other open processes in the 1960s). The other musicians in this book held the copyright to their compositions (melodies, harmonies, rhythms, lyrics) in line with the historical practices of music publishers who preserved underlying composition as a distinct stream of intellectual property. Coleman and Alice Coltrane understood themselves to be both composers and performers. The Velvets self-consciously rebelled against the straitjacket of notation even as their background bore its imprints. Both Smith and Hell never read music but admired it and surrounded themselves with musicians who were trained to some degree. For all but Tudor, some form of live improvisation and/or multitrack studio-based composition was crucial.

How they learned music varied. Though Tudor and Cale learned through the conservatory model of private lessons, by the mid-1960s, both increasingly turned toward open-ended participatory work outside the domain of Western classical music. Coltrane, who also learned through private lessons, was similar to Coleman in that she learned through gigging in predominantly Black churches and in clubs and sought out ad hoc forms of classical training and professional mentorship outside educational institutions. The rock musicians who came of age in the 1950s and early 1960s were struck by Black or Black-derived revolutionary performances (doo-wop, rock and roll, Dylan, the Stones) on television, radio, and sound recordings before cutting their teeth as gigging musicians. Reed took piano lessons as a child, but Smith and Hell were largely self-taught. All the rock musicians self-consciously avoided notation.

The political economy and social scenes of their work were separate from the Western concert music industry and the academic institutions that supported classical music. All were excluded from the centers of academic musical power. In the history of the arts, this is actually quite re-markable: during a postwar boom in higher education when a considerable number of avant-garde artists, poets, performance artists, and composers could find employment and support, none of the musicians in this book were employable as tenure-track professors. This is true even as all six were featured repeatedly in the *New York Times*. The reason for the exclusion was ideological: the music education industry and professional performing arts organizations were almost exclusively committed to Western classical music. Thus, with Tudor as the lone exception, the musicians in this book worked in commercial and entrepreneurial outside spheres of established power at universities, colleges, and professional performing arts organizations.

Much of their styles, subjectivities, and atmospheric musical worlds would have been impossible without the record industry's unprecedented affective and social power in the postwar period. But no blanket ideologi-cal explanation can characterize these musicians' relationships to the music industry. Their trajectories were complex: the ambivalence of capitalism's unprincipled, exploitative, and biased promotion machine had a way of playing both sides. The culture industry never simply reproduced or dis-seminated ideology. For every instance of revolutionary Black conscious-ness in a Nina Simone song there was a performance of Lynyrd Skynyrd with a confederate flag on stage. When it came to the musicians in this book, record companies tended to maintain distance from the creative pro-cess. Those who signed to major labels (Coleman, the Velvets, Coltrane, Hell, Smith) were understood as "art" or "prestige" signings valuable for their critical weight and cultural capital.[12] And none—except for Reed and Smith—made much money in the music industry. (We can recall that the Velvets played to a number of near-empty rooms before breaking up in 1970.) We might note as well that, though it was hardly immune to patterns of bias and discrimination, the commercial sphere was one of the few places in which artists of color could even attempt to make a living.

The assumption that modernist consciousness exists a priori in a given economic or social sphere (say, among new music performers, opera com-panies, or Guggenheim fellows) or aesthetic criterion (those who know their counterpoint or who can navigate a modular synthesizer) is fraught. Resistance, complexity, and contradiction in the avant-garde exists in any number of cultural spheres. For this reason, this book eschews the assump-tion that academic or grant-based creativity or forms of art approved by the art world have special powers ethically to resist the corruptions of the com-modity form. It instead takes the lead from the work of the studios them-selves: how did these musicians build a language with and against the norms and pathologies of society? Assuming no axiomatic sphere for autonomy or reliable technicity for comprehending a fracture of stylistic norms, this book instead listens to the social tensions of modernisms perpetually caught between commerce and art and in social fields structured by inequality and persistent hierarchies. Under these conditions, second-order modernisms sought to elevate and dissolve the self by thwarting consensus on the stylistic criteria for a fracture.

∵

At the close of the historical period of this book, two significant books were published about the meaning and value of music history. One was written by Jacques Attali, an economist influenced by Western Marxism, cybernetics, and information theory.[13] His book, *Noise: The Political Economy of Music* (1977) was a brazen, speculative, countercultural work of critical theory. In it Attali proposed a metanarrative of music history as an anticipatory form of socioeconomic change. That same year, the center-right West German humanist Carl Dahlhaus published *Foundations of Music History* (*Grundlagen der Musikgeschichte*), a book that became a key text for scholars entering the field of historical musicology.[14] Dahlhaus held that the center of a music history was the autonomous form of musical works, which he presumed were published scores with enduring significance. As he presented it, the goal of a music history was to enrich and complicate our understanding of privileged works. Dahlhaus was an aesthetic conservative with humanizing liberal inclinations. His adversaries were on the Left: he opposed a music history that turned attention to events and social history (musicologist Georg Knepler in the GDR for example) or that falsely hypostatized musical works as having immanent capacities to resist social and political malaise (Adorno, and the field of Western Marxism).[15]

The new, or "critical" musicology of the 1980s and 1990s was sympathetic to Attali's mode of reading music as a social text. They leveled an influential critique of the centrality of the work concept while emphasizing music's status as a culturally embedded and meaningful activity. And yet, for almost thirty years, any genuinely progressive or materialist—let alone Marxist—approach to music historiography has remained marginal. Meanwhile, even if Dahlhaus's *Foundations* is less often read today, the Dahlhausian model of music history, with some modifications, has remained a dominant force in musicology. In his *Oxford History of Western Art Music*, Richard Taruskin preserves the outlines of Dahlhaus's historiography, though he expands engagement with contextual and social history to weaken the metanarrative of style history and the traditional myth of aesthetic autonomy. In the last decade, a continued decentering of style history, musical works, and their creators has emerged in the field's leading edges. Glenda Goodman exemplifies a new generation of scholars turning attention to social and material cultures as a focus point of music history.[16] The latest debates on historiography have followed the material and affective turns and "dehumanized" historiography by centering objects, instruments, media, techniques, processes, actor-networks, and affects.[17] Recent calls to address racial justice and subjugated voices have finally begun to elevate voices and perspectives from the epistemic periphery.

This book, of course, shares the collective goal of a far more inclusive and socially minded music history. But a new risk has emerged in some quarters; that the gospel of contextualism has left the music and its history of style underexplained as its own distinct kind of historical agent. In all his zeal to rid music history of style history and metanarrative, Taruskin, for instance, took a misstep when claiming that "agents can only be people."[18] In saying so, he proposed a history in which musical scores, genres, styles, movements, recordings, and performances themselves are drained of agency as aesthetic objects. But ought not the agency of musical sound be the central problem addressed in a music history? That is, How does music steer desires, beliefs, and structures of the collective imagination in ways that are independent of the conscious action of individuals?[19] Once music is recognized as an agent, as a medium of desire, as enmeshed in Raymond Williams's "structure of feeling," one can turn away from the pious appreciation of treasured works and instead think the medium as immanent to the work of social and historical change.[20]

This is a thesis with intuitive appeal. The music of the 1960s was foundational to calls for social change; the tumultuous and revolutionary decade is unthinkable without considering its powers. Think only of the musicians who circulated widely in the US mass media: Simone, Dylan, Odetta, Hendrix. Among the musicians themselves, this was also a period when thinking about music history was inseparable from the way people made it; these musicians thought of themselves as inheriting, intermixing, and revolutionizing various forms of music drawn from the historical past. In these ways, music evidently *was* at once an agent and a carrier of social history. What would it mean, then, to revive a version of style history, specifically a style history that periodizes and diagnoses changes in music's relation to structural and historical trajectories? It would have to be a style history that dispensed with ideological attachments to institutional authority, compositional discipline, and whiteness and instead presumed the openness of Piekut's "mixed scriptural economy." It would be one that foregrounded the imaginary traffic of feeling like one could be another. To escape the accusation of Whiggish teleology, it would also have an accurate and honest grounding in political economy and complex, layered histories of social power. That is, before we grant Babbitt, Boulez, and Stockhausen unquestioned status as heroic resistors of the commodity form, we would need to know the extent to which their paychecks and assets were tied to capital, which, we can surmise, would be no less encompassing than that of Smith in her record deals with Clive Davis. When one can carefully and equitably compare the privileged social networks bestowing tenure-track labor on a trusted generation of intellectuals to the nepotisms and networks of the music industry, one would be able to see that each survives on distinct patterns of extraction and exploitation.

This book narrated, at some subterranean level, its own version of style history: a crisis, an electrification, and a historical opening of what counts as musical literacy. As noted in the previous section, the 1960s witnessed a revolutionary expansion in the various modes of musical writing. There was an explosion of the hyperfracture—that spirited, notated esotericism—at a time when it was still the cognitive backdrop for new music with Tudor in Town Hall or Coleman at the Five Spot. The hyperfracture scrambled and overdetailed itself out of existence during the 1960s and was sublated into new forms of empiricist tinkering. Technology allowed new rules to be made via Walter Benjamin's surgical interventions into the sensorium and the Afro-futurist grammars of Kodwo Eshun's beat masters.[21] Stylistic innovations were enabled by problems immanent to what Adorno once called the *Tendenz des Materials*, which was revealed to be broader and more plural, Black, and vernacular than Adorno was ever willing to imagine. After all, when the definition of what counts expands, so does the definition of who counts. It was a precise lesson of Baraka's *Blues People* (1963): a style history is a social history, and vice versa. The details of the studio mattered because questions immanent to form, style, and social history were rethought at one and the same time. And it was in these details, decisions, and the numinous trajectory of their atmospheres that the messy history of desire, imagination, and social change were palpably brought to life.

# Acknowledgments

The research for this book stretched over fifteen years; it required immeasurable help and support from my friends and colleagues. There were a few people whose provocations steered me to write this book in the first place. First among these was a graduate school mentor, Suzanne Cusick, who slowed down my early writing on music and philosophy by asking, Who is really doing all this thinking? The stubborn young graduate student in me was, of course, focused on the value of studying philosophical questions for their own sake. But her question stuck with me. Over time, I began to realize the answer might be much more complicated and interesting than I originally imagined—that it would open up the rich terrain of how philosophy circulated as a social practice, a topic that would begin to feel inexhaustible. A second influence has been my amazing partner, the art historian Emily Ruth Capper. She opened my ears and my eyes to history and to archives in a way that has permanently changed the trajectory of my work. And finally, many provocations came from my late friend and collaborator Ahmed Janka Nabay, to whom I dedicate this book. Janka revealed to me new vistas of music and social life while subtly (or not so subtly) reminding me the limits of what I would be able to understand. His many provocations were also injunctions, injunctions to listen. He also showed me that listening and philosophizing at the same time would be really hard. I do not know whether I have succeeded here, but I hope the effort has at least opened some suggestive and illustrative paths for the reader.

The thinking here, as it took shape, was aided by many other interlocutors near and far who read versions of the chapters or listened to me deliver some of the material orally. Others provoked me more indirectly, either by talking with me about the underlying ideas in this project or simply by collaborating on musical projects. In a somewhat aleatoric order I would like to thank Carolyn Abbate, Tamara Levitz, Seth Brodsky, Berthold Hoeckner, Richard Leppert, Brian Kane, George Lewis, Michael Veal, Glenda Goodman, Jairo Moreno, Brigid Cohen, Ryan Dohoney, Steven Rings, Amy

Cimini, David Novak, Elliott Powell, Sumanth Gopinath, Stephen Decatur Smith, Jessica Schwartz, Patrick Deer, Jacques Lezra, Pooja Rangan, Naomi Waltham-Smith, Martin Scherzinger, Gavin Steingo, Matthew Rahaim, Joshua Pilzer, Alisha Lola Jones, Braxton Shelley, Marc Hannaford, Benjamin Steege, Emily Dolan, Ian Balfour, Phil Ford, Beth Snyder, Martha Feldman, Gary Tomlinson, Holly Watkins, Jess Kaiser, Bob King, Lawrence Zbikowski, Jennifer Iverson, Roger Grant, Bob Fink, Arun Saldanha, Peter Mercer-Taylor, Fred Moten, Ana María Ochoa, Richard Taruskin, Alexander Rehding, Daniel Chua, Christopher Hasty, Benjamin Tausig, You Nakai, Anne Shreffler, John Deathridge, Charles Kronengold, Kwami Coleman, Anna Seastrand, Nanette Nielsen, Jennifer Ronyak, Patrick Nickleson, Tomas McAuley, Sherry Lee, Eric Drott, Ted Gordon, Benjamin Piekut, Judith Peraino, John Hicks, Meredith Gill, Mariel Oliveira, Jackie Beckey, Nate Nelson, Andy Rockwood, Jonathan Leland, Adam Patterson, Paul Borman, John Colpitts, Clara Latham, Rob Thacher, Boshra AlSaadi, Jonathan Leland, Baby Jane, Shahin Motia, Barry London, Matthew Mehlan, Whitney Johnson, Joe Burns, Jon Coe, James Currie, Natilee Harren, Nathan Brown, Lauren Stone, Erica Weitzman, Travis Workman, Robert Lehman, Audrey Wasser, Martin Hägglund, Benjamin McKean, Erin Graff Zivin, David Ferris, and Aisha Ghani. I am also very indebted to the anonymous readers recruited by the University of Chicago Press, who gave the manuscript a thorough and generous read.

My colleagues in the department of Cultural Studies and Comparative Literature have provided me with the most free-form, wild, and brilliant workplace I could imagine anywhere. We think and work intensely, without rules or parameters. It is as close to a utopia as I can imagine. Many thanks to Tim Brennan, Tony Brown, Cesare Casarino, Keya Ganguly, Maggie Hennefeld, Alice Lovejoy, Laurie Ouellette, Shaden Tageldin, and Christian Uwe. The many students I have worked with during this time have been a constant source of provocation. I could not have refined any work here without conversations with Mark Mahoney (who kindly read a number of chapters and provided valuable feedback), Kathryn Huether, Luke Martin, Cole Pulice, Mikkel Vad, Jordan Brown, Kai Yin Lo, Ryan O'Dell, Runchao Liu, Denise Maria Malauene, Matthew Gilmore, Jeremy Smith, Matthew Tchepikova-Treon, Evan Fraser, Dominic Valadez, Joseph Sannicandro, Heidi Jensen, Hon Ki Cheung, Clare Harmon, Laurie Lee, Audrey Slote, Hiroaki Cho, William Levine, Mary Scott, Conor Greenberg, Max Lindholm, Anthony Miller, among many others. I also thank the graduate students of my seminar as a visiting faculty member at the University of Chicago in 2021, "Music, Philosophy, Praxis." They helped me think through a number of key principles and ideas related to this book at a key stage.

· As a social person and as a musician, I often crave connecting with people about the ideas and histories in this book. I want to thank the institutions who invited me to speak and deliver various versions of and seminars on these chapters when they were at different stages of completion. In each case, conversations spun out that immeasurably improved the manuscript. Many thanks to friends and colleagues at Cornell University, Harvard University, Yale University, Indiana University, University of Southern California, University of Chicago, University of Pennsylvania, Carleton College, University of California, San Diego, University of California, Santa Barbara, Northwestern University, University of Texas at Austin School of Music, Eastman School of Music, University of Colorado at Boulder, University of Oxford, University of Cambridge, Radcliffe Institute for Advanced Study; Petar Milat, Nathan Brown, the Center for Expanded Poetics, and the Mama Multimedia Institute for the summer Symposium on Form in Dubrovnik; Rob Lehman, Jess Kaiser, and the Mahindra Humanities Center at Harvard (for support of their workshop on Dialectical Thinking in the Humanities); Bianet Castellanos at the Institute for Advanced Studies at the University of Minnesota; and Jennifer Awes Freeman at the United Theological Seminary of the Twin Cities for their generous invitations for talks and seminars on the material in this book. Conversations at conferences with many friends and colleagues were of equally essential importance: two American Comparative Literature Association (ACLA) annual meetings in 2014 (a panel on punk run by Patrick Deer and Bryan Waterman) and 2021 (in a panel on Art as Knowledge with Rob Lehman); a panel at the 2017 Society for Cinema and Media Studies (SCMS) annual meeting with Berthold Hoeckner, Amy Skjerseth, and Seth Kim-Cohen; two papers at the American Musicological Society (AMS); a paper on the Velvet Underground at the Royal Musical Association (RMA) Music and Philosophy Study Day in 2017; and a paper on Richard Hell at a conference on popular music and marginality at University of North Carolina at Chapel Hill in 2017.

I have particular debts to librarians, editors, curators, and archivists who helped me work with sources and images. I am grateful to Jessica Abbazio, music librarian at the University of Minnesota; Adriana Cuervo at the Institute for Jazz Studies at Rutgers University; Marvin Taylor at the Fales Library and Special Collection at New York University; the staff at the Velvet Underground Collection at the Division of Rare and Manuscript Collections in the Cornell University Library; Jennie Thomas at the Rock and Roll Hall of Fame Museum and Archives; and Danielle Cordovez at the New York Public Library for the Performing Arts. The amazing staff at the Getty Research Institute have, for years, been tireless supporters and collaborators, namely, Greg Albers, Gail Feigenbaum, Nancy Perloff, Marcia Reed,

Sarah Cooper, Michele Ciaccio, Karen Ehrmann, Pauline Lopez, Adriana Romero, Chloe Millhauser, Dina Murokh, Victoria Barry, Janelle Gatchalian, Eric Gardner, and Torsten Edstam. Thanks as well to Liz Olson, Kristen St. Michel, and the staff in our department for their exceptional support and camaraderie.

I am also grateful to the institutions that gave financial support for this book to be written. Throughout the period I spent writing this book, the dean of the College of Liberal Arts, John Coleman, as well as associate deans Jane Blocker and Josephine Lee, were extraordinarily helpful in supporting our life in Minnesota. A number of fellowships and leaves provided me the time and resources I needed to finish the manuscript. Namely, a National Endowment for the Humanities Summer Stipend, a Talle Faculty Research Award and a Sabbatical Supplement from the College of Liberal Arts, the McKnight Presidential Fellowship and the Imagine Fund at the University of Minnesota (the former supported by the McKnight Foundation), a subvention from the American Musicological Society, housing and travel support from the Getty Research Institute on several occasions, and a fellowship from the Center for Popular Music Studies at Case Western Reserve University. Many thanks to Alexandra Brown in the College of Liberal Arts for her invaluable help with fellowship applications.

I owe so much to the support of my editor, Elizabeth Branch Dyson, and the University of Chicago Press, whose thoughtful conversation and honest critical feedback have become essential to my identity as an intellectual. Many thanks as well to Mollie McFee, her editorial assistant, to Steve LaRue for excellent copyediting, and to June Sawyers for a fantastic index. And finally, this book would have been impossible to complete without the love and support of Emily, our tireless and supportive moms, and little Dario, the greatest force of joy I have ever known.

With much love, and many debts, this book is dedicated to Janka.

# Archival Collections

David Tudor Papers. Getty Research Institute, Los Angeles.

George Avakian and Anahid Ajemian Papers. New York Public Library, Music Division.

James Brawley Collection. Rock n' Roll Hall of Fame Library and Archives, Cleveland, Ohio.

Mary Caroline Richards Papers. Getty Research Institute, Los Angeles.

Ornette Coleman Press Archive. Institute for Jazz Studies, Rutgers University Libraries, Newark, New Jersey.

Richard Hell Papers. New York University Fales Library and Special Collections.

Sire Records Collection. Rock n' Roll Hall of Fame Library and Archives, Cleveland, Ohio.

Velvet Underground Collection. Division of Rare and Manuscript Collections, Cornell University Library, Ithaca, New York.

# Notes

### INTRODUCTION

1. Benjamin Piekut, *Henry Cow: The World Is a Problem* (Durham, NC: Duke University Press, 2019), 391.

2. For more on the varied role of music education, institutions, and notation, see the conclusion of this book, particularly pages 219–21.

3. Joanna Demers, *Drone and Apocalypse: An Exhibit Catalog for the End of the World* (Winchester: Zero Books, 2015), 4.

4. Brigid Cohen, "Enigmas of the Third Space: Mingus and Varèse at Greenwich House, 1957," *Journal of the American Musicological Society* 71, no. 1 (Spring 2018), 157.

5. Cohen, "Enigmas of the Third Space," 159.

6. Cf. Jonathan F. Eburne, *Outsider Theory: Intellectual Histories of Unorthodox Ideas* (Minneapolis: University of Minnesota Press, 2018).

7. Herbert Marcuse, "Philosophy and Critical Theory," in *Negations: Essays in Critical Theory*, trans. Jeremy J. Schapiro (New York: Penguin Press, 1968), 99–118. For two methodological studies of the works of others who either repress (Richard Taruskin) or eschew (Rita Felski) gestures of critique, see Michael Gallope, "Why Was This Music Desirable? On a Critical Explanation of the Avant-Garde," *Journal of Musicology* 31, no. 2 (Spring 2014): 199–230, and "Music and Postcritique," *Nonsite*, no. 35 (April 2, 2021), https://nonsite.org/responses-to-hooked-art-and-attachment/.

8. On the racialized character of these ideological restrictions over what counts as music in modern music disciplines, see Philip Ewell, "Music Theory's White Racial Frame," *Music Theory Spectrum* 43, no. 2 (Fall 2021): 324–29; Philip Ewell, *On Music Theory, and Making Music More Welcoming for Everyone* (Ann Arbor: University of Michigan Press, 2023); Danielle Brown, "An Open Letter on Racism in Music Studies," June 12, 2020, https://www.mypeopletellstories.com/blog/open-letter; and Dylan Robinson, *Hungry Listening: Resonant Theory for Indigenous Sound Studies* (Minneapolis: University of Minnesota Press, 2020).

9. Frank Kofsky, "Interview with John Coltrane," in *Coltrane on Coltrane: The John Coltrane Interviews*, ed. Chris De Vito (Chicago: Chicago Review Press, 2010), 287. Originally published in *Jazz & Pop*, September 1967, 23–31.

10. Ryan Dohoney, *Saving Abstraction: Morton Feldman, the de Menils, and Rothko Chapel* (New York: Oxford University Press, 2019), 3.

11. On music and affect as a social force with a certain regularity and ideological power, see Raymond Williams, "Structures of Feeling" in *Marxism and Literature* (Oxford: Oxford University Press, 1978), 128–35.

12. On affective and ideological contradictions in musical experience, see William Cheng, *Loving Music till It Hurts* (New York: Oxford University Press, 2019).

13. "David Tudor: Interview with Peter Dickinson, Ibis Hotel, London, July 26, 1987" in Peter Dickinson, ed., *CageTalk: Dialogues with & about John Cage* (Rochester, NY: University of Rochester Press, 2006), 91.

14. See, for example, Alonso-Minutti, Ana R. Herrera, Eduardo Herrera, and Alejandro L. Madrid, *Experimentalisms in Practice: Music Perspectives from Latin America* (New York: Oxford University Press, 2018); Brigid Cohen, *Musical Migration and Imperial New York: Early Cold War Scenes* (Chicago: University of Chicago Press, 2022); and Anthony Reed, *Soundworks: Race, Sound, and Poetry in Production* (Durham, NC: Duke University Press, 2021).

15. On the importance of periodization in late modernity, see Nathan Brown, "Postmodernity, Not Yet: Toward a New Periodization," *Radical Philosophy* 2, no. 1 (February 2018): 11–27.

16. Stanley Cavell, "Music Discomposed," in *Must We Mean What We Say?* (Cambridge: Cambridge University Press, 2002), 201.

## CHAPTER ONE

1. Susanne Langer, *Philosophy in a New Key*, 3rd ed. (Cambridge, MA: Harvard University Press, 1957), 147.

2. Langer, 147.

3. Langer, 147.

4. Langer, 97.

5. For Langer, the foundations of human societies are cultures of instinct, action, and nondiscursive ideation. In two chapters of *Philosophy in a New Key*, she turns to two key anthropological universals respectively—ritual and myth—and describes them as complex logical expressions and articulations of these affects: "patterns" of human life. Such processes evolve over the course of human history, but in order to understand how this happens it makes sense to lay aside Hegel's *Geist* and its teleology of self-consciousness. In contending that the genesis of abstraction is instinctual, practical, and affective, Langer provincializes Western philosophy as a deductive, idealistic, Platonic discipline.

6. See Langer, "Discursive and Presentational Forms," *Philosophy in a New Key*, 79–102.

7. Langer, *Philosophy in a New Key*, 241.

8. Langer writes strikingly that we have barely begun—in the 1940s—to tap into the latent potentials of music: "Music is our myth of the inner life—a young, vital, and meaningful myth, of recent inspiration and still in its 'vegetative' growth." Langer, *Philosophy in a New Key*, 245. In *Feeling and Form* (New York: Scribner, 1953), Langer develops the slightly more formalist position that music is in essence "the creation of virtual time"—it produces "the sonorous image of passage," and she adds that "the phenomena that fill time are *tensions*—physical, emotional, or intellectual." For a theoretical exploration of music as a "sonic analog for dynamic processes" linked to embodiment and

phenomenologies of experience, see Lawrence M. Zbikowski, *Foundations of Musical Grammar* (New York: Oxford University Press, 2018), and Mariusz Kozak, *Enacting Musical Time: The Bodily Experience of New Music* (New York: Oxford University Press, 2019). Also compare Amy Cimini, "Music, Theory, Feminism, the Body: Mediation's Plural Work," *Contemporary Music Review* 37, no. 5/6 (2018): 666–83.

9. Langer, *Philosophy in a New Key*, 238.

10. Langer, *Philosophy in a New Key*, 100. Mendelssohn, in a letter of 1842: "A piece of music that I love expresses thoughts to me that are not too *imprecise* to be framed in words, but too *precise*." See Peter le Huray and James Day, eds., *Music and Aesthetics in the Eighteenth and Early-Nineteenth Centuries* (Cambridge: Cambridge University Press, 1988), 311. Though literary artisans of inner consciousness such as Virginia Woolf might protest, Langer emphasizes the ineffability of emotional experience and its awkward fit to the denotative powers of language: "Everybody knows that language is a very poor medium for expressing our emotional nature. It merely names certain vaguely and crudely conceived states, but fails miserably in any attempt to convey the ever-moving patterns, the ambivalences and intricacies of inner experience, the interplay of feelings with thoughts and impressions, memories and echoes of memories, transient fantasy, or its mere runic traces, all turned into nameless, emotional stuff."

11. Langer, *Philosophy in a New Key*, 233.

12. Langer, *Feeling and Form*, 118.

13. Friedrich Kittler, "Musik als Medium," in *Wahrnehmung und Geschichte: Markierungen zur Aisthesis Materialis*, ed. Bernhard J. Dotzler and Ernst Martin Müller (Berlin: Akademie, 1995), 83–99.

14. Friedrich Kittler, "Gramophone" from *Gramophone, Film, Typewriter*, trans. Geoffrey Withrop-Young and Michael Wutz (Palo Alto, CA: Stanford University Press, 1999), 21–114.

15. The foundational psychological study is Sylvan Tompkins's *Affect Imagery Consciousness*, vol. 1, *The Positive Affects* (New York: Springer, 1962), and vol. 2, *The Negative Affects* (New York: Springer, 1963). Recent elaborations in the field of critical theory include Jane Bennett, *The Enchantment of Modern Life: Attachments, Crossings, and Ethics* (Princeton, NJ: Princeton University Press, 2001); Brian Massumi, *Parables for the Virtual: Movement, Affect, Sensation* (Durham, NC: Duke University Press, 2002); Eve Kosofsky Sedgwick, *Touching Feeling: Affect, Pedagogy, Performativity* (Durham, NC: Duke University Press, 2003); Kathleen Stewart, *Ordinary Affects* (Durham, NC: Duke University Press, 2007), and *The Affect Theory Reader*, ed. Melissa Gregg and Gregory J. Seigworth (Durham, NC: Duke University Press, 2010); and Judith Lochhead, Eduardo Mendieta, and Stephen Decatur Smith, eds. *Sound and Affect: Voice, Music, World* (Chicago: University of Chicago Press, 2021).

16. Roger Grant has argued that its conceptual history has deeper historical roots in early modern European philosophy than is typically acknowledged. See Roger Mathew Grant, *Peculiar Attunements: How Affect Theory Turned Musical* (New York: Fordham University Press, 2020).

17. Eugenie Brinkema, *The Forms of the Affects* (Durham, NC: Duke University Press, 2014). In the realm of film music and its relationships to affective memory, see Berthold Hoeckner, *Film, Music, Memory* (Chicago: University of Chicago Press, 2020).

18. Lauren Berlant, *Cruel Optimism* (Durham, NC: Duke University Press, 2011). With equal dialectical attention, Sianne Ngai has tracked the way capitalist channelings of affect have led to a deformation of Enlightenment aesthetic categories in late modernity in *Our Aesthetic Categories: Zany, Cute, Interesting* (Cambridge, MA: Harvard University Press, 2015).

19. Anthropology of ritual is another key influence on Langer, particularly that of Franz Boas. See, in particular, Franz Boas, *The Mind of Primitive Man* (New York: Macmillan, 1911).

20. Langer, *Philosophy in a New Key*, 245.

21. Suzanne Cusick, "On a Lesbian Relationship with Music: A Serious Effort Not to Think Straight," in *Queering the Pitch: The New Gay and Lesbian Musicology*, ed. Brett, Philip, Gary Thomas, and Elizabeth Wood (New York: Routledge, 1994), 67–83.

22. Angela Davis, *Blues Legacies and Black Feminism* (New York: Vintage Books/ Random House, 1998), xi.

23. Davis, 13.

24. Davis, 13.

25. With respect to Cusick's question about the equation of music and sex, Fred Moten gives a similar contradictory answer when he writes that Eros in Ellington's music is "not [sexual] but nothing other than sexual." Fred Moten, *In the Break: The Aesthetics of the Black Radical Tradition* (Minneapolis: University of Minnesota Press, 2003), 25–26.

26. Moten, 26.

27. Moten, 25.

28. Moten, 30–31.

29. Moten's discussion relates to Freud's theory of the drives, articulated in Sigmund Freud, *An Outline of Psycho-Analysis*, trans. James Strachey (New York: W. W. Norton, 1949).

30. Both essays are published in Roland Barthes, *Image, Music, Text*, trans. Stephen Heath (New York: Hill and Wang, 1977). "Musica Practica" appears on pages 149–54, and "The Grain of the Voice" appears on pages 179–89.

31. Carolyn Abbate, "Music—Drastic or Gnostic?" *Critical Inquiry* 30, no. 3 (Spring 2004): 505–36.

32. Vladimir Jankélévitch, *Liszt: Rhapsodie et Improvisation*, ed. Françoise Schwab (Paris: Flammarion, 1998). For a discussion, see Carolyn Abbate and Michael Gallope, "The Ineffable (and Beyond)," *Oxford Handbook of Western Music and Philosophy* (New York: Oxford University Press, 2020), 741–62.

33. Stanley Cavell, "Music Discomposed," in *Must We Mean What We Say?* (Cambridge: Cambridge University Press, 2002), 180–212.

34. Clément Rosset, *Joyful Cruelty: Toward a Philosophy of the Real*, trans. David F. Bell (New York: Oxford University Press, 1993).

35. Vladimir Jankélévitch, *Music and the Ineffable*, trans. Carolyn Abbate, (Princeton, NJ: Princeton University Press, 2003).

36. Michel Foucault, "The Unities of Discourse," in *The Archaeology of Knowledge*, trans. A. M. Sheridan Smith, (New York: Routledge, 2002), 23–33.

37. Carolyn Abbate, "Overlooking the Ephemeral," *New Literary History* 48, no. 1 (Winter 2017): 75–102.

38. Lydia Goehr, *The Imaginary Museum of Musical Works: An Essay in the Philosophy of Music* (New York: Oxford University Press, 1992).

39. Alexander Weheliye, *Phonographies: Grooves in Sonic Afro-Modernity* (Durham, NC: Duke University Press, 2005); and Beth Coleman, "Race as Technology," *Camera Obscura*, no. 1 (2009): 177–207.

40. Michael Denning, *Noise Uprising: The Audiopolitics of a World Musical Revolution* (Brooklyn, NY: Verso, 2015).

41. Kodwo Eshun, *More Brilliant Than the Sun* (London: Quartet Books, 1998).

42. For a variant of affective praxis that builds on a metaphysical tradition from Schopenhauer to Deleuze, see Holly Watkins, *Musical Vitalities: Ventures in a Biotic Aesthetics of Music* (Chicago: University of Chicago Press, 2018).

43. Ruth Leys, "The Turn to Affect: A Critique" *Critical Inquiry* 37, no. 3 (Spring 2011): 434–72.

44. Langer, *Feeling and Form*, 14.

45. Andrew Chung, "What Is Musical Meaning? Theorizing Music as Performative Utterance," *Music Theory Online* 25, no. 1 (March 2019), https://mtosmt.org/issues/mto.19.25.1/mto.19.25.1.chung.html.

46. Gary Tomlinson, *A Million Years of Music* (New York: Zone Books, 2015), 173–208.

47. G. W. F. Hegel, *Logic (Encyclopedia I)* (1817), § 81.

48. On immanent critique, see Andrew Buchwalter, "Hegel, Marx, and the Concept of Immanent Critique," *Journal of the History of Philosophy* 29, no. 2 (April 1991): 253–79.

49. Erin Huang, *Urban Horror: Neoliberal Post-Socialism and the Limits of Visibility* (Durham, NC: Duke University Press, 2020), 8.

CHAPTER TWO

1. On the role impressionism played in this evolution toward modernist painting, see Meyer Schapiro, *Impressionism: Reflections and Perceptions* (New York: George Braziller, 1997). On the role of perception in cubism and abstract painting, see David Cottington, *Cubism* (London: Tate, 2001), and Mel Gooding, *Abstract Art* (London: Tate, 2001).

2. In art theory and aesthetics, see Rudolf Arnheim, *Art and Visual Perception: A Psychology of the Creative Eye* (Berkeley: University of California Press, 1960). In film theory, see, *Hugo Münsterberg on Film: The Photoplay: A Psychological Study and Other Writings*, ed. Allan Langdale (New York: Routledge, 2002). Also see Roy R. Behrens, "Art, Design, and Gestalt Theory," *Leonardo* 31, no. 4 (August 1998): 299–303.

3. Miriam Hansen, "The Mass Production of the Senses: Classical Cinema as Vernacular Modernism," *Modernism/modernity* 6. no. 2 (April 1999): 59–77; and Jonathan Crary, *Suspensions of Perception: Attention, Spectacle, and Modern Culture* (Cambridge, MA: MIT Press, 2001).

4. Sara Danius, *The Senses of Modernism: Technology, Perception, and Aesthetics* (Ithaca, NY: Cornell University Press, 2002). On the instances of ordinary and banal

repetitions of the everyday in modernist literature, see Liesl Olson, *Modernism and the Ordinary* (New York: Oxford University Press, 2009).

5. In something of a precursor to second-order modernism, Arnold Schoenberg proposed speculations about the relativity of dissonance in the *Harmonielehre* (1911) and questioned the normativity of the discrete tone through his structural engagement with timbre specifically in his use of *Klangfarbenmelodie* in the *Five Pieces for Orchestra*, op. 16 (1909), and his experimentation with *Sprechstimme* in *Pierrot lunaire*, op. 21 (1912), among other works. By shaping music's timbre as a fundamental element and exploring the liminal speech-like spaces between discrete tones, Schoenberg implicitly questioned our capacities of musical perception. In this, he may have been influenced by modernist painting, namely, his Viennese friend and colleague Wassily Kandinsky's *Concerning the Spiritual in Art* (1911). At the same time, other elements of his musical aesthetics elevated and preserved the unit of the musical tone, most notably his approach to the twelve-tone technique circa 1923.

6. On the history of racism in the history of the jazz musician's workplace, see Gerald Horne, *Jazz and Justice: Racism and the Political Economy of the Music* (New York: New York University Press, 2019). The economic security of families varied significantly by race, which drastically reduced the number of likely artists from Black families and increased precarity for the ones that did persevere. Cage, Babbitt, and Carter all came from white upper-middle-class families; in the 1940s the American Medical Association and the Bar Association did not allow African Americans to join their professional societies, prohibiting Black Americans from two of the largest and most lucrative professions. African Americans had little access to health insurance until Medicaid was passed in the 1960s.

7. Stuart Hall, "What Is Black in Popular Culture?," in *Stuart Hall: Critical Dialogues in Cultural Studies*, ed. David Morley and Kuan Hsing-Chen (New York: Routledge, 1996), 465–75.

8. The term *racial capitalism* was coined by Cedric Robinson in his book *Black Marxism: The Making of the Black Radical Tradition* (Chapel Hill: University of North Carolina Press, 2000).

9. Matthew Morrison has noted the way in which the extraction and exploitation of Black entertainment labor and intellectual property has a deep structural history: "Black performance practices, or the intellectual performance property of black people, have a history of being absorbed into popular entertainment, making them ineligible for copyright and available in the public domain." See Matthew Morrison, "Race, Blacksound, and the (Re)Making of Musicological Discourse," *Journal of the American Musicological Society* 72, no. 3 (Fall 2019): 781–824.

10. The effects of structural racism were no less of an issue for Black composers. Eileen Southern has noted in her field-defining history of African American music that the vast majority of Black composers' works have remained ephemeral and unpublished. See Eileen Southern, preface to *The Music of Black Americans: A History*, 3rd ed. (New York: W. W. Norton, 1997), xx–xxi.

11. As Achille Mbembe describes the result, "Even at the zenith of the logic of race, these two categories were always marked by ambivalence—the ambivalence of repulsion, of atrocious charm and perverse enjoyment." See Achille Mbembe, *Critique of Black Reason* (Durham, NC: Duke University Press, 2017), 129. Blackness as a racialized

other trafficked in "exoticism, frivolity, and entertainment" for white audiences. In this way, Blackness catered to white fantasies of risk and was also often gendered at the hands of white heterosexual men; Black women were routinely framed as "indolent, available, and submissive." See Mbembe, 68, 69.

12. Stuart Hall, "Representation: Cultural Representations and Signifying Practices," in *Representation: Cultural Representation and Signifying Practices*, ed. Stuart Hall (London: Sage; Milton Keynes: Open University, 1997).

13. Tammy Kernodle in conversation with Monica Hairston O'Connell and Maya-Camille Broussard, "Jazz Kitchen: A Woman's Place," Hyde Park Jazz Festival, October 8, 2020, https://www.youtube.com/watch?v=LmpFQPhWgsU&feature=youtu.be. More fully, Kernodle's words: "This is what I realize more and more everyday: People love Black culture; they don't like Black people. They will eat our food, they will wear our clothes, they will wear clothes in the way we do, they will listen to our music, [Monica Hairston O'Connell: They will let us educate them] they let us educate them, but they negate our humanity. They make us invisible when it comes to lived experiences."

14. See John Bramble, *Modernism and the Occult* (New York: Palgrave Macmillan, 2015); Elizabeth Hutchinson, *The Indian Craze: Primitivism, Modernism, and Transculturation in American Art, 1890–1915* (Durham, NC: Duke University Press, 2009). For a primary source reader in the visual arts, see *Primitivism and Twentieth-Century Art: A Documentary History*, ed. Jack Flam with Miriam Deutsch (Berkeley: University of California Press, 2003).

15. See Georgina Born and David Hesmondhalgh, *Western Music and Its Others: Difference, Representation, and Appropriation in Music* (Berkeley: University of California Press, 2000). Even the highest modernists had their fetishistic moments: a primitivism runs through the steady backdrop of tom toms in Karlheinz Stockhausen's *Kreuzspiel* (1951), not to mention the composer's elaborately conceived cosmologies of the 1960s and 1970s; Pierre Boulez's *Le marteau sans maître* (1954) famously trafficked in Asian and African exotica; even Milton Babbitt, who played jazz clarinet in high school and failed at a career in musical theater in 1930s, cultivated a lifelong interest in standards and jazz that irrupted in a skittish work like *All Set* (1957) for jazz combo.

16. Bramble, *Modernism and the Occult*, 3. Also see Roger Griffin, *Modernism and Fascism: The Sense of a Beginning under Mussolini and Hitler* (Basingstoke: Palgrave Macmillan, 2012). Similarly, for Kimberly Jannarone, the politics of such fetishism were explicitly regressive even if we fail to remember them in this way.

17. See Richard Taruskin, "The Apex: Babbitt and Cold War Serialism," *Oxford History of Western Art Music: The Late Twentieth Century* (New York, Oxford University Press, 2010), 103–74 and Peter Bürger, *Theory of the Avant-Garde*, trans. Michael Shaw (Minneapolis, MN: University of Minnesota Press, 1984).

18. On the institutional barriers to the existence of women artists in the visual arts, see Linda Nochlin, "Why Have There Been No Great Women Artists?," *ArtNews* 69, no. 9 (January 1971): 22–39, 67–71.

19. For the canonical theory of the male gaze and its associated phenomena of scopophilia, see Laura Mulvey, "Visual Pleasure and Narrative Cinema," *Screen* 6, no. 3 (Autumn 1975): 6–18. For a male-authored critique of the male gaze, see John Berger, *Ways of Seeing* (1972), Episode 2, available at https://www.youtube.com/watch?v=bZR06JJWaJM.

20. For a historical overview of bias against women in postwar Western popular music, see Sheila Whiteley, *Women and Popular Music: Sexuality, Identity and Subjectivity* (New York: Routledge, 2000), "Introduction," 1–21. See also Diane Railton, "The Gendered Carnival of Pop," *Gender & Sexuality* (October 2001): 321–31; and Jacqueline Warwick, *Girl Groups, Girl Culture: Popular Music and Identity in the 1960s* (New York: Routledge, 2013).

21. The Harlem Renaissance (1918–1930s) was a site for Afro-modernist reappropriation of primitivism by Black artists, playwrights, and authors. See Edward Marx, "Forgotten Jungle Songs: Primitivist Strategies of the Harlem Renaissance," *Langston Hughes Review* 14, nos. 1/2 (1996): 79–93; David Krasner, *A Beautiful Pageant: African American Theatre, Drama, and Performance in the Harlem Renaissance, 1910–1927* (New York: Palgrave Macmillan, 2002); and Cherene Sherrard-Johnson, *Portraits of the New Negro Woman: Visual and Literary Culture in the Harlem Renaissance* (New Brunswick, NJ: Rutgers University Press, 2007). See also Kobena Mercer, ed., *Cosmopolitan Modernisms* (Cambridge MA: MIT Press, 2005); Partha Mitter, *The Triumph of Modernism: India's Artists and the Avant-Garde 1922–1947* (London: Reaktion, 2007); Elaine O'Brien, Everlyn Nicodemus, Melissa Chiu, Benjamin Genocchio, Mary K. Coffey, and Roberto Tejada, eds., *Modern Art in Africa, Asia, and Latin America: An Introduction to Global Modernism* (Malden, MA: Wiley-Blackwell, 2013); and Ruth B. Phillips, "Aesthetic Primitivism Revisited: The Global Diaspora of 'Primitive Art' and the Rise of Indigenous Modernisms," *Journal of Art Historiography*, no. 12 (June 2015), 1–25.

22. See Eileen Southern, *The Music of Black Americans: A History* (New York: W. W. Norton, 1971); Samuel Floyd, *The Power of Black Music* (New York: Oxford University Press, 1993). On the sidelining of Black artists of the Harlem Renaissance in surveys of art history, see Alphonso Walker Grant and Jessica Baker, "Black Artists of the Harlem Renaissance in Western Survey Textbooks: Narratives of Omission and Representation," *Visual Inquiry* 2, no. 3 (September 2013): 233–46.

23. Laura Doyle, "Modernist Studies and Inter-imperiality in the Longue Durée," in *The Oxford Handbook of Global Modernisms*, ed. Mark Wollaeger (New York: Oxford University Press, 2018), 685.

24. Chika Okeke-Agulu, *Postcolonial Modernism: Art and Decolonization in Twentieth-Century Nigeria* (Durham, NC: Duke University Press, 2015). For an illuminating discussion of Okeke-Agulu, Doyle, and the historiography of global modernisms, see Tamara Levitz and Benjamin Piekut, "The Vernacular Avant-garde: A Speculation," *ASAP Journal*, September 3, 2020, http://asapjournal.com/the-vernacular-avant-garde-a-speculation-tamara-levitz-and-benjamin-piekut/.

25. In Doyle's words, "the anxious vision of a fractured 'modernist' world, with its discrepant time lines and perspectives, was always already 'known' among the dispossessed and simply awaited the emergence among them of artists with access to print or other media. In fact, instead of considering early canonical Anglo-European and Anglo-American modernists the world pioneers, it might be fair to say that they grasped the world situation belatedly at the turn of the century—as compared to the long-standing knowledge of the many thousands living in colonial territories or repeatedly invaded and disenfranchised communities." Doyle, "Modernist Studies," 684.

26. See John Litweiler, *Ornette Coleman: A Harmolodic Life* (New York: William and Morrow, 1992), 106–10.

27. George E. Lewis, *A Power Stronger than Itself: The AACM and American Experimental Music* (Chicago: University of Chicago Press, 2008).

28. Franya Berkman, *Monument Eternal: The Music of Alice Coltrane* (Wesleyan, CT: Wesleyan University Press, 2010), 23–24.

29. Soon after, an edgier and more strident hipster was made "punk" by Lester Bangs's garage rock imaginary in the late 1960s and early 1970s. See, for example, Lester Bangs, "James Taylor Marked for Death," in *Psychotic Reactions and Carburetor Dung*, ed. Greil Marcus (New York: Vintage, 1988), 53–81. Also see Patrick Burke, *Tear Down These Walls: White Radicalism and Black Power in 1960s Rock* (Chicago: University of Chicago Press, 2021).

30. Norman Mailer, "The White Negro: Superficial Reflections on the Hipster," *Dissent* 4 (1957): 276–93; and James Baldwin, "The Black Boy Looks at the White Boy Norman Mailer," *Esquire*, May 1, 1961. Also see Ingrid Monson, "The Problem with White Hipness: Race, Gender, and Cultural Conceptions in Jazz Historical Discourse," *Journal of the American Musicological Society* 48, no. 3 (Fall 1995): 396–422.

31. Arthur Rimbaud, "A Season in Hell" (1873), in *Rimbaud: Complete Works, Selected Letters, A Bilingual Edition*, trans. Wallace Fowlie, updated and rev. Seth Whidden (Chicago: University of Chicago Press, 2005), 271.

32. Simon Frith and Angela McRobbie, "Rock and Sexuality" (1978), in *On Record: Rock, Pop, & The Written Word*, ed. Simon Frith and Andrew Goodwin (New York: Routledge, 1990), 371–89; Robert Walser, *Running with the Devil: Power, Gender, and Madness in Heavy Metal Music* (Hanover, NH: University Press of New England, 1993); Steve Waksman, *Instruments of Desire: The Electric Guitar and the Shaping of Musical Experience* (Cambridge, MA: Harvard University Press, 1999); Philip Auslander, *Performing Glam Rock: Gender and Theatricality in Popular Music* (Ann Arbor: University of Michigan Press, 2006). Edward Comantale's *Sweet Air: Modernism, Regionalism, and American Popular Song* (Urbana: University of Illinois Press, 2013) frames the social revolutions associated with postwar popular music as dependent on the ineffable cipher of the LP format, a uniquely affect-saturated and abstract—even modernist or formalist—medium.

33. On the postwar economic miracle and its relationships to musical repetition as a broader cultural form, see Robert Fink, *Repeating Ourselves: American Minimal Music as Cultural Practice* (Berkeley: University of California Press, 2005).

34. For a critical account of the "liberal" function of jazz in the context of US empire, see Jairo Moreno, "Imperial Aurality: Jazz, the Archive, and US Empire," in *Audible Empire: Music, Global Politics, Critique*, ed. Ronald Radano and Tejumola Olaniyan (Durham, NC: Duke University Press), 135–60. On the "cultural sophistication" of avant-garde liberalism as a function of US cultural diplomacy, see Danielle Fosler-Lussier, "American Cultural Diplomacy and the Mediation of Avant-garde Music," in *Sound Commitments: Avant-Garde Music and the Sixties*, ed. Robert Adlington (New York: Oxford University Press, 2009), 232–53.

35. Stanley Cavell, "A Matter of Meaning It," in *Must We Mean What We Say?* (Cambridge: Cambridge University Press, 2002), 221.

36. Before modernism, this was not the case. In music, Cavell claims that common practice tonality once felt like an improvisation built on expressive and intentional

conventions such that one could hear why one thing would work and not another. In the age of modernism, this is no more. Because of an excess of medium-specific, highly mathematical, and formula-driven methods of musical composition, "the entire enterprise of action and of communication has become problematic." Stanley Cavell, "Music Discomposed," in *Must We Mean What We Say?* (Cambridge: Cambridge University Press, 2002), 201.

37. Cavell, "A Matter of Meaning It," 219.

38. Cavell, 219.

39. Cavell, "Music Discomposed," 201–2.

40. Theodor Adorno and Max Horkheimer, *The Dialectic of Enlightenment*, ed. Gunzelin Schmid Noerr, trans. Edmund Jephcott (Palo Alto, CA: Stanford University Press, 2002); and Martin Heidegger, "Letter on Humanism," *Heidegger: Basic Writings*, ed. David Farrell Krell, trans. Frank A Capuzzi and J. Glenn Gray (New York: Harper Collins, 1993), 213–66.

41. For an account of this tension between emergent discourses of dehumanization and a seemingly paradoxical renewal for human authenticity during the postwar era, see Howard Brick, *Age of Contradiction: American Thought & Culture in the 1960s* (Ithaca, NY: Cornell University Press, 1998), particularly "Authenticity and Artifice," 66–97, and "Systems and the Distrust of Order," 124–45.

42. Jacques Rancière, *The Politics of Aesthetics: The Distribution of the Sensible* (London: Bloomsbury, 2013).

43. See James H. Cone, *The Spirituals and the Blues: An Interpretation* (Maryknoll, NY: Orbis Books, 1972); Alexander Weheliye, *Phonographies: Grooves in Sonic Afro-Modernity* (Durham, NC: Duke University Press, 2005); Shana L. Redmond, *Social Movements and the Sound of Solidarity in the African Diaspora* (New York: New York University Press, 2014); Daphne Brooks, *Liner Notes for the Revolution: Black Feminist Sound Cultures* (Cambridge, MA: Harvard University Press, 2020); Emily Lordi, *The Meaning of Soul: Black Music and Resistance Since the 1960s* (Durham, NC: Duke University Press, 2020).

44. Richard Goldstein, "A Quiet Night at the Balloon Farm," *New York* (October 1966), in Clinton Heylin, ed., *All Yesterday's Parties: The Velvet Underground in Print: 1966–1971* (Cambridge, MA: Perseus Books, 2005), 30.

45. On the complex psychic traffic of mimicry, see Homi Bhabha, *The Location of Culture* (New York: Routledge, 1994).

46. On the unconscious racialization of music among listeners, see Jennifer Lynn Stoever, *The Sonic Color Line: Race and the Cultural Politics of Listening* (New York: New York University Press, 2016), and Nina Eidsheim, *The Race of Sound: Listening, Timbre, and Vocality in African American Music* (Durham, NC: Duke University Press, 2019).

47. Georg Wilhelm Friedrich Hegel, *The Phenomenology of Spirit*, ed. and trans. Terry Pinkard, (Cambridge: Cambridge University Press, 2014), 114. Hegel's discussion of the master-slave dialectic spans pages 108–16.

48. Alexandre Kojève, *Introduction to the Reading of Hegel: Lectures on the Phenomenology of Spirit*, assembled by Raymond Queneau, ed. Allan Bloom, trans. James H. Nichols Jr. (Ithaca, NY: Cornell University Press, 1980).

49. Cedric J. Robinson, *Black Marxism: the Making of the Black Radical Tradition* (Chapel Hill: University of North Carolina Press, 2005). Also see Sylvia Wynter, "Unsettling the Coloniality of Being/Power/Truth/Freedom: Towards the Human, After Man, Its Overrepresentation—An Argument," *New Centennial Review* 3, no. 3 (2003): 257–37.

50. On Du Bois's interest in Hegel, see Joel Williamson, "W.E.B. Du Bois as a Hegelian," in *What Was Freedom's Price*, ed. David G. Sansing (Jackson: University Press of Mississippi, 1978), 21–50. Also see Paul Taylor, *Black Is Beautiful: A Philosophy of Black Aesthetics* (Malden, MA: Wiley-Blackwell, 2016). For a Lacanian perspective on double consciousness see Sheldon George, *Trauma and Race: A Lacanian Study of African American Racial Identity* (Waco, TX: Baylor University Press, 2016).

51. Frantz Fanon, *White Skin, Black Masks*, trans. Charles Lam Markmann (New York: Grove Press, 1968), 12.

52. Fanon, 8.

53. For a feminist and queer reading of Fanon's views of sexuality, see Diana Fuss, "Interior Colonies: Frantz Fanon and the Politics of Identification," *Diacritics* 24, no. 2/3 (1994): 20–42.

54. Fanon explores this theme at length. See, especially, Fanon, *White Skin, Black Masks*, 60.

55. Fanon, 100.

56. Mbembe, *Critique of Black Reason*, 2.

57. Mbembe writes that the other inspires no compassion at the hands of a racism preoccupied by "fears and torments, of disturbed thoughts and terror" and "infinite sufferings and, ultimately catastrophe" (10).

58. Mbembe, 10.

59. Mbembe, 11.

60. Mbembe describes the utopian strain as a historicizing revival of an African imaginary: "African art—and to some extent jazz—appeared as a celestial path of return to one's origins, a kind of grace by which sleeping powers could be awakened, myths and rituals reinvented, tradition rerouted and undermined, and time reversed" (41).

61. Fred Moten's approach is, however, negative and fractured. In passages of *Black and Blur* (Durham, NC: Duke University Press, 2017) and *The Universal Machine* (Durham, NC: Duke University Press, 2018), Moten reads the resistant capacities of Black ontology back into a sustained critique of Emmanuel Levinas's ethical metaphysics.

62. See Saidiya V. Hartman, *Scenes of Subjection: Terror, Slavery, and Self-making in Nineteenth-Century America* (New York: Oxford University Press, 1997), and Fred Moten, *In the Break: The Aesthetics of the Black Radical Tradition* (Durham, NC: Duke University Press, 2003).

63. Simone de Beauvoir, *The Second Sex*, intro. by Judith Thurman, trans. Constance Borde and Sheila Malovany-Chevallier (New York: Vintage Books, 2011), 9.

64. See Judith Butler, *Gender Trouble* (New York: Routledge, 1990); and *Bodies That Matter: On the Discursive Limits of "Sex"* (New York: Routledge, 1993). Other lineages of feminism investigated the social and material underpinnings of the dynamics of recognition and representation; care labor feminism sought to theorize the uniqueness and

gender specificity of feminized labor and, in a more Marxist vein, social reproduction theory that, in Silvia Federici's words, acknowledged that surplus value was "also extracted from the workday of millions of unwaged house-workers as well as many other unpaid and un-free labourers." See Silvia Federici, "Social Reproduction Theory: History, Issues, and Present Challenges," *Radical Philosophy* 2, no. 4 (Spring 2019): 55–57.

65. See for example, Sumi Cho, Kimberlé Williams Crenshaw, and Leslie McCall, "Toward a Field of Intersectionality Studies: Theory, Applications, and Praxis," *Signs* 38, no. 4 (Summer 2013): 785–810. See also Patricia Hall Collins, *Intersectionality as Critical Social Theory* (Durham, NC: Duke University Press, 2019).

66. Amia Srinivasan, *The Right to Sex: Feminism in the Twenty-First Century* (New York: Farrar, Straus, and Giroux, 2021).

67. George E. Lewis, "Improvised Music after 1950: Afrological and Eurological Perspectives," *Black Music Research Journal* 16, no. 1 (Spring 1996): 91–122.

68. W. E. B. Du Bois, *The Souls of Black Folk* (Chicago: A. C. McClurg, 1903), 8.

69. Similarly for Nina Eidsheim's constructivist ethics of listening to voice in her book *The Race of Sound: Listening, Timbre, & Vocality in African American Music* (Durham, NC: Duke University Press, 2019). Eidsheim espouses an ethical skepticism that is attentive to the unknowable inconsistency of the other's voice. She writes, "We think that we already know, but in fact we know very little [about the voice of the other]." (3). And later, "I seek to disassemble any promise of 'accuracy.' I will go as far as to argue that its pursuit is a dead-end street." (21). At the same time, she also proposes to critique existing social constructions and norms of the voice (both passively ideologically and ethically actively): "I aim to confront the continually developing understanding of meaning, the choices and power structures at its base, and the selective choices even the most conscientious listeners must carry out in order to make sense of a voice" (21).

70. Édouard Glissant, *Poetics of Relation*, trans. Betsy Wing. (Ann Arbor: University of Michigan Press, 2010), 189.

71. Michael Taussig, *Mimesis and Alterity: A Particular History of the Senses* (New York: Routledge, 1993).

72. Quincy Troupe, *Miles: The Autobiography* (New York: Picador, 1989), 250. Davis made this statement with references to Ornette Coleman.

73. On Coleman's harmolodics, see Peter Niklas Wilson, *Ornette Coleman: His Life and Music* (Berkeley, CA: Berkeley Hills Books, 1999).

74. Cf. Olúfẹ́mi O. Táíwò, "Being-in-the-Room Privilege: Elite Capture and Epistemic Deference," *Philosopher* 108, no. 4 (Autumn 2020), https://www.thephilosopher1923.org/essay-taiwo.

75. For a collection of essays exploring the emergence of atmospheric aesthetics in music since Debussy, see David Toop, *Ocean of Sound: Ambient Sound and Radical Listening in the Age of Communication* (London: Serpent's Tail, 1995). Also see Gernot Böhme, *The Aesthetics of Atmospheres* (New York: Routledge, 2017), trans. Jean-Paul Thibaud and ed. Frederica Scassillo, *Resounding Spaces: Approaching Musical Atmospheres* (n.p.: Mimesis International, 2020); Friedlind Riedel and Juha Torvinen, *Music as Atmosphere: Collective Feelings and Affective Sounds* (London: Routledge, 2020); and Victor Szabo, *Turn On, Tune In, Drift Off: Ambient Music's Psychedelic Past* (New York: Oxford University Press, 2022).

76. Jean Baudrillard, *The System of Objects*, (Brooklyn, NY: Verso, 2006), 47.

77. See A. H., "David Tudor in Piano Recital," *New York Herald Tribune*, Friday March 20, 1959; and Harold C. Schonberg, "The Far Out Pianist," *Harper's*, June 1960, 49–54.

78. George Hoefer, "Caught in the Act," *Down Beat*, January 7, 1960. Quoted in Litweiler, *Ornette Coleman*, 78.

79. John Cale, *What's Welsh for Zen: The Autobiography of John Cale* (New York: Bloomsbury, 1999), 93.

80. Even Cage, who could be hostile toward sound recording as a medium, was enthusiastic about his Town Hall concert taking the form of a commercially released album. The concert that included Tudor's premiere of the *Concert for Piano and Orchestra* was Cage's first major release. It was adorned with liner notes and was produced, promoted, and even distributed by George Avakian, a major-label executive who worked largely in the jazz industry. On Cage's hostility toward recorded music and its relevance for 1960s experimentalism that was not particularly influenced by or related to recording, see David Grubbs, *Records Ruin the Landscape: John Cage, The Sixties, and Sound Recording* (Chicago: University of Chicago Press, 2014).

81. See Michael E. Veal, *Dub: Soundscapes and Shattered Songs in Jamaican Reggae* (Middletown, CT: Wesleyan University Press, 2007), 19.

82. Veal, 13.

83. Amiri Baraka (then LeRoi Jones), *Blues People* (1963; reprint, New York: Harper Perennial, 2002), 202.

84. Baraka, 213.

85. See Phil Ford, *Dig: Sound and Music in Hip Culture* (New York: Oxford University Press, 2013). Ford's introduction offers a synthesis of the philosophical conundrums surrounding the phenomenon of hipness. He writes of its proximity to negative theology and ineffability: "It is woven into the very fabric of hipness that it not offer itself up to analysis, and if it does somehow find itself analyzed, those items under examination would shrivel, losing whatever hip aura they might have had" (4).

86. James Baldwin, "The Black Boy Looks at the White Boy Norman Mailer," *Esquire*, May 1, 1961.

87. The term *compliance* is drawn from Nelson Goodman, *Languages of Art: An Approach to a Theory of Symbols* (Indianapolis, IN: Hackett, 1976), 186–92.

88. On traditional "harmonic improvisation" in jazz, particularly in the work of Coleman Hawkins, see Scott DeVeaux, "The Making of a Virtuoso" in *The Birth of Bebop: A Social Musical History* (Berkeley: University of California Press, 1997), 72–115.

89. Nat Hentoff. Liner Notes for *Live at the Village Vanguard Again!*, interview with Coltrane in summer or early fall of 1966.

90. The iconic phrase "sheets of sound" was coined by journalist Ira Gitler in 1958. See "Trane on the Track," *Down Beat*, October 16, 1958.

91. Lawrence M. Principe, *The Secrets of Alchemy* (Chicago: University of Chicago Press, 2013).

92. The passage from fracture to hyperfracture to alchemy is prefigured in Adorno's study of Mahler. There, once Adorno realizes that Mahler's harmonies are not

particularly fractured, nor is the music revealing historical cognitions through its use of, say, learned linear counterpoint (as Schoenberg does with the twelve-tone technique), he begins to sense that the criteria for resistance have become murky, inconsistent, and atmospheric. See Theodor Adorno, *Mahler: A Musical Physiognomy*, trans. Edmund Jephcott (Chicago: University of Chicago Press, 1992).

93. Georgina Born, "On Musical Mediation: Ontology, Technology, and Creativity," *Twentieth-Century Music* 2, no. 1 (March 2005): 7–36.

94. Richard Hell Papers, MSS.140, box 4, folder 142, New York University Fales Library Special Collections.

95. For a rich study of the multiplicity of voices and shifting forms in Dylan's work, see Steven Rings, "A Foreign Sound to Your Ear: Bob Dylan Performs 'It's Alright, Ma (I'm Only Bleeding),' 1964–2009," *Music Theory Online* 19, no. 4 (December 2013): https://mtosmt.org/issues/mto.13.19.4/mto.13.19.4.rings.php.

96. See Alice Coltrane, *World Spirituality Classics*, vol. 1, *The Ecstatic Music of Alice Coltrane: Turiyasangitananda* (New York: Luaka Bop, 2017).

97. On Bangs's admiration of Quine, see Jim DeRogatis, *Let It Blurt: The Life and Times of Lester Bangs, America's Greatest Rock Critic* (New York: Broadway Books, 2008), 147–48.

98. Benjamin Piekut, "The Vernacular Avant-Garde," in *Henry Cow: The World Is a Problem* (Durham, NC: Duke University Press, 2019), 387–408; and Anthony Reed, *Soundworks: Race, Sound, and Poetry in Production* (Durham, NC: Duke University Press, 2020), 9–13. Also see Michael Gallope, "A Paradox of the Vernacular," in *Deep Refrains: Music, Philosophy, and the Ineffable* (Chicago: University of Chicago Press, 2017), 243–60, and Philip Rupprecht, "Bedford and Souster as Pop Musicians," in *British Musical Modernism: The Manchester Group and Their Contemporaries* (Cambridge: Cambridge University Press, 2015), 365–442.

### CHAPTER THREE

1. Kenneth Silverman, *Begin Again: A Biography of John Cage* (New York: Knopf, 2010), 152.

2. George Avakian, "About the Concert," from *The 25-Year Retrospective Concert of the Music of John Cage*, liner notes, produced by George Avakian, New York (Independent Release, 1959) (personal copy).

3. Quoted in Silverman, *Begin Again*, 153.

4. Miles Kastendieck, "Cage's Music Still a Phenomenon," *New York Journal-American*, May 16, 1958, David Tudor Papers, 980039, box 62, folder 13, Getty Research Institute, Los Angeles.

5. Cage read about the *bhāva* in two books by Ananda Coomaraswamy: *The Transformation of Nature in Art* (New Delhi: Munshiram Manoharlal, 2014), 52; and *The Dance of Shiva: Fourteen Indian Essays*, rev. ed. (New York: Noonday Press, 1957), 36–38. During this period Cage was also influenced by the music of Indian singer and pakhavaj player Gita Sarabhai, who had been visiting the US. Cage and Sarabhai studied with one another in 1946; she presented in him with his copy of *The Gospel of Sri Ramakrishna*, which he read the following year. He credits her (via her teacher) with the

statement that the purpose of music is "to sober and quiet the mind, thus rendering it susceptible to divine influences." See Cage, *Indeterminacy*, story no. 79 (1959), https://www.lcdf.org/indeterminacy/s/79.

6. Fred Grunfeld, "Cage without Bars," *Reporter*, February 4, 1960, 35, 37. David Tudor Papers, 980039, box 63, folder 1, Getty Research Institute, Los Angeles.

7. Edward James Crooks, "John Cage's Entanglement with the Ideas of Coomaraswamy" (PhD diss, University of York, 2011).

8. Ananda K. Coomaraswamy, *The Transformation of Nature in Art* (New Delhi: Munshiram Manoharlal, 2014), 15.

9. For Cage's 1940s perspective on the proper appropriation of Asian compositional techniques into Western music, see John Cage, "The East in the West," *Asian Music* 1, no. 1 (1947): 18; originally published in *Modern Music* 23, no. 2 (1946): 111–15. The article draws a parallel between twelve-tone music and Hindu ragas; in Cage's view, both emphasize horizontal linearity over vertical harmony.

10. See David W. Patterson, "Cage and Asia: History and Sources," in *The Cambridge Companion to John Cage*, ed. David Nicholls (New York: Cambridge University Press, 2002), 41–62.

11. Robert Sharf, "Suzuki, D. T.," in *Encyclopedia of Religion*, 2nd ed. (Detroit: Macmillan Reference, 2005), 8884–87.

12. In particular, see John Cage, "Composition as Process: III. Communication," in *Silence* (Wesleyan, CT: Wesleyan University Press, 1961): 46–47.

13. Thanks to Martin Iddon for clarification on this point. In a letter from M. C. Richards to Tudor, Richards tells Tudor that Cage received a payment of $125 from the Stable Gallery sometime in August or September 1958. David Tudor Papers, 980039, box 58, Getty Research Institute, Los Angeles.

14. Dore Ashton, "Art Review: Cage, Composer, Shows Calligraphy of Note," *New York Times*, May 6, 1958.

15. Yong Chen, *Chop Suey, USA: The Story of Chinese Food in America* (New York: Columbia University Press, 2021).

16. See "David Tudor: Interview with Peter Dickinson, Ibis Hotel, London, July 26, 1987," in Peter Dickinson, ed., *CageTalk: Dialogues with and about John Cage* (Rochester, NY: University of Rochester Press, 2006), 91.

17. Program for Cage's 25-Year Retrospective Concert at Town Hall, David Tudor Papers, 980039, box 71, folder 7, Getty Research Institute, Los Angeles.

18. Harold C. Schonberg, "The Far Out Pianist," *Harper's Magazine*, June, 1960, 51, David Tudor Papers, 980039, box 63, folder 1, Getty Research Institute, Los Angeles.

19. Press release, Retrospective Concert of the Music of John Cage. George Avakian Papers, boxes 19–20, New York Public Library.

20. John Cage and Daniel Charles, *For the Birds: John Cage in Conversation with Daniel Charles* (London: Marion Boyars, 1995).

21. Schonberg, "The Far Out Pianist," 52.

22. See Martin Iddon and Philip Thomas, *John Cage's Concert for Piano and Orchestra* (New York: Oxford University Press, 2020), 1–10. Holzaepfel has compiled a code

for determining the multiple copies of Tudor's realization. Tudor prepared his first realization of Cage's *Solo for Piano* in the spring of 1958 for the premiere at Town Hall (R1). In the David Tudor Papers, there are a couple dozen loose realization sheets that he would have swapped into the binder to produce alternate sequences (R1S). This first realization extensively works through most of the graphs in Cage's score. In 1959 Tudor made a second realization of sparse "single ictus" attacks culled from his own first realization. This second realization has four versions (the first three are drafts). They are as follows: (1) a nineteen-page pencil sketch draft without proportional notation (R2I, at Northwestern University); (2) a complete forty-five-page pencil draft in proportional notation (R2S, GRI); (3) a sixteen-sheet incomplete score in ink as well as blue, black, and red pencil (R2D, GRI); and (4) the forty-eight-page final copy on unlined white paper and collected in a binder (R2F, GRI). For these manuscripts, see David Tudor Papers, 980039, box 6, folders 11–12, Getty Research Institute, Los Angeles.

23. When backing out of a performance of Jean Barraque's *Sonate* (1950–52) at the 1957 Festival de l'art d'avant-garde in Marseille, France, Tudor claimed that the composer failed, on a technical-pianistic level, to live up to their own Platonic aspirations of the work's structure. Tudor writes to André Hodeir, "Indeed, I have been forced to the conclusion that the writing for piano is most unsuccessful—or that perhaps a good deal of the music of this *Sonate* remains in the composer's thought and is not expressed on paper. Behind this piece is a magnificent structural thought that lures one always onward in the hope of bringing it to realization." David Tudor Papers, 980039, box 54, folder 4 Getty Research Institute, Los Angeles.

24. See Brigid Cohen, *Stefan Wolpe and the Avant-Garde Diaspora* (Cambridge: Cambridge University Press, 2012).

25. On Tudor's recollections of Stefan Wolpe, see Austin Clarkson, ed., "Recollections of Stefan Wolpe by Former Students and Friends," 86–89. https://sites.evergreen .edu/arunchandra/wp-content/uploads/sites/395/2020/08/wolpeRecollections.pdf. See also Austin Clarkson, "David Tudor's Apprenticeship: The Years with Irma and Stefan Wolpe," *Leonardo Music Journal* 14 (2004): 5–10.

26. Dickinson, *CageTalk*, 88.

27. ". . . performing is very much like cooking: putting it all together, raising the temperature," interview with David Tudor by John David Fullemann in Stockholm, May 31, 1984, https://davidtudor.org/Articles/fullemann.html.

28. "I smile when the sound is singing through the space," interview with David Tudor by Teddy Hultberg in Dusseldorf May 17–18, 1988, https://davidtudor.org/Arti cles/hultberg.html .

29. David Tutor, interview by John David Fullemann, Stockholm, May 31, 1984, https://davidtudor.org/Articles/fullemann.html.

30. In "The Far Out Pianist,", Harold Schonberg also cites Henry Cowell and Stefan Wolpe as corroborating his claim that Tudor was an exceptional sight reader.

31. John Holzaepfel, "Reminiscences of a Twentieth-Century Pianist: An Interview with David Tudor," *Musical Quarterly* 78, no. 3 (Autumn 1994): 633.

32. Holzaepfel, 633.

33. Many thanks to Martin Iddon for alerting me to this influence on Tudor.

34. Schonberg "The Far Out Pianist," 54.

35. Holzaepfel, "Reminiscences of a Twentieth-Century Pianist," 634.

36. Holzaepfel, 633–34.

37. Holzaepfel, 633.

38. Holzaepfel, 635–36.

39. For an extended discussion, see Martin Iddon and Philip Thomas, *John Cage's Concert for Piano and Orchestra* (New York: Oxford University Press, 2020), 100–121.

40. Avakian's recording of the Town Hall premiere was a stereo recording made in the room, making the redress of balance problems impossible during mixing. Avakian initially released three hundred copies in stereo and three hundred in mono, and did so independently, fronting his own money and handling the album promotion entirely on his own, and he followed up with potential reviewers. As of 1982 Cage had earned about $3,400 in royalties from sales of the LP. See George Avakian Papers, box 19, folders 3–11, New York Public Library.

41. Avakian and Cage both remark on the buzz of the scene at Town Hall that night. Avakian notes this in his liner notes for the self-produced Cage LP. The stage itself was also visually memorable, which Silverman describes aptly as "a stage crammed with percussion instruments, tape machines, an electronic carillon, and unfamiliar contraptions." Silverman, *Begin Again*, 153.

42. Ross Parmenter, "Music: Experimenter: Zounds! Sound by John Cage at Town Hall," *New York Times*, May 16, 1958, 20, David Tudor Papers, 980039, box 62, folder 13, Getty Research Institute, Los Angeles.

43. *The Hartford Times* remarks of Tudor's "meticulous attention to the varying details of the music" and praised his skill in executing extended techniques as well as conventional virtuosity. See George W. Stowe, "David Tudor Program Opens Sunday Afternoon Series," *Hartford Times*, November 1, 1953. In a 1959 recital at New York University's La maison française, a critic for the *New York Times* remarked, "in the past, [Tudor] has proved he can read, comprehend, and perform music of almost incredible chromatic, rhythmic, and digital complexity." See A. H., "David Tudor in Piano Recital," *New York Times*, Friday March 20, 1959.

44. For an argument linking Cage's *4'33"* and Wittgenstein's *Tractatus*, see James M. Fielding, "An Aesthetics of the Ordinary: Wittgenstein and John Cage," *Journal of Aesthetics and Art Criticism* 72. no. 2 (Spring 2014), 157–67.

45. John Cage, "Counterpoint" (1934), 15. Echoing a traditional nationalist stereotype of aesthetics, Cage praises the French orientation toward the impersonal, the contrapuntal, the linear, the baroque, and the inexpressive as opposed to the expressive Germanic tradition of harmonic experimentation (Wagner's music dramas, Strauss's tone poems). Cage prefers compositional styles that refrain from overtly infusing their work with intentionality. Instead, he insists that one's "way of life" should come alive more impersonally through their music. Cage could be extending basic principles of Wittgenstein's *Tractatus* (1921, English trans. 1922) to the sphere of musical composition. In his personal library, Cage kept almost two dozen editions and publications of works by Wittgenstein, more than any other philosopher. By the later 1940s, Cage was reading more positive thinkers of the ineffable, in particular Meister Eckardt's mystical Neoplatonic dialectics.

46. Cage, "Counterpoint," *Dune Forum* 1, no. 2 (February 5, 1934): 42–44. Republished in Richard Kostelanetz, ed. *Writings about John Cage* (Ann Arbor: University of Michigan Press, 1993): 15.

47. Cage, "Counterpoint," 16.

48. Cage became exposed to Jung's work principally through two friends: Nancy Wilson Ross (1938–39) and Joseph Campbell (1942–late 1950s). On this history, see Edward James Crooks, "John Cage's Entanglement with the Ideas of Coomaraswamy" (PhD diss, University of York, 2011), chap. 3, pp. 86–119. Cage once gave an ultimatum to himself that he would either undertake Jungian psychoanalysis or reach into the id through the indeterminate oracle of the *I Ching*.

49. Carl Jung, foreword to *The I Ching or Book of Changes*, trans. Richard Wilhelm, rendered into English by Cary F. Baynes. (New York: Bollingen Foundation, 1950), xxii.

50. On the "Counter-Enlightenment," see Kimberly Jannarone, "Reactionary Modern," in *Artaud and His Doubles* (Ann Arbor: University of Michigan Press, 2010), 50–71.

51. Jung, "Foreword," xxiii.

52. In Joan Retallack's interview with Cage, the composer insists she find the Richard Wilhelm translation of the *I Ching*, and he explicitly mentions the importance of Jung's introduction. See Joan Retallack and John Cage, *Musicage: Cage Muses on Words, Art, Music* (Wesleyan, CT: Wesleyan University Press, 1996).

53. Jung continues: "The ancient Chinese mind contemplates the cosmos in a way comparable to that of the modern physicist, who cannot deny that his model of the world is a decidedly psychophysical structure. The microphysical event includes the observer just as much as the reality underlying the *I Ching* comprises subjective, i.e., psychic conditions in the totality of the momentary situation. Just as causality describes the sequence of events, so synchronicity to the Chinese mind deals with the coincidence of events." Carl Jung, "Foreword," xxiv.

54. Cage, "Indeterminacy," from "Composition as Process: III. Communication," reprinted in *Silence* (Wesleyan, CT: Wesleyan University Press, 1961), 35. Cage continued: "One evening Morton Feldman said that when he composed he was dead; this recalls to me the statement of my father, an inventor, who says he does his best work when he is sound asleep. The two suggest the 'deep sleep' of Indian mental practice. The ego no longer blocks action. A fluency obtains which is characteristic of nature. The seasons make the round of spring, summer, fall, and winter, interpreted in Indian thought as creation, preservation, destruction, and quiescence. Deep sleep is comparable to quiescence. Each spring brings no matter what eventuality. The performer then will act in any way. Whether he does so in an organized way or in any one of the not consciously organized ways cannot be answered until his action is a reality. The nature of the composition and the knowledge of the composer's own view of his action suggest, indeed, that the performer act sometimes consciously, sometimes not consciously and from the Ground of Meister Eckhart, identifying there with no matter what eventuality."

55. Nelson Goodman, *Languages of Art: An Approach to a Theory of Symbols* (Indianapolis, IN: Hackett, 1976), 143–48.

56. *The 25-Year Retrospective Concert of the Music of John Cage* (Independent Release, 1959).

57. Martin Iddon and Philip Thomas, https://solo.cageconcert.org/app/, University of Huddersfield and University of Leeds, 2023.

58. For the sketches to Graph J (among many other graph sketches), see David Tudor Papers, 980039, box 7, folders 4–5, Getty Research Institute, Los Angeles.

59. Benjamin Piekut, "Not So Much a Program of Music as the Experience of Music," in *Merce Cunningham CO:MM:ON TI:ME*, ed. Fionn Meade and Joan Rothfuss (Minneapolis, MN: Walker Art Center, 2017), 114–29. Also see You Nakai, *Reminded by the Instruments: David Tudor's Music* (New York: Oxford University Press, 2021), chap. 2, "Amplified Piano."

60. Pauline Oliveros organized the concerts at Mills College in honor of Tudor and played horn and tuba. Morton Subotnick, a cofounder with Oliveros of the San Francisco Tape Music Center, played the clarinet part.

61. *Music from the Tudorfest: San Francisco Tape Music Center, 1964* (New World Records, 2014).

62. "I smile when the sound is singing through the space," interview with David Tudor by Teddy Hultberg in Dusseldorf May 17–18, 1988, https://davidtudor.org/Articles/hultberg.html.

63. Paul Henry Lang, "What Is Offered by the Electronic Age?" *New York Herald-Tribune*, April 10, 1960, David Tudor Papers, 980039, box 63, folder 2, Getty Research Institute, Los Angeles.

64. A. H., "David Tudor in Piano Recital," *New York Times*, March 20, 1959. For a study of the Japanese reception of Cage and Tudor as both parallel and distinct from the US reception, see Serena Yang, "Against 'John Cage Shock': Rethinking John Cage and the Post-war Avant-Garde in Japan," *Twentieth-Century Music* 18, no. 3 (2021): 341–62. Yang notes that the phrase "Cage Shock" that circulated in the Japanese press in 1962 masks the underlying reality that similar indeterminate and experimental work was already taking place in Japan during the 1950s.

65. Cage writes to Boulez on December 18, 1950, the day after the premiere of Boulez's sonata, "Tudor had spontaneously devoted himself to the labor of understanding and playing the *Sonata*; I loaned him the original which you had given me with the sketches. He studied French in order to read your articles in *Contrepoint* and *Polyphonie* (by the way, they never sent me these,—although I subscribed), and he has made a collection and study of Artaud. He is an extraordinary person, and at the concert (as I was turning pages for him) I had feeling of an exaltation equal to that you had introduced me to at 34 rue Beautreillis. Naturally the audience was divided (for the various reasons audiences are), but I can tell you with joy that you have here a strong and devoted following. Your music gives to those who love it an arousing and breathtaking enlightenment. I am still always trembling afterwards. . . . My music too is changing. . . . Composition becomes 'throwing sound into silence,' and rhythm which in my *Sonatas* had been one of breathing becomes now one of a flow of sound and silence. I will send you soon some results. . . . Your *Sonata* is still in our ears, and gratitude will ever cease. Those who had no courage to directly listen are troubled; you have increased the danger their apathy brings them to. But now I am no longer one of a few Americans who are devoted to you, but one of many." *Selected Letters of John Cage*, ed. Laura Kuhn (Middleton, CT: Wesleyan University Press, 2016), 139–41. Writing to Tudor in late September 1951, Cage, in addition to recommending "the Sutras, Eckhardt" for the possibility of "no longer clinging," writes that he has enjoyed whatever Tudor and Richards sent him regarding Artaud: "Your gleanings from Debussy and Artaud gave much pleasure" (160–61).

66. Cage, *Selected Letters*, 139–41.

67. Dickinson, *CageTalk*, 84.

68. Dickinson, 83.

69. Boulez famously wrote of Artaud's influence on him, "I think that music should be collective hysteria and magic, violently modern—along the lines of Antonin Artaud and not in the sense of a simple ethnographic reconstruction in the image of civilizations more or less remote from us." Pierre Boulez, *Stocktakings from an Apprenticeship* (New York: Oxford University Press, 1991), 54 (originally published 1948). On Artaud's influence on Tudor and Boulez, see Eric Smigel, "Recital Hall of Cruelty: Antonin Artaud, David Tudor, and the 1950s Avant-Garde," *Perspectives of New Music* 45, no. 2 (Summer 2007): 171–202.

70. For more on Artaud's influence on Cage and the postwar avant-garde more broadly, see Lucy Bradnock, *No More Masterpieces: Modern Art after Artaud* (New Haven, CT: Yale University Press, 2021).

71. Cage's teaching of Artaud is evident in George Brecht's notebooks for Cage's course. See in particular, George Brecht, *George Brecht: Notebooks I (June–September, 1958)*, ed. Dieter Daniels and Hermann Braun (Cologne: Walter König, 1991), 41.

72. On M. C. Richards's overlooked role as an artist, pedagogue, translator, interlocutor, collaborator, and advocate for communally based experimentation, see Jenni Sorkin, "M. C. Richards's Vanishing Point," in *Live Form: Women, Ceramics, and Community* (Chicago: University of Chicago Press, 2016), 147–97.

73. M. C. Richards, "A Lecture Given at the Living Theater, NYC, 1959," Mary Carline Richards Papers, box 30, Getty Research Institute, Los Angeles.

74. David Tudor Papers, box 67, folder 11, Getty Research Institute, Los Angeles. In *Reminded by the Instruments*, You Nakai has also shown how Tudor's lecture notes from his Darmstadt seminars in 1959 reveal that he discussed musical time in terms of breath, mirroring Artaud's theory of "affective athleticism," Steiner's interest in eurhythmy, and the importance of breathing in yoga. You Nakai, *Reminded by the Instruments: David Tudor's Music* (Oxford University Press, 2021), 82–93. Tudor's Darmstadt lecture notes are available in David Tudor Papers, box 107, folder 10, Getty Research Institute, Los Angeles.

75. Antonin Artaud, "An Affective Athleticism," in *Theater and Its Double*, trans. Mary Caroline Richards (New York: Grove Press, 1958), 133–41.

76. Artaud, "An Affective Athleticism," 133.

77. For a discussion of Artaud's importance for Tudor's theory of discontinuous time, see John Holzaepfel, "David Tudor and the Performance of American Experimental Music," (PhD diss., City University of New York, 1993), chap. 2, "A Change in Musical Perception," 19–45.

78. David Tudor, "From Piano to Electronics," *Music and Musicians* 20 (August 1972): 24.

79. Dickinson, *CageTalk*, 91.

80. Tudor, "From Piano to Electronics," 24.

81. Tudor, 24.

82. Tudor, 24, emphasis in original.

83. Dickinson, *CageTalk*, 91.

84. Ananda K. Coomaraswamy, *The Transformation of Nature in Art* (New Delhi: Munshiram Manoharlal, 2014), 7.

85. Coomaraswamy, 7.

86. Dickinson, *CageTalk*, 91.

87. Dickinson, 90.

88. For more on Tudor and his relationship to Anthroposophy and other esoteric traditions, see Eric Smigel, "Alchemy of the Avant-Garde: David Tudor and the New Music of the 1950s" (PhD diss., University of Southern California, 2003), 198–255. David Tudor and his partner, M. C. Richards, were keenly interested in Steiner's Anthroposophy from the mid-1950s. In a letter to Tudor dated September 29, 1959, Richards read to John Cage one of Tudor's 1959 letters that discussed the topic of the occult. This was news to Cage, and he asked to read Steiner's work. Richards lent him a copy of Steiner's *How to Attain Knowledge of Higher Worlds*. Soon after, Richards reported that Cage "had been doing little other than reading the book—with great interest." She continued: "He is already finding it useful in his teaching, he said! His only trouble is with the images ('auras' 'lotus,' etc.). No trouble with concepts. He was especially dwelling on that part about regarding yourself as you would a stranger." David Tudor Papers, box 58, folder 9, Getty Research Institute, Los Angeles.

89. For a synoptic account of Anthroposophy, see Robert McDermott, "Rudolf Steiner and Anthroposophy," in *The Cambridge Handbook of Western Mysticism and Esotericism*, ed. Glenn Alexander Magee (Cambridge: Cambridge University Press, 2016), 260–71.

90. Rudolf Steiner, *The Way of Initiation; or, How to Attain Knowledge of Higher Worlds*, trans. Max Gysi (Perth: Compass Circle, 2019), 53.

91. Steiner, 52.

92. Steiner, 50.

93. On Jung and race, see Fanny Brewster, *African Americans and Jungian Psychology: Leaving the Shadows* (New York: Routledge, 2017), and Carrie B. Dohe, *Jung's Wandering Archetype: Race and Religion in Analytical Psychology* (New York: Routledge, 2016).

94. Carl Jung, "The Complications of American Psychology" (1939), in Carl Jung, *The Collected Works of Carl Jung*, vol. 10, ed. and trans. Gerhard Adler and R. F. C. Hull (Princeton, NJ: Princeton University Press, 1964), 502–14.

95. On the relationship of Theosophy to Nazism, see Nicholas Goodrick-Clarke, *The Occult Roots of Nazism: Secret Aryan Cults and Their Influence on Nazi Ideology* (New York: New York University Press, 2004).

96. Edward Dingle, "Treatise No. 3: The Mystery Supreme," 5, David Tudor Papers, box 101, folder 7, Getty Research Institute, Los Angeles.

97. Dingle, 4.

98. "Young India" from Ananda K. Coomaraswamy, *The Dance of Shiva: Fourteen Indian Essays*, rev. ed. (New York: Noonday Press, 1957), 165.

99. On Suzuki, Zen, and Japanese fascism, see Brian Daizen Victoria, *Zen at War*, 2nd ed. (Oxford: Roman and Littlefield: 2006).

100. George E. Lewis, "Improvised Music after 1950: Afrological and Eurological Perspectives," *Black Music Research Journal* 16, no. 1 (Spring 1996): 91–122. Also see

Rebecca Y. Kim, "John Cage in Separate Togetherness with Jazz," *Contemporary Music Review* 31, no. 1 (February 2012): 63–89.

101. For Cage's critiques of jazz, see Michael Zwerin, "A Lethal Measurement," *Village Voice* (New York), January 6, 1966, and "Social Philosophy," in *John Cage in Conversation with Richard Kostelanetz* (New York: Limelight, 1988), 257–84. Despite Cage's disavowal of jazz, it was haunting his work during the 1950s. Earle Brown, who Cage ultimately criticized for being too open ended in his use of indeterminacy, was heavily influenced by jazz. The press release for the premiere (probably produced in collaboration with Emile de Antonio and George Avakian, who worked in the jazz industry) ironically compared Cage's indeterminate works to the "freedom for the performers characteristic of improvised jazz." Press Release, Retrospective Concert, George Avakian Papers, boxes 19–20, New York Public Library.

102. Kimberly Jannarone, "Reactionary Modern," in *Artaud and His Doubles* (Ann Arbor: University of Michigan Press, 2010), 68.

103. Even as Cage and Tudor seemed to have accepted elements of the socially regressive mythos of the time, Richards, for her part, expressed concern about the racism of the American South in her private correspondence with Tudor. See David Tudor Papers, 980039, box 58, folders 5–10, Getty Research Institute, Los Angeles.

104. Louis Biancolli, "John Cage Gives Review of Work" *World-Telegram and Sun*, May 16, 1958, 25, David Tudor Papers, 980039, box 62, folder 13, Getty Research Institute, Los Angeles.

105. Miles Kastendieck, "Cage's Music Still a Phenomenon," *New York Journal-American*, May 16, 1958, David Tudor Papers, 980039, box 62, folder 13, Getty Research Institute, Los Angeles. Kastendieck divides the devotees, who believe him to be a prophet of musical futures, from the onlookers, who see Cage as merely a "sophisticated primitivist." From here, the review is critical.

106. John K. Sherman, "Music to Hear—and Unhear," *Minneapolis Star*, 1961, David Tudor Papers, 980039, box 63, folder 3, Getty Research Institute, Los Angeles.

107. On Leonard Bernstein's approach to Cage and the New York avant-garde in 1964, see Benjamin Piekut, "When Orchestras Attack! John Cage Meets the New York Philharmonic," in *Experimentalism Otherwise: The New York Avant-Garde and Its Limits* (Berkeley: University of California Press, 2011), 20–64.

108. Virgil Thomson, "John Cage Late and Early," *Saturday Review*, January 30, 1960, 38–39.

109. Alfred Frankenstein, "In Retrospect—The Music of John Cage," *High Fidelity* 10, no. 4 (April 1960): 63.

110. Mary Caroline Richards Papers, 960036, boxes 26 and 114, Getty Research Institute, Los Angeles.

111. Paul Henry Lang, "What Is Offered by Our Electronic Age?," *Herald Tribune*, April 10, 1960.

112. Fred Grunfeld, "Cage without Bars," *Saturday Review*, February 4, 1960.

113. Stanley Cavell, "Music Discomposed," in *Must We Mean What We Say?* (Cambridge: Cambridge University Press, 2002), 180–212. On "fraudulence" and modernism, see 188–19.

114. Branden Joseph associates Cage's emancipatory permissiveness with the advent of intermedia as well as philosophical resonances of Bergsonian and Deleuzian qualitative multiplicities and temporalities. See Branden Joseph, *Experimentations: John Cage in Music, Art, and Architecture* (London: Bloomsbury, 2016). Liz Kotz associated Cage with the advent of the Fluxus event-score. See Liz Kotz, *Words to Be Looked At* (Cambridge, MA: MIT Press, 2007).

115. On the productivity of the score format for the artists associated with Fluxus, see Natilee Harren, *Fluxus Forms: Scores, Multiples, and the Eternal Network* (Chicago: University of Chicago Press, 2020).

116. George Avakian gave special thanks to Garry Moore, host of the CBS television show *I've Got a Secret*, for featuring Cage performing his own work, *Water Walk* (1959). Avakian also thanked Moore for his "bravery" in featuring Cage on television and likened it to his own bravery in underwriting the release of the LP. The LP went through a number of small pressings over the years. See George Avakian Papers, boxes 19–20, New York Public Library.

117. You Nakai's book *Reminded by the Instruments* persuasively shows that what defined Tudor's career was a rigorous attention to the affordances and parameters of various musical instruments. His book features chapters on Tudor's piano, amplified piano, sound systems, the bandoneon, and his installations for the *Pepsi Pavilion* (1970), *Island Eye Island Ear* (1974), and *Neural Synthesis* (1992).

118. John Cage, "The East in the West" (1947), *Asian Music* 1, no. 1 (1968–69): 18.

119. George Avakian Papers, boxes 19–20, New York Public Library.

## CHAPTER FOUR

1. "Beyond the Cool," *Time Magazine*, June 27, 1960, Coleman Press Archive, 1960 April–August, II, 25–50, Institute of Jazz Studies (hereafter IJS), John Cotton Dana Library, Rutgers University, Newark, New Jersey. The two Baraka quotes come from *Digging: the Afro-American Soul of American Classical Music* (Berkeley: University of California Press, 2009), "Black History Month Rediscovers 'the Music' in New York City," 287, and "New York Art Quintet," 395.

2. Mildred Fields, Press Release for Five Spot Café, December 4, 1959. Coleman Press Archive, June 1958–March 1960, I, 1–24, IJS.

3. On Coleman's debut at the Five Spot, see David Neil Lee, *The Battle of the Five Spot: Ornette Coleman and the New York Jazz Field* (Hamilton, ON: Wolsak & Wynn, 2006).

4. George Hoefer, "Caught in the Act: Ornette Coleman," *Down Beat*, January 7, 1960, 40–41, Coleman Press Archive, June 1958–March 1960, I, 1–24, IJS.

5. John Mehegan, "The Question of Coleman," *Down Beat*, December 24, 1959, 7, Coleman Press Archive, June 1958–March 1960, I, 1–24, IJS.

6. See a series of collected review clippings of Coleman's early performances and recordings (1958–60), Coleman Press Archive, June 1958–March 1960, I, 1–24, IJS.

7. "Enigma: Ornette Coleman" December 3, 1960, Coleman Press Archive, June 1958–March 1960, I, 1–24, IJS.

8. "Five Spot N. Y.," December 1959, Coleman Press Archive, June 1958–March 1960, I, 1–24, IJS.

9. For biographies of Coleman, see Maria Golia, *Ornette Coleman: The Territory and the Adventure* (London: Reaktion Books, 2020), and John Litweiler, *Ornette Coleman: A Harmolodic Life* (New York: William Morrow, 1992).

10. See Scott DeVeaux, *The Birth of Bebop: A Social and Musical History* (Berkeley: University of California Press, 1997), "Wartime Highs–And Lows," 236–69. This chapter contains an account of racism and segregation in Black music of the 1940s.

11. See Ted Gioia, *The History of Jazz*, 2nd ed. (Oxford: Oxford University Press, 2011), "Modern Jazz," 185–252.

12. On the genesis of bebop, see DeVeaux, *The Birth of Bebop*; Brent Hayes Edwards, Farah Jasmine Griffin, and Robert O'Meally, eds., *The Jazz Cadence of American Culture* (New York: Columbia University Press, 1998); Robin Kelley, *Thelonious Monk: The Life and Times of an American Original* (New York: Free Press, 2009).

13. An argument for Coleman's "pan-tonality" appears in George Russell and Martin Williams, "Ornette Coleman and Tonality," *Jazz Review*, June, 1960, Coleman Press Archive, 1960 April–August 1960, II, 25–50, IJS.

14. Kwami Coleman, "Free Jazz and the 'New Thing': Aesthetics, Identity, and Texture, 1960–1966," *Journal of Musicology* 38, no. 3 (2021): 263.

15. Kwami Coleman, 276.

16. Amiri Baraka (then LeRoi Jones), *Blues People: Negro Music in White America* (1963; reprint, New York: Harper Perennial, 2002), 137.

17. Ruth Ross and Paul D. Zimmerman, "The New Jazz," *Newsweek*, December 12, 1966, 102, Coleman Press Archive, 1965 July–1969, V, 96–116, IJS.

18. Baraka, *Blues People*, 136.

19. Baraka, *Blues People*, 152–53. He continues with a remarkable distinction between music and language as media for Black social history: "Thought is largely conditioned by reference; it is the result of consideration or speculation against reference, which is largely arbitrary. There is no *one* way of thinking, since reference (hence value) is as scattered and dissimilar as men themselves. If Negro music can be seen to be the result of certain attitudes, certain specific ways of thinking about the world (and only ultimately about the *ways* in which music can be made), then the basic hypothesis of this book is understood. The Negro's music changed as he changed, reflecting shifting attitudes or (and this is equally important) *consistent attitudes within changed contexts*. And it is *why* the music changed that seems most important to me."

20. Amiri Baraka, "Jazz and the White Critic," in *Black Music: Essays by LeRoi Jones (Amiri Baraka)* (Brooklyn, NY: AkashiClassics, 2010), 14.

21. Baraka, *Blues People*, 39.

22. Baraka, 87.

23. Baraka, 63.

24. Baraka, 139.

25. Baraka firsts defines the Black "citizen" in *Blues People*, 4, and refers to it repeatedly thereafter.

26. Baraka, 148.

27. For an account of Adorno's view of Paul Whiteman's highly commoditized jazz, see Richard Leppert, "Commentary: Music and Mass Culture," in *Essays on Music*, ed. Theodor Adorno and Richard Leppert (Berkeley: University of California Press, 2002), 350–55.

28. For Baraka's view of "Black cool," see Baraka, *Blues People*, 213. On "procuring his 'shit,'" see 202.

29. Baraka, *Blues People*, 188.

30. Norman Mailer, "The White Negro: Superficial Reflections on the Hipster," *Dissent* 4 (1957): 276–93.

31. Baraka, *Blues People*, 219.

32. Baraka, 199.

33. Baraka, 227.

34. Baraka, "Jazz and the White Critic," 17.

35. Eric Porter argues that bebop exemplified a "critical ecumenicalism" that represented an "artistic challenge" that also reflected a broader desire for social change and Black progress, though without any particular militant politics at its forefront. See Eric Porter, *What Is This Thing Called Jazz? African American Musicians as Artists, Critics, and Activists* (Berkeley: University of California Press, 2002), "Dizzy Atmosphere," 54–100. Also see DeVeaux, "Introduction: Stylistic Evolution or Social Revolution?" in *The Birth of Bebop*, 1–34.

36. Isabelle Leymarie Ortiz, "A Conversation with Ornette Coleman," *New York Arts Journal* (1979): 9, Coleman Press Archive, 1977 November–1981 December, VII, 139–62, IJS.

37. This phrase comes from a conversation Coleman had with his son Denardo in Shirley Clarke's film, *Ornette: Made in America* (1984): "What really makes me want to play music is when I really hear an individual thought pattern placed in an environment to make something come about that is not an obvious thing that everyone is doing."

38. See Fred Moten, *In the Break: The Aesthetics of the Black Radical Tradition* (Minneapolis: University of Minnesota Press, 2003); Fumi Okiji, *Jazz as Critique: Adorno and Black Expression Revisited* (Stanford, CA: Stanford University Press, 2018).

39. Charlie L. Russell, "Coleman Sounds Off," *Liberator* 5, no. 7 (July 1965): 13, Coleman Press Archive, 1965 July–1969, V, 96–116, IJS.

40. Robert Fulford, "Negroes Make Jazz, Whites Make Money," November 9, 1966, Coleman Press Archive, 1965 July–1969, V, 96–116, IJS.

41. Porter, *What Is This Thing Called Jazz?*, 198.

42. On Afro-modernist movements to escape the dictates of the commercial sphere during the 1960s and onward, see Porter, *What Is This Thing Called Jazz?*, "Practicing 'Creative Music,'" 191–239; George E. Lewis, *A Power Stronger Than Itself: The AACM and American Experimental Music* (Chicago: University of Chicago Press, 2008); Naomi Beckwith and Dieter Roelstraete, *The Freedom Principle: Experiments in Art and Music 1965 to Now* (Chicago: University of Chicago Press, 2015); Michael Heller, *Loft Jazz: Improvising New York in the 1970s* (Berkeley: University of California Press, 2016);

Paul Steinbeck, *Message to Our Folks: The Art Ensemble of Chicago* (Chicago: University of Chicago Press, 2017).

43. Ornette Coleman, "To Whom It May Concern" *Down Beat*, June 1, 1967, 19, Coleman Press Archive, 1965 July–1969, V, 96–116, IJS.

44. Dizzy Gillespie offered this phrase in a 1988 interview for Jan Horne's documentary *To Bop or Not To Be: A Jazz Life* (1990), available at https://www.youtube.com/watch?time_continue=256&v=mdQfIEHlrKc&feature=emb_logo.

45. George E. Lewis, "Improvised Music after 1950: Afrological and Eurological Perspectives," *Black Music Research Journal* 16, no. 1 (Spring 1996): 91–122.

46. Ian Burn, "The Sixties: Crisis and Aftermath," *Art and Text* 1 (Autumn 1981): 52. Quoted in Benjamin H. D. Buchloh, *Neo-Avantgarde and Culture Industry: Essays on European and American Art from 1955 to 1975* (Cambridge, MA: MIT Press, 2000). For further discussion of deskilling in art, see Jasper Bernes, *The Work of Art in the Age of Deindustrialization* (Palo Alto, CA: Stanford University Press, 2017).

47. Litweiler, *Ornette Coleman*, 117.

48. For the oral history of Coleman's lessons with Schuller, see Litweiler, 93–94.

49. Charlie L. Russell, "Coleman Sounds Off," *Liberator* 5, no. 7 ( July 1965): 13, Coleman Press Archive, 1965 July–1969, V, 96–116. IJS.

50. Shelly Manne, "Round the Empty Foxhole," *Down Beat*, October 5, 1967, 17, Coleman Press Archive, 1965 July–1969, V, 96–116, IJS.

51. Ornette Coleman, Pete Welding, Shelly Manne, and Cannonball Adderley, "Round the Empty Foxhole," *Down Beat*, October 5, 1967, 17, Coleman Press Archive, 1965 July–1969, V, 96–116, IJS.

52. Coleman, liner notes to *The Empty Foxhole* (Blue Note, 1966).

53. Jan Horne, *To Bop or Not To Be*.

54. Coleman, liner notes to *The Empty Foxhole* (Blue Note, 1966).

55. Coleman, liner notes to *The Empty Foxhole*.

56. Coleman, liner notes to *The Empty Foxhole*. For rehearsal footage of "The Empty Foxhole," see an excerpt in the opening fifteen minutes of Shirley Clarke's film, *Ornette: Made in America* (1984).

57. Coleman, liner notes to *The Empty Foxhole*.

58. On the emergence of event-scores in the 1960s, see Liz Kotz, *Words to Be Looked At: Language in 1960s Art* (Cambridge, MA: MIT Press, 2007), and Natilee Harren, *Fluxus Forms: Scores, Multiples, and the Eternal Network* (Chicago: University of Chicago Press, 2020).

59. See George Lewis, "Commentary: Benjamin Patterson's Paper Piece (1960)," in *The Scores Project*, ed. Michael Gallope, Natilee Harren, and John Hicks (Los Angeles: Getty Publications, forthcoming).

60. Ortiz, "A Conversation with Ornette Coleman," *New York Arts Journal* (1979): 8, Coleman Press Archive, 1977 November–1981 December, VII, 139–62, IJS.

61. For a rich interpretation of *Skies of America* in dialogue with the genre of the concerto, see Charles Kronengold, *Living Genres in Late Modernity: American Music of the Long 1970s* (Berkeley: University of California Press, 2022), 234–40.

62. For more technical reconstructions of the general features of Coleman's general compositional style of harmolodics, see Peter Niklas Wilson, *Ornette Coleman: His Life and Music* (Berkeley, CA: Berkeley Hills Books, 1999), 34–40, and Stephen Rush, *Free Jazz, Harmolodics, and Ornette Coleman* (New York: Routledge, 2017). Rush's book is grounded in a number of revelatory interviews with Coleman and insightful connections between harmolodics and the civil rights era.

63. Coleman, liner notes for *Skies of America* (Columbia Records, 1972).

64. Coleman, as quoted in Robert Palmer, "Ornette! Harmolodic Stompdown," *New York Rocker*, [1980?], 12. Also appears in Steve O'Leary, "Hendrix Comparisons Are Valid," *Romulus Roman*, December 2, 1981, and in Gary Giddens, "Harmolodic Hoedown," *Village Voice*, March 27, 1984, Coleman Press Archive, 1977 November–1981 December, VII, 139–62, IJS.

65. Coleman, as quoted in Palmer, "Ornette! Harmolodic Stompdown," 12.

66. Coleman states, "Everyone has the freedom to express rhythm and time equally . . . since the rhythm is more adapted to a broken consistency of time. It just sounds like rhythm, but rhythm is a time and rhythm is without a time. So when you play something slow and then play it fast, it becomes rhythm. Just because of the speed accelerating." Ben Watson, *The Wire*, no. 205, March 2001, 35–40.

67. Howard Mandel, "Ornette Coleman: The Creator as Harmolodic Magician," *Down Beat*, October 5, 1978, 54. "[I] find that it's much easier when a person can take a melody, do what they want to do with the melody, then bring his expression to yours, then combine that for a greater expression." Also see Andy Hamilton, "A Question of Scale," *The Wire*, no. 257, July 2005, 22–5. There he states, "So when I found that out, I started analyzing what people call melody for ideas." Also see Graham Lock, "Harmolodic Haberdashing," *The Wire*, no. 52, June 1988, 37. There he states, "when you think of it like that [harmolodic equality], you have more things to choose from at once than just one single melody. All of those things can become a melody."

68. Gene Santoro, "Dancing in Your Head," *The Nation*, August 12, 1991, 199. Coleman contrasts harmolodics with the orderly soloing of jazz: "Bebop deals with only one solo at a time. Even Dixieland, although it's similar to harmolodics, still deals with one solo at a time, because it's using the same device [a chord sequence] to play the way they're playing. . . . In harmolodics someone might be playing minor, someone else augmented, someone else major—all at the same time."

69. Santoro, "Dancing in Your Head," 199.

70. Andy Hamilton, "A Question of Scale," 24.

71. Ben Watson, *The Wire*, no. 205, March 2001, 38. Here Coleman explains: "I think you might have three of these notes and three of these notes, everything is a chromatic, everything starts going up there and starts coming down here. . . . So these are three changes—C major seventh, E flat minor seventh, D, F, A flat, and A [all twelve notes]—and you can play the violin, and nobody in music can play an idea unless they use one of these notes if they're playing a tempered scale. And since there's 12 of them in the form of chords, if you took the same scales you have now and call this whatever you want to call it, and now play them in this sequence, put anything wherever you want to and realise that you're coming in this sequence, you won't say you can't play no more."

72. Hamilton, "A Question of Scale," 23. "Because I found out that in Western culture you have the B♭, the C, the E♭ and the F instruments—those are the four dominant transpositions."

73. Hamilton, "A Question of Scale," 23.

74. Hamilton, "A Question of Scale," 25. "[An E on the piano is] a sound that has been applied to the piano, to represent a concept of other instruments playing in unison with the piano. The piano doesn't transpose."

75. Hamilton, "A Question of Scale," 23. "And yet one instrument [the piano] has to transpose those other three notes for it to sound like one [compositional] idea more than four different harmonies—and that's the piano. So all of a sudden I started understanding the role of the piano [everything has to be brought under one system]."

76. Hamilton, "A Question of Scale," 23. "The note of the saxophone is different [idiosyncratic] to the sound of the saxophone. The note that you hear is not the sound of the instrument [it's doing its own thing]. It's the idea of the notes that you hear being applied to the instrument."

77. Coleman states, "To this very day, I've been working on a concept called harmolodics, which means that the four basic notes of Western culture [B♭, C, E♭, F] are all the same sound on four different instruments. I call that harmolodics." Regarding allowed transposition, especially with piano, Coleman states, "[Transposition is] going to happen, but no one has come to the conclusion that you don't have to transpose an idea. But if you want to play with the piano . . . if you want to play an idea you have to [transpose]." Hamilton, "A Question of Scale," 23.

78. One of Coleman's producers, John Snyder, described this unison phenomenologically: "His unison is any group of notes that suddenly come together and have a purity of sound—a clarity, almost a ringing." Quoted in Whitney Balliett, "Jazz: Ornette," *New Yorker*, August 30, 1982, 67, Coleman Press Archive, 1981 December–1986 February, VIII, 163–86, IJS.

79. Bill Shoemaker, "Dialing Up Ornette," *Jazz Times*, December 1995.

80. Coleman, "Prime Time for Harmolodics," *Down Beat*, July 1983, 54–55. Quoted in Ted Gioia, *The Imperfect Art: Reflections on Jazz and Modern Culture* (New York: Oxford University Press, 1990), 43.

81. Coleman explains, "When you said you 'couldn't play' . . . what you were describing is repeating an idea that you heard someone play, but that idea didn't come from notes, it came from an idea. So when you think the idea comes from the notes, that makes you withdraw, because the idea cannot be repeated the way that person had. It it's like me telling you a lie." Ben Watson, *The Wire*, no. 205, March 2001, 40.

82. Ortiz, "Conversation with Ornette Coleman," 9.

83. Coleman, as quoted in Balliett, "Jazz: Ornette," 66. "I try and play a musical idea that is not being influenced by any previous thing I have played before. You don't have to learn to spell to talk." Noam Chomsky has remarked similarly about language acquisition: "Your actual language nobody teaches you." "The Concept of Language," on *Upon Reflection* with interviewer Al Page (1989), https://www.youtube.com/watch?v=hdUbIlwHRkY.

84. In his 1993 liner notes for the *Beauty Is a Rare Thing* box set of his recordings on Atlantic (1959–61), Coleman writes, "When I started to form a Harmolodic Band, I

auditioned a young kid who did not read or write music that played the Bass (electric). I asked him to play whatever he wanted. As he started to play, I joined him and when we stopped I thought I would offer him a job and teach him Harmolodics. He told me he did not want to play the kind of music we were playing although I was playing with him (what an example of personal interest). This confirmed my belief in Harmolodics." In another instance, he writes, "I just thought music was something that anyone does naturally, which I really believe is true today—that someone who's never picked up an instrument can pick up an instrument and play something that someone who's been playing all his life never thought of playing." Interview with Stefan Lamby, Quoted in Wilson, *Ornette Coleman*, 74.

85. Mandel, "Ornette Coleman," 55, Coleman Press Archive, 1977 November–1981 December, VII 139–62, IJS.

86. Hamilton, "A Question of Scale," 23.

87. Hamilton, 24. Coleman states, "Classical music is related to the past more than it is related to the creative part of sound. Like those songs that I'm writing, you can hear any kind of structure, classical, blues and whatever. . . . The music I'm writing is not in any style, it's not in the style of jazz, classical, nothing. But you get all of that coming through, because of memory and the past."

88. Ben Watson, *The Wire*, no. 205, March 2001, 38.

89. Coleman, liner notes to *Beauty Is a Rare Thing: The Complete Atlantic Recordings* (Rhino Records, 1993).

90. With respect to nonresolution in harmolodics, Coleman stated in 2001, "I tell Denardo and Charnett, 'When you play, do not resolve your idea.' You don't have to re-solve. The reason we resolve music is because there's a method of composing chromatic notes, they go a certain way but sound doesn't have that. Because what is a melody?" Watson, *The Wire*, no. 205, March 2001, 40.

91. For more on the social ideals underpinning harmolodics, see Litweiler, *Ornette Coleman*, 149.

92. Watson, *The Wire*, no. 205, March 2001, 40.

93. Interview with Ralph Quinke, 1987, in Wilson, *Ornette Coleman*, 87. In full: "Harmolodics means transposing any sound whatsoever into your own playing, with-out having to give up your own identity in the process. . . . I believe that this is probably one of the most democratic ways of expressing artistic contents there is."

94. "The Other's Language: Jacques Derrida Interviews Ornette Coleman, 23 June 1997," trans. Timothy S. Murphy, *Genre* 37, no. 2 (2004): 323. Originally appeared in *Les Inrockuptibles* no. 115 (August 20–September 2, 1997): 37–40, 43.

95. Howard Mandel, *Miles, Ornette, Cecil: Jazz beyond Jazz* (New York: Routledge, 2008), 186. Cited in Maria Golia, *Ornette Coleman: The Territory and the Adventure* (London: Reaktion Books, 2020), 230.

96. See Daniel López-Pérez, *Pattern-Thinking* (Zurich: Lars Müller, 2019), and R. Buckminster Fuller, *Operating Manual for Spaceship Earth* (Zurich: Lars Müller, 2019).

97. Peter Watrous, "The Return of Jazz's Greatest Eccentric," *New York Times*, June 23, 1991, 26–36.

98. Howard Mandel, "Driven to Abstraction," *The Wire*, no. 140, October 1995, 37–39.

99. Mandel, 37–39. "Harmolodics is like a colour that has sound, alphabets, it has a gravity in that it works the same way that thinking is to talking, or the five senses are to presence. If you think of the five senses in a harmolodic way, smell is presence, taste is clarity, hearing is receiving, touch is action and sight is territories. In harmolodics those five things each also have five different things, as in music the four basic voices that have to do with sound—soprano, bass, alto and tenor—each has the same four sounds. . . . I discovered what makes every musician unique is when they line up those voices into sound. Some people call it chords, some call it changes, some call it modulations, some call it melody, but that's really what it is . . . that's harmolodics."

100. Mandel, "Driven to Abstraction," 37–39.

101. This quote emphasizes Coleman's turn from nongrammar toward combinatorics and poetics: "Singular compositions are more like the one we use to express language. When someone writes a song, they're writing music to fit a grammar. The grammar of songs is not as free as the grammar of sounds. A sound is free of grammar. When I found that out, I decided that I would try and become more clear how to write and play that kind of relationship to tempered music, to non-tempered music, to melody, to harmony and to poetry." Watson, *The Wire*, no. 205, March 2001, 35–40. A year earlier, he emphasizes the turn toward vernacular affirmation and collaboration: "Only language has grammar . . . because words have meaning. But sound is free of grammar. That allows me to play with people from any setting—a spoon tapping on a jar, it doesn't matter." Gene Santoro, "Freedom Song" *The Nation*, July 10, 2000, 41.

102. Watson, *The Wire*, no. 205, March 2001, 35–40.

103. Hamilton, "A Question of Scale," 24.

104. Hamilton, 24.

105. Hamilton, 24.

106. Coleman once described a young girl saying to him, "You just apply your feelings to sound." Coleman responded that it required a form of intuitive openness: "she was right—if you apply your feelings to sound . . . you'll probably make good music." Mandel, "Ornette Coleman," 54.

107. Greg Tate, "Why the Hell Ornette Went All Up in Eden," *Walker Art Center Fourth Wall*, June 11, 2015, https://walkerart.org/magazine/why-hell-ornette-went -all-eden.

108. Regarding the role of harmolodics in intellectually justifying his own work, Stanley Crouch wrote, "The original inspiration for Coleman's harmolodic theory seems to have been his desire to prove himself more than the intuitive genius he was taken for when he arrived in New York to revolutionize jazz 22 years ago. At first Coleman called for an art based on emotion rather than technique. But eventually, miffed at being thought an illiterate primitive, he both established his credentials as an intellectual to the white critics, musicians, and musicologists who condescended to him ('Ornette sounds great but he doesn't know what he's doing') and separated his art from that of the legions of fakes who followed his lead the way counterfeit modernists like Salvador Dali used Picasso's innovations to justify their garbage." Stanley Crouch, "Ornette Coleman's Jet-Age Jump Band," *Village Voice*, July 1, 1981, Coleman Press Archive, 1977 November–1981 December, VII, 139–62, IJS.

109. Santoro, "Freedom Song," 41.

110. Santoro, 41.

111. Interview with Peter Watrous, "The Return of Jazz's Greatest Eccentric," *New York Times*, June 23, 1991. Quoted in Litweiler, *Ornette Coleman*, 150. Coleman claims here that Harmolodics is "not supposed to be a secret; it's supposed to be something that anyone should be able to do."

112. Interview with Ralph Quinke, 1987. "The reason I haven't published it yet is that I would actually like to write it like a novel so that even people who don't make music would be interested in it and then maybe would want to make music themselves." Quoted in Wilson, *Ornette Coleman*, 73.

113. Interview with Stefan Lamby. "It deals with inspiring the layman as well as the professional person to take an interest in their own creativity." Quoted in Wilson, *Ornette Coleman*, 74.

114. Mandel, "Ornette Coleman: The Creator as Harmolodic Magician," *Down Beat*, October 5, 1978, 19. "You try to make sure that people absorb what you're saying . . . for themselves. More than trying to be at a specific point to give *me* security. I don't think that musical security is useful to the individual." And elsewhere, "I haven't been able to publish it because I haven't worked with an editor to get all of the grammar and everything. . . . I want it to be understood, more than confuse. I want a non-musician reader to be able to understand what a performer will get from reading it." On Coleman being too busy performing to finish the book, see Watson, *The Wire*, no. 205, March 2001, 35–40.

115. Balliett, "Jazz: Ornette," 66.

116. Mandel, "Driven to Abstraction," 37–39.

117. Mandel, "Ornette Coleman," 54. "It is possible to express something that has to do with the way you hear, or feel, or think with another individual without that person having to give you the information before you do what you want to express."

118. Mandel, "Ornette Coleman," 55.

119. Ortiz, "Conversation with Ornette Coleman," 9.

120. Ortiz, 8.

121. Coleman, as quoted in Balliett, "Jazz: Ornette," 66, emphasis in original.

122. Mandel, "Ornette Coleman," 19.

123. Michael Gallope, "A Paradox of the Vernacular," in *Deep Refrains: Music, Philosophy, and the Ineffable* (Chicago: University of Chicago Press, 2017), 244–59.

124. Charles Kronengold, *Living Genres in Late Modernity*, 240.

125. Kwami Coleman, "Free Jazz and the 'New Thing': Aesthetics, Identity, and Texture, 1960–66," *Journal of Musicology* 38, no. 3 (2021): 261–95.

126. George Kanzler, "Guitarist Enjoys Untying Chords," *Star-Ledger*, September 6, 1997, 26.

127. Ornette Coleman, *The Empty Foxhole* liner notes (Blue Note, 1966).

128. Dan Morganstern, *Down Beat*, April 8, 1965, 18.

129. Michael Bourne, "Ornette's Interview," *Down Beat*, November 22, 1973. Quoted in Litweiler, *Ornette Coleman*, 108.

## CHAPTER FIVE

1. For an overview, see Steven Watson, *Factory Made: Warhol and the Sixties* (New York: Pantheon Books, 2003).

2. On the Exploding Plastic Inevitable, see Branden Joseph, "'My Mind Split Open': Andy Warhol's Exploding Plastic Inevitable," *Grey Room* no. 8 (Summer 2002): 80–107.

3. Grace Glueck, "Syndromes Pop at Delmonico's: Andy Warhol and His Gang Meet the Psychiatrist," *New York Times*, January 14, 1966, in Clinton Heylin, ed., *All Yesterday's Parties: The Velvet Underground in Print: 1966–71* (Cambridge, MA: Perseus Books, 2005), 4–5.

4. Glueck, 4–5.

5. Larry McCombs, "Chicago Happenings," *Boston Broadside*, July 1966, in Heylin, ed., *All Yesterday's Parties*, 26.

6. When tasked with melody and lyric transcription for their publishing agreement, Reed and Morrison found the task tedious because of their minimal experience with traditional Western notation. Morrison reports that Cale could have done it easily but refused out of principle. See the interview with Sterling Morrison on a thirty-minute episode of the television show *Arsenal: The Velvet Underground: Feed Back* (originally aired May 19, 1986), season 1, episode 27, available at https://www.youtube.com/watch?v=ZY4PTXR-vg0.

7. Ramblin' Jim Martin, "Interview with Lou Reed," *Open City* 78 (November 1968), in Heylin, ed., *All Yesterday's Parties*, 109.

8. Victor Bockris and Gerard Malanga, *Up-Tight: The Velvet Underground Story* (New York: Cooper Square Press, 2003), 74.

9. Young mentions his 1950s jazz collaborators in a 1984 interview on *UbuWeb*. See Russ Jennings, Interview with La Monte Young and Marian Zazeela (1984), *UbuWeb*, http://www.archive.org/download/AM_1984_08_XX/AM_1984_08_XX_ed_vbr.mp3.

10. On Young's experiences at Darmstadt in 1959, see Jeremy Grimshaw, *Draw a Straight Line and Follow It: The Music and Mysticism of La Monte Young* (Oxford: Oxford University Press, 2011), 57.

11. Grimshaw, *Draw a Straight*, 48–83, "Getting Inside the Sound: The Works from 1959 to 1960."

12. Benjamin Piekut, commentary for chapter 5 on La Monte Young and Jackson Mac Low, "An Anthology for Chance Operations" (1963), in *The Scores Project* (Los Angeles: Getty Publications, forthcoming).

13. Dick Higgins, "Synesthesia and Intersenses: Intermedia" (1965), originally published in *Something Else Newsletter* 1, no. 1 (1966). Also available on *UbuWeb*, https://www.ubu.com/papers/higgins_intermedia.html. Natilee Harren, *Fluxus Forms: Scores, Multiples, and the Eternal Network* (Chicago: University of Chicago Press, 2020). On the climate of experimentalism in and around the year 1964, see Benjamin Piekut, *Experimentalism Otherwise: The New York Avant-Garde and Its Limits* (Berkeley: University of California Press, 2011).

14. The Orientalia Bookstore on East 12th street in Greenwich Village where Cale worked alongside Warhol documentarian Billy Name to ship books out to universities

and scholars carried scholarly books on Asian Religions, Asian Philosophy, Egyptology, Central Asia, Africa, Cartography, Manuscripts and Calligraphy, Zoroastrianism, Bahai, Islam, Literature and Folklore, Languages, History, and Archaeology. See "Bookstores Specializing in Second Hand Books on the Middle East," *Middle East Studies Association Bulletin* 5, no. 3 (October 1, 1971): 45–47.

15. Harold Schonberg, Richard F. Shepard, and Raymond Ericson, "Music: A Long, Long, Long Night (and Day) at the Piano," *New York Times*, September 11, 1963, 45, 48.

16. *I've Got a Secret*, September 16, 1963, available at https://www.youtube.com/watch?v=0mqO-xsRyTM.

17. As early as 1960, Young and Terry Jennings were playing Coltrane-inspired improvisations after the Yoko Ono loft sessions. Henry Flynt interviewed by Kenneth Goldsmith on WFMU, February 26, 2004, https://media.sas.upenn.edu/pennsound/authors/Flynt/Henry_Flynt_Interviewed_by_Kenneth_Goldsmith_WFMU_2.25.04.mp3. Billy Name (Warhol's archivist) was an early collaborator in Young's Theatre of Eternal Music in July and August 1962, performing on acoustic guitar. Conrad said of this 1962 group, "The music was formless, expostulatory, meandering; vaguely modal, arrhythmic, and very unusual. . . . I found it exquisite." From Tony Conrad, *Early Minimalism: Volume 1* (New York: Table of the Elements, 1997), 14–15, CD booklet; quoted in Branden Joseph, *Beyond the Dream Syndicate* (New York: Zone Books, 2008), 27.

18. The recordings of the Theatre of Eternal Music that feature Young on sopranino saxophone (and have circulated informally) stretch from September 1963 to April 1964 and were all recorded in New York. They are often titled as follows: [September 29] (title unknown); [October 19] "19 X 63—Fifth Day of the Hammer—B♭ Dorian Blues"; [October 30] "30 X 63—Day Of Hummingbird Night"; [November 28] "28 XI 63—The Overday (B♭ Dorian Blues)"; [December 17] "17 XII 63—The Fire Is a Mirror"; [December 24] "24 XII 63—Third Day of Yule—Early Tuesday Morning Blues"; [January 12] "12 I 64—The First Twelve—Sunday Morning Blues"; [April 2–3] "2 IV 64—Day of the Holy Mountain—The Pre-Tortoise Dream Music." For a list of the Theatre's recording dates from 1963 to 1964, see Richie Unterberger, *White Light/White Heat: The Velvet Underground Day-by-Day* (London: Jawbone Press, 2009), 22–37. Recordings are in the personal collection of the author, with thanks to Patrick Nickleson. All recordings besides the second were featured on a 1984 WKCR-FM 89.9 (NYC) broadcast honoring La Monte Young titled *The La Monte Young Festival.*

19. Branden Joseph discusses Young's initial preference for the flat seventh (9:5) and the way Conrad pushed him toward using the harmonic seventh (7:4). See Joseph, *Beyond the Dream Syndicate*, 30.

20. La Monte Young and the Forever Bad Blues Band, *Just Stompin'/Live at the Kitchen* (Gramavision CD R279487, 1993), liner notes, cited in Grimshaw, *Draw a Straight Line*, 24n19.

21. Steven Watson, *Factory Made*, 161.

22. Amiri Baraka, *Blues People* (1963; reprint, New York: Harper Perennial, 2002), 202.

23. For a discussion of the tuning of Young's *The Well-Tuned Piano*, see Kyle Gann, "La Monte Young's The Well-Tuned Piano," *Perspectives of New Music* 31, no. 1 (Winter 1993), 134–62.

24. Grimshaw connects this choice of the harmonic seventh to Young's background in the blues. See Grimshaw, *Draw a Straight Line*, 23–25. Quotation about "discipline" is drawn from the interview with La Monte Young and Marian Zazeela in James Marsh, dir., *John Cale* (1998), 59 min.

25. Theatre of Eternal Music performances involving John Cale (1963–65) occurred at the Philadelphia College of Art (October 9, 1964), The Pocket Theatre, 100 3rd Avenue. (October 31–November 1, November 20–22, and December 12–13, 1964); East End Theatre (now KGB Bar), 85 East 4th Street (March 7, 1965); Church St. Loft, 275 Church Street (April 25 and August 15, 1965); Theatre Upstairs at the Playhouse, Pittsburgh, Pennsylvania (October 16, 1965); and the Film-Makers' Cinematheque, New York (December 4–5, 1965). See Unterberger, *White Light/White Heat*, 24–61.

26. For Branden Joseph, Young and the Theatre's obsessive orientation on just-intonation harmony represented an opposite pole to that of Cage's adamant refusal of harmony as an organizing principle and emphasis on time, rhythm, and noise. See Joseph, *Beyond the Dream Syndicate*, 31.

27. Tom Johnson, "In Their 'Dream House,' Music Becomes a Means of Meditation," *New York Times*, April 28, 1974.

28. The Theatre of Eternal Music played small theater, film, and loft shows and recorded their work informally on tape and had no commercial or legal agreements at the time; in fact, they never broached the topic of intellectual property until 1987. Thus, the legacy over authorship of the band's work has remained contested. For a comprehensive account of this topic, see Patrick Nickleson, *The Names of Minimalism: Authorship, Art Music, and Historiography in Dispute* (Ann Arbor: University of Michigan Press, 2023).

29. Swami Satchidananda, "Who Is the Guru?," from *To Know Your Self: The Essential Teachings of Swami Satchidananda*, ed. Philip Mandelkorn (Yogaville, VA: Integral Yoga Publications, 1978), 45.

30. Clement Greenberg, "Avant-Garde and Kitsch," *Partisan Review* (Fall 1939): 34–49. Note that Warhol himself never abandoned the avant-garde; after moving beyond painting, Young's minimalism allegedly inspired Warhol to turn to the time-based medium of film and explore the subtleties and strange realism of long, unedited takes of glamorous individuals. Warhol had attended some of Young's concerts and heard Cale play in the Theatre of Eternal Music on March 7, 1965. See Richie Unterberger, *White Light/White Heat*, 43.

31. Cf. Diana Crane, *The Transformation of the Avant-Garde: The New York Art World, 1940–1985* (Chicago: University of Chicago Press, 1987).

32. Though never really commercial, Henry Flynt's antiestablishment celebrations of musical vernaculars took a protesting stance against the political and aesthetic conservatism of the avant-garde. On Henry Flynt, see Benjamin Piekut, "Demolish Serious Culture! Henry Flynt Meets the New York Avant-Garde," in Piekut, *Experimentalism Otherwise*, 65–101; and Branden Joseph, "Concept Art," in Joseph, *Beyond the Dream Syndicate*, 153–212.

33. Richard Cándida Smith, "The Beat Phenomenon: Masculine Paths of Maturation," *Utopia and Dissent: Art, Poetry, and Politics in California* (Berkeley: University of California Press, 1995), 145–71.

34. See Bernard Gendron, *Between Montmartre and the Mudd Club* (Chicago: University of Chicago Press, 2002), 161–226, "The Cultural Accreditation of the Beatles (1963–68)."

35. Anthony De Curtis, *Lou Reed: A Life* (New York: Little, Brown, 2017), 21–22.

36. Martin Scorsese, dir. *No Direction Home: Bob Dylan* (2005), 208 min.

37. De Curtis, *Lou Reed*, 29.

38. Reed's sister has pushed back against the claim that Reed's parents consented to electroconvulsive therapy to treat his homosexual tendencies. Amanda Holpuch, "Lou Reed's Sister: Singer's Electroshock Therapy Wasn't for Homosexuality," *Guardian*, April 15, 2015, https://www.theguardian.com/music/2015/apr/15/lou-reed-sister-mental-health-homosexuality-rumors.

39. See Richard Witts, *The Velvet Underground* (Bloomington: Indiana University Press, 2006), 18.

40. Witts, 18–19.

41. Reed would recruit Don Cherry to join him on a gig in 1976 following a chance meeting at LAX. See De Curtis, *Lou Reed*, 249–50. Coleman would contribute his saxophone playing to Reed's 2003 project *The Raven*.

42. On Reed's literary background, particularly his relationship with Schwartz, see De Curtis, *Lou Reed*, 50–55.

43. De Curtis, *Lou Reed*, 38. Also see Dylan Segelbaum and Erik van Rheenan, "'I'll be your mirror': Lou Reed's Time at SU Shapes Career as Musical Legend," *Daily Orange*, October 2013, http://dailyorange.com/2013/11/ill-be-your-mirror-lou-reeds-time-at-su-shapes-career-as-music-legend/.

44. De Curtis, *Lou Reed*, 38.

45. See Unterberger, *White Light/White Heat*, 35–36 for a comprehensive account of Cale and Conrad's meeting of Reed.

46. Conrad left the Primitives with drummer and sculptor Walter De Maria and went back to working with Young's Theatre full-time in 1965. See Unterberger, *White Light/White Heat*, 40.

47. Billy Name makes this observation in James Marsh, *John Cale* (1998), available at https://www.youtube.com/watch?v=LwNpOXFvCNE.

48. Michael Leigh, *The Velvet Underground* (New York: Macfadden Books, 1963). A number of sources mistakenly refer to this book as a novel.

49. Cale's role in the Theatre of Eternal Music lasted through December 1965 when Cale finally cut ties to play with the Velvets full-time. Cale made his own experimental recordings during this time (1964–66), sometimes with Conrad and MacLise, other times as a soloist. Among these, Cale's "Loop" for solo guitar and feedback is best known. It was released as side B of a split 7″ with Peter Walker, *Aspen* 1, no. 3 (December 1966) (Americom, NYC), vinyl sound recording.

50. The Velvet Underground, *Peel Slowly and See* (Polydor, 1995), five-disc box set.

51. Tucker's remark is taken from an interview in Kim Evans's *The South Bank Show: Velvet Underground* (1986); excerpts of the film are currently available at https://www.youtube.com/watch?v=LuxZ7iV2UoA. The critic was Phil Morris, "The Velvet

Underground: Musique and Mystique Unveiled," *Circus* ( June 1970), in Heylin, ed., *All Yesterday's Parties*, 169. Tucker reported, "What I'd always wanted to do was get an African drum sound, so I got a bass drum and turned it on its side, so I'd sit on the floor and play that." Bockris and Malanga, *Up-Tight*, 37.

52. Moe Tucker makes this point in James Marsh, *John Cale* (1998), available at https://www.youtube.com/watch?v=LwNpOXFvCNE.

53. Tucker remarked that Warhol himself remained the draw for the EPI shows: "But during this time [1966] the audience wasn't primarily there to see us. Andy was pretty much the focus of the whole thing, and they were there more to see what he was up to. We were getting an older artist-type of crowd." Bockris and Malanga, *Up-Tight*, 37.

54. Having been turned down by a number of major labels, Reed stated that the only reason that MGM/Verve signed them was because Warhol planned to do the artwork. Ironically, so effective was the publicity that people thought Warhol was a guitarist in the band. In James Marsh, *John Cale* (1998).

55. Cale uses the term *intellectual location* in Marsh, *John Cale*.

56. Andy Warhol and Paul Morrissey, *The Velvet Underground and Nico: A Symphony of Sound* (1966), available at https://www.youtube.com/watch?v=2YXhut_ITLwThis film was made to be projected during Exploding Plastic Inevitable performances.

57. Quoted in Greil Marcus, *Lipstick Traces* (Cambridge, MA: Harvard University Press, 1989), 61.

58. Lita Eliscu, "The Velvet Underground: A Rock Band Can Be a Form of Yoga," *Crawdaddy*, January 1970. Velvet Underground Collection, 8105, box 12, folder 6, 1964–2015, Division of Rare and Manuscript Collections, Cornell University Library.

59. Friedrich Kittler, "Gramophone," *Gramophone, Film, Typewriter*, trans. Geoffrey Winthrop-Young (Palo Alto, CA: Stanford University Press, 1999), 21–114.

60. John Cale reported in his Autobiography, "We were really excited. We had this opportunity to do something revolutionary—to combine the avant-garde and rock and roll, to do something symphonic. No matter how borderline destructive everything was, there was real excitement there for all of us. We just started playing and held it to the wall. I mean, we had a good time." John Cale, *What's Welsh for Zen: The Autobiography of John Cale* (New York: Bloomsbury, 1999), 92.

61. The initial sessions took place at Scepter Studios in midtown. The sessions were engineered by Columbia Records sales executive Norman Dolph and engineer John Licata who worked at Scepter. Their approach was that of hands-off facilitators. For a comprehensive overview of the session details, see Richard Buskin, "Classic Tracks: The Velvet Underground 'Heroin,'" *Sound on Sound* (November 2013). Producer Tom Wilson was brought in a month later by MGM. Wilson produced new recordings of "Venus in Furs," "I'm Waiting for The Man," and "Heroin" in Los Angeles that May and produced the final November recording of "Sunday Morning," in New York.

62. Unterberger, *White Light/White Heat*, 85–91.

63. In Reed's words, "'Passion—REALISM—realism was the key. . . . The records were letters. Real letters from me to certain other people. I'd harbored the hope that the intelligence that once inhabited novels and films would ingest rock. I was, perhaps,

wrong.'" Bockris and Malanga, *Up-Tight*, 124. In another interview, Reed reports similarly: "Andy told me that what we were doing with music was the same thing he was doing with painting and movies and writing, i.e., not kidding around. To my mind nobody
in music was doing anything that even approximated the real thing, with the exception
of us. We were doing a specific thing that was very, very real. It wasn't slick or a lie in
any conceivable way, which was the only way we could work with him. Because the first
thing I liked about Andy was that he was very real." Bockris and Malanga, 26. Also see
James Michael Martin, "The Velvet Underground: Music to Watch Warhol By," *Coast
FM & Fine Arts* (September 1969), who writes: "the Velvets were hardly interested in
proselytizing for a lifestyle or a sensibility; they only wanted to expose themselves, to
make people *see* life instead of merely looking at it. . . . The Velvets want to confront us
with a grotesqueness of our own making. . . . Here is the music of the City, the music of
caged animals imprisoned by concrete and steel. The Velvets sing of alienation, with a
stark, chiaroscurist imagery that had been found only in the novels of Burroughs and
Trocchi and in the [Artaud's] Theater of Cruelty. Seldom have the bleaker, more unsettling and unsightly aspects of big city life been portrayed with such immediacy and
impact." Velvet Underground Collection, 8105, box 5, folder 4, 1964–2015. Division of
Rare and Manuscript Collections, Cornell University Library.

    64. Reed's label proposed something similar regarding his 1973 concept album, *Ber-
lin*, describing it as "film for the ear." See Anthony DeCurtis, "My Brilliant and Troubled Friend Lou Reed," *Guardian*, October 1, 2017, https://www.theguardian.com
/music/2017/oct/01/my-brilliant-troubled-friend-lou-reed-a-life-anthony-decurtis
-berlin.

    65. On a Factory rehearsal of "Heroin," the only percussion is tambourine (which
turns the song into a bit of a barn dance). In an earlier take, Tucker has a more traditional array of drums, though synchronization remained unsteady through the tempo
changes. See "Heroin—The Factory Rehearsal," on *The Velvet Underground & Nico
45th Anniversary (Deluxe Edition)* (Polydor, 2012), 2 CD set. Later in Reed's career,
hired drummers would keep a precise groove during live performances of "Heroin." In
a 1972 tour for *Transformer*, he refers to this as the "rock" version. See "Heroin," from
Lou Reed, *American Poet* (Pilot, 2001).

    66. Norman Dolph reported of the Scepter sessions, "I don't know that anybody re-
ally told Lou Reed what to do or what they thought, but you had the feeling that musical decisions were being made largely by John Cale, sort of in conference with Sterling.
Moe was very quiet in the whole thing. I don't think I heard her speak ten words." The
fact that Tucker was actually uncertain was also a product of sexism (she was typically
the last to know when a decision was made, and often remained silent in the studio and
on her own wavelength). See Unterberger, *White Light/White Heat*, 88.

    67. Tucker's quote is taken from an interview with her in Kim Evans, *The South
Bank Show: Velvet Underground* (1986), available at https://www.youtube.com/watch
?v=LuxZ7iV2UoA.

    68. One critic noted that the Velvets' extensive use of repetition made it difficult to
discern their level of skill: "the Velvet's repetition scene makes it hard to tell whether
they're playing badly or not (hypnosis plus practice makes perfect), which was an
always pressing problem for the Banana album." Sandy Pearlman, "Round Velvet Underground," *Crawdaddy* 16 (June 1968): 36.

69. See, for example, Timothy Jacobs, "Review of *The Velvet Underground & Nico*," *Vibrations* 2 (July 1967), in Heylin, ed., *All Yesterday's Parties*, 51, and Richard Williams, "It's a Shame That Nobody Listens," *Melody Maker* (October 25, 1969), in Heylin, ed., *All Yesterday's Parties*, 119–21.

70. The tuning of the studio recording is in C♯ minor. The band frequently played it live in C minor, with Reed performing with his A and D strings tuned down a whole step. This would suggest that the tape of the studio version was slightly sped up. Cale performed a solo version of "Venus in Furs" in 2016 in D minor with the viola tuned traditionally.

71. Martin Carthy, "Scarborough Fair" (Fontana Records, 1965).

72. In live recordings of "All Tomorrow' Parties," Tucker hits the downbeat in sync with Reed's guitar.

73. The Velvet Underground, *The Velvet Underground* (Verve/MGM, 1969).

74. The early Velvets allegedly fined band members for playing blues licks. See Witts, *The Velvet Underground*, 31.

75. Lester Bangs, "Dead Lie the Velvets, Underground," *Creem* (May 1971), in Heylin, ed. *All Yesterday's Parties*, 220–43.

76. The Velvet Underground, *Bootleg Series Volume 1: The Quine Tapes* (Polydor, 2001). This was a release of live recordings from performances Robert Quine attended and recorded in San Francisco and St. Louis in 1969.

77. For an interpretation of the Velvet's use of tanpura-derived drone music that emphasizes its resistance to the commodity form of popular song, see Barry Shank, "'Heroin'; or, The Droning of the Commodity," in *The Political Force of Musical Beauty* (Durham, NC: Duke University Press, 2014), 108–46.

78. With Cale's viola in mind, Reed positioned electricity as paradigmatic for the Velvets. In his words: "What the music really has to do with is electricity. Electricity and different types of machines. One of the ideas we had was like, for instance, John would be playing one of his viola solos and we'd have two jack-cords coming out of the viola; in other words, he'd have two, three, four contact-mikes on the viola, put into two, three, four different amplifiers, and then Nico and me and Mo would control each amplifier." Bockris and Malanga, *Up-Tight*, 61–2.

79. See Frank Smith, "How to Play Raga Rock, Part 1," *Down Beat* 35 (June 13, 1968): 26.

80. Phil Ford, *Dig: Sound and Music in Hip Culture* (New York: Oxford University Press, 2013).

81. Grace Glueck, "Syndromes Pop at Delmonico's: Andy Warhol and His Gang Meet the Psychiatrist," *New York Times*, January 14, 1966, in Heylin, ed., *All Yesterday's Parties*, 5.

82. Lita Eliscu, "The Velvet Underground: A Rock Band Can Be a Form of Yoga," in Heylin, ed., *All Yesterday's Parties*, 125–32.

83. Phil Morris, "The Velvet Underground: Musique and Mystique Unveiled," *Circus* (June 1970), in Heylin, ed., *All Yesterday's Parties*, 169. Also in Velvet Underground Collection, 8105, 1964–2015, box 5, folder 4, Division of Rare and Manuscript Collections, Cornell University Library.

84. Barry Lord, "Velvet Underground in Hamilton," *Arts Canada* (February 1967): 17. Velvet Underground Collection, 8105, 1964–2015, box 5, folder 4, Division of Rare and Manuscript Collections, Cornell University Library.

85. Lester Bangs, "Dead Lie the Velvets," in Heylin, ed., *All Yesterday's Parties*, 223.

86. Cf. John Cage, "The East in the West," *Asian Music* 1, no. 1 (Spring 1946): 111–13.

87. Timothy Jacobs, "Review of *The Velvet Underground & Nico*," in Heylin, ed., *All Yesterday's Parties*, 51.

88. Hyman on Reed. De Curtis, *Lou Reed*, 17.

89. Kim Evans, *The South Bank Show: Velvet Underground* (1986).

90. "Pop Art? Is it Art? A Revealing Interview with Andy Warhol," *Art Voices* (December 1962) in *I'll Be Your Mirror: The Selected Andy Warhol Interviews*, ed. Kenneth Goldsmith (New York: Caroll & Graff, 2004), 5.

91. Andy Warhol, *The Philosophy of Andy Warhol (From A to B and Back Again)* (New York: Harcourt, 1975), 7.

92. Bob Dylan press conference in San Francisco, December 3, 1965, available at https://www.youtube.com/watch?v=wPIS257tvoA.

93. Martin Scorsese, *No Direction Home: Bob Dylan* (2005).

94. Lou Reed press conference in Sydney, Australia, August 14, 1974, available at https://www.youtube.com/watch?v=2UrhX1ilwwc.

95. Their strategy echoed Mailer's claim that the art of the jazz-loving midcentury hipster cannot be taught. Mailer writes: "What makes Hip a special language is that it cannot really be taught—if one shares none of the experiences of elation and exhaustion which it is equipped to describe, then it seems merely arch or vulgar or irritating." Norman Mailer, "The White Negro: Superficial Reflections on the Hipster," *Dissent* 4 (1957): 285. Compare Mark Greif, who argues that the Obama-era hipsters of the gentrifying aughts espouse an identity that is routinely denied and thwarted by its adherents. Mark Grief, *What Was the Hipster? A Sociological Investigation* (New York: Harper Collins, 2010), vii–xvii, "Preface."

96. Marquis de Sade, *The 120 Days of Sodom*, trans. Thomas Wynn and Will McMorran (New York: Penguin, 2016), and Leopold Sacher-Masoch, *Venus in Furs*, trans. Joachim Neugroschel, 1st rev. ed. (New York: Penguin Books, 2000).

97. Pauline Réage, *Story of O*, trans. Sabine D'Estrée (New York: Ballantine Books, 2013), and Hubert Selby Jr., *Last Exit to Brooklyn* (New York: Grove Press, 1988).

98. Gilles Deleuze, "Coldness and Cruelty," in *Masochism*, trans. Jean McNeil (New York: Zone Books, 1991), 22.

99. See Michael Gallope with Carolyn Abbate in "The Ineffable (and Beyond)," *Oxford Handbook of Western Music and Philosophy* (New York: Oxford University Press, 2020), 741–62.

100. This did not stop some fans of "Heroin" telling Reed that they shot up the drug to his song, which left him feeling ambivalent at best. See Geoffrey Cannon, "The Insect of Someone Else's Thoughts," *Zigzag*, no. 18 (March 1971), in Heylin, ed., *All Yesterday's Parties*, 197–98, and Bangs, "Dead Lie the Velvets," in Heylin, ed., *All Yesterday's Parties*, 222.

101. Susan Sontag, "Against Interpretation," "On Style," and "One Culture and the New Sensibility," from *Against Interpretation and Other Essays* (New York: Picador, 1966): 3–14, 15–38, and 293–304.

102. Ramblin' Jim Martin, "Interview with Lou Reed," in Heylin, ed., *All Yesterday's Parties*, 109.

103. For a historical study of male homosexuality and the New York art scene from 1948 to 1963, see Gavin Butt, *Between You and Me: Queer Disclosures in the New York Art World, 1948–1963* (Durham, NC: Duke University Press, 2005).

104. Kathleen Frances Burke, "Exploitation, Women and Warhol." PhD dissertation. (California State University, Northridge, 1986).

105. See K. Allison Hammer, "'Just Like a Natural Man': The B.D. Styles of Gertrude 'Ma' Rainey and Bessie Smith," *Journal of Lesbian Studies* 23, no. 2 (2019): 279–93; and Tyina Steptoe, "Big Mama Thornton, Little Richard, and the Queer Roots of Rock 'n' Roll," *American Quarterly* 70, no. 1 (2018): 55–77.

106. See Philip Auslander, *Performing Glam Rock: Gender and Theatricality in Popular Music* (Ann Arbor, MI: University of Michigan Press, 2006).

107. For a detailed, queer reading of a tape made by Reed for Warhol that included live performances of Reed's and recorded sketches for an unfinished album based in Warhol's *Philosophy of Andy Warhol*, see Judith Peraino, "I'll Be Your Mixtape: Lou Reed, Andy Warhol, and the Queer Intimacies of Cassettes," *Journal of Musicology* 36, no. 4 (2019): 401–36. On Reed's relationship with Humphreys, see Harron Walker, "Lou Reed Dated a Trans Woman: That Doesn't Mean He Treated Her Well." *Vice* May 7, 2020, https://www.vice.com/en/article/akzw9k/lou-reed-trans-girlfriend-rachel -humphreys-complicated-relationship.

108. The Nietzschean character of the Velvets music was noted by Wayne McGuire in *Crawdaddy*. He wrote, "The Velvet Underground is the most vital and significant group in the world today. They are at the fiery center of the twentieth century dilemma, as was Nietzsche. For Nietzsche foresaw that moment in the future when the spiritual citadels of the Judeo-Christian West would crumble silently to dust. And at that moment our poor human souls will be rent with a pain greater than the heat of a hundred hydrogen bombs." Wayne McGuire, "The Boston Sound," *Crawdaddy* 17 (August 1968): 43–48, in Heylin, ed., *All Yesterday's Parties*, 65–78.

109. Lita Eliscu is among the critics associating the Velvet Underground with the "Age of Aquarius" and "The New Age." See Eliscu, "The Velvet Underground." in Heylin, ed., *All Yesterday's Parties*, 125–32.

110. Interview between Iggy Pop, David Bowie, and Dinah Shore on *Dinah!*, April 15, 1977.

111. Jacobs, "Review of *The Velvet Underground & Nico*," in Heylin, ed., *All Yesterday's Parties*, 51 Ironically, the very musicians Reed and Cale admired—particularly Coleman—espoused a politics more aligned with the hippies and the universalisms of the civil rights movement. Perhaps they read Coleman as more negative than he actually was, as a dissonance-obsessed protopunk rather than the gentle utopian artist he presented himself as.

112. On Morrison and his lack of concern for civil rights, see Witts, *The Velvet Underground*, 33–4.

113. Simon Reynolds, "From the Velvets to the Void," *Guardian*, March 16, 2007, https://www.theguardian.com/music/2007/mar/16/popandrock3.

114. For recent discussions see Jon Jackson, "Eric Clapton's Past Racist Comments Surface after Announcement of 'Anti-Lockdown' Song," *Newsweek*, November 27, 2020, https://www.newsweek.com/clapton-morrison-lockdown-single-1550863; and Cameron Crowe, *Playboy* (September 1976), 57–72, https://www.playboy.com/read /playboy-interview-david-bowie. Also see Stephen Duncombe and Maxwell Tremblay, eds. *White Riot: Punk Rock and the Politics of Race* (Brooklyn, NY: Verso, 2011).

115. Mailer, "The White Negro," 280.

116. Mailer, 285.

117. Cf. Perry Meisel, *The Cowboy and the Dandy: Crossing Over from Romanticism to Rock and Roll* (New York: Oxford University Press, 1999).

118. Amiri Baraka, *Blues People* (1963; reprint, New York: Harper Perennial, 2002), 202.

119. The Velvet Underground, *The Velvet Underground* (MGM/Verve, 1969).

120. Ritchie Unterberger, *White Light/White Heat*, 282.

121. Theodor Adorno, "Form of the Phonograph Record," trans. Thomas Y. Levin, *October* 55 (Winter 1990): 56–61.

122. Theodor Adorno, *Aesthetic Theory*, trans. Robert Hullot-Kentor (Minneapolis: University of Minnesota Press, 1998), 81.

123. Nan R. Piene, "Light Art," *Art in America* (May 1967): 24–47, Velvet Underground Collection, 8105, 1964–2015, box 4, folder 4, Division of Rare and Manuscript Collections, Cornell University Library.

124. "The New Flashy Bedlam of the Discothèque," *Life*, May 27, 1966, 72–6. Velvet Underground Collection, 8105, 1964–2015, Box 12, Folder 13, Division of Rare and Manuscript Collections, Cornell University Library.

125. On Warhol's films, see David E. James, "Andy Warhol: Producer as Author," *Allegories of Cinema: American Film in the Sixties* (Princeton, NJ: Princeton University Press, 1989), 58–84.

## CHAPTER SIX

1. See Richie Unterberger, *White Light/White Heat: The Velvet Underground Day-by-Day* (London: Jawbone Press, 2009), 29–37 for his coverage of the year 1964. On Tucker's influences see 59.

2. Don DeMichael, "Record Reviews: Terry Gibbs, Hootenanny My Way," *Down Beat*, January 2, 1964, 25.

3. Harvey Pekar, "Record Reviews: Terry Gibbs, El Nutto," *Down Beat* March 11, 1965, 26.

4. For a detailed account of the development of Coltrane's keyboard style out of her early work with Gibbs, see Franya Berkman, *Monument Eternal: The Music of Alice Coltrane* (Weslcyan, CT: University of Wesleyan Press, 2010), 19–46, "God's Child in the Motor City."

5. Nat Hentoff, liner notes for *Live at the Village Vanguard Again!* interview with Coltrane in summer or early fall of 1966.

6. Dan Morganstern, "Caught in the Act: Titans of the Tenor Sax," *Down Beat*, April 7, 1966, 35–37.

7. Pete Wending, "Record Reviews: Coltrane Live at the Village Vanguard Again!" *Down Beat*, February 23, 1967, 26–27.

8. Wending, 26.

9. Berkman writes, "her church training provided [Coltrane] with many of the requisite skills for life as a professional jazz musician: she was required to sight read, arrange spontaneously from a lead sheet, and listen and respond intently to a soloist or the pastor. She was also required to improvise musical statements and continually adapt her aesthetics, depending on the communal energy of the moment." Berkman, *Monument Eternal*, 23–4.

10. Alice Coltrane interview with Franya Berkman, in Berkman, 36.

11. The performance is with Lucky Thompson's quintet's performance of Dizzy Gillespie's "Woody n' You" (1942) at the Blue Note in Paris, https://jazzonthetube.com/video/woodyn-you/. Coltrane was working as an intermission pianist at the time.

12. See Shankari C. Adams, *Portrait of Devotion: The Spiritual Life of Alice Coltrane Swamini Turiyasangitananda* (n.p.: published by the author, 2016), 15.

13. On Afrocentric spirituality in the 1960s, see Melani McAlister, "One Black Allah: The Middle East in the Cultural Politics of African American Liberation, 1955–1970," *American Quarterly* 51, no. 3 (1999): 622–56, and for a discussion of the Coltrane's relationship to this movement, see Franya J. Berkman, "Appropriating Spirituality: The Coltranes and 1960s Spirituality," *American Studies* 48, no. 1 (Spring 2007): 41–62.

14. See Nathaniel Deutsch, "'The Asiatic Black Man': An African American Orientalism?," *Journal of Asian American Studies* 4, no. 3 (October 2001): 193–208.

15. Jayna Brown, "Lovely Sky Boat: Alice Coltrane and the Metaphysics of Sound," in *Black Utopias: Speculative Life and the Music of Other Worlds* (Durham, NC: Duke University Press, 2021), 71.

16. Helena Petrovna Blavatsky, *The Key to Theosophy*, ed. Joy Mills (Wheaton, IL: Theosophical Publishing House, 1972), 2.

17. Philip Deslippe, "The Swami Circuit: Mapping the Terrain of Early American Yoga," *Journal of Yoga Studies* 1 (2018): 5–44. Yogis and Swamis were relatively few earlier in the twentieth century, as immigration laws prevented most South Asians from living in the United States until 1965.

18. See Philip Deslippe, "The Hindu in Hoodoo: Fake Yogis, Psuedo-Swamis, and the Manufacture of African American Folk Magic," *Amerasia Journal* 40, no. 1 (2014): 34–56.

19. See Vivek Bald, *Bengali Harlem and the Lost Histories of South Asian America* (Cambridge, MA: Harvard University Press, 2013), for a historical account of South Asian Muslim immigration to African American and Puerto Rican communities between the 1880s and the 1960s. Endless thanks to Elliott Powell for orienting me with many references on the complex history of Afro–South-Asian interaction.

20. Paul A. Kramer, "The Importance of Being Turbaned," *Antioch Review* 69, no. 2 (Spring 2011): 208–31.

21. Deslippe, "The Hindu in Hoodoo," 43.

22. See the recent documentary film directed by John Turner, *Korla* (2015). For a comprehensive look at the politics, aesthetics, and cultural dynamics of late modern Afro-Asian musical collaborations, see Elliott H. Powell, *Sounds from the Other Side: Afro-South Asian Collaborations in Black Popular Music* (Minneapolis: University of Minnesota Press, 2020).

23. See Nico Slate, *Colored Cosmopolitanism: The Shared Struggle for Freedom in the United States and India* (Cambridge, MA: Harvard University Press, 2012). The exchange was a two-way street of influences. Swami Vivekananda was mistaken for an African American in the US and took a position opposing American racism. Du Bois understood the struggle against racism to be international. Though he never visited the US, Gandhi drew on American abolitionism when exploring the practice of civil disobedience and admired the assimilationist work of Booker T. Washington, which helped him move past his early racial prejudices against black Africans. Note, however, Afro-Asiatic analogies and solidarities were mobile and far from tidy; among individuals, hypocrisies abounded. For some, it could be easier to critique the injustices of another society than it was to challenge racism at home.

24. Daniel Immerwahr, "Caste or Colony? Indianizing Race in the United States," *Modern Intellectual History* 4, no. 2 (2007): 275–301. The Coltranes' focus on India placed their spiritual thinking at a remove from the contemporaneous Black Power movement (Baraka included), who had understood Gandhi and King to be too beholden to passivity and nonviolence and preferred Cuba, China, and Vietnam as international points of reference. On this see Immerwahr, "Caste or Colony?," 299.

25. See Nicholas Goodrich-Clark, *The Occult Roots of Nazism: Secret Aryan Cults and Their Influence on Nazi Ideology* (New York: New York University Press, 1992).

26. Thanks to Anna Seastrand for her help decoding the iconography of this album art.

27. See David W. Stowe, "Both American and Global: Jazz and World Religions in the United States," *Religion Compass* 4, no. 5 (2010): 312–23. For a broad narrative highlighting the spiritual and religious charge of various moments in jazz history, see Jason Bivins, *Spirits Rejoice! Jazz and American Religion* (New York: Oxford University Press, 2015).

28. Cf. William Sites, *Sun Ra's Chicago: Afrofuturism and the City* (Chicago: University of Chicago Press, 2020), and John Szwed, *Space Is the Place: The Lives and Times of Sun Ra* (Durham, NC: Duke University Press, 2020).

29. Stowe, "Both American and Global," 318.

30. See Paramahansa Yogananda's widely read memoir *Autobiography of a Yogi* (New York: Philosophical Library, 1946). On Rollins's interest in Asian spirituality see Richard Palmer, *Sonny Rollins: The Cutting Edge* (New York: Continuum, 2005), 93.

31. Ingrid Monson, "Russell, Coltrane, and Modal Jazz," in *In the Course of Performance: Studies in the World of Musical Improvisation*, ed. Bruno Nettl and Melinda Russell (Chicago: University of Chicago Press, 1998), 149–68. Notably, Russell's book had its own metaphysical influences: Monson has remarked that Russell's theory reflects his broader interest in a new global spirituality that was in turn influenced by the writings of Armenian-Greek mystic philosopher George Grudjieff (1866–1949). Shankar himself noted this difference between Indian music and traditional jazz harmony in 1968.

In Shankar's words, "Jazz is restricted by the need to follow prescribed rules of harmony. . . . In Indian music one does not have to follow prescribed rules of harmony, the music is based entirely on melodic form—it is free to invent its own course." Bill Quinn, "The Impact of Ravi Shankar," *Down Beat*, March 7, 1968, 17, 38.

32. Scholars have long remarked on the influence of Indian ragas and modes on John's music of the early 1960s; modal jazz had come through his work with Miles Davis in the late 1950s and exposure to the work of Ravi Shankar by at least 1961. See Carl Clements, "John Coltrane and the Integration of Indian Concepts in Jazz Improvisation," *Jazz Research Journal* 2, no. 2 (2008): 155–75.

33. Frank Kofsky, "John Coltrane," in *Coltrane on Coltrane: The John Coltrane Interview*, ed. Chris De Vito (Chicago: Chicago Review Press, 2010), 286. Original interview published as Frank Kofsky, "John Coltrane," *Pop & Jazz* (August 1966): 23–31.

34. Ennosuke Saito, "Interviews with John Coltrane: First Interview: Magnolia Room, Tokyo Prince Hotel," in De Vito, *Coltrane on Coltrane*, 270.

35. Shoichi Yui, Kiyoshi Koyama, Kazuaki Tsujimoto, et. al. [unidentified interviewer], "Interviews with John Coltrane: Second Interview: Magnolia Room, Tokyo Prince Hotel," De Vito, *Coltrane on Coltrane*, 271.

36. Frank Kofsky, "John Coltrane," De Vito, *Coltrane on Coltrane*, 311.

37. Kazuaki Tsujimoto, "Interviews with John Coltrane: Third Interview: Coltrane's Hotel Room, Tokyo Prince Hotel" in De Vito, *Coltrane on Coltrane*, 270.

38. The announcement of the personnel switch appeared in "News and Views," *Down Beat*, March 10, 1966, 8–9.

39. Alice Coltrane, liner notes to *A Monastic Trio* (Impulse!, 1968).

40. Tammy Kernodle, "Freedom Is A Constant Struggle," in *John Coltrane and Black America's Quest for Freedom: Spirituality and the Music* (New York: Oxford University Press, 2010), 85.

41. Howard Singerman, *Art Subjects: Making Artists in the American University* (Berkeley: University of California Press, 1999).

42. Elliott H. Powell, *Sounds from the Other Side: Afro–South Asian Collaborations in Black Popular Music* (Minneapolis: University of Minnesota Press, 2020), 7.

43. See Powell, *Sounds from the Other Side*, 19–40, "A Desi Love Supreme."

44. For Jun, Black Orientalism is not simply appropriative in the manner of historically powerful white colonizers; more equivocally and affirmatively, it is a "heterogeneous and historically variable discourse" that "encompasses a range of black imaginings of Asia that are in fact negotiations with the limits failures, and disappointments of black citizenship." H. H. Jun, *Race for Citizenship: Black Orientalism and Asian Uplift from Pre-Emancipation to Neoliberal America* (New York: New York University Press, 2011), 18. Quoted in Kara Keeling, *Queer Times, Black Futures* (New York: New York University Press, 2019), 202.

45. John Coltrane was interested in the French harpist Carlos Salzedo. On Alice's adoption of the harp, see Alice Coltrane's words in St. Clair Bourne, "Black Journal: 26; Alice Coltrane," 16 mm motion picture film of Alice Coltrane (1970), Collection of the Smithsonian National Museum of African American History and Culture, gift of

Pearl Bowser, https://nmaahc.si.edu/object/nmaahc_2012.79.1.16.1a. Thanks to Elliott Powell for the reference.

46. A. Coltrane-Turiyasangitananda, *Monument Eternal* (Los Angeles: Vedantic Book Press, 1977), 42.

47. On Coltrane's harp playing, see Berkman, *Monument Eternal*, 70–1.

48. Coleman was a friend of Coltrane's by 1969 and had inquired about her interest in solo work after John's death. In her words, "The day before these were to be prepared I had a conversation with Ornette Coleman. During the course of the conversation, the subject of solo recording came up. He said he had been thinking about recording solo, and asked me whether I had ever thought about it. I replied that I had considered doing a solo album myself. On many occasions, I find that playing alone is aesthetically beautiful; bereft of distractions and outside interference, your concentration is more complete and there are fewer hindrances to self-expression." Alice Coltrane, *Huntington Ashram Monestary* (1969), liner notes. In 1970, Coleman's quartet shared a bill with Alice Coltrane's band at the Village Gate, and she sat in on harp with Coleman's quartet. In spring 1971 Coleman contributed the violin arrangements to the recording sessions for Coltrane's *Universal Consciousness*. See John Litweiler, *Ornette Coleman: A Harmolodic Life* (New York: William and Morrow, 1992), 140.

49. Alice Coltrane, liner notes for *Universal Consciousness* (Impulse!, 1971).

50. On the new religious movements associated with the New Age, see Paul Heelas, *The New Age Movement* (Oxford: Blackwell, 1996), and Wouter J. Hanegraaff, *New Age Religion and Western Culture: Esotericism in the Mirror of Secular Thought* (Albany: State University of New York Press, 1998). Though its actual communities often proved ephemeral, the New Age movements made significant impacts in the emergence of environmentalism, the information age, organic farming, vegetarianism and veganism, wellness and holistic medicine, yoga, and workplace democracy. The New Age flourished as a culture industry by the mid- to late 1970s, particularly in book publishing, music, metaphysical novelty stores, organic food and nutrition, and commercial yoga studios. The New Age also included conservative variants—particularly during the 1980s and beyond—that emphasized prosperity, career success, and individual social power.

51. See Alice Bailey, *Education in the New Age* (New York: Lucis Trust, 1954).

52. Swami Satchidananda and Philip Mandelkorn, ed., *To Know Your Self: The Essential Teachings of Swami Satchidananda* (Buckingham, VA: Integral Yoga Publications, 2018), 4.

53. Satchidananda and Mandelkorn, *To Know Your Self*, 45.

54. Satchidananda and Mandelkorn, *To Know Your Self*, 17.

55. Two important works for the immanence and scientism of the New Age were Fritjof Capra's *The Tao of Physics* (1975) and the writings of Gregory Bateson, which linked cybernetics to nonlinear models of mind and ecology. New Age immanence was also allied with Coleman's harmolodics and its relationship to systems theory that had emerged in the 1950s and 60s that held that the creatures of the universe were endlessly interrelated, independent, and networked. This moment has affinities with Sun Ra's metaphysics and later discourses of Afro-futurism. Coltrane is, by comparison, more of

a traditionally transcendent thinker, though her metaphysics relies on a material basis of atomic physics up through human technologies and cosmic consciousness.

56. Coltrane-Turiyasangitananda, *Monument Eternal*, 20. Further on in the book Coltrane accounts for the experience of the divine as an "indescribable state of manifested formlessness" (37). The second quote is from Alice Coltrane-Turiyasangitananda, *Endless Wisdom Vol. 1* (Los Angeles: Avatar Book Institute, 1981), 37.

57. Coltrane-Turiyasangitananda, *Endless Wisdom Vol. 1*, 1:16.

58. Satchidananda and Mandelkorn, *To Know Your Self*, 43.

59. Alice Coltrane/Swamini A. C. Turiyasangitananda, *Turiya Speaks: Divine Discourses* (Los Angeles: Avatar Book Institute, 2007), 1:50.

60. Coltrane/Turiyasangitananda, 1:53, emphasis added.

61. For a discussion of the idealized association of Bhatki and Christianity among Orientalists, see the introduction to Karen Pechilis Prentiss, *The Embodiment of Bhakti* (Oxford University Press, 1999).

62. Coltrane-Turiyasangitananda, *Endless Wisdom Vol. 1*, 1:37.

63. Quoted in Berkman, *Monument Eternal*, 81.

64. Alice Coltrane, liner notes, *World Galaxy* (Impulse!, 1972). Will Smith gave *World Galaxy* a mixed review for its string arrangements, dullness, and deliberate use of tape noise. See Will Smith, "Review: Alice Coltrane, *World Galaxy*" *Down Beat*, May 25, 1972, 21.

65. Alice Coltrane, Liner Notes, *Lord of Lords* (Impulse!, 1972). In *Monument Eternal*, Coltrane elaborates on *kundalini*: "The raising of the sacred *kundalini*, the fire energy at the base of the spinal column, to the thousand-petalled lotus in the brain, is also a part of this very same Consciousness—Realization. Physically, when this fire is released, usually its force and heat are too fierce to be endured in the waking state. The Lord had to put me to sleep before its ascent. Although physically asleep, my back was on fire, and aching with pain. Suddenly, my spirit leaped out of me and stood ceiling-high, away from the burning body. The mysterious *kundalini* deposits upon the ascetically initiated, millions of keys which unlock the doors to many of the mysteries of life. *Kundalini* energy also transcends the lower nature, and it brings the soul into consummation with the Supreme Lord" (41). Smith gave *Lord of Lords* three stars in *Down Beat*, remarking that "Ms. Coltrane's works are made up of little more than strung-together arpeggios and glissandi . . . a massive swaying smear." He seems to have been totally disengaged from the spiritual injunctions, remarking, "She seldom allows herself to get into anything deeply here," and that "The liner notes by Ms. Coltrane are pretty strange, particularly her 'visitation' from the late Igor Stravinsky. Oh well." Will Smith, "Review: Alice Coltrane, *Lord of Lords*," *Down Beat*, February 15, 1973, 20.

66. Adams's *Portrait of Devotion*. Adams's book describes the educational philosophy of Coltrane's Vedantic Center, which she established in 1976. Among the key texts studied at the center was the *Bhagavad Gita*, often given in Sanskrit. See Adams, 36.

67. Following the release of *Monument Eternal* (Los Angeles: Vedantic Book Press, 1977), Coltrane scheduled public readings and radio appearances in 1978, including at Kanya Vashon McGhee's The Tree of Life bookstore in Harlem. See promotional poster in the clippings file for Alice Coltrane (1978 May) at the Institute of Jazz Studies, Rutgers University.

68. For Coltrane, the devotional experience of the divine is paradoxically unique and novel, similar across various instances, and obscure or esoteric: "each soul will experience the Lord in a similar, yet different, secret, ever-new way." Coltrane-Turiyasangitananda, *Monument Eternal*, 37. Coltrane writes similarly in *Endless Wisdom Vol. 2* "Blessed are they that have been anointed with the sacrosanct oil of esoteric knowledge; for they are endowed with true perception and understanding of My hidden Meaning in any scripture, any revelation, or divine dispensation of My Words, statues, and ordinances." Alice Coltrane-Turiyasangitananda, *Endless Wisdom Vol. 2* (Los Angeles: Avatar Book Institute, 1998), 31.

69. Coltrane-Turiyasangitananda, *Monument Eternal*, 27, 38.

70. Coltrane-Turiyasangitananda, *Monument Eternal*, 13.

71. St. Clair Bourne, "Black Journal: 26; Alice Coltrane," 16 mm motion picture film of Alice Coltrane (1970), Collection of the Smithsonian National Museum of African American History and Culture, gift of Pearl Bowser. https://nmaahc.si.edu/object/nmaahc_2012.79.1.16.1a, June 18, 2020. Thanks to Elliott Powell for the reference.

72. Coltrane-Turiyasangitananda, *Endless Wisdom Vol. 1*, 61–68.

73. Alongside the writings of Kodwo Eshun, Alondra Nelson was also a key voice in articulating the scope of Afro-futurism. See Alondra Nelson, ed., *Afrofuturism: A Special Issue of* Social Text (Durham, NC: Duke University Press, 2002).

74. Coltrane-Turiyasangitananda, *Monument Eternal*, 19, 22. On Coltrane's use of the Oberheim, see Geeta Dayal, "Higher State of Consciousness: How Alice Coltrane Finally Got Her Dues," *Guardian*, May 5, 2017, https://www.theguardian.com/music/2017/may/05/alice-coltrane-turiyasangitananda-higher-state-of-consciousness. Eshun describes her organ: "Her startling title track *Universal Consciousness* doesn't so much update the archetypal Hollywood 50s score as archaize it even further. Celestial strings invests the Biblical sublime with a sudden seriousness. Like a Bronx accent in Bethlehem BC, it anachronizes you. 50s widescreen Biblical epic pitchbent into Bollywood tones. Coltrane turns the organ into a solar engine. Her lead instrument is the organ pedal, generating sheets of feedback, of angels on fire. The electrified organ floods you in sensations of ceremonial solemnity, the regal procession of swaying paladins. . . . On *Universal Consciousness*, jazz becomes turbulence, stratospheric organ chords that open a horizon in the ear, stretch the sun line to the clouds. Violins, harp, percussion are sucked upwards, wrenching the calm into a perplexing tsunami" Kodwo Eshun, *More Brilliant Than the Sun* (London: Quartet Books, 1998), 168.

75. Eshun, 165.

76. Eshun, 164–65.

77. Kara Keeling, *Queer Times, Black Futures* (New York: New York University Press, 2019), 202.

78. Keeling, 201, 203.

79. Brown, *Black Utopias*, 62. Brown offers a powerful and clear account of the spiritual dimensions of Afro-futurism in *Black Utopias: Speculative Life and the Music of Other Worlds* (Durham, NC: Duke University Press, 2021).

80. Baraka, *Blues People* (1963; reprint, New York: Harper Perennial, 2002), 202.

81. Baraka, 213.

CHAPTER SEVEN

1. Ornette Coleman, "What Reason Could I Give," *Science Fiction* (New York: Columbia Records, 1972).

2. Patti Smith and Lenny Kaye, "Patti Smith's First Performance, St. Mark's Church 2/10/71," available at https://www.youtube.com/watch?v=klpUlOZyGIs&t=2s.

3. In a 1976 interview, Smith remarked that her most famous line was not about hostility to Christianity but about the authenticity and responsibility of the self: "Jesus died for somebody's sins, but not mine,' you know, to shock the Catholic church or the Christian church. I say something like that because I believe that people shouldn't you know, that we form our own lives, you know, that when I do evil or if I do something socially evil or something, I know I'm doing it. *I* do it by my own free will. Someone else isn't going to accept the blame or accept the rewards of what I do." Mick Gold, "Interview with Patti Smith," May 10, 1976, in Aidan Levy, ed., *Patti Smith on Patti Smith: Interviews and Encounters* (Chicago: Chicago Review Press, 2021), 63.

4. For Smith's account see Patti Smith, *Just Kids* (New York: HarperCollins, 2010), 181–82.

5. Richard Hell, *I Dreamed I Was a Very Clean Tramp: An Autobiography* (New York: HarperCollins, 2013), 109.

6. Hell, *I Dreamed I Was a Very Clean Tramp*, 109.

7. Dave Thompson, *Dancing Barefoot: The Patti Smith Story* (Chicago: Chicago Review Press, 2016), 88.

8. For footage of their rehearsal tapes, see "Television: The Full Ork Loft Tapes," available at https://www.youtube.com/watch?v=srn98FdXI4E. On Ork's archive, see "Terry Ork's Punk Rock Time Capsule Celebrates a Nihilistic Niche," *New York Times*, October 23, 2015.

9. Patti Smith, "Television: Escapees from Heaven," *Soho Weekly News*, June 27, 1974.

10. Hell's impression of Smith's reaction: "Patti was the underground girl of the year in 1974, as Edie Sedgwick had once been, and Bette Midler after that, and Madonna later. When Patti saw us she realized she had company. She saw that we were as fresh and good in our area as she was in hers and it was time for her to connect to us and move more fully into music." Hell, *I Dreamed I was a Very Clean Tramp*, 146. In Smith's recollection: "We had promised the poet Richard Hell that we would come to see the band in which he played bass, Television. We had no idea what to expect, but I wondered how another poet would approach performing rock and roll. . . . The band had a ragged edge, the music erratic, angular and emotional. I liked everything about them, their spasmodic movements, the drummer's jazz flourishes, their disjointed, orgasmic musical structures. I felt kinship with [Verlaine] the alien guitarist on the right. He was tall, with straw-colored hair, and his long, graceful fingers wrapped around the neck of his guitar as if to strangle it. Tom Verlaine had definitely read *A Season in Hell*. In between sets Tom and I did not talk of poetry but of the woods of New Jersey, the deserted beaches of Delaware, and flying saucers hovering in the western skies. It turned out that we were raised twenty minutes from one another, listened to the same records, watched the same cartoons, and both loved the *Arabian Nights*." Smith, *Just Kids*, 239–40.

11. Richard Hell, Journal from Patti Smith (June 1974), Richard Hell Papers, MSS.140, box 1, folder 3, Fales Library and Special Collections, New York University. In 1992 Hell published the diary from Patti Smith as a small format book. See Richard Hell, *Artifact: Notebooks from Hell, 1974–80* (New York: Hanuman Books, 1992).

12. On the importance of the French bohemian tradition of cabaret on Smith's work, see Philip Shaw, "Rock 'n' Rimbaud, 1973–75," in *Patti Smith's* Horses, 33⅓ Series (New York: Bloomsbury, 2008), 67–90.

13. For Smith's account of her collaboration with Verlaine, see Smith, *Just Kids*, 240–42.

14. Smith recalls, "Over the weeks we spent at CBGB, it had become apparent to us all that we were evolving under own terms into a rock and roll band. On May Day, Clive Davis offered me a recording contract with Arista Records, and the seventh I signed." Smith, *Just Kids*, 247.

15. John Rockwell, "The Pop Life: Patti Smith Plans Album with Eyes on Stardom," *New York Times* (March 28, 1975). Rock journalists first used the term *punk* early in the 1970s to describe 1960s garage rock, the MC5, and Iggy Pop.

16. Hell, *I Dreamed I Was a Very Clean Tramp*, 148.

17. "Music: Anthems of the Blank Generation," *Time*, July 11, 1977.

18. Richard Hell, 1977–80, Sire Records Collection, ARC-0002, series 1, subseries 1, box 6, folder 7, Rock and Roll Hall of Fame Library and Archives, Cleveland, Ohio.

19. Hell remixed and rereleased *Destiny Street* in 2021. On the rerelease, see Daniel Kreps, "Richard Hell and the Voidoids Ready 'Destiny Street Complete' Reissue," *Rolling Stone*, November 19, 2020, https://www.rollingstone.com/music/music-news/richard-hell-the-voidoids-destiny-street-complete-reissue-1092478/.

20. Richard Hell, journal from Patti Smith, November 19, 1976, Richard Hell Papers, MSS.140, box 1, folder 3, Fales Library and Special Collections, New York University. Published in Hell, *Artifact*, 70–71.

21. Hell noted in a 2013 interview, "Most musicians are thoroughly musicians. For me, being a musician was a kind of decision. It wasn't something that just welled up in me, that carried me along in the wave of my confidence in my unique skills as a composer-bass player. No—I decided I wanted to make music, and then I decided to stop." James Sullivan, "Richard Hell on New Memoir: 'I Never Really Thought of Anything I Did As 'Punk,'" *Rolling Stone*, March 27, 2013.

22. Erin Graff Zivin, "Transmedial Noise: Babel and the Translation of Radio," *Yearbook of Comparative Literature* 63 (June 5, 2020): 160–78.

23. For a discussion of the Black roots of punk and rock n' roll, see Evan Rapport, *Damaged: Musicality and Race in Early American Punk* (Jackson: University of Mississippi Press, 2020), particularly pp. 35–62.

24. Lenny Kaye, prod., *Nuggets: Original Artyfacts from the First Psychedelic Era 1965–68* (Elektra, 1972).

25. Greil Marcus, *Lipstick Traces* (Cambridge, MA: Harvard University Press, 1989), 8.

26. Richard Hell, Journal from Patti Smith, August 19, 1976, Richard Hell Papers, MSS.140, box 1, folder 3, Fales Library and Special Collections, New York University. Published in Hell, *Artifact*, 56.

27. Richard Hell, "Blank Generation," from *Blank Generation* (New York: Sire, 1977). On the relationship between "blank generation" and ineffability, see Hell, *I Dreamed I was a Very Clean Tramp*, 222.

28. William S. Burroughs, "When Patti Rocked," *SPIN* (April 1988); the interview took place in March 1979. Also published in Aidan Levy, ed., *Patti Smith on Patti Smith: Interviews and Encounters* (Chicago: Chicago Review Press, 2021): 150–52.

29. On the avant-garde roots of punk, see Evan Rapport, "'Ignorance of Your Culture Is Not Considered Cool': Reconsidering the Avant-Garde Impulse in American Punk," in Rapport, *Damaged*, 63–92.

30. Richard Hell, Letter to John Cage, series II, box 5, folder 196, and Richard Hell, Letter to Marcel Duchamp, box 5, folder 231, Richard Hell Papers, MSS.140, Fales Library and Special Collections, New York University.

31. Richard Hell, Journal from Patti Smith, December 13, 1976, Richard Hell Papers, MSS.140, box 1, folder 3, Fales Library and Special Collections, New York University. Also see Hell, *Artifact*, 82.

32. Richard Hell, Early 70s Music Notebook, Richard Hell Papers, MSS.140, series 1F, box 4, folder 134, Fales Library and Special Collections, New York University.

33. Richard Hell, Materials from "Music" Notebook, Richard Hell Papers, MSS.140, series 1F, box 4, folder 142, Richard Hell Papers, MSS.140, Fales Library and Special Collections, New York University.

34. Richard Hell, *I Dreamed I was a Very Clean Tramp*, 36.

35. Henri Murger, *Scènes de la Bohème* (1851); available in English as *Bohemians of the Latin Quarter*, Project Gutenberg, https://www.gutenberg.org/ebooks/18445.

36. See Cedric J. Robinson, *Black Marxism: The Making of the Black Radical Tradition* (Chapel Hill: University of North Carolina Press, 2000). On the devaluing uses of the category of the "human" in this epistemic and colonial history, see Sylvia Wynter, "Unsettling the Coloniality of Being/Power/Truth/Freedom: Towards the Human, After Man, Its Overrepresentation," *New Centennial Review* 3, no. 3 (Fall 2003): 257–37.

37. Jerrold Siegel, *Bohemian Paris: Culture, Politics, and the Boundaries of Bourgeois Life, 1830–1930* (New York: Penguin Books, 1986).

38. Arthur Rimbaud, "A Season in Hell," in *A Season in Hell & The Drunken Boat*, trans. Louise Varèse (New York: New Directions, 1961), 17–18.

39. Kristen Ross, "Rimbaud and the Resistance to Work," *Representations* 19 (Summer 1987): 63.

40. Jack Hamilton, *Just around Midnight: Rock and Roll and the Racial Imagination* (Cambridge, MA: Harvard University Press, 2016).

41. Afro-modernism of the 1960s was only an indirect influence on Smith and Hell: Smith mentions Coltrane in an interview but claimed in *Just Kids* to have not had the money to hear Coleman at the Five Spot. Though it is instructive to note that she felt, writing her memoir, that she had to demonstrate her knowledge of Coleman and account for her absence at the premiere. Smith, *Just Kids*, 48.

42. See Lester Bangs, "Dead Lie the Velvets Underground R.I.P Long Live Lou Reed," *Creem* (May 1971), quoted in Rapport, *Damaged*, 50. Reed reports to Bangs, "Sister Ray's jam came about right there in the studio—we didn't use any splices or anything. I had

been listening to a lot of Cecil Taylor and Ornette Coleman, and wanted to get something like that with a rock 'n' roll feeling. And I think we were successful, but I also think that we carried that about as far as we could, for our abilities as a band that was basically rock 'n' roll. Later, we continued to play that kind of music and I was really experimenting a lot with guitar, but most of the audiences in the clubs just weren't receptive to it at all."

43. On Verlaine's interest in free jazz in the early 1960s, see Tim Mitchell, *Sonic Transmission: Television, Tom Verlaine, Richard Hell* (London: Glitterbooks, 2006), 7–9.

44. Ken Shimamoto and The Barman, "Robert Quine Remembered," *I-94 Bar* (June 1, 2016), reprint of May 2000 interview with Robert Quine, https://www.i94bar.com/interviews/robert-quine-remembered.

45. Fred Moten, *In the Break: The Aesthetics of the Black Radical Tradition* (Minneapolis: University of Minnesota Press, 2003), 12.

46. Hamilton, *Just around Midnight*, 3.

47. Lester Bangs, "The White Noise Supremacists," in *Psychotic Reactions and Carburetor Dung*, ed. Greil Marcus (New York: Anchor Books, 2003), 278.

48. Ahmir "Questlove" Thompson, dir., *Summer of Soul ( . . . Or, When the Revolution Could Not Be Televised)* (2021), 117 min.

49. On the Black rock bands of the mid-1980s in New York and Los Angeles, see Maureen Mahon, *Right to Rock: The Black Rock Coalition and the Cultural Politics of Race* (Durham, NC: Duke University Press, 2004). Also see the documentary film by James Spooner, dir., *Afro-Punk* (2003) 66 min.

50. Patti Smith, "Television: Escapees from Heaven," *Soho Weekly News*, June 27, 1974. During Smith's stage banter in a CBGBs show in 1975 in a joint bill with Television, Smith had Verlaine and other members of Television back her on the song "Space Monkey." During the set she noted of the band's guitar tuning, "We have to retune the guitars because it's done in Arabic harmonics. Gotta get that assasinatin' rhythm." See "Patti Smith Plays at CBGD in One of Her First Recorded Concerts," *Open Culture*, July 31, 2015, https://www.openculture.com/2015/07/patti-smith-plays-at-cbgb-in-one-of-her-first-recorded-concerts.html.

51. Smith remarked, "[In 1964], it was all James Brown, all black. I didn't like white music. It was either John Coltrane or Smokey Robinson. We didn't have no time for the Beach Boys or the Beatles. 'Cept when Jagger came out. Then, I was happy to be white. There was nothing like him. I was into James Brown and Smokey but I didn't want to fuck them. All of a sudden I looked at Jagger and I knew. Dylan was the same. There was this whole new consciousness. Lou Reed too." Robin Katz, "Patti Smith: Poetry in Motion" *Sounds*, December 13, 1975, in Levy, ed., *Patti Smith on Patti Smith*, 32. This was partly conditioned by her sense of the white public response. Smith, for example, noted the transgressive impact the Stones had on her father in 1964—not an uncommon experience for white families of the postwar period: "[In 1964] I was totally into black stuff, I didn't wanna see this Rolling Stones crap. But my father acted so nuts [when seeing the Stones on Ed Sullivan], it was like, he was so cool, for him to react so violently attracted me." Dave Marsh, "Patti Smith: Her Horses Got Wings, They Can Fly," *Rolling Stone*, January 1976, in Levy, ed., *Patti Smith on Patti Smith*, 41. Also compare Robert Pattison,

*The Triumph of Vulgarity: Rock Music in the Mirror of Romanticism* (New York: Oxford University Press, 1987), 30–55, "I Am White, But Oh My Soul Is Black: The Origins of Rock in the Romantic Primitive."

52. "[Brian Jones] was a length ahead. He was gonna dig up the great African root and pump it like gas in every Stones hit." Patti Smith, "Jag-arr of the Jungle," *Creem*, January 1973, 54. Regarding Jagger and Richards, Smith remarked, "[My dreams about the Rolling Stones] were so real, and every one was the same. The first one, I was riding in this old Victorian carriage with Mick and Keith and they were talking to each other in this funny language. They kept talking about ritual, it reminded me of voodoo, Haiti or something." Dave Marsh, "Patti Smith,", in Levy, ed., *Patti Smith on Patti Smith*, 43.

53. Dave Marsh, "Patti Smith," in Levy, ed., *Patti Smith on Patti Smith*, 51.

54. Robin Katz, "Patti Smith: Poetry in Motion," *Sounds*, December 13, 1975, in Levy, ed., *Patti Smith on Patti Smith*, 32–33. Smith notes, "That's when I discovered Hendrix. And do you know why I loved him? Because everyone always wanted him to talk about black is beautiful. But he'd talk about how Mars is beautiful." A year later, "[Hendrix] had to become white because it's a white tradition to do high art and Jimi was really into poetry. And Rimbaud was totally into black people, Rimbaud believed totally that he was part n——, because of the Ethiopians being a totally relentless physical race. Jimi Hendrix had to be like that because of synthesizing." Dave Marsh, "Patti Smith," in Levy, ed., *Patti Smith on Patti Smith*, 51.

55. "Rock 'n' Roll N——," *Radio Ethiopia* (Arista, 1978). See also Dave Marsh, "Patti Smith," in Levy, ed., *Patti Smith on Patti Smith*, 41, and Charles M. Young, "Visions of Patti," *Rolling Stone*, July 27, 1978, 51–54.

56. Liner notes to "Rock 'n' Roll N——," *Radio Ethiopia* (Arista, 1978).

57. See Young, "Visions of Patti," 52.

58. In a 1978 interview, Smith also framed her primitivism as a claim to Indigeneity: "I have American Indian in me. I wake up every day and I'm half Apache. It's like I have nowhere to put my tomahawk, so I have to scalp with my electric guitar. My guitar is my instrument of battle. That's why I like rock 'n' roll—it gives a little 100-pound monkey a chance to be a soldier. It's the only machine gun I ever got to hold. I can't help it, we were born out of violent times. I'm a war baby, I was born out of war and never got a chance to be a soldier myself, except now in rock 'n' roll, and my fight is to keep rock 'n' roll alive and to continue rock 'n' roll, now more than ever." John Tobler, "*ZigZag* Articles," *ZigZag*, April and June 1978, in Levy, ed., *Patti Smith on Patti Smith*, 106.

59. Young, "Visions of Patti," 52. "I was raised with black people. It's like, I can walk down the street and say to a kid, 'Hey n——.' I don't have any kind of super-respect or fear of that kind of stuff. When I say statements like that, they're not supposed to be analyzed, 'cause they're more like off-the-cuff humorous statements. I do have a sense of humor, ya know, which is sumpthin' that most people completely wash over when they deal with me. I never read anything where anybody talked about my sense of humor. It's like, a lot of the stuff I say is true, but it's supposed to be funny."

60. Lester Bangs, "James Taylor Marked for Death," (1971) in Greil Marcus, *Psychotic Reactions and Carburetor Dung*, 53–81.

61. See Stephen Duncombe and Maxwell Tremblay, eds., *White Riot: Punk Rock and the Politics of Race* (Brooklyn, NY: Verso, 2011).

62. Lester Bangs, "The White Noise Supremacists," in Greil Marcus, *Psychotic Reactions and Carburetor Dung*, 272–82.

63. Bangs, "The White Noise Supremacists," 277.

64. Bangs, 275–77. Compare Dick Hebdige's modernist interpretation of punk in the same year in *Subculture: Towards the Meaning of Style* (New York: Routledge, 1979).

65. Susan Sontag, "Fascinating Fascism," in *Under the Sign of Saturn* (New York: Farrar, Straus, and Giroux, 1980), 73–105.

66. David E. James notes that midcentury filmmakers strategically thought of themselves as "poets" to frame their filmmaking as artistry and escape the ideologies of the profit-centered studio system. David E. James, *Allegories of Cinema* (Princeton, NJ: Princeton University Press, 1989), 31–32.

67. Victor Bockris and Patti Smith, "The Poetry of Performance: An Interview with Patti Smith," in Levy, *Patti Smith on Patti Smith*, 5.

68. Bockris and Smith, in Levy, ed., *Patti Smith on Patti Smith*, 8–9.

69. Bockris and Smith, in Levy, ed., *Patti Smith on Patti Smith*, 14.

70. Arthur Rimbaud, *Illuminations*, trans. Louise Varèse (New York: New Directions, 1957); Smith, *Just Kids*, 23.

71. Kristen Ross, "Rimbaud and the Resistance to Work," *Representations* 19 (Summer 1987): 62–86.

72. Smith described the misery of working at a factory during the 1960s and noted it was a place of backward anti-intellectualism. See Smith, *Just Kids*, 23–24.

73. Bockris and Smith, "Poetry of Performance," in Levy, ed., *Patti Smith on Patti Smith*, 15–16.

74. Rimbaud, "Letter to Paul Demeny" (1871), *Illuminations*, xxix.

75. Richard Hell, Early 70s Music Notebook, series IF, box 4, folder 134, Richard Hell Papers, MSS.140, Fales Library and Special Collections, New York University.

76. Richard Hell Papers, MSS.140, October 2, 1969–October 2, 1970, series I, box 1, folder 1, Fales Library and Special Collections, New York University.

77. Patti Smith, "Patti Smith's My First Gig: Desecrating a Church with Electric Guitar" *NME*, June 12, 2014, https://www.youtube.com/watch?v=tNOuHNlZwEk.

78. Bockris and Smith, "Poetry of Performance," in Levy, ed., *Patti Smith on Patti Smith*, 18–19.

79. Richard Hell, *I Dreamed I was a Very Clean Tramp*, 127–28.

80. John Cage, *For The Birds*, (Boston: Marion Boyars, 1981), 173.

81. Hell, *I Dreamed I was a Very Clean Tramp*, 127–28.

82. Hell, *I Dreamed I was a Very Clean Tramp*, 225.

83. Bockris and Smith, "Poetry of Performance," and Smith in Levy, ed., *Patti Smith on Patti Smith*, 18.

84. Smith, in Levy, ed., *Patti Smith on Patti Smith*, 18.

85. Robert Christgau, "Patti Smith: Save This Rock and Roll Hero," *Village Voice*, January 17, 1977.

86. Richard Hell, "David Johansen: Secret Messages," *HitParader*, June 1976, 22–23. Also see Richard Hell, interview with David Johansen, Richard Hell Papers, MSS.140, series 1D, box 4, folder 94A, Fales Library and Special Collections, New York University. Hell writes in his notes for the interview: "4. What is distinctive about present / 'cultural' state of consciousness? Interested in any 'medium' other than rock and roll?"

87. "There are privileged moments when it all comes together. I mean you've written a book of poems. But you know that the lyrics of your songs will have an audience far beyond the poems that you might publish because they are carried by music." Victor Bockris, "Susan Sontag Meets Richard Hell," in *Beat Punks*, ed. Victor Bockris (New York: Da Capo Press, 2000), 191.

88. Susin Shapiro, "Patti Smith: Somewhere, Over the Rimbaud," *Crawdaddy*, December 1975, in Levy, ed., *Patti Smith on Patti Smith*, 24.

89. Dave Marsh, "Patti Smith," in Levy, ed., *Patti Smith on Patti Smith*, 42.

90. Bockris and Smith, "Poetry of Performance," in Levy, ed., *Patti Smith on Patti Smith*, 13.

91. Marsh, "Patti Smith," in Levy, ed., *Patti Smith on Patti Smith*, 42. Smith's quote is from her 1967 poem, "Female." The full poem is published online, https://representi mental.tumblr.com/post/2343886014/female-by-patti-smith-1967-female-feel-male.

92. Patti Smith, "Jag-arr of the Jungle," *Creem*, January 1973, 51.

93. Michael Gross, "Patti Smith: Misplaced Joan of Arc," *Blast*, August 1976, 78.

94. Bockris and Smith, "Poetry of Performance," in Levy, ed., *Patti Smith on Patti Smith*, 13.

95. Susin Shapiro, "Patti Smith," in Levy, ed. *Patti Smith on Patti Smith*, 26.

96. Richard Hell, *I Dreamed I was a Very Clean Tramp*, 109.

97. In her memoir, Smith was also forthcoming about her internalized homophobia of the late 1960s. "I thought a man turned homosexual when there was not the right woman to save him, a misconception I had developed from the tragic union of Rimbaud and the poet Paul Verlaine. . . . In my literary imagination, homosexuality was a poetic curse. . . . I knew nothing of the reality of homosexuality. I thought it irrevocably meshed with affectation and flamboyance. I had prided myself on being nonjudgmental, but my comprehension was narrow and provincial. Even in reading Genet, I saw his men as a mystical race of thieves and sailors. I didn't fully comprehend their world." Smith, *Just Kids*, 77.

98. Patti Smith, "Gloria," Live on "Free Music Show" WBAI New York, May 28, 1975, available at https://www.youtube.com/watch?v=bltLbMYS2Hk.

99. In 1969 Kaye wrote an article Smith had read about the revival of a cappella R & B of the 1950s. Lenny Kaye, "The Best of Acapella," *Jazz and Pop* (December 1969).

100. Patti Smith, *Just Kids*, 247.

101. Patti Smith live at the Cirque Royal, filmed for Belgian TV, October 12, 1976, available at https://www.youtube.com/watch?v=GCmhefOpgII.

102. Bockris and Smith, "Poetry of Performance," in Levy, ed., *Patti Smith on Patti Smith*, 19.

103. Richard Hell, "The Velvet Underground vs. the Rolling Stones," in *Massive Pissed Love: Nonfiction 2001–14* (Berkeley, CA: Soft Skull Press, 2015), 15.

104. Hell, *I Dreamed I was a Very Clean Tramp*, 35.

105. Hell, 35.

106. Hell, 101–4.

107. Bangs, "James Taylor Marked for Death."

108. Hell, "Velvet Underground vs. The Rolling Stones," 15.

109. On Hell's haircut and clothes, see Hell, *I Dreamed I was a Very Clean Tramp*, 117–20.

110. For Bangs, deskilled authenticity was inextricable from an inconsistency of intention—punk irony: "All this 'art' and 'bop' and 'rock 'n' roll' and whatever is all just a joke and a mistake, just a hunka foolishness so stop treating it with any seriousness or respect at all and just recognize the fact that it's nothing but a Wham-O toy to bash around as you please in the nursery, it's nothing but a goddam Bonusburger so just gobble the stupid thing and burp and go for the next one tomorrow; and don't worry about the fact that it's a joke and a mistake and a bunch of foolishness as if that's gonna cause people to disregard it as do it in or let it dry up and die, because it's the strongest, most resilient, most *invincible* Superjoke in history, nothing could possibly destroy it ever, and the reason for that is precisely that it *is* a joke, mistake, foolishness. The first mistake of Art is to assume that it's serious. . . . You cannot enslave a fool. No way to regiment the heebie jeebies or make 'em walk a straight line. And nothing better to do from here on out, now that we got cybernation and all such like, but just go to the Party and STAY THERE." Lester Bangs, "James Taylor Marked for Death," in Marcus, *Psychotic Reactions and Carburetor Dung*, 74.

111. Richard Hell and the Voidoids, "Love Comes in Spurts," Live at the Village Gate, set 1, bootleg recording, August 26, 1977. Richard Hell and the Voidoids, The Village Gate, NYC, August 26–27, 1977, box 6, cassette 29, James Brawley Collection, ARC-0045, Rock and Roll Hall of Fame Library and Archives, Cleveland, Ohio.

112. See, for example, Richard Hell and the Voidoids, The Village Gate, NYC, August 26–27, 1977, box 6, cassette 29, and Richard Hell and the Voidoids, CBGB (2nd Avenue), NYC, December 31, 1977 box 10, cassette 3, James Brawley Collection, ARC-0045, Rock and Roll Hall of Fame Library and Archives. Cleveland, Ohio.

113. For a study of Quine and Julian's solos, see Adrian Woodward, "Love Comes in Spurts by Richard Hell & The Voidoids / Guitar Lesson," Anyone Can Play Guitar, July 27, 2018, https://www.youtube.com/watch?v=kjzLA-aphSs.

114. Bangs, "James Taylor Marked for Death," in Marcus, *Psychotic Reactions and Carburetor Dung*, 73.

115. Legs McNeil, "Delicate Delinquent," *Punk*, February 1977, in Levy, ed., *Patti Smith on Patti Smith*, 85.

116. John Rockwell, "The Pop Life," *New York Times*, January 2, 1976.

117. Andy Schwartz, "The Patti Smith Group," *New York Rocker*, June 1979, in Levy, ed., *Patti Smith on Patti Smith*, 138.

118. Mick Gold, "Interview with Patti Smith," May 10, 1976, interview transcript, in Levy, ed., *Patti Smith on Patti Smith*, 68.

119. Richard Hell, Journal from Patti Smith, August 20, 1975, Richard Hell Papers, MSS.140, box 1, folder 3, Fales Library and Special Collections, New York University. Also see Richard Hell, *Artifact: Notebooks from Hell, 1974–80* (New York: Hanuman Books, 1992), 34–35.

120. Richard Hell, Journal from Patti Smith, November 19, 1976, Richard Hell Papers, MSS.140, box 1, folder 3, Fales Library and Special Collections, New York University. Also see Hell, *Artifact*, 66–75.

121. Richard Hell, Journal from Patti Smith, August 29, 1977, Richard Hell Papers, MSS.140, box 1, folder 3, Fales Library and Special Collections, New York University. Also see Hell, *Artifact*, 111–12.

122. As Evan Rapport has noted, "while punks often talk about the ephemerality of their culture, it is hard to imagine a group of people more concerned with documenting themselves." See Rapport, *Damaged*, 24.

123. Michael Gallope, *Deep Refrains: Music, Philosophy, and the Ineffable* (Chicago: University of Chicago Press, 2017), 243–58.

## CONCLUSION

1. David Harvey, *A Brief History of Neoliberalism* (New York: Oxford University Press, 1995).

2. Ernst Mandel, *Late Capitalism*, trans. Joris De Bres (Brooklyn, NY: Verso, 1978)

3. Thomas Frank, *The Conquest of Cool* (Chicago: University of Chicago Press, 1997), 9, 14.

4. Bruce J. Schulman, *The Seventies: The Great Shift in American Culture, Society, and Politics* (New York: Da Capo Press, 2002); Jefferson Cowie, *Stayin' Alive: The 1970s and the Last Days of the Working Class* (New York: New Press, 2010), Andrew Strombeck, *DIY On the Lower East Side: Books, Buildings, and Art After the 1975 Fiscal Crisis* (Albany: State University of New York Press, 2020).

5. Fred Turner, *From Counterculture to Cyberculture: Stewart Brand, the Whole Earth Network, and the Rise of Digital Utopianism* (Chicago: University of Chicago Press, 2008); Mari Dumett, *Corporate Imagination: Fluxus Strategies for Living* (Berkeley: University of California Press, 2017); Joseph Bernes, *The Work of Art in the Age of De-industrialization* (Palo Alto, CA: Stanford University Press, 2017).

6. Martha Feldman and Nicholas Mathew, "Music Histories from the Edge," *Representations* 154 (2021): 1–9.

7. On this characterization of the 1960s, see Frederic Jameson, "Periodizing the 60s," *Social Text*, no. 9/10 (Spring/Summer 1984): 178–209. Also, compare Joan Didion, *The White Album* (New York: Farrar, Straus, and Giroux, 1979), and Todd Gitlin, *The Sixties: Years of Hope, Days of Rage* (New York: Bantam Books, 1987).

8. Amiri Baraka, *Blues People* (1963; reprint, New York: Harper Perennial, 2002), 122–41. Thanks to Jordan Brown for bringing the contradictory tensions of this chapter to my attention. Also see Mike Davis and Jon Weiner, *Set the Night on Fire: L.A. in the Sixties* (Brooklyn, NY: Verso, 2020).

9. Anthony De Curtis, *Lou Reed: A Life* (New York: Little, Brown, 2017), 21–22.

10. Frederic Jameson, "Periodizing the 60s," *Social Text*, no. 9/10 (Spring/Summer 1984), 178–209. A historical condition of this music was an emergent struggle for liberation, justice, and self-consciousness, a process Jameson attributed to Fanon: "A whole theory of cultural revolution as the collective reeducation (or even collective psychoanalysis) of oppressed peoples or unrevolutionary working classes . . . which

have become internalized as a kind of Cultural revolution as a strategy for breaking the immemorial habits of subalternity and obedience second nature in all the laborious and exploited classes in human history."

11. For an exemplary study of praxis as a mode of negotiating and thinking through genre in the late 1960s and 1970s, see Charles Kronengold, *Living Genres in Late Modernity: American Music of the Long 1970s* (Berkeley: University of California Press, 2022).

12. We might recall that George Avakian, producer of Cage's Town Hall recording, was praised for his bravery in taking on Cage's project as an independent release (chap. 1, n. 116).

13. On these influences, see Eric Drott, "Rereading Jacques Attali's *Bruits*," *Critical Inquiry* 41 (Summer 2015): 721–56.

14. Carl Dahlhaus, *Foundations of Music History*, trans. J. B. Robinson (Cambridge: Cambridge University Press, 1983).

15. On Dahlhaus's *Foundations*, see James Hepokoski, "The Dahlhaus Project and Its Extra-Musicological Sources," *19th-Century Music* 14, no. 3 (Spring 1991): 221–46; Anne C. Shreffler, "Berlin Walls: Dahlhaus, Knepler, and Ideologies of Music History," *Journal of Musicology* 20, no. 4 (Fall 2003): 498–525; and Tobias Robert Klein, "On the Foundations of Dahlhaus's Foundations," trans. Stephen Hinton, *Journal of Musicology* 38, no. 2 (Spring 2021): 209–29.

16. Glenda Goodman, *Cultivated by Hand: Amateur Musicians in the Early American Republic* (New York: Oxford University Press, 2020).

17. Emily I. Dolan, *The Orchestral Revolution: Haydn and the Technologies of Timbre* (Cambridge: Cambridge University Press, 2013); Roger Moseley, *Keys to Play: Music as a Ludic Medium from Apollo to Nintendo* (Berkeley: University of California Press, 2016); Alexander Rehding, "Colloquy: Discrete/Continuous: Music and Media Theory after Kittler," *Journal of the American Musicological Society* 70, no. 1 (Spring 2017): 221–56.

18. Richard Taruskin, "Introduction: The History of What?," *Oxford History of Western Music* (New York: Oxford University Press, 2009), x–xix.

19. Richard Taruskin claims historical agents should be regarded as "sentient" in "Agents and Causes, and Ends, Oh My," *Journal of Musicology* 31, no. 2 (2014): 272–93.

20. Raymond Williams, *Marxism and Literature* (New York: Oxford University Press, 1978), 128–35. On music as part of deeper economies of desires, fantasies, and investments, Seth Brodsky's work has been a crucial inspiration. See Seth Brodsky, *From 1989, or European Music and the Modernist Unconscious* (Berkeley: University of California Press, 2017).

21. On the surgeon as analogous to the cinematographer who physically intervenes in the field of representation, see Walter Benjamin, "The Work of Art in the Age of Its Technological Reproducibility," in *The Work of Art in the Age of Its Technological Reproducibility and Other Writings on Media*, ed. Michael W. Jennings, Brigid Doherty, and Thomas Y. Levin, and trans. Edmund Jephcott, Rodney Livingstone, Howard Eiland, and others (Cambridge, MA: Harvard University Press, 2008), 35. Also, compare Kodwo Eshun, *More Brilliant Than the Sun* (London: Quartet Books, 1998), and Jennifer Iverson, *Electronic Inspirations: Technologies of the Cold War Musical Avant-Garde* (New York: Oxford University Press, 2019).

# Index

Printed in Great Britain
by Amazon

40898329R00175